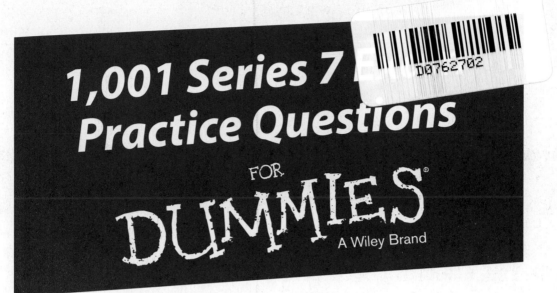

1,001 Series 7 Exam Practice Questions

FOR DUMMIES®

A Wiley Brand

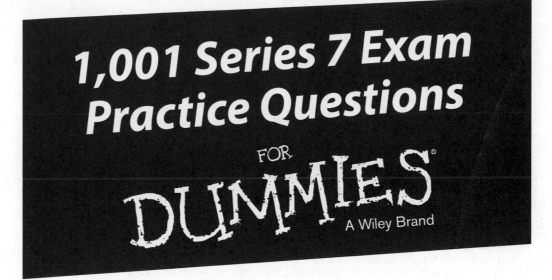

1,001 Series 7 Exam Practice Questions

FOR DUMMIES®
A Wiley Brand

by Steven M. Rice

FOR DUMMIES®
A Wiley Brand

1,001 Series 7 Exam Practice Questions For Dummies®

Published by: **John Wiley & Sons, Inc.,** 111 River Street, Hoboken, NJ 07030-5774, www.wiley.com

Copyright © 2015 by John Wiley & Sons, Inc., Hoboken, New Jersey

Media and software compilation copyright © 2013 by John Wiley & Sons, Inc. All rights reserved.

Published simultaneously in Canada

For general information on our other products and services, please contact our Customer Care Department within the U.S. at 877-762-2974, outside the U.S. at 317-572-3993, or fax 317-572-4002. For technical support, please visit www.wiley.com/techsupport.

Wiley publishes in a variety of print and electronic formats and by print-on-demand. Some material included with standard print versions of this book may not be included in e-books or in print-on-demand. If this book refers to media such as a CD or DVD that is not included in the version you purchased, you may download this material at http://booksupport.wiley.com. For more information about Wiley products, visit www.wiley.com.

Library of Congress Control Number: 2014945056

ISBN 978-1-118-88574-1 (pbk); ISBN 978-1-118-89159-9 (ebk); ISBN 978-1-118-89164-3 (ebk);

Manufactured in the United States of America

10 9 8 7 6 5 4 3 2 1

Contents at a Glance

Table of Contents

Introduction

●●●

*T*his book is designed for people like you who are getting prepared to tackle the Series 7 exam. Make no mistake, the Series 7 can be a gorilla of an exam if you don't prepare adequately. It isn't enough for you to have a good grasp on the material covered on the Series 7; you also need to have completed enough practice questions to go in to take the *real deal* with confidence.

Tackling test questions is a skill. I have tutored many students who could just about recite a Series 7 book from memory, but when it came down to answering questions, they were lost. The only way to get better is to answer a lot of questions. You need to know how to break questions down, focus on the last sentence in the question, and eliminate wrong answers.

This book is broken down into chapters and sections, but you can jump around to whatever topic you need help with. And although I've organized the questions into logical chapters, when you take the real Series 7 exam, the questions are not going to be in chapter order; they will be jumbled. If you want to get a feel for the real exam, you may want to randomly grab 100 questions or so encompassing all the different chapters and subchapters.

This is your book, so feel free to either take each question one by one and check the answer and explanation or complete an entire section before looking at the answers and explanations. Either way you do it, make sure that you give your best effort in answering each question before looking at the answer. Also, keep your eyes from wandering to the answers to questions you haven't completed yet.

Work hard and give yourself the best opportunity to pass the Series 7 exam on the first (or next) attempt.

What You'll Find

The 1,001 Series 7 exam practice problems in the book are divided into 12 chapters with several subsections. Each chapter provides an abundance of question types that you're likely to face when taking the real exam. As on the real exam, some questions will take you a few seconds to answer, and some will take you a couple of minutes.

The last chapter of the book provides the answers and detailed explanations to all the problems. If you get an answer wrong, give it a second attempt before reading the explanation. Eliminating answers that you know are wrong will have a big impact on your score as compared to just "C-ing" your way through (just choosing Choice [C] for every answer you're not sure of).

Beyond the Book

This product comes with an online Cheat Sheet that helps you increase your odds of performing well on the Series 7 exam. Check out the free Cheat Sheet at www.dummies.com/cheatsheet/1001series7.

Where to Go for Additional Help

I wouldn't say that any part of the Series 7 is overly difficult, but the exam itself is tough. The problem is that there is *so* much to remember. Remembering everything and not confusing rules and numbers makes it one of the tougher exams you can take.

In addition to getting help from people who have recently passed the Series 7 exam, Series 7 teachers, or tutors, you can find a variety of questions and study materials online. A simple online search often turns up heaps of information. You can also head to www.dummies.com to see the many articles and books that can help you in your studies.

1,001 Series 7 Exam Practice Questions For Dummies gives you just that — 1,001 practice questions and answers to help you prepare for the Series 7 exam. If you need more in-depth study and direction, check out *Series 7 Exam For Dummies,* written by yours truly (and published by Wiley). This book provides you with the background you need to master the Series 7 exam.

Part I
The Questions

In this part . . .

Make no mistake: Doing well on the Series 7 exam requires a lot of study and practice. Here are the categories of questions you'll face:

- Underwriting securities (Chapter 1)
- Equity securities (Chapter 2)
- Corporate and U.S. government debt securities (Chapter 3)
- Municipal bonds (Chapter 4)
- Margin accounts (Chapter 5)
- Packaged securities (Chapter 6)
- Direct participation programs (Chapter 7)
- Options (Chapter 8)
- Portfolio and securities analysis (Chapter 9)
- Orders and trades (Chapter 10)
- Taxes and retirement plans (Chapter 11)
- Rules and regulations (Chapter 12)

Chapter 1

Underwriting Securities

· ·

A good place to start is at the beginning. Prior to corporations "going public," they must register and have a way of distributing their securities. The Series 7 exam tests your ability to understand the registration process, the entities involved in bringing new issues to market, and types of offerings. In addition, you're expected to know which securities are exempt from Securities and Exchange Commission (SEC) registration.

The Problems You'll Work On

As you work through this chapter, be sure you can recognize, understand, and, in some cases, calculate the following:

- ✔ The process involved with bringing new issues to market
- ✔ Who gets what (distribution of profits)
- ✔ The different types of offerings
- ✔ Exempt securities and transactions

What to Watch Out For

Read the questions and answer choices carefully and make sure that you

- ✔ Watch out for words that can change the answer you're looking for, such as EXCEPT, NOT, ALWAYS, and so on.
- ✔ Recognize that there's a difference between *exempt securities* and *exempt transactions*.
- ✔ If you're not certain of the correct answer, try to eliminate any answers that you can. Doing so may make the difference between passing and failing.

1–34 Bringing New Issues to Market

1. Which of the following types of underwriting agreements specify that any unsold securities are retained by the underwriters?

(A) mini-max

(B) firm commitment

(C) all-or-none (AON)

(D) best efforts

2. Pluto Broker-Dealer is offering an IPO that will not be listed on the NYSE, NASDAQ, or any other exchange. How long after the effective date must Pluto provide a final prospectus to all purchasers?

(A) 20 days

(B) 30 days

(C) 40 days

(D) 90 days

3. The cooling-off period for a new issue lasts approximately how many days?

(A) 20

(B) 30

(C) 40

(D) 60

4. GNU Corporation is planning to issue new shares to the public. GNU has not yet filed a registration statement with the SEC. An underwriter for GNU may do which of the following?

(A) Accept money from investors for payment of the new issue of GNU.

(B) Send a red herring to investors.

(C) Accept indications of interest.

(D) None of the above.

5. Which of the following is NOT a type of bond underwriting?

(A) mini-max

(B) best efforts

(C) standby

(D) AON

6. A tombstone ad would include all of the following names EXCEPT

(A) selling group members

(B) syndicate members

(C) the syndicate manager

(D) the issuer

7. A registered rep may use a preliminary prospectus to

(A) solicit orders from clients to purchase a new issue

(B) show prospective investors that the issue has been approved by the SEC

(C) obtain indications of interest from investors

(D) accept orders and payments from investors for a new issue

8. All of the following are included in the preliminary prospectus EXCEPT

I. the public offering price

II. the financial history of the issuer

III. the effective date

(A) I only

(B) I and II

(C) II and III

(D) I and III

9. What is the underwriting arrangement that allows an issuer whose stock is already trading publicly to time the sales of an additional issue?

    (A) shelf registration

    (B) a standby underwriting

    (C) a negotiated offering

    (D) an Eastern account underwriting

10. A primary offering would do which of the following?

    I. Increase the number of shares outstanding.

    II. Decrease the number of shares outstanding.

    III. Raise additional capital for the issuer.

    IV. Include selling treasury stock.

    (A) I, III, and IV

    (B) II, III, and IV

    (C) I and IV

    (D) I and III

11. Which of the following are types of state securities registration?

    I. filing

    II. communication

    III. qualification

    IV. coordination

    (A) I, III, and IV

    (B) II, III, and IV

    (C) I, II, and III

    (D) I, II, III, and IV

12. Which of the following securities acts covers the registration and disclosure requirements of new issues?

    (A) the Securities Act of 1933

    (B) the Securities Exchange Act of 1934

    (C) the Trust Indenture Act of 1939

    (D) all of the above

13. Which TWO of the following are considered securities under the Securities Act of 1933?

    I. variable annuities

    II. fixed annuities

    III. FDIC insured negotiable CDs

    IV. oil and gas limited partnerships

    (A) I and III

    (B) I and IV

    (C) II and III

    (D) II and IV

14. All of the following would be included on a tombstone ad EXCEPT

    (A) the name of the issuer

    (B) the names of the selling groups

    (C) the names of the syndicate members

    (D) the name of the syndicate manager

15. Under the Securities Act of 1933, the SEC has the authority to

    I. approve new issues of common stock

    II. issue stop orders

    III. review registration statements

    (A) I and II

    (B) II and III

    (C) I and III

    (D) all of the above

16. Stabilizing bids may be entered at

(A) a price at or below the public offering price

(B) the stabilizing price stated in the final prospectus

(C) a price at or slightly above the public offering price

(D) a price deemed reasonable by the Fed

17. All of the following may be determined by the managing underwriter EXCEPT

(A) the takedown

(B) the public offering price

(C) the effective date

(D) the allocation of orders

18. A corporation in the process of issuing stock has not filed a registration statement with the SEC. An account executive may do which of the following relating to the new issue?

(A) Accept money from customers.

(B) Obtain indications of interest.

(C) Guarantee to customers that they will be able to purchase 1,000 shares of the new issue.

(D) Nothing.

19. HIJ Corporation is issuing common stock through an IPO that will trade on the OTCBB when it is first issued. Broker-dealers who execute orders for clients in HIJ common stock must have a copy of a final prospectus available for how long?

(A) 25 days after the effective date

(B) 30 days after the effective date

(C) 40 days after the effective date

(D) 90 days after the effective date

20. Zamzow, Inc., has filed a registration statement and is currently in the cooling-off period. Zowie Broker-Dealer is the lead underwriter for Zamzow and is in the process of taking indications of interest. Which TWO of the following are TRUE regarding indications of interest?

I. They are binding on Zowie.

II. They are binding on customers.

III. They are not binding on Zowie.

IV. They are not binding on customers.

(A) I and II

(B) III and IV

(C) I and IV

(D) II and III

21. A syndicate has just won a bid on a new issue of corporate bonds. The syndicate is expected to start receiving orders for this issue shortly. What is the normal order for filling orders from highest priority to lowest priority?

I. group net

II. member

III. designated

IV. presale

(A) IV, I, III, II

(B) I, III, II, IV

(C) III, II, I, IV

(D) IV, II, I, III

22. All of the following terms apply to a new issue of securities EXCEPT

(A) stabilization

(B) due diligence

(C) matching orders

(D) cooling-off period

23. Which of the following are covered under the Securities and Exchange Act of 1934?

I. margin accounts

II. trust indentures

III. proxies

IV. short sales

(A) I, II, and III

(B) II and IV

(C) III and IV

(D) I, III, and IV

24. An investment banking firm has won a competitive bid for a corporate underwriting of ABCDE common stock. The investment banking firm has agreed to purchase the shares from the issuer. This type of offering is a(n)

(A) all-or-none underwriting

(B) best efforts underwriting

(C) standby underwriting

(D) firm commitment underwriting

25. Silversmith Securities is the lead underwriter for 2 million shares of HIJ common stock. Silversmith has entered into an agreement with HIJ to sell as many shares of their common stock as possible, but HIJ will cancel the offering if the entire 2 million shares are not sold. What type of offering is this?

(A) firm commitment

(B) all-or-none

(C) mini-max

(D) best efforts

26. Which of the following documents details the liabilities and responsibilities of each firm involved in the distribution of new securities?

(A) the registration statement

(B) the letter of intent

(C) the syndicate agreement

(D) the code of procedure

27. Which of the following information must be included in the registration statement to the SEC when registering new securities?

I. the issuer's name and description of its business

II. what the proceeds of sale will be used for

III. financial statements

IV. the company's capitalization

(A) I and III

(B) I, II, and III

(C) I, III, and IV

(D) I, II, III, and IV

28. Which of the following is TRUE?

    I.   The registrar is responsible for making sure that a corporation's outstanding shares do not exceed the amount of authorized shares.

    II. The transfer agent is responsible for making sure that a corporation's outstanding shares do not exceed the amount of authorized shares.

    III. The registrar maintains records of a corporation's stock and bond owners plus mails and cancels old certificates as necessary.

    IV. The transfer agent maintains records of a corporation's stock and bond owners plus mails and cancels old certificates as necessary.

    (A) I and III

    (B) I and IV

    (C) II and III

    (D) II and IV

29. Which of the following securities is subject to the anti-fraud provision of the Securities Act of 1933?

    (A) U.S. government securities

    (B) common stock issued by any corporation

    (C) private placements under Regulation D

    (D) all of the above

30. SEC Rule 145 requires shareholder approval for which of the following events?

    I.   new shares issued for a stock dividend

    II. new shares issued for a stock split

    III. an acquisition

    IV. mergers of consolidations

    (A) I and II

    (B) III and IV

    (C) I, III, and IV

    (D) II and IV

31. One of your clients is interested in purchasing shares of a new issue of DIMM common stock. However, the demand for DIMM has exceeded the number of shares DIMM had intended to offer. You should look to see whether there is a

    (A) Rule 144 exemption

    (B) Rule 145 exemption

    (C) green shoe provision

    (D) way of purchasing the shares privately

32. The main function of an investment banker is to

    (A) advise an issuer on how to raise capital

    (B) raise capital for issuers by selling securities

    (C) help issuers comply with the laws of the Securities Act of 1933

    (D) all of the above

33. Which of the following is NOT determined by the syndicate manager?

    (A) the effective date

    (B) allocation of orders

    (C) syndicate member allotment

    (D) public offering price

34. Which of the following documents would contain the allocation of orders?

(A) official statement

(B) trust indenture

(C) syndicate agreement

(D) preliminary prospectus

35–44 Distribution of Profits

35. Place the following in order from largest compensation to smallest compensation in an underwriting spread.

I. concession

II. manager's fee

III. reallowance

IV. takedown

(A) IV, I, III, II

(B) II, III, I, IV

(C) I, II, III, IV

(D) III, II, I, IV

36. The public offering price to purchase a new issue of DEF Corporate bonds is $1,000. However, the issuer receives only $989 per bond. What is the $11 difference called?

(A) the takedown

(B) the underwriting spread

(C) the additional takedown

(D) the concession

37. Your firm is a syndicate member for an IPO offering of BCDE common stock. If you sell one of your customer's BCDE stock, he will pay the public offering price

(A) plus a commission

(B) plus a markup

(C) without a markup or commission

(D) plus a manager's fee

38. Armbar common stock is being sold to a syndicate during an underwriting for $13.50 per share. The public offering price is $15.00 per share, and the manager's fee is $0.25 per share. If the concession is $0.80 per share, what is the additional takedown?

(A) $0.45 per share

(B) $1.15 per share

(C) $1.25 per share

(D) $1.50 per share

39. Liddell Securities is part of a syndicate that is offering new shares of SLAM Corporation common stock to the public. There are 8 million shares being offered to the public, and Liddell Securities is allocated 1 million shares. After selling its allotment, 800,000 shares remain unsold by other members. How much of the remaining shares would Liddell Securities be responsible for?

I. 100,000 shares if the offering was on an Eastern account basis

II. 100,000 shares if the offering was on a Western account basis

III. 0 shares if the offering was on an Eastern account basis

IV. 0 shares if the offering was on a Western account basis

(A) I and IV

(B) II and III

(C) I and II

(D) III and IV

40. Faber Hughes Corporation is offering 2 million new shares to the public. The shares are being sold to a syndicate for $8 and are being reoffered to the public at $9. The takedown for each share sold is $0.85. The concession is $0.55 a share, and the managing underwriter retains $0.15 in fees for each share sold by anybody. The selling group will assist in selling 500,000 of the 2 million shares offered. If the selling group sells its entire allotment, how much does it make in profits?

(A) $425,000

(B) $150,000

(C) $350,000

(D) $275,000

41. A syndicate is offering 10 million new shares to the public on an Eastern account basis. A member of the syndicate is responsible for selling 2.5 million shares. After selling its entire allotment, 1 million shares are left unsold by other members. How many additional shares is the firm responsible for selling to the public?

(A) 0

(B) 100,000

(C) 250,000

(D) 1 million

42. TUV Corp. is offering 6 million new shares to the public. The shares are being sold to a syndicate for $15 and are being reoffered to the public at $16. The compensation to the underwriters for each share sold is $0.75. The selling group receives $0.30 a share for each share it sells, and the managing underwriter retains $0.25 in fees for each share sold by anybody. The selling group will assist in selling 1 million of the 6 million shares offered. If the selling group sells its entire allotment, how much does the syndicate make on shares sold by the selling group?

(A) $200,000

(B) $300,000

(C) $450,000

(D) $750,000

43. The smallest portion of a corporate underwriting spread is the

(A) concession

(B) takedown

(C) reallowance

(D) manager's fee

44. What is the profit syndicate members make when selling shares of a new issue?

(A) the concession

(B) the takedown

(C) the reallowance

(D) the spread

45–49 Types of Offerings

45. A municipality is offering $20 million of new bonds through a syndicate in a negotiated offering. A firm in a syndicate that is established as a Western account is responsible for selling $2 million of the bonds. After the firm sells $1.8 million of the firm's allotment, the manager of the syndicate determines that there are $4 million of bonds left unsold. How much of the unsold bonds is the firm responsible for selling?

(A) 0

(B) 200,000

(C) 400,000

(D) 600,000

46. A corporation is offering 1 million shares of its common stock to the public. Of those shares, 600,000 are authorized but previously unissued, while insiders of the company are selling the other 400,000 shares. What type of offering is this?

(A) IPO

(B) primary

(C) secondary

(D) combined

47. WXY Corporation is offering a large block of treasury stock. What type of offering is this?

(A) IPO

(B) primary

(C) secondary

(D) split

48. The first time a corporation issues stock is called a(n)

(A) primary offering

(B) secondary offering

(C) split offering

(D) initial public offering

49. SEC Rule 415 outlines rules for

(A) primary offerings

(B) shelf offerings

(C) secondary offerings

(D) IPOs

50–64 Exempt Securities and Transactions

50. Which of the following Securities Act of 1933 exemptions may be used for an initial offering of securities?

   I. Rule 144

   II. Rule 147

   III. Regulation D

   IV. Regulation S

(A) I, II, and III

(B) II and IV

(C) III and IV

(D) II, III, and IV

51. One of your clients purchased unregistered securities overseas from a U.S. corporation under Regulation S. Which of the following is TRUE?

   I. They are exempt transactions.

   II. They are exempt securities.

   III. The securities must be held for 270 days before they can be resold in the United States.

   IV. The securities must be held for one year before they can be resold in the United States.

(A) I and III

(B) I and IV

(C) II and III

(D) II and IV

52. One of your clients wants to purchase a private placement. According to Regulation D, which of the following are the minimum standards for an accredited investor?

   I. a net worth exceeding $1 million excluding primary residence

   II. a net worth exceeding $300,000 excluding primary residence

   III. an annual income exceeding $100,000 in each of the two most recent years and a reasonable expectation of the same income level in the current year

   IV. annual income exceeding $200,000 in each of the two most recent years and a reasonable expectation of the same income level in the current year

(A) I and III

(B) I and IV

(C) II and III

(D) II and IV

53. Which of the following securities are exempt from the full registration requirements of the Securities Act of 1933?

(A) corporate convertible bonds

(B) closed-end funds

(C) real estate limited partnerships

(D) commercial paper

54. A Regulation D private placement is

(A) an offering of securities to no more than 35 unaccredited investors in a 12-month period

(B) an intrastate offering

(C) an offering of securities worth no more than $5 million in a 12-month period

(D) a large offering of commercial paper

55. A Regulation S exemption under the Securities Act of 1933 is for

(A) a non-U.S. issuer issuing new securities to U.S. investors

(B) a U.S. issuer issuing new securities to non-U.S. investors

(C) a U.S. issuer issuing new securities to U.S. investors

(D) a non-U.S. issuer issuing new securities to non-U.S. investors

56. Which of the following are non-exempt securities?

I. municipal GO bonds

II. treasury notes

III. blue chip stocks

IV. variable annuities

(A) I and II

(B) II and III

(C) III and IV

(D) I and IV

57. Which of the following is TRUE of Regulation A offerings?

(A) They are limited to 35 unaccredited investors each year.

(B) They are issued without using a prospectus.

(C) They are limited to raising up to $10 million per year.

(D) They are also known as private placements.

58. A Rule 147 offering is

(A) an offering of securities only within the issuer's home state

(B) an offering of securities worth no more than $5 million within a one-year period

(C) an offering of securities to no more than 35 unaccredited investors within a one-year period

(D) also known as an interstate offering

59. Sig Hillstrand has held shares of Greenhorn restricted stock for more than one year. Greenhorn has 4 million shares outstanding. The most recently reported weekly trading volumes for Greenhorn are as follows:

Week Ending	Trading Volume
May 27	35,000
May 20	50,000
May 13	40,000
May 6	45,000
Apr 29	50,000

What is the maximum number of shares that Sig can sell under Rule 144?

(A) 35,000

(B) 46,250

(C) 44,000

(D) 42,500

60. Which of the following securities is NOT exempt from SEC registration?

(A) limited partnership public offerings

(B) treasury notes sold at auction

(C) Rule 147 offerings

(D) private placements

61. Derrick Diamond has held restricted stock for six months. When must Derrick file a Form 144 with the SEC to sell the stock publicly?

(A) at the time of sale

(B) 30 days after the sale

(C) 60 days after the sale

(D) 90 days after the sale

62. Which of the following are exempt transactions?

I. private placements

II. securities issued by the U.S. government

III. municipal bonds

IV. intrastate offerings

(A) II and III

(B) II, III, and IV

(C) I and IV

(D) I, II, III, and IV

63. Mike Steelhead and his wife, Mary, would like to open a joint account at your firm. They are interested in purchasing a private placement under Regulation D. You should inform them that to be considered accredited investors, they must have a combined annual income of at least

(A) $200,000

(B) $300,000

(C) $500,000

(D) $1 million

64. All of the following are exempt securities under the Act of 1933 EXCEPT

(A) treasury bonds

(B) municipal general obligation bonds

(C) REITs

(D) public utility stocks

Chapter 2

Equity Securities

• •

*T*o be a corporation, you must have stockholders. Both common and preferred stock are considered *equity securities* because they represent ownership of the corporation. A majority of most registered representatives' commission is earned by selling equity securities because, historically, equity securities have outpaced inflation.

Although this isn't the largest section on the Series 7 exam, it does relate to many other chapters, such as packaged securities and options.

The Problems You'll Work On

In this chapter, you're expected to understand and calculate questions regarding the following:

- ✔ The specifics of common stock
- ✔ How stock splits and dividends affect stockholders
- ✔ The difference between common stock and preferred stock
- ✔ The reason for American depositary receipts (ADRs)
- ✔ What rights and warrants are

What to Watch Out For

Read the questions and answer choices carefully, and be sure you

- ✔ Don't assume an answer without reading each question and answer choice completely (twice if necessary).
- ✔ Watch out for key words that can change the answer (EXCEPT, NOT, and so on).
- ✔ Eliminate any incorrect answer choice that you can.
- ✔ Look at questions from the corporation's or the investor's point of view depending on how the question is worded.

65–77 Common Stock

65. Which of the following would be owners of a corporation?

    I. common stockholders

    II. debenture holders

    III. participation preferred stockholders

    IV. equipment trust bondholders

    (A) I and III

    (B) II and IV

    (C) I, III, and IV

    (D) II, III, and IV

66. Which of the following does NOT describe treasury stock?

    (A) It has no voting rights.

    (B) It is stock that was previously authorized but still unissued.

    (C) It is issued stock that has been repurchased by the company.

    (D) It has no dividends.

67. Common stockholders have the right to vote for all of the following EXCEPT

    I. cash dividends

    II. stock dividends

    III. stock splits

    IV. members of the board of directors

    (A) I, II, and III

    (B) III and IV

    (C) I and II

    (D) IV only

68. An individual owns 2,000 shares of TUV common stock. TUV has four vacancies on the board of directors. If the voting is cumulative, the investor may vote in any of the following ways EXCEPT

    (A) 4,000 votes for two candidates each

    (B) 5,000 votes for one candidate and 3,000 votes for another candidate

    (C) 3,000 votes each for three candidates

    (D) 2,000 votes for four candidates each

69. You have a new client who is new to investing. She is concerned about taking too much risk. Which of the following investments could you tell her is the riskiest?

    (A) common stock

    (B) preferred stock

    (C) debentures

    (D) GO bonds

70. Macrohard Corp. was authorized to issue 2 million shares of common stock. Macrohard issued 1.1 million shares and subsequently repurchased 150,000 shares. How many of Macrohard's shares remain outstanding?

    (A) 150,000

    (B) 900,000

    (C) 950,000

    (D) 1.85 million

71. Treasury stock is

    (A) U.S. government stock

    (B) local government stock

    (C) authorized but unissued stock

    (D) repurchased stock

72. WHY Corporation has an EPS of $6.10 and pays an annual dividend of $2.10. At a market price of $42.00, what is the current yield?

(A) 5.0%

(B) 9.2%

(C) 14.5%

(D) 34.4%

73. Common stockholders have which of the following rights and privileges?

I. the right to receive monthly audited financial reports

II. the right to vote for cash dividends

III. the right to vote for stock splits

IV. a residual claim to assets at dissolution

(A) I and II

(B) III and IV

(C) I, III, and IV

(D) II, III, and IV

74. KO Corp., a new company, has held back some of its shares for later use. According to shelf distribution rules, KO can sell the shares over the course of the next _____ without having to reregister the shares.

(A) 180 days

(B) 270 days

(C) 1 year

(D) 3 years

75. Cain Weidman owns 1,000 shares of HIT Corp. HIT issues stock with cumulative voting. What is the maximum number of votes that Cain can cast for one candidate if the board of directors of HIT has four vacancies?

(A) 100

(B) 250

(C) 1,000

(D) 4,000

76. The par value of a common stock is

I. used for bookkeeping purposes

II. one dollar

III. adjusted for stock splits

IV. the amount investors receive at maturity

(A) I and III

(B) I, II, and III

(C) II, III, and IV

(D) I, II, III, and IV

77. Which of the following investments exposes an investor to the greatest risk?

(A) TUV subordinated debentures

(B) TUV mortgage bonds

(C) TUV common stock

(D) TUV preferred stock

78–89 Stock Splits and Dividends

78. JKLM common stock has an EPS of $2 and pays a $0.20 quarterly dividend. If JKLM's market price is $32, what is the current yield?

(A) 0.67%

(B) 2.5%

(C) 5.0%

(D) 10%

79. Which of the following changes the par value of a stock?

(A) a rights offering

(B) the issuer repurchasing some of its outstanding stock

(C) a stock split

(D) a cash dividend

80. Dana Black, an investor, purchased 1,000 shares of ABC at $40. If ABC announces a 5-for-4 split, what is Dana's position after the split?

(A)   800 ABC at $50

(B)   1,250 ABC at $32

(C)   1,250 ABC at $50

(D)   800 ABC at $32

81. How much is the price of a stock reduced for a 4-for-3 split?

(A)   10%

(B)   20%

(C)   25%

(D)   33%

82. A listed stock closed at $24.95 on the business day prior to the ex-dividend date. If the company previously announced a $0.30 dividend, what will be the opening price on the next business day?

(A) $24.35

(B) $24.65

(C) $24.95

(D) $25.25

83. ABC splits its stock 3 for 1. An investor who owns 100 shares would receive

(A)   another certificate representing 200 shares of ABC

(B)   a sticker to be placed on his existing certificate notifying purchasers that the stock was split

(C)   a notice to send back the existing certificate so that it can be replaced with a new one representing 300 shares

(D)   another certificate representing 300 shares of ABC and a notice to destroy the existing certificate

84. A corporation would announce all of the following dates EXCEPT

(A)   the declaration date

(B)   the ex-dividend date

(C)   the record date

(D)   the payment date

85. The ex-dividend date as related to cash dividends is

I.   the date that the stock price is reduced by the dividend amount

II.   the date that the stock price is increased by the dividend amount

III.   two business days before the record date

IV.   two business days after the trade date

(A)   I and III

(B)   I and IV

(C)   II and III

(D)   II and IV

86. A corporation announces a dividend with a record date of Monday, February 16. When is the last day an investor can buy the stock the regular way and receive the dividend?

(A)   February 11

(B)   February 12

(C)   February 13

(D)   February 15

87. One of your customers owns 1,000 shares of DIM common stock at $24. DIM declares a 20% stock dividend. On the ex-dividend date, your customer will own

I. 1,000 shares

II. 1,200 shares

III. stock at $20 per share

IV. stock at $24 per share

(A) I and III

(B) I and IV

(C) II and III

(D) II and IV

88. What is the main reason a corporation would split its stock?

(A) to bring in additional funds

(B) to increase the overall market value of its stock

(C) to decrease the amount of dividend paid per share

(D) to increase the demand for its stock

89. ABC undergoes a 1-for-4 reverse stock split; which TWO of the following increases?

I. EPS

II. the market capitalization of ABC

III. the market price of ABC

IV. the number of shares outstanding

(A) I and II

(B) I and III

(C) III and IV

(D) II and IV

90–104 Preferred Stock

90. EYEBM Corp. shares are trading at $55 per share when it declares a 5% stock dividend. After EYEBM pays the dividend, one of your clients who owned 500 shares now owns

(A) 500 shares valued at $57.73 per share

(B) 525 shares valued at $55.00 per share

(C) 550 shares valued at $55.00 per share

(D) 525 shares valued at $52.38 per share

91. TUV Corporation declares a 4-for-3 stock split; an investor who owns 600 shares would receive _____ additional shares.

(A) 100

(B) 200

(C) 400

(D) 600

92. Interest rates have just increased. Investors would expect that the prices of their straight preferred stock would

(A) increase

(B) decrease

(C) remain the same

(D) first increase then decrease

93. The dividend rate on adjustable-rate preferred stock will vary depending on the

(A) Treasury bill rate

(B) Treasury note rate

(C) Treasury bond rate

(D) CPI

94. Which of the following are advantages of holding straight preferred stock over common stock?

    I.   a fixed dividend

    II. more voting power

    III. preference in the event of issuer bankruptcy

    IV. the ability to receive par value at maturity

    (A) I and II

    (B) II and IV

    (C) I and III

    (D) I, III, and IV

95. An investor purchases a DEF 4% convertible preferred stock at $90. The conversion price is $25. If the common stock is trading one point below parity, what is the price of DEF common stock?

    (A) $21.50

    (B) $22.50

    (C) $24.00

    (D) $26.00

96. What is the advantage to a corporation issuing callable preferred stock as compared to non-callable preferred stock?

    (A) It allows the issuer to take advantage of high interest rates.

    (B) The dividend rate on callable preferred stock is lower than that of non-callable preferred stock.

    (C) It allows the issuer to issue preferred stock with a lower fixed dividend after the call date.

    (D) Callable preferred stock usually has a longer maturity date.

97. Which TWO of the following are TRUE of preferred stock?

    I.   Holders have voting rights.

    II. Holders do not have voting rights.

    III. In the event of corporate bankruptcy, preferred stock is senior to common stock.

    IV. In the event of corporate bankruptcy, preferred stock is junior to common stock.

    (A) I and III

    (B) I and IV

    (C) II and III

    (D) II and IV

98. A company has previously issued 4% of $100 par cumulative preferred stock. Over the first three years, the company paid out $9 in dividends. If the company announces a common dividend in the following year, how much does it owe preferred stockholders?

    (A) $3

    (B) $4

    (C) $7

    (D) $16

99. One of your customers wants to purchase preferred stock that would help him reduce inflation risk. Which of the following types of preferred stock would you recommend?

    (A) participating

    (B) convertible

    (C) cumulative

    (D) noncumulative

100. Preferred dividends may be paid in the form of

    I.   cash

    II.   stock

    III.   product

    (A)   I only

    (B)   I and II

    (C)   I and III

    (D)   I, II, and III

101. Callable preferred stock is most advantageous to the issuer because

    (A)   the issuer can issue high-dividend stock

    (B)   the issuer can issue stock with a lower dividend

    (C)   the issuer can call in the stock at a price less than par value

    (D)   the issuer can replace stock with a higher dividend with stock with a lower dividend

102. Platinum Edge Corp. is offering 5% participating preferred stock. The 5% represents the

    (A)   minimum yearly dividend payment

    (B)   average yearly dividend payment

    (C)   maximum yearly dividend payment

    (D)   exact yearly dividend payment

103. With everything else being equal, a preferred stockholder would expect _____ preferred stock to pay the highest dividend.

    (A)   convertible

    (B)   straight

    (C)   callable

    (D)   cumulative

104. One of your clients wants to purchase preferred stock but wants to reduce the risk of inflation. You should recommend

    (A)   straight preferred stock

    (B)   callable preferred stock

    (C)   cumulative preferred stock

    (D)   convertible preferred stock

105–108 American Depositary Receipts

105. An ADR is

    (A)   a receipt for a foreign security trading in the U.S.

    (B)   a receipt for a foreign security trading in the U.S. and overseas

    (C)   a receipt for a U.S. security trading overseas

    (D)   a receipt for a U.S. security trading in the U.S. and overseas

106. All of the following are benefits of investing in ADRs EXCEPT

    (A)   the dividends are received in U.S. currency

    (B)   transactions are completed in U.S. currency

    (C)   it has low currency risk

    (D)   it allows U.S. investors to invest overseas

107. All of the following are characteristics of American depositary receipts EXCEPT

    (A)   they help U.S. companies gain access to foreign dollars

    (B)   investors do not receive the actual certificates

    (C)   investors can't vote

    (D)   dividends are paid in U.S. dollars

108. Holders of American depositary receipts assume which of the following risks?

    I.   liquidity risk

    II.   foreign currency risk

    III.   market risk

    IV.   political risk

    (A)   I, III, and IV

    (B)   II, III, and IV

    (C)   I, II, and III

    (D)   II and III

109–118 Rights and Warrants

109. All of the following are TRUE of warrants EXCEPT

    I.   they pay dividends quarterly

    II.   they are equity securities

    III.   they are used to buy common stock at a fixed price

    IV.   they give the holder a leveraged position

    (A)   I and II

    (B)   II and III

    (C)   II, III, and IV

    (D)   III and IV

110. Which of the following is NOT TRUE regarding warrants?

    (A)   They are marketable securities.

    (B)   They offer investors a long-term right to buy stock at a fixed price.

    (C)   They have voting rights.

    (D)   Investors do not receive dividends.

111. The Hanson Hilstrand Corp. is issuing new stock through a rights offering. If the stock trades at $30 and it costs $24 plus two rights to buy a new share, what is the theoretical value of a right cum-rights (prior to ex-rights)?

    (A) $0.50

    (B) $0.75

    (C) $1.00

    (D) $2.00

112. One of your clients owns 80 shares of common stock of a company issuing new shares in a rights offering. The stock trades at $12 per share. The company requires that investors must submit nine rights plus $10 to purchase a new share of stock. Fractional shares automatically become whole shares. How many additional shares may your client purchase, and what is the amount of money that needs to be paid for the new shares?

    I.   8 shares

    II.   9 shares

    III. $80 paid

    IV. $90 paid

    (A)   I and III

    (B)   I and IV

    (C)   II and III

    (D)   II and IV

113. All of the following are TRUE of warrants EXCEPT

    (A)   they have a longer life than rights

    (B)   they are non-marketable securities

    (C)   they are typically issued in units

    (D)   the exercise price is above the current market price of the common stock when issued

114. Which of the following are TRUE regarding warrants?

    I.   Warrants are often issued with a corporation's other securities to make an offering more attractive to investors.

    II.   Warrants provide a perpetual interest in an issuer's common stock.

    III.   Holders of warrants have no voting rights.

    (A) I and II

    (B) I and III

    (C) II and III

    (D) I, II, and III

115. Global International World Corporation is proposing an additional public offering of its common stock. According to the terms of its rights offering, current shareholders can purchase the stock for $35 per share plus five rights. If the market price of Global International is $45 after the ex-right date, what is the value of one right?

    (A) $1.00

    (B) $1.50

    (C) $2.00

    (D) $5.00

116. All of the following are TRUE about rights offerings EXCEPT

    (A) they are short-term

    (B) each share of outstanding common stock receives one right

    (C) they typically have a standby underwriter

    (D) rights are automatically received by preferred stockholders

117. HIJK Corp. wants to sell additional shares of common stock to its existing stockholders through a rights offering. Stockholders who want to subscribe to the rights offering must send the purchase amount with the rights certificate to the

    (A) registrar

    (B) transfer agent

    (C) rights agent

    (D) standby underwriter

118. A corporation needs to raise additional capital. Which of the following would help the corporation meet its goal?

    (A) declaring a stock dividend to existing shareholders

    (B) a rights distribution to existing shareholders

    (C) calling in their convertible bonds

    (D) splitting their stock 2 for 1

Chapter 3

Corporate and U.S. Government Debt Securities

•••

*W*hen issuers want to borrow money from the public, they issue debt securities. These issuers include corporations, local governments (municipal bonds), and the U.S. government. Unlike equity securities, holders of debt securities are creditors, not owners.

The Problems You'll Work On

In this chapter, you'll work on questions regarding the following:

- ✔ Understanding the different types of bonds

- ✔ Determining bond prices and yields

- ✔ Comparing the different types of bonds

- ✔ Seeing the benefits and risks of convertible bonds

- ✔ Recognizing the different types of U.S. government securities and their tax benefits

- ✔ Comparing money market instruments

- ✔ Calculating accrued interest when bonds are sold in between coupon dates

- ✔ Understanding collateralized mortgage obligations (CMOs) and collateralized debt obligations (CDOs)

What to Watch Out For

Keep the following tips in mind as you answer questions in this chapter:

- ✔ Be aware of words that can change the answer you're looking for, such as EXCEPT or NOT.

- ✔ Don't jump too quickly to answer a question. Make sure you read each question and answer choice completely before choosing an answer.

- ✔ Make sure you understand which type of bond the question is talking about prior to answering because there are many differences.

- ✔ Double-check your math when doing calculations.

119–129 Types of Bonds

119. Corporations may issue which of the following debt securities?

   I.   equipment trust bonds

   II.   mortgage bonds

   III.   double-barreled bonds

   IV.   revenue bonds

   (A)   I and IV

   (B)   I and II

   (C)   II, III, and IV

   (D)   I, II, III, and IV

120. Term bonds are quoted according to

   (A)   a percentage of dollar price

   (B)   its nominal yield

   (C)   its yield to call

   (D)   its yield to maturity

121. Which of the following BEST describes a guaranteed bond?

   (A)   one that is mainly issued by transportation companies

   (B)   one that is backed by the assets of another company

   (C)   one that is issued by corporations in bankruptcy

   (D)   one that is backed by stocks and bonds held by the issuer

122. The call premium on a callable bond is

   (A)   the amount an investor must pay above par value when calling the bonds early

   (B)   the amount an issuer must pay above par value when calling its bonds early

   (C)   the amount of interest an issuer must pay on its callable bonds

   (D)   the difference in interest an issuer must pay on its callable bonds over its non-callable bonds

123. The type of secured bond typically issued by transportation companies is called

   (A)   a guaranteed bond

   (B)   a mortgage bond

   (C)   an equipment trust bond

   (D)   a collateral trust bond

124. HIJ Corp. has issued $30 million worth of convertible mortgage bonds, which are convertible for $25. The bonds are callable beginning in March 2020, while the maturity date is March 2040. The bond trades at 98, and the stock trades at $24. The bonds are secured by

   (A)   rolling stock

   (B)   the full faith and credit of HIJ Corp.

   (C)   securities owned by HIJ Corp.

   (D)   a lien on property owned by HIJ Corp.

125. Which of the following are TRUE regarding Eurodollar bonds?

   I.   They must be registered with the SEC.

   II.   They are U.S.-dollar denominated.

   III.   They are issued by non-American companies outside of the U.S. and the issuer's home state.

   IV.   They are subject to currency risk.

   (A)   II, III, and IV

   (B)   I, II and IV

   (C)   I, II, and III

   (D)   I, III, and IV

126. Which of the following has become the most common form of delivery for corporate and U.S. government bonds?

   (A)   fully registered

   (B)   partially registered

   (C)   bearer

   (D)   book entry

127. A collateral trust bond is

(A) mainly issued by transportation companies

(B) backed by stocks and bonds owned by the issuer

(C) issued by corporations in bankruptcy

(D) backed by the assets of a parent company

128. One of your clients is interested in bonds with a relatively high level of regular income with only a moderate amount of risk. Which of the following would you recommend?

(A) high-yield bonds

(B) convertible bonds

(C) mortgage bonds

(D) income bonds

129. Rank the following mortgage bonds from safest to riskiest.

I. open-end

II. closed-end

III. prior lien

(A) I, II, III

(B) II, III, I

(C) III, II, I

(D) II, I, III

130–140 Price and Yield Calculations

130. What is the current yield on a T-bond with an initial offering price of $1,000, a current market price of $101.16, and a coupon rate of 4.25%?

(A) 4.19%

(B) 4.25%

(C) 4.37%

(D) 4.41%

131. A 4% bond has a basis of 3.30%. The bond is trading at

(A) a discount

(B) a premium

(C) par

(D) a price that could be at a discount, at a premium, or at par value depending on the maturity

132. A 6% corporate bond is trading at 101. What yield could an investor expect if purchasing the bond at the current price and holding it ten years until maturity?

(A) 4.76%

(B) 5%

(C) 5.24%

(D) 6%

133. A 4% bond is purchased at 92 with 25 years until maturity, What is the current yield?

(A) 3.65%

(B) 4%

(C) 4.35%

(D) 4.66%

134. Which of the following is TRUE of bonds selling at a discount?

I. The market price is lower than par value.

II. The current yield is greater than the coupon rate.

III. Interest rates most likely declined after the bonds were issued.

IV. The yield to maturity is greater than the current yield.

(A) I and III

(B) II and III

(C) II, III, and IV

(D) I, II, and IV

135. ABC Corporate Bonds are quoted at 101⅜. How much would an investor purchasing ten of these bonds pay?

(A) $1,013.75

(B) $1,013.80

(C) $10,137.50

(D) $10,138.00

136. A bond has increased in value by 50 basis points, which is equal to which TWO of the following?

   I.   0.50%

   II. 5%

   III. $5

   IV. $50

(A) I and III

(B) I and IV

(C) II and III

(D) II and IV

137. One of your clients purchased a 4% ABC convertible bond yielding 5% and convertible at $50. If your client holds the bond until maturity, how much will she receive?

(A) $1,000

(B) $1,020

(C) $1,025

(D) $1,050

138. An investor purchases a bond with a 6% coupon. The bond is callable in ten years at par. The maturity of the bond is 15 years. If the bond is purchased at 102, which of the following is TRUE?

(A) The yield to maturity is higher than the yield to call.

(B) The yield to call is higher than the yield to maturity.

(C) Because the bond is callable at par, the yield to maturity and the yield to call are the same.

(D) The current yield is higher than the nominal yield.

139. An investor buys a 5% callable corporate bond at 95 with 20 years until maturity. The bond was called five years later at 105. What is the yield to call?

(A) 4.3%

(B) 5.7%

(C) 6.3%

(D) 7.0%

140. An investor purchased a 4 percent corporate bond at 98 with ten years to maturity. If the bond is currently trading at 101, how much interest will the investor receive next time he gets paid?

(A) $19.60

(B) $20.00

(C) $20.20

(D) $40.00

141–155 Comparing Bonds

141. Which of the following would affect the liquidity of a bond?

    I.   the rating

    II. the coupon rate

    III. the maturity

    IV. call features

    (A) I and II

    (B) I, II, and III

    (C) II, III, and IV

    (D) I, II, III, and IV

142. A corporate bond indenture would include which of the following?

    I.   the nominal yield

    II. the rating

    III. any collateral backing the bond

    IV. the yield to maturity

    (A) I and II

    (B) I and III

    (C) I, III, and IV

    (D) III and IV

143. Which of the following BEST describes the call premium for debt securities?

    (A) the amount that investors paid above par value to purchase the bond in the primary market

    (B) the amount that investors paid above par value to purchase the bond in the secondary market

    (C) the amount that investors must pay to the issuer for having the bond called early

    (D) the amount that the issuer must pay to investors for calling its bonds early

144. If an official statement has a dated date of January 15 but the first coupon payment is set at August 1, the first payment is a(n)

    (A) short coupon

    (B) intermediate coupon

    (C) long coupon

    (D) discount payment

145. The indenture of a corporate bond includes the

    (A) current yield

    (B) yield to maturity

    (C) yield to call

    (D) nominal yield

146. Which TWO of the following would make a corporate bond LEAST subject to liquidity risk?

    I.   bonds with a high credit rating

    II. bonds with a low credit rating

    III. bonds with a long-term maturity

    IV. bonds with a short-term maturity

    (A) I and III

    (B) I and IV

    (C) II and III

    (D) II and IV

147. One of your clients wants to purchase a corporate bond with a high degree of safety. You have recommended four different bonds with varying credit ratings. Place the following S&P bond ratings from highest to lowest:

    I.   A+

    II. AA–

    III. AA

    IV. AAA

    (A) IV, III, II, I

    (B) IV, I, III, II

    (C) I, IV, III, II

    (D) I, II, III, IV

148. Which of the following is the MOST appealing to the issuer of a corporate bond?

- (A) a high coupon rate
- (B) a put feature
- (C) a high call premium
- (D) little call protection

149. If a bond's YTM is 5%, which of the following would MOST likely be refunded by the issuer?

- I. Coupon 5.5%, maturing in 2030, callable in 2021 at 103
- II. Coupon 4.5%, maturing in 2030, callable in 2020 at 103
- III. Coupon 4.5%, maturing in 2030, callable in 2020 at 100
- IV. Coupon 5.5%, maturing in 2030, callable in 2021 at 100

- (A) I and II
- (B) II and IV
- (C) III only
- (D) IV only

150. Which of the following is rated by Moody's and Standard & Poor's?

- (A) default risk
- (B) market risk
- (C) systematic risk
- (D) all of the above

151. Which of the following securities is exempt from the Trust Indenture Act of 1939?

- I. T-bonds
- II. GO bonds
- III. equipment trust bonds
- IV. revenue bonds

- (A) I only
- (B) II and III
- (C) I, II, and IV
- (D) I, III, and IV

152. Mrs. Jones wants to put away money for her 8-year-old child's college tuition. Which of the following investments would be MOST suitable to meet her needs?

- (A) zero-coupon bonds
- (B) growth company common stocks
- (C) growth company preferred stocks
- (D) certificates of deposit

153. Which of the following Moody's bond ratings are considered investment grade?

- I. Aa
- II. A
- III. Baa
- IV. Ba

- (A) I and II
- (B) I and III
- (C) I, II, and III
- (D) I, II, III, and IV

154. You have a customer who is risk-averse and wants to start investing in bonds. Which of the following should you NOT recommend?

- (A) TIPS
- (B) income bonds
- (C) AAA rated corporate bonds
- (D) T-bonds

155. Which type of bond issue has an equal amount of debt maturing each year?

- (A) term
- (B) series
- (C) serial
- (D) balloon

156–164 Convertible Bonds

156. A bond is convertible into common stock for $25. If the stock trades at $28, what is the parity price of the bond?

(A) $990

(B) $1,020

(C) $1,040

(D) $1,120

157. Curly Fry Lighting Corporation bonds are convertible at $50. If DIM's common stock is trading in the market for $42 and the bonds are trading for 83, which of the following statements are TRUE?

I. The bonds are trading below parity.

II. The stock is trading below parity.

III. Converting the bonds would be profitable.

IV. Converting the bonds would not be profitable.

(A) I and III

(B) I and IV

(C) II and III

(D) II and IV

158. Dee Plump, an investor, owns a TUB 5% convertible bond purchased at 103 with five years until maturity. If she holds the bond until maturity, Dee will receive

(A) $970

(B) $1,000

(C) $1,015

(D) $1,030

159. One of your clients holds ABC convertible bonds in his portfolio. ABC bonds are convertible into 40 shares of ABC common stock. Your client has the choice of converting the bonds while ABC common stock is trading at $28.50 or allowing the bond to be called at 104. The situation being faced by your client is called

(A) a forced conversion

(B) an arbitrage situation

(C) risk arbitrage

(D) a refunding call

160. A bond is convertible into 25 shares of common stock. The bond trades at 98, and the stock trades at $40. If the bond is called at 102, which of the following is the BEST alternative for an investor?

(A) Allow the bond to be called.

(B) Sell the bond in the market.

(C) Convert the bond and sell the stock.

(D) None of the above.

161. TUV Corp. has issued $10 million worth of convertible mortgage bonds, which are convertible for $40. The bonds are callable beginning in March 2020, while the maturity date is March 2030. The bond trades at 110, and the stock trades at $48. What is the conversion ratio of the bonds?

(A) 10

(B) 16.66

(C) 20

(D) 25

162. TUV convertible bonds are trading at 98. TUV is convertible into common stock at $20. If the common stock is 10% below parity, what is the price of the common stock?

(A) $8.82

(B) $9.80

(C) $17.64

(D) $19.60

163. An anti-dilution clause is important to holders of which of the following debt securities?

(A) adjustment bonds

(B) convertible bonds

(C) income bonds

(D) zero-coupon bonds

164. DUD Corp. previously issued $5 million par value of convertible bonds. The bonds are convertible at $25 and are issued with an anti-dilution covenant. If DUD Corp. declares a 5% stock dividend, which of the following are TRUE on the ex-dividend date?

I. The conversion price will increase.

II. The conversion price will decrease.

III. The conversion ratio will increase.

IV. The conversion ratio will decrease.

(A) I and III

(B) I and IV

(C) II and III

(D) II and IV

165–181 U.S. Government Securities

165. Which of the following are part of the Federal Farm Credit System?

I. Federal Home Loan Banks

II. Federal Intermediate Credit Banks

III. Bank for Cooperatives

IV. Federal Land Banks

(A) II, III, and IV

(B) I, III, and IV

(C) I, II, and III

(D) I, II, and IV

166. All of the following are TRUE of T-bills EXCEPT

I. they make semiannual interest payments

II. they are issued with three-, six-, and nine-month maturities

III. most T-bills are callable

IV. they are traded on a discount yield basis

(A) I and II

(B) I, II, and III

(C) II and IV

(D) II, III, and IV

167. One of your customers purchased ten 4.5% Treasury bonds at 100-12. What was the total dollar amount of the purchase?

(A) $1,001.20

(B) $1,003.75

(C) $10,012.00

(D) $10,037.50

168. A security is quoted as follows:

0.090 – 0.080

This is the quote for a

(A) Ginnie Mae

(B) Treasury bill

(C) Treasury note

(D) Treasury bond

169. Treasury bonds have initial maturities of

(A) 1 month to 1 year

(B) more than 1 year to 10 years

(C) between 10 and 30 years

(D) between 1 and 30 years

170. Which of the following is TRUE of GNMAs?

I. They are considered safer than FHLMCs.

II. They are backed by the U.S. government.

III. They pay interest semiannually.

IV. The interest received by investors is state tax-free.

(A) I and II

(B) II, III, and IV

(C) I and IV

(D) I, II, III, and IV

171. The maximum maturity on a T-note is

(A) one year

(B) two years

(C) five years

(D) ten years

172. An investor has $10,000 to invest. Which of the following investments would expose the investor to the LEAST amount of capital risk?

(A) blue chip stocks

(B) warrants

(C) investment grade bonds

(D) call options

173. If an investor is purchasing a T-bond quoted $102.04 to $102.24, what would he be expected to pay for the bond, excluding commission?

(A) $1,021.25

(B) $1,022.40

(C) $1,024.00

(D) $1,027.50

174. Which of the following securities earns interest?

I. Treasury bills

II. Treasury bonds

III. Treasury stock

IV. Treasury STRIPS

(A) II only

(B) I, II, and IV

(C) II and III

(D) II and IV

175. Place the following U.S. government securities in order of initial maturity from shortest term to longest term.

I. Treasury notes

II. Treasury bonds

III. Treasury bills

(A) I, II, III

(B) III, II, I

(C) III, I, II

(D) II, I, III

176. Which of the following statements is TRUE relating to Series EE savings bonds?

(A) The interest is exempt from federal taxes.

(B) The default risk is higher than GO bonds.

(C) They are sold at face value.

(D) They can be purchased only in multiples of $1,000.

177. Treasury bonds issued by the U.S. government are issued in what form?

(A) book entry

(B) bearer

(C) fully registered

(D) partially registered

178. Which TWO of the following are TRUE regarding T-STRIPS?

    I.   Holders do not pay taxes on the interest earned until maturity.

    II. Holders must pay taxes on the interest earned annually.

    III. Holders receive the principal and interest at maturity.

    IV. Holders receive interest semiannually, and principal is paid at maturity.

    (A) I and III

    (B) I and IV

    (C) II and III

    (D) II and IV

179. All of the following are benefits of investing in TIPS EXCEPT

    (A) a guaranteed profit

    (B) they are low-risk investments

    (C) the principal keeps pace with inflation

    (D) they can be purchased directly through the Treasury Direct system

180. Which of the following are U.S. government securities?

    I.   T-bills

    II. TIPS

    III. I savings bonds

    IV. FRNs

    (A) I and II

    (B) I and III

    (C) I, II, and III

    (D) I, II, III, and IV

181. One of your clients is interested in purchasing U.S. debt securities. She is looking for securities that are non-marketable, but she is concerned about purchasing power risk. You should recommend that she consider purchasing

    (A) EE bonds

    (B) HH bonds

    (C) I bonds

    (D) TIPS

182–189 Money Market Instruments

182. This money market instrument is guaranteed by a bank and provides capital for importing and exporting.

    (A) American depositary receipts

    (B) bankers' acceptance

    (C) Eurodollar bonds

    (D) Fed funds

183. One of your smaller clients is interested in purchasing negotiable CDs. You may tell him that this may not be an appropriate investment because the minimum denomination for negotiable CDs is

    (A) $25,000

    (B) $50,000

    (C) $100,000

    (D) $500,000

184. Money market instruments are

    (A) short-term debt

    (B) long-term debt

    (C) common stock

    (D) preferred stock

185. Your broker-dealer enters a repurchase agreement with a large institutional customer. Which of the following is TRUE regarding this agreement?

(A) Your broker-dealer bought securities from the customer with an agreement to sell them back at a predetermined date.

(B) Your broker-dealer sold securities to the customer with an agreement to buy them back at a predetermined date.

(C) Your broker-dealer purchased securities from the customer with an arrangement to sell them to a third party.

(D) Your broker-dealer sold securities to the customer who had an arrangement to sell them to a third party.

186. Which of the following is NOT TRUE regarding Eurodollar deposits?

(A) They pay a higher rate of interest than U.S. banks.

(B) The interest rate is determined from the discount rate set by the Federal Reserve Board (FRB).

(C) The deposit is denominated in U.S. dollars but held in foreign banks.

(D) The risk is higher than depositing money in U.S. banks.

187. Corporate commercial paper has a maximum maturity of

(A) 30 days

(B) 45 days

(C) 90 days

(D) 270 days

188. Which of the following money market instruments trades with accrued interest?

(A) Treasury bills

(B) bankers' acceptance

(C) jumbo CDs

(D) commercial paper

189. Which of the following is TRUE about commercial paper?

I. It trades without accrued interest.

II. It is backed by the issuer's assets.

III. It is an exempt security.

IV. It matures in 270 days or less.

(A) I, III, and IV

(B) II and IV

(C) II, III, and IV

(D) I, II, and III

190–197 Accrued Interest

190. An investor buys a new municipal bond on Tuesday, February 18, with coupon dates March 1 and September 1 and a dated date of January 1. How many days of accrued interest does the investor owe?

(A) 47 days

(B) 48 days

(C) 49 days

(D) 50 days

191. One of your clients buys a corporate bond on Monday, May 10, with coupon dates February 15 and August 15. How many days of accrued interest does your client owe?

(A) 85 days

(B) 86 days

(C) 87 days

(D) 88 days

192. Accrued interest is calculated

(A) from the previous coupon date up to but not including the settlement date

(B) from the settlement date up to the following coupon date

(C) from the previous coupon date up to and including the settlement date

(D) from the trade date up to and including the next coupon date

193. The dated date is best described as

(A) the trade date

(B) the settlement date

(C) the date on which a bond begins accruing interest

(D) the issue date

194. Accrued interest on U.S. government securities is calculated by using

I. actual day per month

II. 30-day months

III. a 360-day year

IV. actual days in a year

(A) I and III

(B) I and IV

(C) II and III

(D) II and IV

195. On Tuesday, March 17, one of your customers purchases one 5.4% corporate bond maturing in 2030. If the bonds pay interest on January 1 and July 1, how much accrued interest is added to the purchaser's price?

(A) $9.42

(B) $10.18

(C) $10.65

(D) $11.85

196. On Thursday, October 19, one of your customers purchases one 4.6% U.S. government bond maturing in 2035. If the coupon dates are January 15 and July 15, how many days of accrued interest does your customer owe?

(A) 94 days

(B) 95 days

(C) 97 days

(D) 101 days

197. Which of the following bonds normally trades without accrued interest?

(A) Treasury notes

(B) subordinated debentures

(C) debentures

(D) income bonds

198–208 CMOs and CDOs

198. You are making recommendations to a client. If your client is interested in CMOs, you may compare them to which of the following?

(A) certificates of deposit

(B) mortgage bonds

(C) other CMOs only

(D) FNMAs

199. All of the following are TRUE of collateralized debt obligations EXCEPT

(A) they are known as asset-backed securities

(B) they are always backed by mortgages

(C) they are backed by credit cards, auto loans, and so on

(D) they are liquid investments

200. CMOs typically have one of these TWO S&P ratings:

I. AAA

II. AA

III. A

IV. BBB

(A) I and II

(B) II and III

(C) III and IV

(D) II and IV

201. One of your clients is interested in investing in CMOs for the first time. If your client's main concern is safety, which of the following tranches would you recommend?

(A) Z

(B) TAC

(C) companion

(D) PAC

202. When recommending CDOs to one of your clients, you may state which of the following?

I. The loans that determine the value of the CDOs are liquid.

II. CDOs have tranches that have different forms of prepayment and extension risk.

III. CDOs are not suitable for all investors.

IV. They represent the securitization of non-mortgage loans, including credit cards and auto loans.

(A) I only

(B) I and III

(C) II and IV

(D) II, III, and IV

203. All of the following are part of a CMO EXCEPT

(A) GNMA

(B) FNMA

(C) SLMA

(D) FHLMC

204. The minimum denomination of a CMO is

(A) $500

(B) $1,000

(C) $10,000

(D) $25,000

205. Which TWO of the following are TRUE regarding prepayment of CMOs?

I. As interest rates rise, prepayments increase.

II. As interest rates rise, prepayments decrease.

III. As interest rates fall, prepayments increase.

IV. As interest rates fall, prepayments decrease.

(A) I and III

(B) I and IV

(C) II and III

(D) II and IV

206. One of your customers is interested in investing in collateralized mortgage obligations for the first time. You should disclose to your customer that

(A) because they are made up of GNMA, FNMA, and FHLMC securities, they are guaranteed by the U.S. government

(B) all CMOs carry an equal amount of risk

(C) they are triple tax-free investments

(D) they are subject to prepayment and extension risk

207. Which of the following is NOT TRUE about GNMAs?

(A) They issue pass-through certificates.

(B) They are backed by commercial, FHA, and VA mortgages.

(C) They pay interest semiannually.

(D) The interest received is subject to federal, state, and local taxes.

208. Which of the following CMO tranches is supported by a companion tranche?

(A) PAC

(B) Z

(C) PO

(D) IO

Chapter 4

Municipal Bonds

• •

Municipal bonds are ones issued by state governments, local governments, or U.S. territories. Municipalities may issue many types of municipal bonds, but the two main types are GO (general obligation) bonds and revenue bonds. Municipal bonds may be backed by taxes or by a revenue-producing facility.

After you become a licensed registered rep, you may not spend a lot of time selling municipal bonds, but you need to know about them for the Series 7 exam and expect to be tested heavily.

The Problems You'll Work On

When working through the questions in this chapter, be prepared to

- ✔ Compare the differences between GO bonds and revenue bonds.
- ✔ Compare other municipal bonds and notes.
- ✔ Understand the tax treatment of municipal bonds.
- ✔ Determine how new issues of municipal bonds come to market (primary market).
- ✔ Analyze municipal bonds and make recommendations.
- ✔ Remember rules relating to municipal bonds.

What to Watch Out For

This chapter includes a lot of municipal bond questions, so watch out for questions that require you to

- ✔ Recognize the difference between taxable and non-taxable municipal bonds.
- ✔ Understand an investor's needs when answering questions regarding recommendations.
- ✔ Pay attention to key words, like EXCEPT and NOT, that would change your answer choice.

209–224 GO and Revenue Bonds

209. One of your clients is interested in purchasing municipal GO bonds and is looking for guidance. You can inform him that

   I. they are issued to fund revenue-producing facilities

   II. they are backed by the taxing power of the municipality

   III. they need approval of voters to be issued

   IV. they are subject to a debt ceiling

   (A) I and IV

   (B) II, III, and IV

   (C) II and III

   (D) I, III, and IV

210. Why should an investor NOT trade municipal GO bonds short?

   (A) because they are usually thin issues

   (B) because municipal securities do not trade on an exchange

   (C) because MSRB rules prohibit the short selling of municipal bonds

   (D) because the SEC prohibits the short selling of municipal bonds

211. Which of the following municipal bodies receives no revenue from ad valorem taxes?

   (A) school districts

   (B) county governments

   (C) state governments

   (D) town governments

212. Uriah Silva is interested in purchasing Miami municipal general obligation bonds. The bonds were originally issued with a serial maturity. If Uriah believes that interest rates are going to drop over the next 20 to 30 years, which maturity would you advise him to buy?

   (A) short-term

   (B) intermediate-term

   (C) long-term

   (D) a combination of long-term, short-term, and intermediate-term

213. A municipality decides to call its general obligation bonds due to mature in 2022 and to finance the call by issuing bonds with a maturity date of 2035. This is known as

   (A) pre-refunding

   (B) advance refunding

   (C) redeeming

   (D) refunding

214. Plano, Texas, is issuing $30 million worth of callable general obligation bonds. All of the following are TRUE about the call feature of these bonds EXCEPT

   (A) the call feature makes the bonds less marketable

   (B) callable bonds have a higher coupon rate than non-callable bonds

   (C) the call feature makes the bonds more marketable

   (D) callable bonds are issued with certain degree of call protection

215. The largest source of backing for a local GO bond is

   (A) property tax

   (B) sales tax

   (C) income tax

   (D) traffic fines and parking tickets

216. In which of the following instances would a municipal issuer require voter approval prior to bonds being issued?

    I. bonds being issued to build a public school

    II. bonds being issued to build a county jail

    III. bonds being issued to build a toll road

    IV. bonds being issued to build a new airport

  (A) II and IV

  (B) I and II

  (C) III and IV

  (D) I, III, and IV

217. An individual owns property with a market value of $220,000 and an assessed value of $235,000. If the tax rate of the municipality is 14 mills, what is the ad valorem tax?

  (A) $3,080

  (B) $30,800

  (C) $3,290

  (D) $32,900

218. Which of the following municipal securities is backed by the full faith and credit of the issuer?

    I. GO

    II. revenue

    III. double-barreled

    IV. moral obligation

  (A) I and II

  (B) I and III

  (C) II and IV

  (D) I, III, and IV

219. Which of the following is NOT a source of funding for municipal revenue bonds?

  (A) airports

  (B) tolls

  (C) property taxes

  (D) user fees

220. Municipal revenue bonds may be issued to fund which of the following projects?

    I. a toll road

    II. a sports stadium

    III. a public library

    IV. an airport

  (A) I, II, and III

  (B) I, III, and IV

  (C) I and IV

  (D) I, II, and IV

221. A municipality issues revenue bonds. The revenues are not sufficient to meet the debt service payments. If the municipality is able to meet the debt service obligation of the revenue bonds by backing it with its taxing power, the debt is termed

  (A) moral obligation bonds

  (B) special situation bonds

  (C) special tax bonds

  (D) double-barreled bonds

222. Which of the following would be found on the indenture of a revenue bond?

    I. the legal opinion

    II. the rating

    III. covenants

    IV. flow of funds

  (A) I, II, and III

  (B) I, III, and IV

  (C) II, III, and IV

  (D) I, II, III, and IV

223. All of the following statements regarding municipal revenue bonds are TRUE EXCEPT

    (A) the maturity date of the issue will typically exceed the useful life of the facility backing the bonds

    (B) they are not subject to a debt ceiling

    (C) they may be issued by interstate authorities

    (D) the principal and interest is paid from revenues received from the facility backing the bonds

224. All of the following are sources of funding for municipal revenue bonds EXCEPT

    (A) property taxes

    (B) toll bridges

    (C) sewer and water fees

    (D) toll roads

225–244 Other Municipal Bonds and Notes

225. Special tax bonds are

    (A) backed by charges on the property that benefits

    (B) backed by excise taxes

    (C) types of general obligation bonds

    (D) types of moral obligation bonds

226. Which of the following is TRUE of industrial development revenue bonds?

    (A) They are backed by municipal taxes.

    (B) They are backed by municipal revenues.

    (C) They are backed by a corporation.

    (D) None of the above.

227. Which of the following is TRUE of special assessment bonds?

    (A) They are backed by charges on the benefitted property.

    (B) They are backed by excise taxes.

    (C) They require legislative approval to be issued.

    (D) They are backed by a revenue-producing facility.

228. Which of the following municipal bonds allows municipality to receive from the U.S. government tax credit payments of 35% of the amount of interest paid?

    (A) IDRs

    (B) direct payment BABs

    (C) tax credit BABs

    (D) special assessment bonds

229. A double-barreled bond is a combination of

    I. revenue bonds

    II. special tax bonds

    III. build America bonds

    IV. general obligation bonds

    (A) I and II

    (B) II and III

    (C) II and IV

    (D) I and IV

230. Which of the following types of municipal bonds would MOST likely be issued to build a bridge?

    (A) BABs

    (B) PHAs

    (C) IDRs

    (D) LRBs

231. When purchasing a limited tax general obligation bond, what is limited?

(A) the number of taxpayers backing the bond issue

(B) the type of tax that can be used to back the bond issue

(C) the number of investors who are able to purchase the bond issue

(D) the number of syndicate members who are allowed to sell the bond issue

232. Clint, one of your clients, is interested in investing in municipal bonds for the first time. He is primarily interested in safety. Which of the following should you recommend?

(A) moral obligation bonds

(B) public housing authority bonds

(C) special assessment bonds

(D) double-barreled bonds

233. For clients looking for a safe investment, new housing authority bonds would be acceptable because

(A) they are backed by U.S. government subsidies

(B) they are backed by the taxing power of the municipal issuer

(C) they are backed by rental income, which remains constant

(D) they are typically backed by AMBAC insurance

234. RANs, BANs, TANs, and CLNs are issued by municipalities to

(A) provide short-term financing

(B) provide intermediate-term financing

(C) provide long-term financing

(D) provide flexible-term financing

235. All of the following are types of municipal notes EXCEPT

(A) PNs

(B) AONs

(C) TRANs

(D) CLNs

236. Which of the following is the highest rating for a bond anticipation note?

(A) AAA

(B) Aaa

(C) MIG1

(D) MIG4

237. All of the following municipal securities could have a rating of MIG3 EXCEPT

(A) PNs

(B) TRANs

(C) CLNs

(D) GOs

238. Suffolk County is experiencing a temporary cash flow shortage that is expected to last about three months. Which of the following would Suffolk County MOST likely issue to meet its current obligations?

(A) construction loan notes

(B) tax anticipation notes

(C) revenue bonds

(D) general obligation bonds

239. MIG ratings are applied to

(A) municipal GO bonds

(B) municipal notes

(C) municipal revenue bonds

(D) build America bonds

240. Which of the following are types of municipal notes?

    I.   PNs

    II. TRANs

    III. GANs

    IV. RANs

    (A) II and IV

    (B) I, III, and IV

    (C) III and IV

    (D) I, II, III, and IV

241. Which of the following is TRUE of municipal certificates of participation?

    I.   They require voter approval prior to being issued.

    II. They do not require voter approval prior to being issued.

    III. They are a type of revenue bond.

    IV. They are a type of GO bond.

    (A) I and III

    (B) I and IV

    (C) II and III

    (D) II and IV

242. A client is interested in purchasing municipal bonds but is concerned about the price of the bonds dropping due to anticipated rising interest rates. Which of the following securities would BEST meet his needs?

    (A) reset bonds

    (B) double-barreled bonds

    (C) general obligation bonds

    (D) industrial development revenue bonds

243. Akron, Ohio, has issued revenue bonds to build a local stadium. The indenture of the bonds states that emergency funding from the Ohio State legislature would be pursued in the event that the debt service exceeds revenues. What type of bond is this?

    (A) a moral obligation bond

    (B) a double-barreled bond

    (C) debentures

    (D) BABs

244. Which of the following is TRUE about auction rate securities (ARS) issued by a municipality?

    (A) They have stable prices and a fixed coupon rate.

    (B) They have stable prices and a variable coupon rate.

    (C) They have volatile prices and a fixed coupon rate.

    (D) They have volatile price and a variable coupon rate.

245–259 Tax Treatment of Municipal Bonds

245. Dallas, Texas, is issuing $100 million general obligation bonds at a discount from par with a coupon rate of 2.5%. If the bonds are issued at 90 and there are 30 years until maturity, how is the discount treated to purchasers of the new issue if the bond is held to maturity?

    (A) The discount is accreted annually and not taxed on the federal level.

    (B) The discount is accreted annually and treated as federally taxable income each year.

    (C) The discount is not accreted annually but treated as taxable income at maturity.

    (D) The amount of the discount is treated as a long-term capital gain subject to tax on both the state and federal level.

246. All of the following is subject to federal taxation EXCEPT

    I.   interest on municipal bonds

    II. interest on U.S. government bonds

    III. capital gain on municipal bonds

    IV. cash dividends on stocks

    (A) I only

    (B) I and III

    (C) II, III, and IV

    (D) II and III

247. Gary Golden is a resident of Atlantic City, New Jersey. Gary purchased 20 New Jersey municipal bonds. What is the tax treatment of the interest that Gary earns on his New Jersey bonds?

    (A) It is exempt from local taxes only.

    (B) It is exempt from state taxes only.

    (C) It is exempt from federal taxes only.

    (D) It is exempt from federal, state, and local taxes.

248. Which of the following bonds generally have the lowest yields?

    (A) AA rated corporate bonds

    (B) GO bonds

    (C) T-bonds

    (D) cannot be determined

249. Tito Sonnen lives in Oregon and is considering purchasing a bond. He has settled on either a 4% municipal bond offered by Oregon or a 6% corporate bond offered by Ground and Pound Corp., which has headquarters in Oregon. Tito needs some guidance and would like you to help him determine which bond will provide him with the greatest return. Which of the following information do you need before you can make the appropriate recommendation?

    (A) Tito's place of employment

    (B) Tito's tax bracket

    (C) how long Tito has lived in Oregon

    (D) Tito's other holdings

250. One of your clients purchases a new OID municipal GO zero-coupon bond for 70 with ten years until maturity. If your client holds the bond until maturity, what is her tax consequence?

    (A) $0

    (B) $300 ordinary income divided by the ten years until maturity

    (C) $300 capital gain

    (D) It is impossible to determine without knowing the client's tax bracket.

251. Which of the following investments would provide the BEST after-tax return for an individual in the 28% tax bracket?

    (A) 4.25% treasury bond

    (B) 5% AA rated corporate bond

    (C) 4% GO bond

    (D) 5.5% preferred stock

252. Holders of which of the following municipal securities may be subject to alternative minimum tax?

    (A) BANs

    (B) special assessment bonds

    (C) GO Bonds

    (D) IDRs

253. One of your clients who is in the 28% tax bracket is interested in two different debt securities. One of them is a 6% corporate bond, and the other is a 5% municipal general obligation bond. Which of the following is TRUE regarding his investment choices?

(A) The general obligation bond has a higher after-tax yield.

(B) The corporate bond has a higher after-tax yield.

(C) The corporate bond and municipal bond have an equivalent after-tax yield.

(D) There is not enough information given to determine the after-tax yield.

254. Mr. Jones is in the 31% tax bracket and owns a 6% corporate bond. What is the municipal equivalent yield?

(A) 3.96%

(B) 4.14%

(C) 5.11%

(D) 5.42%

255. A client is interested in purchasing tax-free municipal bonds on margin. You should let your client know that

(A) the interest charges on the debit balance are not tax-deductible

(B) the interest charges on the debit balance are tax-deductible

(C) the interest charges on the debit balance are not tax-deductible unless approved by the MSRB

(D) the interest charges on the debit balance are tax-deductible if subject to AMT

256. Which of the following municipal securities might be included in the AMT calculation?

(A) GO bonds

(B) special assessment bonds

(C) special tax bonds

(D) industrial development revenue bonds

257. An investor purchased a 4% municipal GO bond in the secondary market at 95 with ten years until maturity. What are the yearly tax consequences for this investor?

(A) $45 federally tax-free interest

(B) $40 federally tax-free interest

(C) $40 federally tax-free interest and $5 taxable accretion

(D) $40 federally tax-free interest and $5 tax-free accretion

258. A customer purchased an OID 4% municipal bond with ten years to maturity at 90. If the bond is held to maturity, what are the tax consequences?

(A) $900 return of capital, $400 federally tax-free interest, and $100 of taxable accretion over the life of the bond

(B) $900 return of capital and $500 federally tax-free interest over the life of the bond

(C) $1,000 return of capital and $400 federally tax-free interest over the life of the bond

(D) $900 return of capital, $400 taxable interest, and $100 of non-taxable accretion over the life of the bond

259. You are in the process of convincing one of your clients to invest in triple tax-free municipal bonds. Which of the following U.S. territories issues municipal bonds that are triple tax-free?

　I.　U.S. Virgin Islands

　II.　Puerto Rico

　III.　Guam

　IV.　Hawaii

(A) I and IV

(B) I, II, and IV

(C) I, II, and III

(D) I, II, III, and IV

260–272 Primary Market

260. Suffolk County, New York, is issuing bonds through a competitive offering; how do they determine the winning syndicate?

(A) the proposal with the highest payment

(B) the proposal with the longest maturity

(C) the proposal with the lowest interest cost

(D) the proposal with the lowest spread

261. An official notice of sale contains all of the following EXCEPT

(A) the bond rating

(B) interest and payment dates

(C) method and place of settlement

(D) the name of the bond counsel

262. If interest rates are high and expected to decrease in the near future, which of the following bond maturities would a municipality MOST likely issue?

(A) short-term bonds

(B) intermediate-term bonds

(C) long-term bonds

(D) cannot be determined

263. Which of the following factors affect the marketability of municipal bonds?

　I.　the maturity

　II.　the rating

　III.　the issuer's name

　IV.　the dated date

(A) II and III

(B) II, III, and IV

(C) I, II, and III

(D) I, II, III, and IV

264. Smithtown, New York, is auctioning a block of new bonds to underwriters. What document will Smithtown use to notify potential underwriters about the auction?

(A) the indenture

(B) official statement

(C) notice of sale

(D) agreement among underwriters

265. All of the following are important factors when examining the rating of a general obligation bond EXCEPT

(A) the debt ceiling

(B) overlapping debt

(C) debt per capita

(D) covenants

266. Which of the following items can be found on the official notice of sale?

　I.　call provisions

　II.　the name of the bond counsel providing the legal opinion

　III.　maturity structure

　IV.　type of bond

(A) II and IV

(B) I, II, and IV

(C) II and III

(D) I, II, III, and IV

267. When accepting bids for a municipal bond offering, what is the municipality looking for?

(A) a syndicate that could sell the issue at the highest price

(B) a syndicate that could sell the issue at the lowest price

(C) a syndicate that could sell the issue with the lowest cost to the municipality

(D) a syndicate that could help the issuer with day-to-day operations

268. A municipal bond syndicate member has committed to sell $2 million of a new $20 million issue. The member sells the $2 million that he is committed to. However, $1 million of the issue still remains unsold. What percentage of the unsold amount is the member responsible for if the syndicate is formed on a divided account basis?

(A) 0%

(B) 5%

(C) 10%

(D) 20%

269. All of the following are required when a municipal bond underwriter submits a bid on a competitive issue EXCEPT

(A) a good faith deposit

(B) the net interest cost or true interest cost

(C) reoffering yields

(D) a properly signed form

270. A municipality placed a notice of sale in *The Bond Buyer*. The municipal issuer will take into consideration the timing of interest payments when comparing bids. Which of the following methods of interest cost is the issuer using?

(A) net interest cost

(B) true interest cost

(C) actual interest cost

(D) approximate interest cost

271. Which of the following is the BEST source of information about municipal bonds in the primary market?

(A) the *Blue List*

(B) *The Bond Buyer*

(C) Thomson Municipal News

(D) EMMA

272. What is the primary purpose of a firm with a recall option quote?

(A) to get assistance from another brokerage firm in selling unsold securities

(B) to obtain the assistance of a broker's broker in the sale of securities

(C) to allow another brokerage firm to sell the securities at a different price

(D) to recall the securities within five minutes in the event of receiving an unsolicited order

273–324 Analysis and Recommendations

273. All of the following are important in analyzing a general obligation bond issued by a school district EXCEPT

(A) debt ceiling

(B) traffic fines

(C) insurance covenants

(D) property taxes

274. Park City, Utah, decides to issue general obligation bonds to build an expansive children's park. Which of the following characteristics of the issuer should an investor consider when analyzing this issue of bonds?

    I.   overall debt

    II. efficiency of the government

    III. rate covenants

    IV. flow of funds

    (A) I and II

    (B) II, III, and IV

    (C) III and IV

    (D) I, II, III, and IV

275. Where would you tell a potential investor that she can find the most information about a municipal bond issue?

    (A) the official notice of sale

    (B) the final prospectus

    (C) the bond indenture

    (D) the official statement

276. *The Bond Buyer's* 11-Bond Index is comprised of which of the following grades of bonds?

    I.   AAA

    II. AA

    III. A

    IV. BBB

    (A) I only

    (B) I and II

    (C) I, II, and III

    (D) I, II, III, and IV

277. The BEST indication for the demand for new municipal issues would be found by analyzing

    (A) the placement ratio

    (B) the visible supply

    (C) *The Bond Buyer's* Index

    (D) the 11-Bond Index

278. All of the following could have overlapping debt EXCEPT

    (A) a town

    (B) a city

    (C) a county

    (D) a state

279. A municipal revenue bond was issued under a net revenue pledge. The following numbers are reported for the current year:

    $76 million in gross revenues

    $40 million in operating and maintenance expenses

    $10 million in interest expenses

    $2 million in principal repayment

What is the debt service coverage ratio?

    (A) 2 to 1

    (B) 3 to 1

    (C) 4 to 1

    (D) 5 to 1

280. The flow of funds found on the trust indenture is used for municipal

    (A) revenue anticipation notes

    (B) general obligation bonds

    (C) industrial development revenue bonds

    (D) revenue bonds

281. Phoenix owes $500 million in debt while Arizona's debt is $2 billion. Phoenix has a population of 1.4 million and has an assessed property value that is 18% of Arizona's. What is Phoenix's direct debt per capita?

(A) $357.14

(B) $537.14

(C) $1,428.57

(D) $1,785.71

282. Which of the following is important when analyzing the credit of a municipal revenue bond?

I. direct debt per capita

II. net debt to assessed valuation

III. debt service coverage ratio

IV. flow of funds

(A) I and II

(B) III and IV

(C) I, II and III

(D) I, III, and IV

283. A municipal bond counsel is responsible for all of the following EXCEPT

(A) making sure the issue is valid and binding on the issuer

(B) making sure that the issue will be federally tax-free

(C) preparing the legal opinion

(D) guaranteeing timely payment of interest

284. White's Rating Service is mainly concerned with a municipal bond's

(A) risk of default

(B) debt service coverage ratio

(C) liquidity

(D) yield

285. Variable rate municipal bonds are subject to which of the following risks?

I. interest rate

II. liquidity

III. market

IV. default

(A) I only

(B) II and IV

(C) II, III, and IV

(D) I, II, III, and IV

286. Investors would be able to find information about a municipal issuer's financial condition by examining the

(A) official statement

(B) indenture

(C) notice of sale

(D) prospectus

287. Which of the following is NOT an important factor when evaluating a revenue bond?

(A) feasibility study

(B) property taxes

(C) flow of funds

(D) rate covenants

288. Municipal bond insurance protects investors against

(A) market risk

(B) liquidity risk

(C) default risk

(D) inflation risk

289. When considering credit rating, municipal general obligation bonds are usually second only to

(A) collateralized mortgage obligations

(B) Treasury bonds

(C) IBM

(D) mortgage bonds

290. Which of the following would NOT affect the credit rating of a general obligation bond?

(A) rate covenants

(B) per capita debt

(C) assessed property values

(D) the tax collection history of the municipality

291. Municipal revenue bonds are often insured because

(A) revenue bond issues in excess of $10 million are required to be insured under MSRB rules

(B) it increases the credit rating and marketability of the bonds

(C) it is required under most state laws

(D) revenue bond issues in excess of $10 million are required to be insured under SEC rules

292. *The Bond Buyer's* 11-Bond Index shows the average yield of 11 general obligation bonds rated

I. AAA

II. AA

III. A

IV. BBB

(A) I only

(B) I and II

(C) I, II, and III

(D) I, II, III, and IV

293. One of your customers is interested in getting the latest up-to-the-minute pricing information on municipal securities. This information can best be found on

(A) Thomson Municipal News

(B) EMMA

(C) the National Quotation Bureau

(D) MSRB RTRS

294. Geographical diversification of municipal bonds would protect against which of the following risks?

I. interest rate

II. business

III. purchasing power

IV. economic

(A) I, II, and IV

(B) I and III

(C) II and IV

(D) I, II, III, and IV

295. Which of the following factors should you determine before recommending a municipal bond to a client?

I. the client's state of residence

II. the client's tax bracket

III. the client's investment objectives

(A) I and II

(B) II and III

(C) I and III

(D) I, II, and III

296. Which of the following sources would provide investors the best information about municipal bonds in the primary market?

(A) *Forbes*

(B) *The Bond Buyer*

(C) Munifacts

(D) the *Blue List*

297. Where would a municipal securities broker-dealer find the visible supply?

(A) *The Bond Buyer*

(B) the *Blue List*

(C) the Yellow Sheets

(D) Munifacts

298. All of the following could be used to help measure the marketability of a new municipal general obligation bond EXCEPT

(A) credit ratings

(B) the placement ratio

(C) the RevDex

(D) the visible supply

299. All of the following are factors that would affect the marketability of municipal bonds EXCEPT

(A) the credit rating

(B) the dated date

(C) the maturity

(D) the issuer's name

300. When comparing municipal revenue bonds, your client found one that's covered by a gross revenue pledge. This means that the FIRST expense to be paid is

(A) bond principal and interest

(B) operation and maintenance

(C) debt service reserve

(D) renewal and replacement

301. An unqualified legal opinion for a municipal bond indicates that

(A) a bond attorney did not examine the indenture

(B) the bond attorney guarantees all interest payments will be made

(C) the issuer meets conditions with restrictions

(D) the issuer meets all conditions without restrictions

302. When helping a client compare municipal general obligation bonds from different issuers, you should compare

I. population trends

II. the home state

III. wealth of the community

IV. diversity of industry within its tax base

(A) II and III

(B) II, III, and IV

(C) I and II

(D) I, II, III, and IV

303. An investor is interested in purchasing insured municipal bonds because of the higher credit rating. Which of the following insurance companies insure municipal bonds?

I. National Public Finance Guarantee Corp.

II. AMBAC

III. SIPC

IV. FGIC

(A) I and III

(B) II, III, and IV

(C) I, II, and IV

(D) I, II, III, and IV

304. An investor is comparing several different issues of revenue bonds and sees that most of them have a net revenue pledge. The first priority under a net revenue pledge is

(A) debt service

(B) operation and maintenance

(C) the sinking fund

(D) the reserve fund

305. Which of the following provides a free online site that stores key information about municipal securities for retail, non-professional investors?

(A) EMMA

(B) RTRS

(C) *The Bond Buyer*

(D) the *Blue List*

306. One of your clients is interested in purchasing municipal securities for the first time. You would like to help him purchase a diversified portfolio of municipal securities. All of the following factors are important in municipal diversification EXCEPT

(A) type

(B) rating

(C) amount

(D) geographical

307. Where could a retail investor find electronic copies of official statements?

(A) RTRS

(B) EMMA

(C) TM3

(D) FGIC

308. An investor primarily interested in safety should purchase which of the following bonds?

(A) pre-refunded municipal GO

(B) industrial development revenue

(C) COP

(D) revenue

309. Which of the following securities is subject to the LEAST market risk?

(A) GNMA

(B) AAA rated GO bonds

(C) AAA rated corporate bonds

(D) bond anticipation notes

310. One of your clients is interested in adding additional bonds to her portfolio. You may suggest variable rate municipal bonds over other municipal bonds because

(A) they are non-callable

(B) the bond price should remain stable

(C) they are typically puttable bonds

(D) the interest is exempt from federal taxes

311. When comparing revenue bonds from different issuers, a customer is interested in examining the flow of funds. He would be able to find the flow of funds in the

(A) official notice of sale

(B) syndicate agreement

(C) bond indenture

(D) legal opinion

312. A bond resolution includes the covenants between the issuer and the

(A) trustee acting for the bondholders

(B) MSRB

(C) syndicate manager

(D) bond counsel

313. In which of the following circumstances may the issuer of a municipal revenue bond issue a catastrophe call?

(A) A drop in interest rates occurred.

(B) The facility backing the bond has been condemned due to a hurricane.

(C) The revenues from the facility backing the bonds has dropped by 20% or more from the previous year's revenues.

(D) The bonds have reached the first call date.

314. One of your new clients is interested in purchasing municipal bonds for the first time. Which of the following information should you take into consideration prior to making a recommendation?

    I.   your client's tax bracket

    II.   your client's home state

    III. the bond's rating

    IV. the bond's maturity

    (A) I and III

    (B) I, II and III

    (C) II, III, and IV

    (D) I, II, III, and IV

315. A municipality generates $30 million in revenues from a facility. The municipality must pay bond interest of $1.5 million, principal of $3 million, and operating and maintenance expenses of $12 million. What is the debt service coverage ratio?

    (A) 4 to 1

    (B) 6.67 to 1

    (C) 10 to 1

    (D) 20 to 1

316. Richmond has $200 million in debt, and Virginia has $800 million in debt. If Richmond's assessed property value is 20% of Virginia's, what is Richmond's net overall debt?

    (A) $160 million

    (B) $200 million

    (C) $360 million

    (D) $1 billion

317. New Jersey decides to issue revenue bonds to construct a new highway. The highway will charge tolls to pay off the revenue bond debt. Which of the following are important factors in assessing the safety of the revenue bond being issued?

    I.   feasibility reports

    II.   debt limitations

    III. flow of funds

    IV. debt per capita

    (A) I and III

    (B) II and IV

    (C) I, III, and IV

    (D) II, III, and IV

318. Fort Myers has $50 million in debt, while Florida has $1 billion in debt. Fort Myers has a population of 65,000 and has an assessed property value that is 3% of Florida's. What is Fort Myers's direct debt per capita?

    (A) $769.23

    (B) $1,230.77

    (C) $15,384.62

    (D) $16,153.85

319. You have a client who is in a high income tax bracket and is looking for income for his investment account. Which of the following should you recommend?

    (A) municipal zero-coupon bonds

    (B) municipal GO bonds

    (C) AAA rated corporate bonds

    (D) aggressive growth funds

320. Mr. Mullahy owns the following investments:

25 New Jersey 5% GO bonds maturing in 2030 and rated AA

25 Florida University 6% revenue bonds maturing in 2031 and rated AA

25 Utah turnpike 6% revenue bonds maturing in 2030 and rated AA

What type of diversification does Mr. Mullahy have?

- (A) maturity
- (B) quality
- (C) quantity
- (D) geographical

321. To help with the analysis of municipal revenue bonds, investors and professionals can find out theoretical yields by looking at the Revenue Bond Index. The Revenue Bond Index consists of

- (A) 25 various revenue bonds with 30-year maturities
- (B) 30 various revenue bonds with 25-year maturities
- (C) 25 various revenue bonds with 25-year maturities
- (D) 30 various revenue bonds with 30-year maturities

322. *The Bond Buyer* Municipal Bond Index is an index of 40 revenue and GO bonds with an average maturity of

- (A) 15 years
- (B) 20 years
- (C) 25 years
- (D) 30 years

323. When a municipal bond trade occurs between a broker-dealer and a bank-dealer, the trade takes place in

- (A) the secondary market
- (B) the institutional market
- (C) the retail market
- (D) the interdealer market

324. Which of the following BEST describes the visible supply?

- (A) 20-year general obligation bonds with 30-year maturities
- (B) 20-year general obligation bonds rated AA or better
- (C) 30-year revenue bonds with 25-year maturities
- (D) the total dollar amount of municipal bonds expected to reach the market in the next 30 days

325–352 Municipal Bond Rules

325. According to MSRB Rule G-37, what is the maximum contribution allowed for a municipal finance professional to a person running for local government office?

- (A) $250 per year
- (B) $250 per election
- (C) $2,500 per year
- (D) $2,500 per election

326. According to MSRB rules, a municipal securities broker-dealer opening an account for the employee of another firm must

- I. notify the employing firm in writing
- II. notify the SEC at the time of each trade
- III. obtain the approval of the employing firm prior to each trade
- IV. send the employing firm a duplicate confirmation after each trade

- (A) I and IV
- (B) I, III, and IV
- (C) II and III
- (D) I, II, III, and IV

327. According to MSRB rules, which of the following constitutes a control relationship?

(A) More than one employee of a broker-dealer lives in the issuer's municipality.

(B) At least one officer of a broker-dealer lives in the issuer's municipality.

(C) An employee of a broker-dealer holds a position of authority over the municipal issuer.

(D) All of the above.

328. Under MSRB rules, which of the following is TRUE regarding a registered representative's apprenticeship period?

I. During the 180-day apprenticeship period, registered reps may not transact business with public customers or be compensated for any municipal securities transactions.

II. During the 90-day apprenticeship period, registered reps may not transact business with public customers or be compensated for any municipal securities transactions.

III. Registered reps must pass their exam within 180 days of the beginning of the apprenticeship period.

IV. Registered reps must pass their exam within 90 days of the beginning of the apprenticeship period.

(A) I and III

(B) I and IV

(C) II and III

(D) II and IV

329. Under MSRB rules, account transfers must be validated within

(A) one business day of receipt of an ACAT form, and transfers must be completed within three business days of validation

(B) one business day of receipt of an ACAT form, and transfers must be completed within five business days of validation

(C) five business days of receipt of an ACAT form, and transfers must be completed within five business days of validation

(D) three business days of receipt of an ACAT form, and transfers must be completed within four business days of validation

330. If each of the following municipal bonds is callable at par, which confirmation must show yield to call?

(A) 4% bond trading at a 4.5% basis maturing in 2025

(B) 5% bond trading at a 5.5% basis maturing in 2030

(C) 5% bond trading at a 4.5% basis maturing in 2025

(D) 4.5% bond trading at a 4.5% basis maturing in 2030

331. Which of the following is considered a gift violation according to MSRB Rule G-20?

(A) a $320 round-trip airline ticket for a client to come to the firm

(B) spending $120 on business lunch with a client

(C) buying a client season passes to the Yankees

(D) sending a client a picture of yourself in an $80 frame

332. Advertisements relating to municipal GO bonds must be approved by

(A) the Fed

(B) the SEC

(C) the MSRB

(D) a municipal securities principal

333. Which TWO of the following are TRUE of broker's brokers?

I. They deal only with public customers.

II. They deal only with institutional customers and municipal brokers.

III. They maintain no inventory of municipal bonds.

IV. They maintain an inventory of municipal bonds.

(A) I and III

(B) I and IV

(C) II and III

(D) II and IV

334. The legal opinion for municipal bonds is prepared by the

(A) trustee

(B) municipal issuer

(C) syndicate manager

(D) bond counsel

335. According to MSRB rules, disputes between a customer and a member should be decided by

(A) arbitration

(B) litigation

(C) mediation

(D) code of procedure

336. All of the following are governed by MSRB rules EXCEPT

(A) issuers

(B) registered reps

(C) broker-dealers

(D) bank-dealers

337. According to MSRB rules, a municipal finance professional is

I. an associated person of a broker-dealer who is engaged in municipal securities activities other than retail sales to customers

II. an associated person of a broker-dealer who is engaged in municipal securities activities relating to retail sales to customers

III. an associated person of a broker-dealer who solicits municipal securities business for the broker-dealer

IV. an associated person of a broker-dealer whose main function is to educate the broker-dealers' registered reps about MSRB rules

(A) I and III

(B) I and IV

(C) II and III

(D) II and IV

338. A principal at a municipal securities firm must approve all of the following EXCEPT

(A) each new account

(B) each transaction

(C) advertisements sent out by the firm

(D) the preliminary official statement

339. Municipal dealers must disclose control relationships in which of the following situations?

    I.   when executing trades for institutional buyers

    II.   when executing trades for public customers

    III.   when executing trades for discretionary accounts

    (A)   I only

    (B)   II and III

    (C)   III only

    (D)   I, II, and III

340. All of the following enforce MSRB rules EXCEPT

    (A)   FINRA

    (B)   the SEC

    (C)   the Fed

    (D)   the MSRB

341. An investor purchases a municipal bond on Thursday, October 4. What is the regular-way settlement date?

    (A)   Thursday, October 4

    (B)   Friday, October 5

    (C)   Monday, October 7

    (D)   Tuesday, October 8

342. Which of the following must be included on a customer's confirmation of a municipal securities transaction?

    I.   the customer's name

    II.   the capacity of the broker-dealer

    III.   par value

    IV.   trade date and time of execution

    (A)   I and IV

    (B)   I, II and III

    (C)   I, II, and IV

    (D)   I, II, III, and IV

343. A client has written a letter of complaint to your municipal securities firm regarding a markup. Upon receiving the complaint, which of the following must be done FIRST?

    (A)   Put the complaint in the circular file.

    (B)   Accept the complaint and record any action taken.

    (C)   Accept the complaint and send a copy to the MSRB.

    (D)   Refund the markup charged.

344. According to MSRB rules, complaints must be kept on file by a broker-dealer for

    (A)   two years

    (B)   three years

    (C)   six years

    (D)   the lifetime of the firm

345. Which of the following is TRUE of broker's brokers?

    I.   They do not rate the credit of any bonds.

    II.   They maintain the anonymity of clients.

    III.   They underwrite new issues.

    IV.   They do not carry any inventory.

    (A)   I, II, and III

    (B)   I, II, and IV

    (C)   II, III, and IV

    (D)   II and III

346. A delivery of which of the following would be considered a fail to deliver?

    (A)   the delivery of an ex-legal bond without a legal opinion attached

    (B)   the delivery of a mutilated bond certificate

    (C)   the delivery of a bond with a legal opinion attached

    (D)   all of the above

347. A quote on municipal securities between one municipal dealer and another is assumed to be

(A) a subject quote

(B) a workout quote

(C) a bona fide quote

(D) a nominal quote

348. One of your customers purchased a pre-refunded municipal bond. The bond will be called in two years at 101. What yield must be shown on the customer's confirmation?

(A) yield to maturity or yield to call, whichever is lower

(B) yield to maturity or yield to call, whichever is higher

(C) yield to call

(D) yield to maturity

349. An investor looking to purchase new municipal bonds can find them in which form?

I. bearer

II. registered as to principal only

III. fully registered

IV. book entry

(A) IV only

(B) II, III, and IV

(C) III and IV

(D) I, II, III, and IV

350. An investor purchases a municipal bond for cash on Friday, October 4. What is the settlement date?

(A) Friday, October 4

(B) Monday, October 7

(C) Tuesday, October 8

(D) Wednesday, October 9

351. Accrued interest on municipal bonds is calculated by using

I. actual days in a month

II. 30-day months

III. actual days in a year

IV. a 360-day year

(A) I and III

(B) I and IV

(C) II and III

(D) II and IV

352. According to MSRB Rule G-39, telemarketing calls cannot be made

(A) before 8:00 a.m. or after 9:00 p.m. local time of the person being called

(B) before 8:00 a.m. or after 9:00 p.m. local time of the telemarketer

(C) before 9:00 a.m. or after 8:00 p.m. local time of the person being called

(D) before 9:00 a.m. or after 8:00 p.m. local time of the telemarketer

Chapter 5

Margin Accounts

● ●

*I*nstead of paying for securities in full, investors may buy (or sell short) certain securities on margin. Margin accounts are ones in which the broker-dealer covers a percentage of the securities purchased by investors. The good news is that it gives investors leverage to purchase more securities than they might without margin accounts. In turn, that means a larger commission or markup for you, the registered rep.

Margin isn't a huge topic on the Series 7 exam, but you can score some quick points if you're familiar with its nuances and the math.

The Problems You'll Work On

In this chapter, you'll need to have a good handle on the following:

- ✔ The paperwork required to open a margin account
- ✔ The initial margin required when opening a margin account
- ✔ Long account calculations
- ✔ Short account calculations
- ✔ How to deal with customers who have combined margin accounts
- ✔ How to determine the amount of excess equity
- ✔ Rules for restricted accounts
- ✔ The various margin rules

What to Watch Out For

This chapter involves more math than most of the other chapters, so you have to be careful of

- ✔ Using the correct formula for long accounts and short accounts
- ✔ Making careless math mistakes
- ✔ Remembering the Regulation T requirement and minimum maintenance requirements
- ✔ Making sure you read each question thoroughly before attempting to answer the question

353–356 Paperwork

353. You are opening a long margin account for one of your customers. You should inform her that she will have to sign

    I.   a credit agreement

    II.   a risk disclosure document

    III.   a hypothecation agreement

    IV.   a loan consent form

    (A)   I and II

    (B)   I, II, and IV

    (C)   I, III, and IV

    (D)   II, III, and IV

354. Which of the following margin documents discloses the interest rate to be charged on the debit balance?

    (A)   the credit agreement

    (B)   the hypothecation agreement

    (C)   the loan consent form

    (D)   the margin interest rate form

355. A margin loan consent form

    (A)   allows the broker-dealer to provide a loan to the customer

    (B)   allows the broker-dealer to loan a customer's margined securities to other investors

    (C)   allows the broker-dealer to borrow money from a bank for margin accounts

    (D)   is required for both cash and margin accounts

356. Which of the following documents must be sent to a margin customer prior to the signing of the margin agreement?

    (A)   credit agreement

    (B)   hypothecation agreement

    (C)   loan consent form

    (D)   risk disclosure document

357–366 Initial Margin Requirements

357. One of your customers wants to open a margin account by selling short 100 shares of GHI at $15. What is the margin call?

    (A) $750

    (B) $1,500

    (C) $2,000

    (D) $3,000

358. In an initial transaction in a margin account, a customer purchases 100 shares of RRR at $18 per share. What is the margin call?

    (A) $900

    (B) $1,800

    (C) $2,000

    (D) $2,900

359. An investor opens a margin account by selling short $5,000 worth of securities. What is the margin call?

    (A) $1,500

    (B) $2,000

    (C) $2,500

    (D) $5,000

360. Which of the following securities are exempt from the Regulation T margin requirement?

    (A)   U.S. Treasury bills

    (B)   municipal bonds

    (C)   U.S. government agency securities

    (D)   all of the above

361. Which of the following securities can be purchased on margin by depositing the Regulation T margin requirement?

   I.   exchange-listed stocks

   II. exchange-listed bonds

   III. mutual funds

   IV. IPOs

   (A) I and II

   (B) III and IV

   (C) I and III

   (D) III only

362. The deadline for meeting margin calls is

   (A) on the trade date

   (B) one business day after the trade date

   (C) three business days after the trade date

   (D) five business days after the trade date

363. What is the minimum equity requirement for a pattern day trader?

   (A) $5,000

   (B) $10,000

   (C) $25,000

   (D) $50,000

364. A customer sells short 1,000 shares of Sketchy Corporation common stock at $3.80 per share. What is the margin call?

   (A) $1,900

   (B) $2,000

   (C) $3,800

   (D) $5,000

365. An investor opens a margin account by purchasing 1,000 shares of ABC at $15 per share and shorting 1,000 shares of DEF at $12 per share. What is the investor's margin call as a result of these transactions?

   (A) $1,500

   (B) $3,000

   (C) $13,500

   (D) $27,000

366. An investor opens a margin account by purchasing 100 shares of UPP at $50 per share. What is the margin call if the house margin requirement is 60% and house maintenance is set at 30%?

   (A) $1,250

   (B) $1,500

   (C) $2,500

   (D) $3,000

367–372 Long Account Calculations

367. Riley Moneyhaul opens a margin account by purchasing 500 shares of TTT Corporation at $24 per share. The broker-dealer Regulation T margin requirement is 60%, and Riley deposits the full margin requirement. How much of this account can the broker-dealer rehypothecate?

   (A) $4,800

   (B) $6,700

   (C) $7,200

   (D) $8,460

368. One of your clients has a margin account with $30,000 in securities, a $22,000 debit balance, and $3,000 SMA. How much equity does your client have in her account?

(A) $3,000

(B) $5,000

(C) $8,000

(D) $11,000

369. One of your clients has a long margin account with the following positions:

100 TUV at $15

200 XYZ at $30

500 LMN at $25

What is the minimum maintenance for his account?

(A) $4,000

(B) $5,000

(C) $6,667

(D) $10,000

370. Mr. Flanagan's margin account holds the following securities:

100 shares of CSA at $60 per share

200 shares of TUV at $24 per share

100 shares of LMN at $18 per share

How much equity is in Mr. Flanagan's margin account if the debit balance is $7,200?

(A) $5,400

(B) $6,300

(C) $7,200

(D) $7,450

371. All of the following would reduce the debit balance in a long margin account EXCEPT

(A) cash deposits

(B) cash dividends

(C) stock dividends

(D) liquidation of stock held in the account

372. Which of the following would increase the debit balance on a long margin account?

I. interest charges

II. withdrawing SMA

III. an increase in the market value of the securities held

IV. a decrease in the market value of the securities held

(A) I and II

(B) I, II, and III

(C) I, II, and IV

(D) I and III

373–375 Short Account Calculations

373. Mr. DiScala owns a short margin account with a short market value of $34,500, and equity of $17,500, and a credit balance of $52,000. How high can the market value go before Mr. DiScala receives a maintenance call?

(A) $36,000

(B) $38,000

(C) $40,000

(D) $42,000

374. An investor sells short 1,000 shares of LMN at $30. What is the credit balance?

(A) $15,000

(B) $30,000

(C) $45,000

(D) $60,000

375. What is the minimum maintenance requirement for a short account with a current market value of $25,000?

(A) $6,250

(B) $7,500

(C) $10,000

(D) $12,500

376–377 Combined Accounts

376. One of your clients has a combined margin account with the following dollar figures:

Long market value = $30,000

Short market value = $25,000

Debit balance = $18,000

Credit balance = $40,000

Long account SMA = $1,500

With Regulation T set at 50%, what is the combined equity in your client's account?

(A) $25,500

(B) $27,000

(C) $28,500

(D) $30,000

377. An investor has a combined margin account with a long market value of $35,000 and a short market value of $28,000. The long market value increased to $38,000, and the short market value decreased to $26,000. What change occurs to the equity in the account?

(A) $1,000 increase in equity

(B) $1,000 decrease in equity

(C) $5,000 increase in equity

(D) $5,000 decrease in equity

378–382 Excess Equity

378. Mrs. Diamond sells short 1,000 shares of HIJ at $80. If HIJ drops to $70, what is the buying (shorting) power?

(A) $0

(B) $7,500

(C) $15,000

(D) $30,000

379. An investor has a margin account with $50,000 market value and $18,000 debit balance. If the investor wants to purchase an additional $25,000 of stock in this account, what amount must the investor deposit?

(A) $5,500

(B) $7,000

(C) $12,500

(D) cannot be determined

380. An investor has a margin account with market value $46,000 and debit balance $19,500. What is the buying power?

(A) $3,500

(B) $7,000

(C) $8,500

(D) $17,000

381. Mr. Jones has a margin account with $60,000 market value and $22,000 debit balance. If Mr. Jones wants to purchase an additional $30,000 of stock in this account, what amount must Mr. Jones deposit?

(A) $5,500

(B) $7,000

(C) $8,000

(D) $15,000

382. One of your clients wants to use the excess equity in his margin account and wants to know what will happen to his debit balance. You can inform him that his debit balance will

(A) increase

(B) decrease

(C) remain the same

(D) fluctuate

383–386 Restricted Accounts

383. Mr. Steyne sells short 1,000 shares of LMN at $42. If LMN goes up to $44.50, how much is his account restricted?

(A)   0
(B) $2,500
(C) $3,100
(D) $3,750

384. An investor buys 1,000 shares of LMN at $50 in a margin account. If LMN drops to $40, by how much is the account restricted?

(A) $1,000
(B) $3,000
(C) $7,000
(D) $10,000

385. A client has a restricted long margin account with a market value of $60,000 and a debit balance of $36,000. How far can this client's market value drop before receiving a maintenance call?

(A) $30,000
(B) $45,000
(C) $48,000
(D) $51,000

386. The margin account of one of your customers is restricted. This means that

I.   the equity in her margin account has fallen below 50% of the long market value

II.   the equity in her margin account has fallen below 25% of the long market value

III.   she cannot borrow any additional money until the margin account is taken out of restricted status

IV.   she has 24 hours to deposit funds to bring it out of restricted status

(A)   I only
(B)   I, III, and IV
(C)   II and III
(D)   II, III, and IV

387–392 Rules

387. Which of the following regulations of the Federal Reserve Board regulates how much credit a bank can allow a customer for the purposes of purchasing securities on margin?

(A)   Regulation T
(B)   Regulation G
(C)   Regulation U
(D)   Regulation B

388. Under Regulation T, what are the initial and maintenance requirements for long margin accounts?

(A)   50% initial and 25% maintenance
(B)   50% initial and 30% maintenance
(C)   75% initial and 25% maintenance
(D)   70% initial and 30% maintenance

389. Maintenance calls must be paid:

(A) on demand

(B) within one business day

(C) within three business days

(D) within five business days

390. A customer has a restricted long margin account. If the customer is purchasing new securities on margin and fails to pay for the new purchase, the broker-dealer will sell stock worth

(A) the margin call

(B) twice the margin call

(C) three times the margin call

(D) securities cannot be purchased in restricted margin accounts

391. The prohibited action of mixing a customer's securities with the account of the broker-dealer is called

(A) free riding

(B) hypothecation

(C) commingling

(D) conjoining

392. One of your clients opens a long margin account and fills out the required paper-work. Which of the following are TRUE regarding this account?

I. The securities in the account will be held in street name.

II. Your client will be required to pay interest on the debit balance.

III. A decrease in market value would lower the debit balance.

IV. A portion of the securities may be pledged as collateral for a loan.

(A) II and III

(B) I and IV

(C) II, III, and IV

(D) I, II, and IV

Chapter 6

Packaged Securities

• •

*P*ackaged securities include investment companies (mutual funds and closed-end funds), real estate investment trusts, annuities, and so on. The idea is to provide investors a way to diversify their portfolios with a relatively small outlay of cash. Pretty much all investors have packaged securities in their portfolio. What's also nice about packaged securities for investors is that usually the funds are professionally managed, and the management fee is relatively small.

In this chapter, you should be aware of which funds are best for which investors according to their investment objectives.

The Problems You'll Work On

In this chapter, you'll work on questions that deal with the following:

- ✔ Understanding the different types of funds and making appropriate investment recommendations
- ✔ Knowing when investors are eligible for discounts and different methods of investing
- ✔ Determining the sales charge and public offering price
- ✔ Figuring out how funds are taxed and the rules
- ✔ Understanding information about real estate investment trusts (REITs)
- ✔ Comparing the differences between fixed and variable annuities

What to Watch Out For

Keep the following tips in mind as you work through this chapter:

- ✔ When you're dealing with questions regarding investment recommendations, make sure you take the customer's investment objectives into consideration first.
- ✔ Know the difference between open- and closed-end funds.
- ✔ Make sure you have a good handle on variable annuities.
- ✔ Get a good grasp of what the question is asking, and read all the answer choices before picking an answer.

393–415 Types of Funds and Investment Recommendations

393. Which of the following is NOT TRUE of open-end investment companies?

(A) They offer shares to the public continuously.

(B) Their public offering price can't be below the net asset value.

(C) They charge commissions to customers who purchase shares.

(D) They may not lend money to customers to purchase shares.

394. You may tell one of your clients that closed-end investment companies

 I. continuously issue new shares

 II. make a one-time offering of new shares

 III. may issue preferred stock

 IV. may issue bonds

(A) II only

(B) I only

(C) I, III, and IV

(D) II, III, and IV

395. Which of the following types of investment companies invests in a fixed portfolio of securities and charges no management fees?

(A) UIT

(B) REIT

(C) face amount certificate company

(D) mutual fund

396. While reading a newspaper, an investor notices that the NAV of a fund increased by $0.80 while the POP decreased by $0.20. What type of fund does this have to be?

(A) open-end

(B) closed-end

(C) no-load

(D) balanced

397. Blommerman closed-end fund has an NAV of $27.65 and a POP of $27.52. Purchasers of this fund would pay

(A) $27.52

(B) $27.52 plus a sales charge

(C) $27.52 plus a commission

(D) $27.65

398. Which of the following is TRUE about closed-end funds?

 I. They may issue only common stock.

 II. They are generally listed on an exchange.

 III. They have a fixed number of shares outstanding.

 IV. They are redeemable.

(A) II and III

(B) I and IV

(C) I, III, and IV

(D) II, III, and IV

399. You have a client who has never invested in mutual funds and doesn't know where to start. You should inform her that the MOST important thing is a fund's

(A) sale's charge

(B) 12b1 fees

(C) management fees

(D) investment objectives

400. All of the following are TRUE about money market funds EXCEPT

(A) They offer a check-writing feature as a way of redeeming shares.

(B) Investors are prohibited from redeeming the money market fund for a year.

(C) They are no-load.

(D) They compute dividends daily and credit them monthly.

401. John Lavinsky purchased 500 shares of a municipal bond fund; which of the following statements are TRUE?

   I. Dividends are taxable.

   II. Dividends are not taxable.

   III. Capital gains distributions are taxable.

   IV. Capital gains distributions are not taxable.

(A) I and IV

(B) I and III

(C) II and III

(D) II and IV

402. You have a new 35-year-old client who is interested in investing in a mutual fund. He is looking to invest $400 per month and wants a fund that will minimize his risk as he gets older. You should recommend a(n)

(A) aggressive growth fund

(B) life-cycle fund

(C) money market fund

(D) tax-free municipal bond fund

403. One of your clients would like to invest in a mutual fund that has capital appreciation as its main investment objective. Which of the following types of funds should you recommend?

(A) specialized

(B) income

(C) balanced

(D) money market

404. An investor is looking to invest in a mutual fund that has a high rate of current income. Her BEST choice would be a

(A) hedge fund

(B) growth fund

(C) aggressive growth fund

(D) income fund

405. Which of the following investments would be MOST suitable for a married couple in their mid-20s who have already maxed out their IRA contributions?

(A) DPPs

(B) commodities

(C) growth funds

(D) buying index call options

406. You have a client who has a high current income and is in the top federal income tax bracket. He is interested in purchasing a bond fund. The BEST suggestion would be

(A) a U.S. government bond fund

(B) a municipal bond fund

(C) a money market fund

(D) cannot be determined

407. Which of the following funds allows investors to receive voting rights of the stocks purchased and to trade the stocks purchased separately?

(A) HOLDRs

(B) ETFs

(C) ETNs

(D) private-equity funds

408. Which of the following investment companies specifies what percentage of asset will be allocated for stocks and for bonds for the life of the fund?

(A) a blind-pool fund

(B) a life-cycle fund

(C) a private-equity fund

(D) a structured fund

409. An individual primarily interested in current income would LEAST likely buy which of the following funds?

(A) a municipal bond fund

(B) a sector fund investing in high-tech stocks

(C) a high-yield bond fund

(D) an income fund

410. One of your clients would like to purchase a mutual fund on margin. You should inform her that

(A) mutual funds can't be purchased on margin

(B) to purchase on margin, she must sign a letter of intent

(C) the minimum deposit to purchase mutual funds on margin is $25,000

(D) the minimum deposit to purchase mutual funds on margin is $100,000

411. One of your clients is bearish on the market. Which of the following investment choices would be appropriate for this client?

(A) selling short an index fund

(B) an inverse exchange-traded fund

(C) a hedge fund

(D) selling short a dual-purpose fund

412. A mutual fund holds a portfolio of securities that consists of stocks of corporations in the process of releasing new products. This type of fund is a

(A) specialized fund

(B) dual-purpose fund

(C) special situation fund

(D) life-cycle fund

413. One of your clients is interested in purchasing a fund. If liquidity is high on his list of investment objectives, which of the following would be the LEAST suitable recommendation?

(A) ETFs

(B) inverse ETFs

(C) hedge funds

(D) money market funds

414. A 60-year-old investor is interested in purchasing a fund that provides tax-free income and a high degree of safety. Which of the following funds would you recommend?

(A) an insured municipal bond fund

(B) a high-yield bond fund

(C) a money market fund

(D) a fund of hedge funds

415. When explaining the difference between exchange-traded funds and mutual funds, you can say that unlike mutual funds, exchange-traded funds

 I. can be sold short

 II. can be purchased on margin

 III. represent a basket of securities

 IV. provide real-time pricing

(A) I, II, and III

(B) II and III

(C) II, III, and IV

(D) I, II, and IV

416–419 Discounts and Methods of Investing

416. One of your clients deposits $1,000 on the first of each month into AGG Aggressive Growth Fund. The purchase price per share for AGG Aggressive Growth Fund on the first of each month for the time the client has been purchasing is as follows:

Month 1: $20

Month 2: $25

Month 3: $40

Month 4: $50

Month 5: $50

What is the average cost per share paid by your client?

(A) $32.26

(B) $35.22

(C) $37.00

(D) $40.00

417. An investor who purchases 50 shares of the same mutual fund each month is executing which method of investment?

(A) dollar cost averaging

(B) fixed share averaging

(C) a constant dollar plan

(D) market timing

418. A letter of intent may be backdated up to

(A) 30 days

(B) 60 days

(C) 90 days

(D) 120 days

419. A client invests $15,000 into ABC Balance Fund and signs a letter of intent for $20,000 to qualify for a breakpoint. ABC has been doing quite well, and, even without additional investments, 12 months later, your client's shares are worth $22,000. Which of the following is TRUE?

(A) ABC will sell shares held in escrow to make up for the lost sales charge revenue.

(B) Because your client has more than $20,000 invested, his letter of intent contract is satisfied.

(C) You should remind your client that he has another month to invest an additional $5,000 into ABC.

(D) All shares will be redeemed at the NAV, and the proceeds less the adjusted sales charge will be returned to your client.

420–423 Determining the Sales Charge and Public Offering Price

420. DIMCO Growth Fund has an NAV of $13.20 and a POP of $14.00. What is the sales charge percent?

(A) 4.3%

(B) 5.7%

(C) 6.9%

(D) 7.8%

421. AMP Growth Fund has a net asset value (NAV) of $29.26 and a public offering price of $31.40. If there is a 5% sales charge for investments of $20,000 and up, how many shares can an investor who is depositing $40,000 purchase?

(A) 1,273.885 shares

(B) 1,298.701 shares

(C) 1,301.956 shares

(D) 1,311.423 shares

422. What is the maximum sales charge for mutual funds?

(A) 5% of the NAV

(B) 8.5% of the NAV

(C) 5% of the amount invested

(D) 8.5% of the amount invested

423. The public offering price of a mutual fund is

(A) the net asset value + the sales charge

(B) the net asset value − the sales charge

(C) the net asset value × the sales charge

(D) the net asset value ÷ the sales charge

424–434 Taxation and Rules

424. After a mutual fund's tenth year, performance statistics must show results for which of the following periods?

I. one year

II. three years

III. five years

IV. ten years

(A) II and III

(B) I, III, and IV

(C) I, II, and IV

(D) II, III, and IV

425. Who is responsible for the safekeeping of the securities owned by a mutual fund?

(A) the custodian bank

(B) the registrar

(C) the investment adviser

(D) the transfer agent

426. How much money must a mutual fund raise before a public offering?

(A) $50,000

(B) $100,000

(C) $500,000

(D) $1,000,000

427. An investor decides to redeem shares of a mutual fund; at what price will the trade be executed?

(A) the current bid price

(B) the current ask price

(C) the next computed bid price

(D) the next computed ask price

428. The maximum sales charge for a mutual fund is

(A) 7% of the amount invested

(B) 7.5% of the amount invested

(C) 8% of the amount invested

(D) 8.5% of the amount invested

429. Mr. Diamond invests money into a front-end load mutual fund and chooses to automatically reinvest the dividends and capital gains. Which TWO of the following are TRUE?

I. The capital gains distributions will be reinvested at the NAV.

II. The capital gains distributions will be reinvested at the POP.

III. The dividend distributions will be reinvested at the NAV.

IV. The dividend distributions will be reinvested at the POP.

(A) I and III

(B) I and IV

(C) II and III

(D) II and IV

430. A mutual fund announces that it will pay a dividend to shareholders of record Friday, May 10. When is the ex-dividend date?

(A) Thursday, May 9

(B) Wednesday, May 8

(C) Tuesday, May 7

(D) on the date set by the board of directors

431. Redemptions of mutual funds must be completed within

(A) one business day

(B) three business days

(C) five business days

(D) seven calendar days

432. How often must a regulated investment company distribute any income earned on investments in the fund?

(A) monthly

(B) quarterly

(C) semiannually

(D) annually

433. Mutual funds must send financial statements to shareholders

(A) monthly

(B) quarterly

(C) semiannually

(D) annually

434. An investor wants to transfer his holdings from DIMCO Aggressive Growth Fund to DIMCO Balanced Fund. What would be his tax consequences?

(A) Any gains or losses would be deferred until he redeems DIMCO shares.

(B) Any gains or losses on DIMCO Aggressive Growth Fund would be recognized for tax purposes.

(C) Any losses on DIMCO Aggressive Growth Fund would be recognized for tax purposes, but gains would be deferred.

(D) Any gains on DIMCO Aggressive Growth Fund would be recognized for tax purposes, but the losses would be deferred.

435–440 Real Estate Investment Trusts

435. A REIT must distribute at least _____ of its income to shareholders to avoid being taxed as a corporation.

(A) 25%

(B) 75%

(C) 90%

(D) 95%

436. Which of the following is TRUE of mortgage real estate investment trusts (REITs)?

(A) The REIT must generate at least 75% of income from construction and mortgage loans.

(B) The REIT must generate at least 75% of income from ownership of properties.

(C) The REIT must generate at least 75% of income from a combination of ownership of properties and construction loans.

(D) The REIT may not invest in securities such as stocks and bonds.

437. Which of the following securities is actively traded in the secondary market?

(A) open-end funds

(B) unit investment trusts

(C) REITs

(D) all of the above

438. Which of the following are TRUE about REITs?

I. At least 75% of the trust's gross income must be earned from real estate–related projects.

II. They may not use any of their assets to purchase securities.

III. They don't have to be registered with the SEC.

IV. They are redeemable securities.

(A) I only

(B) I, II, and III

(C) II, III, and IV

(D) I, III, and IV

439. All of the following are types of REITs EXCEPT

(A) equity

(B) mortgage

(C) double-barreled

(D) hybrid

440. All of the following are types of real estate investment trusts EXCEPT

(A) equity

(B) raw land

(C) hybrid

(D) mortgage

441–456 Fixed and Variable Annuities

441. A 25-year-old investor has just received a very large inheritance and wants to purchase a variable annuity. Which of the following purchase options would be BEST for this investor?

(A) immediate annuity with deferred payment

(B) periodic payment deferred annuity

(C) single payment immediate annuity

(D) single payment deferred annuity

442. Which TWO of the following are TRUE about variable life insurance policies?

I. The minimum death benefit is guaranteed.

II. The minimum death benefit is not guaranteed.

III. The minimum cash value is guaranteed.

IV. The minimum cash value is not guaranteed.

(A) I and III

(B) II and III

(C) I and IV

(D) II and IV

443. A 68-year-old investor owns a non-qualified variable annuity. She invested a total of $38,000. The annuity now has a value of $47,000. She decides to take a lump-sum withdrawal of $12,000. What is her tax liability if she is in the 28% tax bracket?

(A) $0

(B) $840

(C) $2,520

(D) $3,360

444. One of your clients has a variable annuity contract with an AIR of 4.25%. Last month, the actual net return to the separate account was 5.75%. If your client is currently in the payout phase, how would this month's payment compare to the AIR?

(A) It will be the same.

(B) It will be higher.

(C) It will be lower.

(D) It cannot be determined until this month is over.

445. One of your clients is interested in purchasing a variable annuity that would provide the largest monthly payment. Which of the following options would be MOST suitable for this client?

(A) life income annuity

(B) life with period certain annuity

(C) joint and last survivor annuity

(D) not enough information given to answer this question

446. All of the following securities are covered under the Investment Company Act of 1940 EXCEPT

(A) open-end funds

(B) fixed annuities

(C) closed-end funds

(D) variable annuities

447. The owner of a variable annuity dies during the accumulation phase; the death benefit will be paid to

(A) the IRS

(B) the account holder's estate

(C) the insurance company

(D) the designated beneficiary

448. All of the following are TRUE of variable annuities EXCEPT

(A) the securities held in the separate account are professionally managed

(B) securities held in the separate account may be mutual funds

(C) investors are protected against capital loss

(D) they are more likely to keep pace with inflation than fixed annuities

449. Investors holding a variable annuity receive payments for life. This is called a(n)

(A) life-payment guarantee

(B) mortality guarantee

(C) deferred guarantee

(D) post-payment guarantee

450. Which of the following annuity options would hold accumulation units?

I. single payment deferred annuity

II. periodic payment deferred annuity

III. immediate annuity

(A) II only

(B) I and II

(C) II and III

(D) I, II, and III

451. Which of the following payout options for variable annuities would provide the largest monthly payment to annuitants?

(A) straight life annuity

(B) life annuity with period certain

(C) joint and survivor annuity

(D) unit refund

452. Which of the following would be BEST suited for a variable annuity?

(A) Mr. Gold, an unemployed prospector who is 42 years old

(B) Mr. Silver, who is 56½ years old, has thousands available to invest, and has been investing the maximum into his IRA and 401(k) plan

(C) Mrs. Platinum, who is 81 years old, has been retired for 16 years, has enough money to live comfortably, and wants to leave all of her investments to her adult children

(D) Ms. Diamond, a 25-year-old jeweler who is saving to buy her first house

453. The investment risk in a variable annuity is assumed by

(A) the holder of the policy

(B) the insurance company

(C) 60% by the insurance company and 40% by the policyholder

(D) none of the above

454. Variable annuities must be registered with

I. the SEC

II. the State Banking Commission

III. the State Insurance Commission

IV. the NYSE

(A) I and II

(B) II and IV

(C) I and III

(D) II, III, and IV

455. John Silverhouse has been investing in a variable annuity for 30 years and is about to retire. When receiving payouts from his variable annuity, he will receive

(A) a variable number of accumulation units based on the value of his annuity units

(B) a variable number of annuity units based on the value of his accumulation units

(C) a fixed number of accumulation units based on the value of his annuity units

(D) a fixed number of annuity units based on the value of his accumulation units

456. A 55-year-old investor has previously invested $60,000 into a variable annuity. The separate account is now worth $70,000. If the investor withdraws $20,000 from the account, what is the tax liability if the investor is in the 31% tax bracket?

(A) $4,100

(B) $6,200

(C) $8,200

(D) $25,000

Chapter 7

Direct Participation Programs

· ·

Direct participation programs (DPPs) are more commonly known as limited partnerships. DPPs raise money to invest in projects such as real estate, oil and gas, and equipment leasing. DPPs aren't for everyone because investors (limited partners) need to be prescreened by the registered representative and then accepted by the general partner.

DPPs are unique to other investments and even have their own tax category (passive). You should be prepared to answer questions about what makes these investments different.

The Problems You'll Work On

In this chapter, you should be ready to answer questions regarding

- ✔ The roles and responsibilities of the general partner and limited partners
- ✔ The different partnership paperwork
- ✔ The difference between partnership taxes and other investment taxes
- ✔ The three main types of partnerships

What to Watch Out For

Be careful not to get tripped up by common mistakes, such as the following:

- ✔ Mixing up the roles of the general and limited partners
- ✔ Not reading each question thoroughly before choosing an answer
- ✔ Not understanding that the limited partnerships have their own unique tax category
- ✔ Thinking that everyone is eligible to (or should) invest in a direct participation program

457–462 General and Limited Partners

457. Which of the following is NOT a legitimate use of partnership democracy in limited partnerships?

(A) voting to remove a general partner

(B) voting on which partnership assets should be liquidated to pay creditors

(C) voting to end the limited partnership

(D) allowing the general partner to manage more than one partnership as long as it isn't a conflict of interest

458. The ones who assume the most risk in an oil and gas limited partnership are

(A) limited partners

(B) general partners

(C) limited partners and general partners assume equal amount of risk

(D) it depends on how the partnership is set up

459. A general partner has

(A) an active role and unlimited liability

(B) an active role and limited liability

(C) an inactive role and unlimited liability

(D) an inactive role and limited liability

460. Which of the following is TRUE regarding a limited partner assisting a general partner to solicit new investors to the partnership?

(A) It is permitted as long as the limited partner is not compensated.

(B) It could jeopardize the status of the limited partner.

(C) It is allowed as long as outlined in the agreement of limited partnership.

(D) None of the above.

461. The general partner of an oil and gas developmental program is responsible for all of the following EXCEPT

(A) paying the partnership's expenses

(B) managing the partnership

(C) providing a bulk of the capital for the partnership

(D) accepting new limited partners

462. Limited partners may

  I. compete with the partnership

  II. inspect the partnership books

  III. vote to terminate the partnership

  IV. make management decisions for the partnership

(A) I, II, and III

(B) I, III, and IV

(C) II, III, and IV

(D) I, II, and IV

463–467 Partnership Paperwork

463. Which of the following documents are required by a limited partnership?

  I. subscription agreement

  II. certificate of limited partnership

  III. registration form

  IV. partnership agreement

(A) I, II, and III

(B) II, III, and IV

(C) I, II, and IV

(D) I, II, III, and IV

464. Which of the following would require an amendment to a certificate of limited partnership?

    I.   a change in the sharing arrangements between the limited and general partners

    II. a typographical error on the exiting certificate of limited partnership

    III. an increase in the contributions made by the limited and/or general partner

(A) I and II

(B) II and III

(C) I and III

(D) I, II, and III

465. Which of the following investments would require written proof of the client's net worth?

(A) a variable annuity contract

(B) an aggressive growth fund

(C) a face amount certificate company

(D) an oil and gas limited partnership

466. Which of the following documents must a general partner sign to accept a new limited partner?

(A) a prospectus

(B) a certificate of limited partnership

(C) an agreement of limited partnership

(D) a subscription agreement

467. Which of the following partnership documents needs to be filed with the SEC prior to making a public offering?

(A) certificate of limited partnership

(B) agreement of limited partnership

(C) subscription agreement

(D) all of the above

468–481 Partnership Taxes

468. Which of the following real estate direct participation programs allows for tax credits to investors?

(A) raw land

(B) existing property

(C) historic rehabilitation

(D) new construction

469. Oil and gas program depletion deductions are based on the amount of oil

(A) stored

(B) extracted

(C) lost

(D) sold

470. Losses from a real estate direct participation program can be used to offset which of the following?

    I.   income from an oil and gas partnership

    II. earned income

    III. portfolio income

    IV. capital gains from a REIT

(A) I only

(B) IV only

(C) II and III

(D) I, II, III, and IV

471. Which of the following partnerships are limited partners allowed to claim non-recourse debt as a tax deduction?

(A) equipment leasing

(B) oil and gas wildcatting

(C) oil and gas developmental

(D) real estate

472. Which of the following does NOT describe the tax status of a limited partnership?

(A) Any gains generated are taxed as capital gains.

(B) Any income generated is taxed as ordinary income.

(C) The partnership is fully taxed by the IRS.

(D) The tax liability flows through to the limited and general partners.

473. Matt Serano deposited $150,000 to become a limited partner of an oil and gas limited partnership. In addition, he deposited $40,000 in recourse debt. For the calendar year, he reports a $20,000 cash distribution, $60,000 in depreciation, and $50,000 in depletion. What is Matt's cost basis?

(A) $20,000

(B) $30,000

(C) $60,000

(D) $70,000

474. Which of the following would NOT be considered a tax advantage of investing in an oil and gas DPP?

(A) depletion deductions

(B) depreciation recapture

(C) IDCs

(D) accelerated depreciation deductions

475. One of your clients buys into an oil and gas limited partnership. He makes an initial contribution of $25,000 and signs a recourse note for $35,000. What is his cost basis?

(A) $10,000

(B) $25,000

(C) $35,000

(D) $60,000

476. A limited partner's cost basis in a real estate program could be increased by all of the following EXCEPT

(A) cash contributions

(B) cash distributions

(C) non-recourse debt

(D) property contributions

477. The point in a limited partnership where revenues exceed deductions is called

(A) the crossover point

(B) functional allocation

(C) phantom income

(D) the cash-flow point

478. Which of the following types of partnerships has the highest IDCs?

(A) exploratory

(B) raw land

(C) existing property

(D) income

479. Which of the following partnerships could claim depletion deductions?

I. real estate

II. oil and gas

III. equipment leasing

(A) I only

(B) II only

(C) I and III

(D) II and III

480. One of your clients sells her interest in an oil and gas limited partnership. To determine her gain or loss, she must determine the difference between

(A) the sales proceeds and the original cost basis

(B) the sales proceeds and the tax-deductible losses

(C) the sales proceeds and the adjusted cost basis

(D) the sales proceeds and the cumulative depletion allowance

481. A limited partnership program shows the following results for the current year:

Revenues: $2,000,000

Operating expenses: $800,000

Interest expense: $150,000

Depreciation: $1,200,000

Management fees: $180,000

What is the cash flow?

(A) $800,000

(B) $870,000

(C) $1,200,000

(D) $2,000,000

482–496 Checking Out Types of Partnerships

482. An investor in an undeveloped land limited partnership is mostly concerned with

(A) depletion

(B) depreciation

(C) appreciation

(D) cash flow

483. Which of the following is TRUE of an oil and gas blind-pool offering?

(A) It invests a large portion of its income into real estate partnerships.

(B) It purchases interest only in other real estate limited partnerships.

(C) It may not claim depletion deductions.

(D) It is one in which 25 percent or more of its sites have not been identified at the time of the offering.

484. All of the following are advantages of investing in a real estate limited partnership EXCEPT

(A) appreciation potential

(B) depreciation deductions

(C) depletion deductions

(D) cash flow

485. All of the following are likely to be part of an equipment leasing partnership EXCEPT

(A) computers

(B) oil well drill heads

(C) construction equipment

(D) moving trucks

486. Rank the following oil and gas limited partnerships from safest to riskiest.

I. income

II. developmental

III. exploratory

(A) I, II, III

(B) II, I, III

(C) III, I, II

(D) III, II, I

487. John Wegner is a limited partner in a real estate DPP that invests in public housing. John receives passive income that exceeds the passive deductions by a significant amount, and he would like to shelter more of his passive income. Which of the following recommendations would be appropriate for John?

(A) oil and gas exploratory program

(B) oil and gas developmental program

(C) oil and gas income program

(D) real estate program that invests in existing properties

488. One of your wealthy clients would like to invest in a real estate partnership that provides stability of income. Which of the following should you recommend?

(A) raw land

(B) condominiums

(C) Section 8

(D) new construction

489. Which of the following is NOT a benefit of investing in a long-term equipment leasing program?

(A) a steady stream of income

(B) depreciation deductions

(C) capital appreciation potential

(D) operating expenses to help offset revenues

490. Marge is a 54-year-old investor from Utah who is looking to add some liquidity to her portfolio. All of the following investments would help Marge meet that goal EXCEPT

(A) an aggressive growth fund

(B) an oil and gas limited partnership

(C) blue chip stocks

(D) Treasury bills

491. Frack-for-Life Oil and Gas partnership drills only in proven areas. This is considered a(n)

(A) exploratory program

(B) developmental program

(C) income program

(D) combination program

492. One of your risk-averse clients is interested in investing in an oil and gas limited partnership. Which of the following types of partnerships should you recommend?

(A) a wildcatting program

(B) a developmental program

(C) an income program

(D) a combination program

493. Mary Gold is interested in investing $25,000 in a real estate limited partnership. Her main investment objective is capital growth potential. If all of the rest of Mary's money is tied up in non-liquid investments, which of the following types of partnerships should you recommend?

(A) raw land

(B) new construction

(C) existing properties

(D) You should not recommend a limited partnership.

494. A real estate limited partnership goes bankrupt. Place the following in order of repayment.

   I. limited partners

  II. general partners

 III. a bank that holds a mortgage on the property owned by the partnership

 IV. a bank that provided an unsecured loan to the partnership

(A) III, IV, I, II

(B) I, III, IV, II

(C) I, II, III, IV

(D) III, I, IV, II

495. Which of the following investments does NOT require written verification of an investor's financial status?

(A) oil and gas partnerships

(B) real estate limited partnerships

(C) equipment leasing partnerships

(D) real estate investment trusts

496. Tito Rousey wants a diversified oil and gas investment portfolio. Which of the following oil and gas partnerships offers the MOST diversification?

(A) an exploratory program

(B) an income program

(C) a combination program

(D) a developmental program

Chapter 8

Options

O ptions are also known as derivatives because they derive their value from the value of an underlying security. Options give the holder the right to buy or sell the underlying security at a fixed price for a fixed period of time. Options give holders a leveraged position because they have an interest in a large amount of securities for a relatively small outlay of cash. Options are risky investments and aren't for everyone because of the likelihood of losing all the money invested.

Options are one of the more heavily tested areas on the Series 7 exam. Although you may have heard horror stories about how tough options are, using an options chart makes life much easier. You can expect at least as many questions where you don't need an options chart as ones that you do, so don't spend all your time just practicing calculations.

The Problems You'll Work On

To work the problems in this chapter, you need to

- ✔ Be familiar with the option basics, such as what is a put and what is a call.
- ✔ Figure out questions related to straddles and combinations.
- ✔ Understand option spreads, recognize option markets, and remember option rules.
- ✔ Recognize the best option positions for someone who already owns the stock.
- ✔ Calculate maximum gains, losses, and break-even points for investors who own multiple option contracts.
- ✔ Determine what happens when an underlying stock splits or receives a dividend.
- ✔ Know the basics of currency, LEAPS, yield, and index options.

What to Watch Out For

Here are a couple things to watch out for when working with option questions:

- ✔ Don't focus entirely on the calculations; you're likely going to get more questions that don't require an options chart than do.
- ✔ When using an options chart, make sure you put the numbers on the correct side of the chart.

497–519 Option Basics

497. Which of the following transactions may be executed in a cash account?

   I.   the purchase of a call option

   II. the sale of a covered call option

   III. the short sale of a stock

   IV. the sale of a naked option

(A) I only

(B) I and II

(C) I and III

(D) III and IV

498. Mr. Drudge writes a naked put option on WIM common stock. What is the maximum loss per share that Mr. Drudge can incur?

(A) strike price minus the premium

(B) strike price plus the premium

(C) the entire premium received

(D) unlimited

499. Bullish option strategies include

   I.   buying calls

   II. buying puts

   III. writing in-the-money calls

   IV. writing in-the-money puts

(A) I and III

(B) I and IV

(C) II and III

(D) II and IV

500. Which option is out of the money if ABC is at $40?

(A) ABC May 45 put

(B) ABC May 35 call

(C) ABC May 50 call

(D) ABC May 55 put

501. A QRS Dec 50 call is trading for 9 when QRS is at $55. What is the time value of this option?

(A) 0

(B) 4

(C) 5

(D) 9

502. An investor would face an unlimited maximum loss potential if

   I.   writing 3 XYZ Dec 25 puts

   II. shorting 200 shares of XYZ

   III. writing 4 XYZ Dec 30 naked calls

   IV. writing 2 XYZ Dec 30 covered calls

(A) I and II

(B) I and III

(C) II and III

(D) II and IV

503. An investor who is long a call option realizes a profit if exercising the option when the underlying stock price is

(A) above the exercise price plus the premium paid

(B) below the exercise price

(C) below the exercise price minus the premium paid

(D) above the exercise price

504. When selling an uncovered put, an investor would realize a profit in all of the following situations EXCEPT

(A) the price of the underlying stock increases in value above the strike price of the option

(B) the premium of the put option decreases

(C) the option expires unexercised

(D) the option is exercised when the price of the underlying stock is below the strike price minus the premium

505. Which of the following option contracts are in the money when UPP is trading at 43.50?

   I. short UPP 35 call

   II. short UPP 40 put

   III. long UPP 40 call

   IV. long UPP 50 put

(A) I, III, and IV

(B) II and IV

(C) III and IV

(D) I, II, and III

506. If holding which of the following positions would an investor deliver the stock if exercised?

(A) long a call or short a call

(B) long a call or short a put

(C) long a put or short a call

(D) long a put or short a put

507. One of your clients is convinced that DWN common stock will decline in value over the next few months. Which investment strategy would you recommend to your client that would allow him to take advantage of the expected decline with the smallest cash investment?

(A) buying a DWN call option

(B) buying a DWN put option

(C) shorting DWN stock

(D) buying a DWN straddle

508. If an investor sells a covered call on stock owned in an account, which of the following is TRUE?

(A) The premium increases the cost basis.

(B) The premium decreases the cost basis.

(C) The investor has unlimited risk.

(D) The trade must be executed in a margin account.

509. Options of the same series have the same

   I. stock

   II. expiration date

   III. strike price

   IV. type

(A) I only

(B) I and III

(C) I, II, and III

(D) I, II, III, and IV

510. The break-even point for an investor who is short a put is

(A) the market price minus the premium

(B) the market price plus the premium

(C) the strike price minus the premium

(D) the strike price plus the premium

511. The profit on an option transaction will be taxed as

(A) a capital gain

(B) ordinary income

(C) investment income

(D) passive income

512. Unless otherwise stated, a stock option contract represents

(A) 1 share of the underlying security

(B) 10 shares of the underlying security

(C) 100 shares of the underlying security

(D) 1,000 shares of the underlying security

513. When can European-style options be exercised?

(A) any time

(B) one business day prior to expiration

(C) three business days prior to expiration

(D) any time during the expiration month

514. Which of the following would affect the premium of an option?

I. volatility of the underlying security

II. the amount of time until the option expires

III. the intrinsic value

(A) I and II

(B) II and III

(C) I and III

(D) I, II, and III

515. Which of the following is the riskiest option strategy?

(A) buying calls

(B) buying puts

(C) selling uncovered calls

(D) selling uncovered puts

516. An investor who writes a put has the

(A) right to buy stock at a fixed price

(B) right to sell stock at a fixed price

(C) obligation to buy stock at a fixed price if exercised

(D) obligation to sell stock at a fixed price if exercised

517. A LMN Dec 45 put is trading for 3.5 when LMN is at $47.50. What is the time value of this option?

(A) 0

(B) 1

(C) 2.5

(D) 3.5

518. Standard option contracts are issued with an expiration of

(A) 6 months

(B) 9 months

(C) 12 months

(D) 39 months

519. An October 40 call option is two days away from expiration. The current market value of the underlying stock is 52. What is the most likely premium?

(A) 0.754

(B) 2

(C) 12.25

(D) 16

520–528 Standard Option Math

520. An investor sells one HIJ Jun 40 put at 6; what is the break-even point?

(A) 34

(B) 40

(C) 46

(D) cannot be determined

521. An investor writes an RST Dec 60 call for 7. What is this investor's maximum potential gain?

(A) $700

(B) $5,300

(C) $6,700

(D) unlimited

522. An investor with no other position in RST writes one RST Dec 40 put at 3.25. If the put option is exercised when RST is trading at 37.50 and the investor immediately sells the stock in the market, what is her gain or loss excluding commissions?

(A) $75 loss

(B) $75 gain

(C) $575 loss

(D) $575 gain

523. An investor wrote ten uncovered puts on DWN common stock. What is the maximum potential loss?

(A) unlimited

(B) the premium received

(C) (strike price – the premium) × 100 shares × 10 options

(D) (strike price + the premium) × 100 shares × 10 options

524. An investor is sold one WXYZ Jan 35 put at 3.5 when WXYZ was trading at $36.10. What is the investor's break-even point as a result of this transaction?

(A) 31.5

(B) 32.6

(C) 38.5

(D) 39.6

525. Mr. Couture is long one MMA Feb 40 call at 1.75. If MMA is currently trading at $39.50, what is Mr. Couture's break-even point?

(A) $37.75

(B) $38.25

(C) $41.25

(D) $41.75

526. An ABC call option premium increased by 0.65. What is the dollar amount of the increase?

(A) $0.65

(B) $6.50

(C) $65.00

(D) $650.00

527. Use the following exhibit to answer this question:

RST	Strike	Jun	Sep	Dec
50.50	40	12.20	14.40	15.90
50.50	40p	a	0.60	1.30
50.50	50	2.10	3.35	5.10
50.50	50p	1.50	2.80	4.15

p = put   a = not traded

What is the maximum potential gain for an investor who sells an RST Dec 50 put?

(A) $150

(B) $415

(C) $4,585

(D) unlimited

528. With no previous positions in an account, Mr. Jones writes an XYZ May 75 put for 6.62 while XYZ trades at 63.25. If XYZ later closes at 60.88, what is Mr. Jones's break-even point?

(A) 54.25

(B) 56.63

(C) 68.38

(D) 81.63

529–544 Straddles and Combinations

529. An investor buys a DDD Jun 50 put for 5 and buys a DDD Jun 45 call for 2. This investor has created a

(A) long straddle

(B) long combination

(C) short straddle

(D) diagonal spread

530. One of your clients is holding DUD common stock. You and your client believe that DUD's market price will stay at roughly the same price for the next year. Which of the following option positions would you recommend for the client to be able to generate some additional income on DUD?

(A) Buy a DUD combination.

(B) Write a DUD straddle.

(C) Buy a DUD call.

(D) Buy a DUD put.

531. An investor is long one CDE Nov 35 call for 4 and one CDE Nov 35 put for 7. CDE drops to 22 just prior to expiration. The investor buys the stock in the market and exercises the put. After the call expires, what is the gain or loss?

(A) $200 gain

(B) $200 loss

(C) $1,600 gain

(D) $1,600 loss

532. An investor shorts one TUB Aug 40 call for 7 and shorts one TUB Aug 35 put for 3. What are the investor's break-even points?

(A) 32 and 47

(B) 30 and 45

(C) 25 and 50

(D) 28 and 43

533. What is the maximum potential gain for an investor who purchased a straddle?

(A) the premiums

(B) the difference between the exercise price minus the premiums

(C) the difference between the premiums minus the difference between the exercise prices

(D) unlimited

534. One of your customers wants to create a short straddle on TUV common stock. Your customer is already short one TUV Sep 40 call. What other position would you tell your customer she needs?

(A) long one TUV Sep 45 put

(B) long one TUV Sep 40 put

(C) short one TUV Sep 35 put

(D) short one TUV Sep 40 put

535. An investor with no other positions shorts an XYZ Dec 35 straddle while XYZ is trading at 35. This investor is looking for XYZ to

(A) increase in value

(B) decrease in value

(C) remain stable

(D) either Choice (A) or (B)

536. An investor sells a DEF at-the-money straddle. This investor is

(A) bullish on DEF

(B) bearish on DEF

(C) neutral on DEF

(D) cannot be determined

537. These investors are looking for the price of the underlying security to remain stable.

I. buyers of an at-the-money straddle

II. sellers of an at-the-money straddle

III. buyers of an out-of-the-money combination

IV. sellers of an out-of-the-money combination

(A) I and III

(B) I and IV

(C) II and III

(D) II and IV

538. Holders of which of the following option positions face the greatest risk?

(A) long straddle

(B) short combination

(C) short (credit) spread

(D) long (debit) spread

539. An investor buys an ABC May 40 call for 9 and buys an ABC May 40 put for 5 when ABC trades at $45. ABC increases to $60, and the investor exercises the call and allows the put to expire. Two weeks later, the investor sold the stock in the market for $58. What is the gain or loss?

(A) $400 gain

(B) $400 loss

(C) $600 gain

(D) $600 loss

540. Holders of which of the following option positions are looking for volatility?

I. long straddle

II. short straddle

III. long combination

IV. short combination

(A) I and II

(B) III and IV

(C) I and III

(D) II and IV

541. An investor buys one LMN Sep 55 call at 6.5 and one LMN Sep 55 put at 3.2. This investor would see a profit with LMN trading at

(A) $44.70

(B) $55.00

(C) $57.30

(D) $64.70

542. Which of the following positions would be profitable to an investor who is long a straddle?

I. when the market value of the underlying security is above the combined premiums added to the strike price

II. when the market value of the underlying security is below the combined premiums subtracted from the strike price

III. when the market value of the underlying security is above the strike price minus the premiums

IV. when the market value of the underlying security is below the strike price plus the premiums

(A) I or II

(B) I or III

(C) II or III

(D) II or IV

543. An investor who sees a stock with a high beta would most likely apply which of the following option strategies?

(A) bullish spread

(B) short combination

(C) long straddle

(D) short a put

544. A customer buys one HIJ Oct 40 call at 6 and one HIJ Oct 40 put at 2. Six months later, the call is closed for 1, and the put is closed for 4. What is the customer's gain or loss?

(A) $100 gain

(B) $100 loss

(C) $300 gain

(D) $300 loss

545–569 Spreads

545. Which of the following is a bearish spread?

(A) long one DEF Feb 40 call/short one DEF Feb 50 call

(B) long one XYZ Oct 30 put/short one XYZ Dec 40 put

(C) long one TUV Aug 60 put/short one QRS Aug 50 put

(D) long one HIJ Dec 80 call/short one HIJ Nov 70 call

546. Mr. Levin writes one JKL Aug 60 put for 6 and buys one Aug 75 put for 12. What is Mr. Levin's maximum potential gain?

(A) $600

(B) $900

(C) $1,500

(D) unlimited

547. Mrs. Jones bought one DEF Oct 40 put and wrote one DEF Nov 50 put. Mrs. Jones has created a

(A) vertical spread

(B) horizontal spread

(C) diagonal spread

(D) long combination

548. Which of the following would create a short spread?

(A) buying a call at a low strike price and selling a call at a high strike price

(B) buying a put at a high strike price and selling a put at a low strike price

(C) buying a call with a long expiration and selling a call with a short expiration

(D) buying a put at a low strike price and selling a put at a high strike price

549. Mr. Silver purchased an STU Sep 30 put at 2 and also wrote an STU Sep 40 put at 7. Mr. Silver will be able to make a profit if

   I. both options expire unexercised

   II. both options are exercised

   III. the premium difference narrows to less than 5

   IV. the premium difference widens to more than 5

(A) I or III

(B) I or IV

(C) II or III

(D) II or IV

550. Use the following exhibit to answer this question:

	BID	OFFER
ZAM Dec45 call	5	5.25
ZAM Dec45 put	4	4.25
ZAM Dec50 call	1	1.25
ZAM Dec50 put	7	7.25

How much would an investor creating a debit call spread have to pay (disregarding commissions)?

(A) $300

(B) $325

(C) $375

(D) $425

551. What is the maximum potential gain on a debit call spread?

(A) the difference between the exercised strike prices minus the difference between the premiums

(B) the difference between the exercised premiums less the premium received plus the premium paid

(C) the difference between the premium paid less the premium received

(D) the difference between the strike prices plus the cost of the two premiums

552. An investor has created a long (debit) spread. In order to make a profit, this investor wants the

I. option premium difference to narrow

II. option premium difference to widen

III. options to be exercised

IV. options to remain unexercised

(A) I and III

(B) I and IV

(C) II and III

(D) II and IV

553. One of your clients purchased one DEF May 40 call at 8 and sold one DEF May 50 call at 2. You can inform her that her break-even point is

(A) $34

(B) $42

(C) $46

(D) $50

554. Stan Goldhouse sold one XYZ Jul 65 put at 5 and purchased one XYZ Jul 60 put at 2. What is Stan's break-even point?

(A) $53

(B) $62

(C) $67

(D) $72

555. An investor buys a WXY Dec 40 call for 9 and writes a WXY Oct 60 call for 2. What is the maximum gain?

(A) $300

(B) $700

(C) $1,300

(D) $2,000

556. Mrs. Smith buys one HIJ June 60 call for 8 and sells one HIJ June 80 call for 3. Mrs. Smith has established a

(A) vertical spread

(B) horizontal spread

(C) diagonal spread

(D) long straddle

557. A client shorts one LMN Feb 55 put at 6 and longs one LMN Feb 45 put at 1 while LMN is trading at 55. Your client is

(A) bullish on LMN

(B) bearish on LMN

(C) bullish/neutral on LMN

(D) bearish/neutral on LMN

558. An investor purchases an EFG May 70 put for 4 and writes an EFG May 90 put for 12. If the investor closes the 70 put for 6 and the 90 put for 15, what is the gain or loss?

(A) $100 gain

(B) $100 loss

(C) $500 gain

(D) $500 loss

559. An investor sells an HIJ May 50 call and buys an HIJ May 60 call. Which TWO of the following describe this spread?

I. bullish

II. bearish

III. debit

IV. credit

(A) I and III

(B) I and IV

(C) II and III

(D) II and IV

560. Use the following exhibit to answer this question:

	BID	OFFER
GHI Sep 40 call	5	5.25
GHI Sep 40 put	4	4.25
GHI Sep 50 call	2	2.25
GHI Sep 50 put	8	8.25

How much would an investor creating a long (debit) call spread have to pay?

(A) $200

(B) $225

(C) $300

(D) $325

561. A client who wants to create a spread on XYZ and is bullish on XYZ would

I. create a vertical long call spread on XYZ

II. create a vertical short call spread on XYZ

III. create a vertical long put spread on XYZ

IV. create a vertical short put spread on XYZ

(A) I and III

(B) I and IV

(C) II and III

(D) II and IV

562. Which of the following is a credit spread?

(A) long 1 ABC Dec 60 call/short 1 ABC Dec 70 call

(B) long 1 DEF Nov 70 put/short 1 GHI Nov 55 put

(C) long 1 JKL Sep 40 call/short 1 JKL Sep 30 call

(D) long 1 MNO May 30 put/short 1 MNO May 20 put

563. A customer is long one DEF Aug 80 call at 2 and writes one DEF Aug 70 call at 5. This position is called a

(A) bullish call spread

(B) bearish call spread

(C) long straddle

(D) short combination

564. An investor is short one LMN Oct 60 put at 6 and long one LMN Oct 50 put at 2. What is the investor's break-even point?

(A) 46

(B) 54

(C) 56

(D) 64

565. An ABC horizontal call spread has

(A) different expiration months

(B) different strike prices

(C) different securities

(D) Choices (A) and (B)

566. An investor who writes an ABC August 40 put for 9 and buys an ABC October 50 put for 13 has taken which TWO of the following positions?

I. vertical spread

II. diagonal spread

III. credit spread

IV. debit spread

(A) I and III

(B) I and IV

(C) II and III

(D) II and IV

567. What has a customer established who buys three ABC Oct 35 calls at 7 and writes six ABC Oct 45 calls at 2 when ABC is trading at 38?

(A) long combination

(B) short combination

(C) ratio spread

(D) ratio straddle

568. What is the market attitude of a client who establishes a debit put spread?

(A) bullish

(B) bearish

(C) neutral

(D) speculative

569. Which of the following are spreads?

I. long 1 ABC Jun 30 call/short 1 ABC Jun 40 call

II. long 1 ABC Jun 30 call/long 1 ABC Jun 40 call

III. long 1 ABC Sep 30 call/short 1 ABC Jun 30 call

IV. long 1 ABC Sep 30 call/short 1 ABC Sep 40 put

(A) I and III

(B) I and II

(C) II and III

(D) II and IV

570–588 Stock and Options

570. Mr. Goldshack purchases 100 shares of RST at 47.50 per share and sells 1 RST Oct 50 call at 3.25. What is Mr. Goldshack's maximum potential loss?

(A) $250

(B) $4,425

(C) $5,175

(D) unlimited

571. An investor shorts 100 shares of TUV at 44.50 and 1 TUV Aug 40 put at 3. What is the investor's break-even point?

(A) $37.00

(B) $41.50

(C) $43.00

(D) $47.50

572. Buying a put option on a long stock position is an appropriate strategy when the market is expected to

(A) rise sharply

(B) fall sharply

(C) remain stable

(D) become volatile

573. One of your clients purchases 100 shares of DEFG at 45.10 and 1 OEX Sep 790 put at 4.50. A few months later, DEFG is trading at 43.55, and the OEX index is trading at 779. If your client closes the stock position and exercises his OEX put, what is his gain?

(A) $155

(B) $495

(C) $1,100

(D) $3,535

574. Mr. Gold has shorted LMN common stock at 34. LMN common stock has recently dropped to 28, and Mr. Gold expects that the price will continue to decrease over the long term. If Mr. Gold wants to hedge against a possible increase in the price, he should

(A) buy an LMN call option

(B) sell an LMN call option

(C) buy an LMN put option

(D) buy an LMN straddle

575. An investor buys 100 shares of TUV at $40 and writes 1 TUV Jun 50 call for 6. What is this investor's maximum potential gain?

(A) $600

(B) $1,600

(C) $3,400

(D) unlimited

576. Todd Goldflow purchases 100 shares of HLP at 25 and writes a 30 call at 3.25. If HLP stock increases to 40 and the call is exercised, Todd has a(n)

(A) $175 loss

(B) $175 gain

(C) $825 loss

(D) $825 gain

577. Mr. Hendricks owns 100 shares of TUF common stock. The price of TUF has been trading between 51 and 53 for the past year. Mr. Hendricks likes the stock but wants to generate some additional income. You should suggest that he

(A) write a TUF call

(B) buy a TUF put

(C) write a TUF put

(D) buy a TUF call

578. An investor sold short 100 shares of DWN common stock at 47.50 and purchased 1 DWN Oct 50 call at 3.25. What is this investor's break-even point?

(A) $44.25

(B) $46.75

(C) $47.50

(D) $50.75

579. Zeb Zeldin purchased 1 RST 45 put at 2.75 and 100 shares of RST at 51. A few months later, with RST trading at 53.50, Zeb closes his put for 0.50 and sells his stock at the market. What is Zeb's gain or loss as a result of these transactions?

(A) $25 gain

(B) $25 loss

(C) $475 gain

(D) $475 loss

580. One of your clients purchases 100 shares of DEF at $54 per share and subsequently writes a DEF May 60 call for 5. If DEF increases to 73 and the call is exercised, what is your client's gain?

(A) $100

(B) $1,100

(C) $2,400

(D) $2,900

581. One of your clients is long 100 shares of WIZ stock originally purchased at $32.50 per share. Your client subsequently wrote a WIZ Jun 35 call at 3.25 when WIZ was trading at $34.10 per share. What is your client's maximum potential loss?

(A) $2,925

(B) $3,085

(C) $3,575

(D) $3,735

582. The break-even point for covered call writers is

(A) the stock price plus the premium

(B) the stock price minus the premium

(C) the exercise price plus the premium

(D) the exercise price minus the premium

583. Mrs. Gold purchases 500 shares of QRS Corp. at $65 per share and 5 QRS Oct 60 puts at 7. What is her break-even point?

(A) 53

(B) 58

(C) 67

(D) 72

584. An investor who writes a DEF call option would be considered covered if owning any of the following positions EXCEPT

(A) DEF convertible bonds convertible into 100 shares of DEF common stock

(B) an escrow receipt for the stock from a bank

(C) a DEF call option with the same expiration month and a lower strike price

(D) 100 shares of DLQ stock

585. An investor who is long 100 shares of ABC wants to protect himself from too much loss in case ABC declines. He should

(A) buy an ABC call option

(B) buy an ABC put option

(C) sell an ABC call option

(D) sell an ABC put option

586. Which of the following would cover the sale of an XYZ Aug 60 put?

(A) long 100 shares of XYZ

(B) long 1 XYZ Aug 50 call

(C) long 1 XYZ Aug 50 put

(D) long 1 XYZ Aug 70 put

587. Mr. Steele purchased 100 shares of RST at $60 and wrote an RST May 80 call for 5. What is Mr. Steele's break-even point?

(A) 65

(B) 75

(C) 55

(D) 85

588. On the same day, an investor purchases 100 shares of LMN at 48 and 1 LMN Sep 45 put for 3. Nine months later, the put expires unexercised. What is the investor's tax consequence?

(A) owning stock with a cost basis of 45

(B) owning stock with a cost basis of 51

(C) a $300 capital loss

(D) a $300 ordinary loss

589–599 Multiple Option Contracts

589. An investor purchased 400 shares of XYZ at 52 and 4 XYZ Aug 50 protective puts at 3.50 each. What is this investor's maximum potential gain?

(A) $600

(B) $800

(C) $1,400

(D) unlimited

590. A client purchases 500 shares of ABC at 36 and buys 5 ABC Jun 35 puts at 4 each. What is your client's break-even point?

(A) 31

(B) 32

(C) 39

(D) 40

591. An investor buys three HIJ Sep 40 calls for 3 each. When HIJ trades at 46, the investor exercises the three calls in order to buy 300 shares of HIJ for the margin account. How much must the investor deposit in the margin account for the stock purchase?

(A) $6,000

(B) $6,900

(C) $12,000

(D) $13,800

592. One of your clients owns ten HPPY Aug 30 calls, which were initially purchased for $3,000. HPPY increases to $40, and your client exercises the calls. The client tells you to sell the stock immediately after purchase. If all of these trades are executed in a margin account, how much must your client deposit?

(A) $2,000

(B) $15,000

(C) $20,000

(D) No deposit is required.

593. An investor buys two LMN December 40 calls at 9 and sells two LMN December 60 calls at 1. The investor will NOT profit in which TWO of the following situations?

I. The premium difference widens.

II. The premium difference narrows.

III. The options are exercised.

IV. The options expire unexercised.

(A) I and III

(B) I and IV

(C) II and III

(D) II and IV

594. Melissa Goldhouse purchased 300 shares of UPP Corp. at $35 per share and purchased 3 UPP Nov 30 puts at 2. What is Melissa's break-even point?

(A) 28

(B) 32

(C) 33

(D) 37

595. Sandy Silver purchased two GHI 35 calls and pays a premium of 4.5 for each option. Sandy also purchased two GHI 35 puts and pays a premium of 2 for each option. At the time of purchase, GHI was trading at $51.75. Just prior to expiration, GHI is trading at $36.25, and Sandy decides to close her options for their intrinsic value. Excluding commission, Sandy had a

(A) $525 loss

(B) $525 gain

(C) $1,050 loss

(D) $1,050 gain

596. Mike Mineshaft shorted three XYZ Oct 40 calls for a premium of $300 per option. Two months later, Mike closed his option positions for $260 per option. What was Mike's gain or loss?

(A) $40 loss

(B) $40 gain

(C) $120 loss

(D) $120 gain

597. An investor is long two HIJ Oct 40 calls at 6 each and short two HIJ Oct 50 calls at 2 each. What is the investor's maximum potential loss?

(A) $400

(B) $600

(C) $800

(D) $1,200

598. An investor purchases 400 shares of SSS Corp. at $32.50 per share and purchases 4 SSS Nov 30 puts at 4.5. What is the investor's break-even point?

(A) $25.50

(B) $28.00

(C) $34.50

(D) $37.00

599. An investor buys four HOT May 60 puts for 6 each and writes four HOT May 50 puts for 2 each. What is the investor's maximum gain?

(A) $600

(B) $800

(C) $2,400

(D) $3,200

600–604 Splits and Dividends

600. LMN declares a stock dividend. What will happen to LMN option contracts as a result of the dividend?

(A) The number of contacts will increase, and the strike price will decrease.

(B) The number of shares per contract will increase, and the stock price will decrease.

(C) The number of contracts will decrease, and the strike price will increase.

(D) The number of shares per contract will decrease, and the strike price will increase.

601. If a 20% stock dividend is declared for HIJ stock, the owner of one HIJ Aug 30 call will own

(A) one HIJ contract for 100 shares with a strike price of 30

(B) one HIJ contract for 120 shares with a strike price of 25

(C) two HIJ contracts for 60 shares with a strike price of 30

(D) two HIJ contracts for 60 shares with a strike price of 25

602. When a corporation splits its stock evenly, what happens to holders of options on that stock?

(A) The number of contracts will increase, and the strike price will decrease.

(B) The number of shares per contract will increase, and the stock price will decrease.

(C) The price of the stock will increase, and the number of contracts will decrease.

(D) The price of the stock will increase, and the number of shares per contract will decrease.

603. An investor owns four HIJ Oct 40 calls. If HIJ announces a 5-for-2 split, what is the investor's new position after the split?

(A) ten HIJ Oct 40 calls, 250 shares each

(B) ten HIJ Oct 16 calls, 250 shares each

(C) four HIJ Oct 16 calls, 250 shares each

(D) four HIJ Oct 40 calls, 100 shares each

604. An investor owns four LMN Oct 60 calls. If LMN announces a 3-for-1 split, what is the investor's new position?

(A) 4 LMN Oct 20 calls, 300 shares each

(B) 4 LMN Oct 60 calls, 300 shares each

(C) 12 LMN Oct 20 calls, 100 shares each

(D) 12 LMN Oct 60 calls, 100 shares each

605–623 Currency, LEAPS, Yield, and Index Options

605. If a client is bullish on the S&P 500, which of the following option strategies would the client use?

I. Buy SPX calls.

II. Buy SPX puts.

III. Buy VIX calls.

IV. Buy VIX puts.

(A) I and III

(B) I and IV

(C) II and III

(D) II and IV

606. An investor buys one Japanese Yen 120 call at 3. What is the cost of this option?

(A) $300

(B) $3,000

(C) $30,000

(D) $300,000

607. PHLX traded world currency options are available for all of the following currencies EXCEPT

(A) euro

(B) Japanese yen

(C) U.S. dollar

(D) British pound

608. An investor purchases ten DEF Oct 40 call LEAPS at 4. The LEAPS expire in 30 months. If they are purchased on margin, what is the margin call?

(A) $2,000

(B) $3,000

(C) $4,000

(D) Options cannot be purchased on margin.

609. One of your clients purchases three LEAPS in the market with two years left until expiration. If the LEAPS expire out of the money, what is the investor tax consequence at expiration?

(A) short-term capital gain

(B) short-term capital loss

(C) long-term capital gain

(D) long-term capital loss

610. An individual expects interest rates to increase over the next few months. Which of the following would be proper option investments?

I. Buy T-bond calls.

II. Buy T-bond puts.

III. Write T-bond calls.

IV. Write T-bond puts.

(A) I and III

(B) I and IV

(C) II and III

(D) II and IV

611. All of the following are TRUE about LEAPS EXCEPT

    (A)   They have a longer life than other listed options.

    (B)   They are available only on index options.

    (C)   They may be exercised at any time.

    (D)   They have higher premiums than shorter-term options.

612. If an investor exercises an OEX call option, what form of delivery should she expect?

    (A)   100 shares of OEX

    (B)   cash equal to the intrinsic value of the option times 100 shares at the end of the exercise day

    (C)   cash equal to 100 shares of OEX

    (D)   none of the above

613. An investor who buys SPX put options is

    (A)   bearish on the market

    (B)   bullish on the market

    (C)   bearish on SPX common stock

    (D)   bullish on SPX common stock

614. One of your customers believes that the U.S. dollar will weaken against the Canadian dollar. To take advantage of this belief, what should your customer do?

    (A)   Buy U.S. dollar calls.

    (B)   Buy U.S. dollar puts.

    (C)   Buy Canadian dollar calls.

    (D)   Buy Canadian dollar puts.

615. Yield-based options are based on yields of

    (A)   CDs

    (B)   Treasury securities

    (C)   general obligation bonds

    (D)   CMOs

616. England has announced that there was an increase in the gross national product figures for another quarter. Japan just had an earthquake that was devastating to the economy. What would be the appropriate investment strategy for an investor who is aware of this news?

    I.   Buy British pound calls.

    II.   Buy British pound puts.

    III.   Buy Japanese yen calls.

    IV.   Buy Japanese yen puts.

    (A)   I and III

    (B)   I and IV

    (C)   II and III

    (D)   II and IV

617. If a client believes that interest rates will increase, which TWO of the following option positions are MOST appropriate?

    I.   Buy T-bond calls.

    II.   Buy T-bond puts.

    III.   Buy T-bond yield calls.

    IV.   Buy T-bond yield puts.

    (A)   I and III

    (B)   I and IV

    (C)   II and III

    (D)   II and IV

618. A customer holds a portfolio of securities that includes a significant amount of preferred stocks. Which of the following option strategies would you recommend to protect against a decline in the value of the preferred stocks?

    (A)   Buy interest rate calls.

    (B)   Buy interest rate puts.

    (C)   Buy index option calls.

    (D)   Buy index option puts.

619. Which of the following index option strategies would be BEST for an investor who is bullish on the market?

    I.   Buy index call options.

    II. Buy index put options.

    III. Sell index call options.

    IV. Sell index put options.

    (A) I and III

    (B) I and IV

    (C) II and III

    (D) II and IV

620. Listed options for which of the following currencies are available on U.S. exchanges?

    I.   U.S. dollar

    II. Japanese yen

    III. euro

    IV. New Zealand dollar

    (A) II and III

    (B) I, II, and IV

    (C) II, III, and IV

    (D) I, II, III, and IV

621. World currency options trade on the

    (A) NASDAQ OMX PHLX

    (B) Chicago Board Options Exchange

    (C) American Stock Exchange

    (D) New York Stock Exchange

622. What is the maximum potential loss for an investor who is long an index put option?

    (A) the premium paid

    (B) the strike price minus the premium multiplied by 100 shares

    (C) the strike price plus the premium multiplied by 100 shares

    (D) the strike price multiplied by 100 shares

623. If an investor exercises an OEX index call option, which of the following would be acceptable delivery from the seller of the call?

    (A) 100 shares of the OEX index

    (B) cash equal to the market value of 100 shares of the OEX index

    (C) cash equal to the intrinsic value of the option at the end of the day of exercise

    (D) cash equal to the margin requirement for 100 shares of the OEX index

624–640 Option Markets and Option Rules

624. All of the following can be used as collateral in a margin account EXCEPT

    (A) listed stocks

    (B) listed bonds

    (C) call options

    (D) mutual funds

625. When is the last time a customer can exercise a stock option listed on the CBOE?

    (A) 10:59 p.m. CST on the Saturday after the third Friday of the expiration month

    (B) 3:02 p.m. CST on the third Friday of the expiration month

    (C) 4:00 p.m. CST on the third Friday of the expiration month

    (D) 4:30 p.m. CST on the third Friday of the expiration month

626. New options investors must sign an options account agreement

    (A) at or prior to approval of the new account

    (B) at or prior to the investor's first option transaction

    (C) within 15 days after approval of the account

    (D) whenever the investor sees fit

627. You execute the following trades for one of your speculative investors:

> Buy one HIJ Oct 35 call at 7
>
> Write one HIJ Oct 40 call at 2

Would these trades be considered suitable?

(A) It is impossible to say.

(B) No, because it is impossible to profit from these option positions.

(C) Yes, because this investor is looking for risky positions.

(D) No, because these positions are too safe for a speculative investor.

628. One of your customers wants to liquidate a long option. How would you mark the option order ticket?

(A) opening purchase

(B) opening sale

(C) closing purchase

(D) closing sale

629. An investor is long 5,000 GHI calls. Which of the following additional positions may the investor have without violating position limits (position limit = 10,500)?

(A) long 6,000 GHI calls

(B) short 7,000 GHI puts

(C) short 8,000 GHI calls

(D) none of the above

630. One of your clients wants to start trading options. Place the following option transactions in sequential order, from the first to last:

I. The registered options principal approves the account.

II. The client sends in a signed options account agreement.

III. An options risk disclosure document is sent to the client.

IV. The transaction is executed.

(A) III, I, IV, II

(B) II, I, III, IV

(C) I, III, II, IV

(D) I, IV, III, II

631. Listed option transactions settle

(A) in one business day

(B) in two business days

(C) in three business days

(D) in five business days

632. Options are automatically exercised at expiration if the option is at LEAST

(A) 0.01 in the money

(B) 1/2 point in the money

(C) 1 point in the money

(D) 1% in the money

633. The OCC uses which of the following methods when assigning exercise notices?

(A) first-in, first-out

(B) random selection

(C) to the member firm holding the largest position

(D) any of the above

634. When is the last time that an investor can trade an options contract?

   (A) 4:30 p.m. EST on the business day prior to expiration

   (B) 4:30 p.m. CST on the business day prior to expiration

   (C) 3:00 p.m. CST on the business day prior to expiration

   (D) 11:59 p.m. EST on the business day prior to expiration

635. Option confirmations must include

   I.   the option type

   II. the option strike price

   III. the number of contracts

   IV. the premium

   (A) I and III

   (B) I, II, and III

   (C) I, III, and IV

   (D) I, II, III, and IV

636. The individual responsible for approving all options accounts at a firm is

   (A) a registered options principal

   (B) a general securities principal

   (C) an office manager

   (D) the compliance officer

637. Trading is temporarily halted on a listed common stock. What happens to the trading of the listed options on that stock?

   (A) It is halted.

   (B) It is restricted to closing transactions only.

   (C) It continues.

   (D) None of the above.

638. A market maker on the CBOE is an

   (A) OCC

   (B) OAA

   (C) OBO

   (D) ODD

639. Place the following in order from first to last when a customer is opening a new options account.

   I.   Have a ROP approve the account.

   II. Send out an ODD.

   III. Have the customer sign and return the OAA.

   IV. Execute the options trade.

   (A) I, II, III, IV

   (B) II, I, IV, III

   (C) III, I, II, IV

   (D) IV, III, II, I

640. Which of the following are TRUE about options advertisements and sales literature?

   I.   All ads must be preceded or accompanied by an options risk disclosure document.

   II. All sales literature must be preceded or accompanied by an options risk disclosure document.

   III. Advertisements and sales literature must be approved by a CROP.

   (A) I and II

   (B) II and III

   (C) I and III

   (D) I, II, and III

Chapter 9

Portfolio and Securities Analysis

• •

*I*nstead of just randomly recommending securities to customers or potential customers, you're expected to know why you're recommending those securities. Typically, most brokerage firms have their own analysts who are responsible for doing the research and recommending which securities the registered reps should promote. The two main types are fundamental analysts, who examine the specifics of corporations, and technical analysts, who follow the market to determine the best time to buy or sell. As a registered rep, you'll also be responsible for examining your customers' portfolios to help them keep in line with their investment objectives.

The Problems You'll Work On

The questions in this chapter test your ability in the following areas:

- ✔ Making appropriate recommendations based on your customers and their individual needs

- ✔ Understanding a customer's investment objectives so you can accurately help manage his portfolio

- ✔ Grasping the concepts of fiscal policy, money supply, the Fed, and how governmental intervention is likely to affect the market

- ✔ Comprehending certain definitions and economic indicators

- ✔ Recognizing the roles of fundamental analysts and technical analysts

- ✔ Understanding the different types of issues and their risks and rewards

- ✔ Remembering the different indexes and circuit breakers

What to Watch Out For

Simple things can trip you up; here's what you need to watch out for as you work through this chapter:

- ✔ Really make sure you understand an investor's investment objectives and needs.

- ✔ Always be aware of the key words, such as EXCEPT and NOT, that can change an answer.

- ✔ Eliminate answers that you know are wrong to increase your chances of selecting the right one.

- ✔ Perform math calculations carefully to avoid careless errors.

641–648 Knowing Your Customer

641. Which of the following is the MOST important consideration when making investment recommendations to a client?

(A) the client's age

(B) the client's marital status

(C) the client's financial needs

(D) the client's investment objectives

642. One of your new clients has a long-term investment objective of aggressive growth. However, she is planning on purchasing a fixer-upper home within the next year. Which of the following investments would you determine to be MOST suitable for her portfolio?

(A) Treasury bills

(B) high-yield bond fund

(C) aggressive growth fund

(D) an oil and gas wildcatting program

643. A customer of yours has preservation of capital as his primary investment objective. Which of the following securities would you recommend to help him meet his objective?

I. AAA-rated corporate bonds

II. an exploratory direct participation program

III. blue chip stocks

IV. U.S. government bonds

(A) I, II, and III

(B) I, III, and IV

(C) II and IV

(D) II, III, and IV

644. Which of the following investments would be proper for investors interested in capital growth?

(A) T-bonds

(B) municipal bonds

(C) the stock of new corporations

(D) REITs

645. If a client is interested in investing in liquid securities, which TWO of the following would you NOT recommend:

I. municipal bonds

II. direct participation programs

III. mutual funds

IV. blue chip stocks

(A) I and II

(B) III and IV

(C) II and III

(D) I and IV

646. Changing which of the following nonfinancial information might change an investor's investment objectives?

I. the investor growing older

II. getting married or divorced

III. investment experience

IV. family responsibilities

(A) II and IV

(B) I, II, and III

(C) I, II, and IV

(D) I, II, III, and IV

647. A client's investment decisions should be based mostly on her

    I.   investment needs

    II. registered representative's recommendations

    III. risk tolerance

    (A) I and II

    (B) I and III

    (C) II and III

    (D) I, II, and III

648. A client's nonfinancial considerations are typically as important as his financial considerations. Nonfinancial considerations include

    (A) the client's age

    (B) the client's marital status

    (C) the client's employment status

    (D) all of the above

649–659 Portfolio Management

649. Which of the following investment strategies should be recommended for a 60-year-old investor?

    (A) 40% in stocks and 60% in bonds and cash equivalents

    (B) 60% in stocks and 40% in bonds and cash equivalents

    (C) 50% in stocks and 50% in bonds and cash equivalents

    (D) 30% in common stocks, 20% in options, 10% in bonds, and 40% in cash equivalents

650. All of the following securities have reinvestment risk EXCEPT

    (A) Treasury bills

    (B) Treasury notes

    (C) municipal revenue bonds

    (D) municipal GO bonds

651. Your client has an investment objective of total return. He currently has 100% of his portfolio invested in common stocks and common stock mutual funds. What would you suggest he add to his portfolio to help him meet his investment objective?

    (A) blue chip stocks

    (B) preferred stocks

    (C) aggressive growth mutual funds

    (D) corporate bonds

652. Which of the following would be the BEST recommendations for an investor who has an investment objective of speculation?

    I.   sector funds

    II. blue chip stocks

    III. zero-coupon bonds

    IV. technology stocks

    (A) I and II

    (B) II and III

    (C) I and IV

    (D) I, II, and IV

653. One of your 60-year-old clients has a portfolio that consists of 60% invested in stocks, 30% in bonds, and 10% in cash equivalents. Using a standard strategic asset allocation model, he should

(A) sell some of his bonds and purchase more stocks

(B) sell some of his stocks and purchase more bonds

(C) sell his cash equivalents and purchase more stocks and bonds

(D) cannot be determined with the information given

654. Which of the following must occur before a registered representative makes an investment recommendation to his client?

(A) The registered representative must determine the client's suitability.

(B) The registered representative must receive written approval from a principal.

(C) The registered representative must obtain a written power of attorney from the client.

(D) All of the above.

655. One of your wealthy clients is in the highest tax bracket and has a portfolio with a nice mixture of corporate bonds and stocks. What would be the BEST recommendation to help the client round out his portfolio?

(A) U.S. Treasury securities

(B) municipal bonds

(C) REITs

(D) CMOs

656. A customer wants to purchase a security that does not fit his investment objectives. After making him aware of that fact, he decides that he wants to go ahead with the purchase anyway. What should you do?

(A) Refuse the order.

(B) Change the customer's investment objectives.

(C) Talk it over with a principal prior to taking the order.

(D) Take the order and mark the order ticket as "unsolicited."

657. Mr. Steele is a 55-year-old investor who has a couple hundred thousand invested in the market. He would like to add more securities to his portfolio that have a high degree of liquidity. All of the following would be acceptable recommendations EXCEPT

(A) blue chip stocks

(B) mutual funds

(C) DPPs

(D) Treasury bills

658. A client would like to make sure his portfolio is diversified. Which of the following are ways that a portfolio can be diversified?

I. buying different types of securities (equity, debt, options, DPPs, and packaged)

II. buying securities from different industries

III. buying bonds with different ratings

IV. buying securities from different areas of the country or world

(A) I only

(B) I and III

(C) II, III, and IV

(D) I, II, III, and IV

659. A client new to investing has $10,000 to invest and wants to build a diversified portfolio. Which of the following is the BEST investment recommendation?

(A) purchasing several different mutual funds

(B) purchasing three different types of bonds and several different blue chip stocks

(C) purchasing T-bonds and gradually adding stocks to the portfolio with the interest received

(D) waiting until the client has more money to invest because you can't build a diversified portfolio with $10,000

660–672 Fiscal Policy, Money Supply, and the Fed

660. Which of the following actions may the Fed take to tighten the money supply?

I. Increase reserve requirements.

II. Lower reserve requirements.

III. Raise the discount rate.

IV. Lower the discount rate.

(A) I and III

(B) I and IV

(C) II and III

(D) II and IV

661. An inverted yield curve indicates that

I. short-term bonds are yielding less than long-term bonds

II. short-term bonds are yielding more than long-term bonds

III. interest rates have recently increased

IV. interest rates have recently decreased

(A) I and III

(B) I and IV

(C) II and III

(D) II and IV

662. The discount rate is

(A) the interest rate that banks charge their best customers for loans

(B) the interest rate that the Fed charges banks for loans

(C) the interest rate charged in margin accounts

(D) the interest rate that banks charge each other for overnight loans

663. If the Fed increases the discount rate, all of the following would occur EXCEPT

(A) bond yields increase

(B) stock prices decrease

(C) the federal funds rate increases

(D) inflation increases

664. The economic theory that says that less government spending and lower taxes will result in economic growth is

(A) the monetary theory

(B) demand-side theory

(C) supply-side theory

(D) Keynesian theory

665. If the value of the U.S. dollar declines in relation to foreign currencies, all of the following are TRUE EXCEPT

(A) foreign exports become less competitive

(B) U.S. imports of foreign goods increase

(C) foreign imports of U.S. products increase

(D) U.S. exports become more competitive

666. Which of the following outstanding bonds will decrease MOST in price if the Fed increases the discount rate?

(A) T-bills

(B) T-notes

(C) T-bonds

(D) cannot be determined

667. The U.S. dollar has been steadily falling against the euro. If the pattern continues, which of the following statements would be TRUE?

I. The amount of U.S. exports would likely increase.

II. The amount of U.S. exports would likely decrease.

III. This would most likely happen during a tight-money period.

IV. This would most likely happen during an easy-money period.

(A) I and III

(B) I and IV

(C) II and III

(D) II and IV

668. All of the following would indicate that the money supply is tightening EXCEPT an increase in the

(A) prime rate

(B) call loan rate

(C) money available for bank loans

(D) yields on Treasury bills

669. Which of the following is the tool MOST commonly used by the Fed to control the money supply?

(A) open market operations

(B) changing the federal funds rate

(C) changing the discount rate

(D) changing reserve requirements

670. The Federal Reserve Board is responsible for all of the following EXCEPT

(A) open market operations

(B) setting the federal funds rate

(C) setting the discount rate

(D) setting minimum margin requirements

671. Which of the following would cause an increase in the balance of trade deficit?

I. an increase in imports of foreign goods

II. an increase in exports of U.S. goods

III. overseas investors buying land in the United States

IV. U.S. investors buying ADRs

(A) II and III

(B) I and IV

(C) I, III, and IV

(D) II, III, and IV

672. The Fed has been expanding the money supply at an alarming rate, and inflation is getting out of hand. Which of the following is the BEST indicator of inflation?

(A) CPI

(B) M1

(C) M3

(D) GDP

673–677 Definitions and Economic Indicators

673. The United States has been in an economic decline for the past three quarters. Therefore, the U.S. economy is said to be in a

(A) recession

(B) depression

(C) freefall

(D) downgrade

674. Which of the following is measured in constant dollars?

(A) M1 money supply

(B) M2 money supply

(C) CPI

(D) real GDP

675. Which of the following bonds would have the highest duration?

(A) 4% bond with a 5-year maturity

(B) 4.5% bond with a 10-year maturity

(C) 5% bond with a 15-year maturity

(D) 5.5% bond with a 15-year maturity

676. During an easy-money yield curve, which of the following is TRUE?

(A) Short-term interest rates are less volatile than long-term interest rates.

(B) Long-term interest rates are less volatile than short-term interest rates.

(C) Long-term and short-term interest rates are equally volatile.

(D) None of the above.

677. Which of the following is a leading economic indicator?

(A) industrial production

(B) the unemployment rate

(C) building permits

(D) GDP

678–693 Fundamental Analysis

678. A fundamental analyst examines all of the following EXCEPT

(A) earnings per share

(B) balance sheets

(C) income statements

(D) trend lines

679. ABC stock pays an annual dividend of $4, has an earnings per share of $8, and has a market price of $40. What is ABC's PE ratio?

(A) 2

(B) 5

(C) 10

(D) 20

680. A fundamental analyst examines which of the following features of a corporation?

(A) earnings trends

(B) support and resistance

(C) breadth of the market

(D) none of the above

681. Which of the following is NOT considered a quick asset?

(A) inventory

(B) accounts receivable

(C) marketable securities

(D) cash

682. Cash flow equals

(A) net income – depreciation

(B) gross income + depreciation + depletion

(C) net income + depreciation + depletion

(D) gross income – depletion + depreciation

683. PE ratio equals

(A) the market price divided by the earnings per share

(B) annual dividends per common share divided by the market price

(C) annual dividends per common share divided by earnings per share

(D) net income minus preferred dividends divided by the number of common shares outstanding

684. Use the following exhibit to answer this question:

Income Statement for HIJ Corp.	
Net Sales	$10,000,000
Operating Expenses	$7,000,000
EBIT	$3,000,000
Bont Interest	$600,000
Taxable Income	$2,400,000
50% Tax	$1,200,000
Net Income	$1,200,000
Preferred Dividends	$600,000
	$600,000
Common Dividends	$300,000
Retained Earnings	$300,000

The market price of the common stock is - $12
1,000,000 common shares outstanding
$0.30 annual common dividend
Depreciation = $200,000

What is the dividend payout ratio for HIJ Corp.?

(A) 10%

(B) 20%

(C) 50%

(D) 60%

685. A fundamental analyst can view or determine all of the following information from the balance sheet of a corporation EXCEPT

(A) long-term liabilities

(B) EPS

(C) shareholder's equity

(D) inventory

686. A corporation's intangible assets include

I.   inventory

II. patents

III. equipment

IV. goodwill

(A) I and III

(B) I, II, and III

(C) III and IV

(D) II and IV

687. Working capital equals

(A) assets – liabilities

(B) liabilities + stockholder's equity

(C) current assets – current liabilities

(D) net worth – liabilities

688. Use the following balance sheet to answer this question:

Assets		Liabilities	
Cash	$10	Accts Payable	$10
Securities	$10	Bonds Due	
Accts Receivable	$20	This Year	$10
Inventory	$20	Bonds Due	
Machinery	$10	in 10 Years	$30
Land	$10		

What is the current ratio?

(A) 1:1

(B) 2:1

(C) 3:1

(D) 4:1

689. If LMN common stock has a $2.20 dividend, a current yield of 5.0%, and a PE ratio of 6 and is trading at $44, its approximate earnings per share is

(A) $0.44

(B) $2.73

(C) $7.33

(D) $8.80

690. Which of the following equations could NOT be determined by extracting numbers from an income statement?

(A) book value per share

(B) net profit margin

(C) gross profit margin

(D) bond interest coverage

691. When a corporation declares a cash dividend, which of the following is TRUE in relation to the corporation's balance sheet?

(A) Assets decrease.

(B) Liabilities increase.

(C) Working capital remains the same.

(D) The stockholder's equity increases.

692. The money a corporation keeps after paying all expenses, interest, taxes, and dividends is called

(A) paid-in capital

(B) capital surplus

(C) net worth

(D) earned surplus

693. If ABCD Corporation issues new long-term bonds, all of the following would increase on its balance sheet EXCEPT

(A) assets

(B) liabilities

(C) net worth

(D) working capital

694–704 Types of Issues and Risks

694. An investor is interested in purchasing debt securities for the first time. If his biggest concern is credit risk, which of the following bonds should he NOT purchase?

  I. income bonds

  II. high-yield bonds

  III. investment grade bonds

  IV. AAA-rated industrial development revenue bonds

(A) I only

(B) I and II

(C) II and III

(D) II, III, and IV

695. A client owns a large amount of Treasury bonds and long-term investment grade corporate bonds. His main risk concern should be

(A) credit risk

(B) inflationary risk

(C) systematic risk

(D) timing risk

696. If the FDA increases pollution standards that are more costly for oil companies, investors who own shares of oil company stock would most likely see the value of their shares decline due to

(A) purchasing power risk

(B) reinvestment risk

(C) credit risk

(D) regulatory risk

697. Precious metal stocks are considered

(A) countercyclical

(B) defensive

(C) blue chip

(D) growth

698. One of your clients is interested in purchasing the common stock from several companies based in Europe. As his registered representative, you should explain to him the risks of investing in these securities. The risks include

  I. political risk

  II. market risk

  III. currency risk

  IV. interest rate risk

(A) I and III

(B) I, III, and IV

(C) I, II, and III

(D) I, II, III, and IV

699. GLD stock tends to move in the opposite direction of the economy. GLD would be termed

(A) defensive stock

(B) blue chip stock

(C) cyclical stock

(D) countercyclical stock

700. A client wants to strengthen her portfolio by adding some defensive stocks. Which of the following stocks would be the defensive?

  I. appliance company

  II. automotive

  III. pharmaceutical

  IV. alcohol

(A) I and II

(B) III and IV

(C) I, III, and IV

(D) I and III

701. Which of the following types of companies would be most adversely affected by rising interest rates?

(A) alcohol

(B) household appliances

(C) utilities

(D) pharmaceutical

702. Which TWO of the following statements are TRUE regarding portfolio diversification?

    I. Diversification reduces systematic risk.

    II. Diversification doesn't reduce systematic risk.

    III. Diversification reduces non-systematic risk.

    IV. Diversification doesn't reduce non-systematic risk.

(A) I and III

(B) I and IV

(C) II and III

(D) II and IV

703. Which of the following are defensive industries?

    I. household appliances

    II. food

    III. pharmaceutical

    IV. tobacco

(A) II, III, and IV

(B) I, II, and III

(C) III and IV

(D) II and III

704. Which of the following debt securities has no reinvestment risk?

(A) municipal GO bonds

(B) equipment trusts

(C) industrial development revenue bonds

(D) Treasury STRIPS

705–715 Technical Analysis

705. According to the Dow theory, the reversal of a bearish trend would be confirmed by

(A) advance/decline ratio

(B) the amount of short interest

(C) an increase in the DJIA and the DJTA

(D) an increase in investors buying call options

706. A head and shoulders top formation indicates the

(A) reversal of a bullish trend

(B) reversal of a bearish trend

(C) security is consolidating

(D) security is due for a breakout

707. According to a technical analyst, if short interest increases in the market, it is a

(A) bullish indicator

(B) bearish indicator

(C) volatility indicator

(D) none of the above

708. The lower portion of a securities trading range is the

(A) support

(B) resistance

(C) breakout

(D) shoulder

709. One of your clients is interested in purchasing a stock with a beta of 1.6. You can tell him that

(A) the stock is equally volatile to the market

(B) the stock is less volatile than the market

(C) the stock is more volatile than the market

(D) cannot be determined

710. A saucer formation is an indication that a security is

(A) consolidating

(B) breaking out

(C) reversing from a bullish trend

(D) reversing from a bearish trend

711. Technical analysts would be MOST interested in which of the following?

(A) corporate balance sheets

(B) the unemployment rate

(C) the trading volume on the NASDAQ OMX PHLX

(D) corporate profits

712. Which of the following technical market theories is based on the belief that small investors usually buy and sell at the wrong time?

(A) random walk theory

(B) odd-lot theory

(C) short interest theory

(D) modern portfolio theory

713. Which of the following would a technical analyst use to determine whether a security is a good investment?

(A) the price earnings ratio

(B) balance sheets

(C) income statements

(D) trend lines

714. When assessing ABC Corporation's stock, a technical analyst will consider all of the following EXCEPT

(A) the market price

(B) the trading volume

(C) the earnings

(D) market momentum

715. DEF Corporate stock's price has been very volatile over the past few years. However, over the past month, the stock has been trading between $40 and $41. DEF stock is

(A) consolidating

(B) saucering

(C) trend lining

(D) breaking out

716–720 Indexes and Circuit Breakers

716. Which of the following are broad-based indexes?

I. S&P 500

II. Wilshire 5000

III. Value Line Composite Index

IV. Dow Jones Industrial Average

(A) I and III

(B) I and II

(C) I, II, and III

(D) I, II, III, and IV

717. Which of the following is an index of mutual funds?

(A) Wilshire

(B) Russell 2000

(C) S&P 500

(D) Lipper

718. Which of the following Dow Jones indexes is comprised of 20 listed common stocks?

(A) Composite

(B) Industrial

(C) Transportation

(D) Utilities

719. According to NYSE Rule 80B, which of the following would cause the NASDAQ OMX PHLX and NYSE Euronext to halt for the remainder of the trading day?

(A) the DJIA declining by 20% in a day

(B) the S&P 500 declining by 20% in a day

(C) the DJIA declining by 30% in a day

(D) the Dow Jones Composite declining by 30% in a day

720. Which of the following indexes is the most widely used to indicate the performance of the market?

(A) DJIA

(B) S&P 500

(C) NYSE Composite

(D) Wilshire

Chapter 10

Orders and Trades

· ·

As a registered rep, you'll need to know the intricacies of orders and trades and, if needed, be able to explain them to customers or potential customers. This chapter covers questions about the different securities markets, primary and secondary market, the roles of broker-dealers, types of orders, reporting systems, and so on.

The Problems You'll Work On

In this chapter, you should be prepared to answer questions on

- The different securities markets
- The difference between the primary and secondary markets
- The roles of brokers and dealers
- The different types of orders
- The rules and reasons for short sales
- What a market maker's book is
- The consolidated tape
- The different reporting systems and how to report trades
- Some of the rules of the Securities Exchange Act of 1934

What to Watch Out For

As you work through the problems in this chapter, keep the following in mind:

- Make sure you know the difference between the role of a broker and a dealer.
- Read each question and answer choice completely before answering each question.
- Watch out for key words, such as EXCEPT and NOT, that can change the answer you're looking for.
- Focus on the last sentence of each question to make sure you know what's being asked.

721–727 Securities Markets

721. Which of the following are exchange markets?

    I.   NASDAQ OMX PHLX

    II. ECN

    III. NYSE Euronext

    IV. OTCBB

  (A) I and III

  (B) I, II, and III

  (C) II and IV

  (D) II, III, and IV

722. A client has entered a call option order with your broker-dealer. The order could be executed on the

    I.   CBOE

    II. NYSE

    III. NASDAQ OMX PHLX

  (A) I only

  (B) I and II

  (C) I and III

  (D) I, II, and III

723. Which of the following levels of NASDAQ includes subject quotes?

  (A) Level I

  (B) Level II

  (C) Level III

  (D) Level IV

724. The over-the-counter market is best described as

  (A) an auction market

  (B) a negotiated market

  (C) unregulated market

  (D) Choices (A) and (C)

725. Which of the following are considered "auction markets"?

    I.   OTCBB

    II. NYSE Euronext

    III. NASDAQ OMX PHLX

    IV. NYSE Arca

  (A) I, II, and III

  (B) II, III, and IV

  (C) I and IV

  (D) I, II, III, and IV

726. To be listed on the NYSE Euronext, all of the following are required EXCEPT

  (A) a minimum number of publicly held shares

  (B) a minimum number of shareholders

  (C) national interest

  (D) a minimum dividend payout

727. One of your clients is interested in purchasing an OTCBB stock. Right now, only one market maker is displaying a firm quote for this stock. Your broker-dealer must contact how many dealers to determine the prevailing price of the stock?

  (A) 0

  (B) 1

  (C) 2

  (D) 3

728–735 Primary and Secondary Markets

728. Which of the following BEST describes a third market trade?

 (A) listed securities trading on an exchange

 (B) unlisted securities trading OTC

 (C) listed securities trading OTC

 (D) institutional trading without using the services of a broker-dealer

729. DIM, Inc., is offering 1 million shares of new stock and 800,000 shares of stock owned by selling shareholders. This offering is a(n)

 (A) combined offering

 (B) secondary offering

 (C) IPO

 (D) primary offering

730. Which of the following describe the secondary market?

 I. the trading for OTC issues

 II. the trading of listed securities

 III. the trading of outstanding issues

 IV. the underwriting of new issues

 (A) I and III

 (B) II and IV

 (C) I, II, and III

 (D) I, II, and IV

731. A trade of securities between ABC Bank and DEF Insurance Company without using the services of a broker-dealer would be a

 (A) first market trade

 (B) second market trade

 (C) third market trade

 (D) fourth market trade

732. All of the following trades occur in the secondary market EXCEPT

 (A) a syndicate selling new issues of municipal GO bonds to the public

 (B) a designated market maker purchasing common stock for her own account

 (C) a corporation selling its shares of treasury stock to the public using the services of a broker-dealer

 (D) a trade between an insurance company and a bank without using the services of a broker-dealer

733. Which of the following is TRUE regarding dark pools of liquidity?

 I. They represent pools of institutional and large retail clients.

 II. They reduce the amount of transparency of information relating to securities trading.

 III. Firms trading for their own inventory may be included.

 IV. Trades executed by the pools are reported as exchange transactions.

 (A) I and IV

 (B) I, III, and IV

 (C) I, II, and III

 (D) II and III

734. The second market is

 (A) listed securities trading OTC

 (B) listed securities trading on an exchange

 (C) institutional trading without using the services of a broker-dealer

 (D) unlisted securities trading OTC

735. A dealer purchases 1,000 shares of HIJK at $17.50 per share for its own inventory. Several weeks later, HIJK is being quoted at $16.80 to $17.00, and the dealer sells 1,000 shares to one of his customers. Which of the following prices is the basis for the dealer's markup?

(A) $16.80

(B) $17.00

(C) $17.25

(D) $17.50

736–741 Broker-Dealer

736. When a broker-dealer makes a market in a particular security, he is acting as a(n)

(A) agent

(B) broker

(C) principal

(D) syndicate member

737. Which TWO of the following are TRUE relating to a firm that sells securities out of its own inventory?

   I. It is acting as a broker.

   II. It is acting as a dealer.

   III. It charges a commission.

   IV. It charges a markup.

(A) I and III

(B) I and IV

(C) II and III

(D) II and IV

738. A market maker enters a quote of $17.10 to $17.25. A customer wants to purchase 1,000 shares of stock from the market maker. How many shares is the market maker obligated to sell?

(A) 100

(B) 200

(C) 500

(D) 1,000

739. A broker-dealer purchases a large block of corporate bonds in anticipation of drop in the discount rate. The firm is

(A) hedging

(B) position trading

(C) engaged in arbitrage

(D) all of the above

740. When a customer purchases a stock from a dealer, she pays a price that

(A) includes a markup

(B) includes a commission

(C) includes a commission and a markup

(D) any of the above

741. Which of the following customer orders are discretionary?

   I. "Buy 1,000 shares of a growth company."

   II. "Buy or sell 500 shares of LMN."

   III. "Buy or sell as many shares of TUV as you think I can handle."

(A) I and II

(B) II and III

(C) I and III

(D) I, II, and III

742–755 Types of Orders

742. One of your clients has an unrealized gain from selling short FFF common stock. If your client wants to protect his profit, you should recommend that he enter a

(A) buy stop order on FFF

(B) buy limit order on FFF

(C) sell stop order on FFF

(D) sell limit order on FFF

743. Which of the following orders guarantee the order is executed at a specific price or better?

(A) buy limits and sell stops

(B) buy limits and sell limits

(C) sell limits and buy stops

(D) buy stops and sell stops

744. A client enters a sell stop order for LMN at $25.00. The ticker following entry of the order is as follows:

$25.25, $24.88, $25.25, $25.00

The order was

(A) triggered at $25.25, executed at $24.88

(B) triggered at $24.88, executed at $25.00

(C) triggered at $24.88, executed at $24.75

(D) triggered at $24.88, executed at $25.25

745. Which TWO of the following are TRUE regarding immediate-or-cancel orders?

I. They must be executed entirely.

II. They allow for partial execution.

III. They must be executed in one attempt immediately.

IV. They may be executed in several attempts.

(A) I and III

(B) I and IV

(C) II and III

(D) II and IV

746. Why would an investor place a stop order?

I. to protect the profit on a long position

II. to protect the profit on a short position

III. to limit the loss on a long position

IV. to limit the loss on a short position

(A) I and II

(B) II and IV

(C) III and IV

(D) all of the above

747. Darla Diamond purchases 1,000 STU at $42. After STU increases to $47, Darla would like to protect the profit on her investment. Out of the following choices, which of the following orders should you recommend?

(A) sell limit at $50

(B) sell limit at $45

(C) sell stop at $46

(D) sell stop at $48

748. A client enters an order to sell HIJK at $20.50 stop $20.40 limit. The ticker following entry of the order is as follows:

$20.75, $20.60, $20.50, $20.30, $20.35, $20.40, $20.50

The order was

(A) triggered at $20.75, executed at $20.50

(B) triggered at $20.60, executed at $20.40

(C) triggered at $20.50, executed at $20.40

(D) triggered the first time it hit $20.50, executed the second time it hit $20.50

749. All-or-none orders

(A) must be executed in their entirety immediately or the order is canceled

(B) must be executed in their entirety or the order is canceled

(C) must be at least partially executed immediately or the order is canceled

(D) must be at least partially executed or the order is canceled

750. Which of the following orders becomes a market order as soon as the underlying security passes a specific price?

(A) limit

(B) stop limit

(C) market

(D) stop

751. Sell stop orders are entered

(A) below the current market price

(B) at the current market price

(C) above the current market price

(D) either at or above the current market price

752. Which TWO of the following are TRUE of fill-or-kill orders?

I. They must be executed entirely.

II. They allow for partial execution.

III. They must be executed in one attempt immediately.

IV. They may be executed in several attempts.

(A) I and III

(B) I and IV

(C) II and III

(D) II and IV

753. A client has entered an order to purchase 500 shares of DEF at 30 stop. DEF declares a 20% stock dividend. On the ex-dividend date, the order will read

(A) buy 500 shares at 30 stop

(B) buy 600 shares at 25 stop

(C) buy 500 shares at 25 stop

(D) buy 600 shares at 30 stop

754. Early in the afternoon, a customer gives a registered rep a market order to buy 200 shares of HIJ at the close of the market. What should be done in regard to the order?

(A) The registered rep should refuse the order.

(B) The registered rep should hold the order until ten minutes before the close of the market.

(C) The order should be sent to the floor broker immediately.

(D) The order should be held until after the market closes.

755. A customer places an order to buy 100 shares of RST at 50. Which TWO of the following are TRUE of this order?

I. It is a limit order.

II. It is a market order.

III. It is good for the day.

IV. It is good until canceled.

(A) I and III

(B) I and IV

(C) II and III

(D) II and IV

756–762 Short Sales

756. Short sellers are

(A) bullish

(B) bearish

(C) bullish/neutral

(D) bearish/neutral

757. Which of the following are TRUE about short sales against the box?

I. They allow investors to defer taxes.

II. They hedge long positions.

III. They are executed in margin accounts.

IV. The securities being sold short are already owned by the investor.

(A) I and IV

(B) I, II, and IV

(C) II, III, and IV

(D) I, II, III, and IV

758. Regulation SHO covers

(A) margin requirements for municipal and U.S. government securities

(B) the short sale of securities

(C) margin requirements for commodities

(D) portfolio margining rules

759. Which of the following is TRUE regarding short sales?

I. They must be executed in margin accounts.

II. OTCBB stocks may be sold short.

III. Listed securities may be sold short.

IV. They have unlimited risk.

(A) I, III, and IV

(B) II, III, and IV

(C) I, II, and III

(D) I, II, III, and IV

760. All of the following securities are typically sold short EXCEPT

(A) over-the-counter common stock

(B) preferred stock

(C) exchange-listed stock

(D) municipal bonds

761. An investor sells short 1,000 shares of DWN at $35. If the investor buys back 1,000 shares of DWN at $30 five years later to cover the short position, what is the gain or loss?

(A) $5,000 short-term gain

(B) $5,000 short-term loss

(C) $5,000 long-term gain

(D) $5,000 long-term loss

762. All of the following are TRUE of short sales EXCEPT

    (A) they must be executed in margin accounts

    (B) securities listed on an exchange may be sold short

    (C) short sellers have unlimited risk

    (D) OTCBB stocks may be sold short

763–773 Market Maker's Book

763. Which of the following is NOT TRUE about a DMM stopping stock?

    (A) The DMM is guaranteeing a price.

    (B) The DMM needs permission from an exchange official.

    (C) This may be done only for public orders.

    (D) All of the above.

764. Which of the following are used by a designated market maker (DMM) in determining the order of trading?

    I. priority

    II. profit

    III. precedence

    IV. parity

    (A) I, II, and III

    (B) II, III, and IV

    (C) I, III, and IV

    (D) I, II, and IV

765. Using the following table, what is the inside market of LMN?

BID	LMN	OFFER
5 Hurricane B/D	46.00	10 Firefly B/D (stop)
3 Tornado Sec	46.01	
9 Tide B/D 12 Lowland B/D	46.02	
	46.03	
	46.04	
	46.05	
	46.06	5 Mississippi Sec. 8 Tippy Top B/D 12 Overland Sec.
7 Highpoint Sec. (stop GTC)	46.07	7 Hudson B/D

    (A) 46.00 to 46.07

    (B) 46.02 to 46.06

    (C) 46.00 to 46.06

    (D) 46.02 to 46.07

766. Which of the following orders can a designated market maker (DMM) NOT accept?

    (A) NH

    (B) FOK

    (C) IOC

    (D) AON

767. Which TWO of the following open orders in a designated market maker's order display book would be adjusted on the ex-dividend date for a cash dividend?

I. buy stop

II. buy limit

III. sell stop

IV. sell limit

(A) I and III

(B) I and IV

(C) II and III

(D) II and IV

768. All of the following orders could be placed in a NYSE Display Book EXCEPT

(A) limit orders

(B) stop orders

(C) GTC orders

(D) market orders

769. Who is responsible for maintaining a fair and orderly market on the NYSE trading floor?

(A) floor brokers

(B) designated market makers

(C) two-dollar brokers

(D) order book officials

770. All of the following are TRUE about SDBK EXCEPT

(A) it may be used to enter market, stop, or limit orders

(B) it is used for orders on the NYSE

(C) any order can be entered regardless of the amount of shares traded

(D) orders bypass the floor broker and go directly to the DMM

771. If a customer has entered an open order to sell 10,000 shares of LMN at $20 and LMN announced a 2-for-5 split that is allowed by stockholders, how will the order be adjusted by the designated market maker on the ex-split date?

(A) Sell 10,000 shares of LMN at $20.

(B) Sell 4,000 shares of LMN at $50.

(C) Sell 25,000 shares of LMN at $8.

(D) The order would be canceled.

772. A client wants to enter an order to purchase 2,000 shares of DEF at 35. If the client wants this order to be canceled if not executed within the week, how would it be placed in the market maker's order book?

(A) as a good-for-week (GFW) order

(B) as a day order that must be reconfirmed each day by a floor broker

(C) as a good-till-canceled (GTC) order

(D) as a not held (NH) order

773. A NYSE Display Book indicates the following for TUV common stock:

BID	TUV	OFFER
4 Northwest B/D	30.00	
5 Northeast B/D	30.01	12 Pacific B/D (stop)
8 Southwest B/D 14 Southeast B/D	30.02	
	30.03	
	30.04	
	30.05	4 Atlantic Sec. 9 Gulf B/D (GTC)
9 Midland Sec. (stop GTC)	30.06	6 Mississippi Sec.

What is the size of the market?

(A) 14 x 4

(B) 22 x 13

(C) 31 x 19

(D) 40 x 31

774–780 Consolidated Tape

774. An order to buy at 40.25 stop limit is entered prior to the opening. Trades following the opening are as follows:

40.15, 40.25, 40.30, 40.35, 40.45

What can you conclude about the order?

(A) It was executed at 40.15.

(B) It was executed at 40.25.

(C) It was executed at 40.30.

(D) It has not been executed.

775. Which of the following is NOT shown on the consolidated tape?

(A) common stocks

(B) preferred stocks

(C) bonds

(D) warrants

776. Reports on trades made to the consolidated tape

(A) include markups or commissions

(B) do not include markups or commissions

(C) include markups but not commissions

(D) do not include markups but do include commissions

777. A client enters an order to sell 100 shares of HIJ at 27 stop limit. Before your client entered the order, HIJ was trading at 27.30. Trades following the placement of the order are reported on the tape as follows:

HIJ 26.80, 26.85, 26.95, 27, 27.10

Which trade caused the order to be triggered?

(A) 26.80

(B) 26.95

(C) 27

(D) 27.10

778. What does the symbol SLD on the ticker tape indicate?

(A) There is a special offer on the stock.

(B) The stock has stopped trading.

(C) The trade is reported out of sequence.

(D) There is an offer on the stock.

779. Who is responsible for reporting trades to the consolidated tape?

(A) buyers

(B) sellers

(C) the SEC

(D) FINRA and the exchanges

780. What do the letters OPD on the consolidated tape indicate?

(A) a delayed opening print

(B) a trade reported out of sequence

(C) a short sale

(D) an options trade

781–786 Reporting Systems

781. Which TWO of the following are TRUE regarding TRACE reports?

I. Only the buyer needs to report the transaction.

II. Both the buyer and seller need to report the transaction.

III. TRACE reports trades of corporate debt securities.

IV. TRACE reports trades of corporate stocks.

(A) I and III

(B) I and IV

(C) II and III

(D) II and IV

782. The Order Audit Trail System tracks the

(A) execution of an order only

(B) cancellation of an order only

(C) entire life of an order from entry to execution

(D) none of the above

783. Where could a client find quotes for municipal bonds?

(A) Green sheets

(B) TRACE

(C) OTC Pink Market

(D) RTRS

784. A client wants to know the pricing information for several long-term bonds. Which of the following is a printed source of wholesale information on corporate bonds?

(A) OTC Pink Sheets

(B) TRACE

(C) the Magenta List

(D) EMMA

785. Which of the following is TRUE of FINRA's Trade Reporting Facility?

(A) It facilitates the reporting of trade data for NYSE-listed securities occurring on the floor of the NYSE.

(B) It facilitates the reporting of trade data for NASDAQ-listed securities and exchange-listed securities occurring off the exchange floor.

(C) It facilitates the reporting of trade data for municipal bonds traded on an exchange.

(D) It facilitates the reporting of trade data for U.S. government securities traded on an exchange.

786. The computer system that broker-dealers use to keep track of the routing of over-the-counter orders is

(A) ACT

(B) SDBK

(C) ECN

(D) OATS

787–792 Securities Exchange Act of 1934

787. Market makers for NASDAQ securities are required to report trades

(A) within 30 seconds of the trade

(B) within 90 seconds of the trade

(C) within 5 minutes of the trade

(D) by the end of the business day

788. Which of the following Securities Exchange Act of 1934 rules covers market manipulation?

(A) Regulation T

(B) Regulation S

(C) Regulation M

(D) Regulation D

789. The U.S. Securities and Exchange Commission regulates trading of which of the following securities?

I. stock options

II. commodity futures

III. common stock

IV. corporate bonds

(A) I, III, and IV

(B) III and IV

(C) II and III

(D) I, II, III, and IV

790. All of the following are mandated or regulated under the Securities Exchange Act of 1934 EXCEPT

(A) the creation of the SEC

(B) market manipulation

(C) margin rules

(D) the full and fair disclosure required on new offerings

791. Which of the following securities Acts created the Securities and Exchange Commission?

(A) the Securities Act of 1933

(B) the Securities and Exchange Act of 1934

(C) the Trust Indenture Act of 1939

(D) the Investment Company Act of 1940

792. Which of the following is NOT TRUE of the Securities Exchange Act of 1934?

(A) It regulates the extension of credit.

(B) It regulates trades of securities in the primary market.

(C) It regulates trades of securities in the OTC market.

(D) It regulates trades of securities in the exchange market.

Chapter 11

Taxes and Retirement Plans

. . . .

*T*axes are a part of life. Investors face additional taxes that aren't imposed on your average consumer, including capital gains and dividends. In addition, this chapter covers different retirement plans and how they're taxed. The Series 7 exam tests your ability to understand the tax categories, what happens when you purchase a bond at a discount or premium, qualified versus non-qualified retirement plans, health savings accounts (HSAs), and so on.

The Problems You'll Work On

The types of problems in this chapter require you to

- ✔ Understand the different tax categories and types of income.
- ✔ Calculate interest income and taxes on dividends.
- ✔ Handle capital gains and losses.
- ✔ Compute accretion and amortization.
- ✔ Be familiar with wash sale rules, gift taxes, and estate taxes.
- ✔ Recognize qualified and non-qualified plans.
- ✔ Compare traditional IRAs and Roth IRAs.
- ✔ Understand health savings accounts (HSAs).

What to Watch Out For

Don't let common mistakes trip you up; be careful that you

- ✔ Read each question and answer choice completely before choosing an answer.
- ✔ Eliminate false answers when the correct one doesn't reveal itself right away.
- ✔ Watch out for key words that can change the answer choice you're looking for.
- ✔ Remember the difference between progressive and regressive (flat) taxes.

793–798 Tax Categories and Types of Income

793. Which of the following taxes are regressive?

  I. income

  II. gas

  III. alcohol

  IV. sales

  (A) I and III

  (B) II and IV

  (C) II, III, and IV

  (D) I, II, and III

794. An investor buys 1,000 shares of a stock at $40. If the stock increases in value to $60, how would the result be categorized?

  (A) as a profit

  (B) ordinary income

  (C) appreciation

  (D) capital gain

795. Portfolio income includes

  I. income from an oil and gas DPP

  II. income from stock dividends

  III. interest from corporate bonds

  IV. capital gains from the sale of municipal bonds

  (A) I, II, and III

  (B) II, III, and IV

  (C) II and III

  (D) I, II, III, and IV

796. All of the following taxes are progressive EXCEPT

  (A) personal income

  (B) gift

  (C) estate

  (D) sales

797. Earned income includes all of the following EXCEPT

  (A) capital gains

  (B) salary

  (C) bonuses

  (D) income received from active participation in a business

798. Property tax is a

  I. flat tax

  II. graduated tax

  III. regressive tax

  IV. progressive tax

  (A) I and III

  (B) I and IV

  (C) II and III

  (D) II and IV

799–806 Interest Income and Taxes on Dividends

799. An investor receives interest from a corporate bond that he has held for more than one year. If the investor is in the 28% tax bracket, what tax rate will he be required to pay on the interest received?

  (A) 0%

  (B) 15%

  (C) 20%

  (D) 28%

800. One of your clients who lives in Florida purchased an Atlantic City, New Jersey, municipal revenue bond. The interest is

I. subject to state tax

II. exempt from state tax

III. subject to federal tax

IV. exempt from federal tax

(A) I and III

(B) I and IV

(C) II and III

(D) II and IV

801. Dirk Diamond purchased 100 shares of UPP preferred stock, paying a yearly dividend of $6 per share. Dirk originally purchased the stock one year ago. Exactly one year later to the day, Dirk sold the stock for a profit of $320. Which TWO of the following are TRUE relating to the tax treatment of Dirk's transactions?

I. The dividends will be taxed as ordinary income.

II. The dividends will be taxed as passive income.

III. The sale will be treated as a short-term capital gain.

IV. The sale will be treated as a long-term capital gain.

(A) I and III

(B) I and IV

(C) II and III

(D) II and IV

802. Cain Jones and his wife Meisha received cash dividends in their brokerage accounts as follows:

Cain: $2,000

Meisha: $1,000

Joint: $1,500

How much of these dividends are subject to taxation if they file their taxes jointly?

(A) $0

(B) $1,500

(C) $3,000

(D) $4,500

803. Which of the following are taxable to investors?

I. stock splits

II. stock dividends

III. cash dividends

IV. corporate bond interest

(A) I and II

(B) III and IV

(C) I and III

(D) II, III, and IV

804. One of your U.S. clients purchased stock from a Mexican company. This corporation paid a dividend, and your client and the Mexican government withheld 10% of the dividends as a tax. Which of the following is TRUE regarding the 10% tax?

(A) It will be treated as a tax credit on your client's U.S. tax return.

(B) It will be treated as a tax credit on your client's Mexican tax return.

(C) It will be treated as a reduction of ordinary income on your client's tax return.

(D) It will not impact your client's tax return.

805. What is the tax rate on qualified dividends for investors who are in the 39.6% federal tax rate?

(A) 0%

(B) 15%

(C) 20%

(D) 39.6%

806. Interest on U.S. government T-bonds is subject to

(A) state tax but not federal tax

(B) federal tax but not state tax

(C) neither state tax nor federal tax

(D) both state and federal tax

807–815 Capital Gains and Losses

807. One of your clients has the following investments for the current year:

> Capital gains: $14,500
>
> Capital losses: $21,000

What is the tax status for this investor?

(A) He has a $6,500 loss for the current year.

(B) He has a $3,000 loss for the current year and $3,000 carried over to the following year.

(C) He has a $3,000 loss for the current year and $3,500 carried over to the following year.

(D) He has a $6,500 loss for the current year and $3,000 carried over to the following year.

808. An investor has made the following transactions in the current year:

> Jan. 4: Buy 100 TUV at 30
>
> Feb. 6: Buy 100 TUV at 40
>
> Feb. 13: Sell 100 TUV at 36

What is the investor's gain or loss?

(A) $400 capital loss

(B) $600 capital gain

(C) $600 capital loss

(D) $400 capital gain

809. Dirk Diamond has held 1,000 shares of Armbar common stock for six months and decides to purchase a nine-month call on Armbar. If the Armbar call option expires and Dirk decides to sell the Armbar common stock five months after the expiration of the call, what is Dirk's tax position?

(A) short-term capital gain or long-term capital loss

(B) long-term capital gain or short-term capital loss

(C) long-term capital gain or long-term capital loss

(D) short-term capital gain or short-term capital loss

810. An investor purchases 1,000 shares of common stock at $23. If the stock increases in value to $25, how would the result be categorized?

(A) appreciation

(B) capital gain

(C) passive income

(D) ordinary income

811. A client would like to sell short ABC common stock but is unfamiliar with the tax treatment of short sales. You should inform him that

(A) all gains are taxed as ordinary income

(B) all gains or losses are taxed as passive income or losses

(C) all gains or losses are considered short term

(D) all gains or losses are considered long term

812. A security purchased on September 30 would become long term on

(A) September 30 of the following year

(B) September 31 of the following year

(C) October 1 of the following year

(D) December 31 of the current year

813. If a client is a resident of New Jersey, which of the following investment results would be subject to federal taxation?

I. cash dividends on stock

II. interest on T-notes

III. accretion of a zero-coupon debenture

IV. capital gains on a New Jersey revenue bond

(A) I only

(B) I and II

(C) I, II, and III

(D) I, II, III, and IV

814. Long-term capital gains are taxed at which of the following tax rates?

I. 0%

II. 15%

III. 20%

IV. the investor's tax bracket

(A) II and III

(B) I, II, and III

(C) II, III, and IV

(D) I, II, III, and IV

815. An investor has been purchasing $500 worth of an ABC growth fund each month for the last six years. He needs to sell off some shares to purchase a new car. The price of ABC has fluctuated over the last six years, and the investor wants to minimize his tax liability on the shares sold. When selling the shares, he should use which accounting method?

(A) FIFO

(B) LIFO

(C) average basis

(D) identified shares

816–822 Accretion and Amortization

816. One of your clients purchases ten 6% Albany municipal bonds in the secondary market at 110. If the bonds mature in eight years, what is the approximate amount of amortization after holding the bond for four years?

(A) $50

(B) $125

(C) $500

(D) $1,000

817. Sally Silverhouse purchases a new municipal bond at a price of $970. Which TWO of the following are TRUE?

   I.   The discount on the bond must be accreted.

   II.   The discount on the bond would not be accreted.

   III.   Sally would be subject to a capital gain if she holds the bond until maturity.

   IV.   Sally would not be subject to a capital gain if she holds the bond until maturity.

   (A)   I and III

   (B)   I and IV

   (C)   II and III

   (D)   II and IV

818. An investor buys an equipment trust bond in the secondary market for 106. The bond has 12 years until maturity. Four years later, the investor sells the bond for 104. What is the investor's gain or loss?

   (A) $60 capital loss

   (B) $20 capital gain

   (C) $20 capital loss

   (D)   no gain or loss

819. Mrs. Jones purchased a DEF corporate bond for 92 with ten years until maturity. If Mrs. Jones sells that bond at 94 in six years, what is her gain or loss?

   (A) $28 loss

   (B) $80 loss

   (C) $20 gain

   (D) $60 gain

820. A client purchased a 5% corporate bond at 95 with ten years until maturity. The bond is callable in five years at par value. How much taxable income does the investor have to claim each year?

   (A) $0

   (B) $5

   (C) $50

   (D) $55

821. An investor purchased a municipal bond at a premium. Which TWO of the following are TRUE regarding the amortization of the bond premium?

   I.   It increases the reported bond interest income.

   II.   It decreases the reported bond interest income.

   III.   It increases the cost basis.

   IV.   It decreases the cost basis.

   (A)   I and III

   (B)   I and IV

   (C)   II and III

   (D)   II and IV

822. Which TWO of the following are TRUE?

   I.   Corporate bonds purchased at a discount must be accreted.

   II.   Corporate bonds purchased at a discount may be accreted.

   III.   Corporate bonds purchased at a premium must be amortized.

   IV.   Corporate bonds purchased at a premium may be amortized.

   (A)   I and III

   (B)   I and IV

   (C)   II and III

   (D)   II and IV

823–829 Wash Sales, Gift, and Estate Taxes

823. What is the tax deduction limit for gifts between spouses?

(A) $100

(B) $14,000

(C) $75,000

(D) unlimited

824. Mike Smith purchased 100 shares of TIP common stock for $42.50 per share. Several months later with TIP trading at $57, Mike gives the stock to his sister Michelle. Michelle eventually ended up selling the stock for $60 per share. Michelle would have to claim a capital gain of

(A) $0 because Mike would be responsible for paying taxes on the capital gain

(B) $300

(C) $1,450

(D) $1,750

825. Uriah Florian sold GNP Corporation stock at a $6.50 loss per share and bought GNP call options 23 days later. Which of the following is TRUE?

(A) The $6.50 loss per share deduction is allowed.

(B) The $6.50 loss per share deduction is disallowed.

(C) The $6.50 loss per share deduction can be used to offset capital gains.

(D) The $6.50 loss per share deduction can be used to offset ordinary income.

826. An investor sold DEF common stock at a loss. Which of the following securities may the investor buy back immediately without violating the wash sale rule?

(A) DEF convertible bonds

(B) DEF call options

(C) DEF warrants

(D) DEF preferred stock

827. Gary Goldman purchased 1,000 shares of GGG common stock four years ago at a cost of $42 per share. Gary gives the stock to his son Grant when the market value is $52 per share. Which TWO of the following are TRUE of this transaction?

I. Gary may be subject to a gift tax.

II. Grant may be subject to a gift tax.

III. Grant's cost basis is $42 per share.

IV. Grant's cost basis is $52 per share.

(A) I and III

(B) I and IV

(C) II and III

(D) II and IV

828. Clay Rousey inherits stock valued at $52 on the day of his grandfather's death. His grandfather purchased the stock at $32. If Clay sells the stock at $62, how much of a capital gain per share would Clay claim?

(A) $0

(B) $10

(C) $20

(D) $30

829. Which of the following have unified tax credits?

  I.   estate tax

  II. gift tax

  III. sales tax

  IV. income tax

  (A) I and II

  (B) III and IV

  (C) I, III, and IV

  (D) I, II, and IV

830–848 Qualified and Non-Qualified Plans

830. All of the following are non-qualified retirement plans EXCEPT

  (A) deferred compensation plans

  (B) payroll deduction plans

  (C) 401(k) plan

  (D) 457 plan

831. When an investor starts receiving payments at retirement from a 403(b) plan, they are

  (A) not taxable

  (B) 100% taxable at the investor's tax bracket

  (C) partially taxable at the investor's tax bracket

  (D) either fully taxable or partially taxable depending on the investor's tax bracket

832. All of the following individuals are eligible to participate in a Keogh plan EXCEPT

  (A) a corporate executive who receives $10,000 in stock options from his employer each year

  (B) a self-employed driving instructor who makes $50,000 per year

  (C) a real estate office manager who gets paid to give lectures in her spare time

  (D) a self-employed landscaper

833. Which TWO of the following statements regarding qualified retirement plans are TRUE?

  I.   Distributions are 100% taxable at the holder's tax bracket.

  II. Distributions are partially taxable at the holder's tax bracket.

  III. Contributions are made with pretax dollars.

  IV. Contributions are made with after-tax dollars.

  (A) I and III

  (B) I and IV

  (C) II and III

  (D) II and IV

834. All of the following are types of corporate defined contribution plans EXCEPT

  (A) SIMPLEs

  (B) 401(k)s

  (C) Keogh plans

  (D) profit sharing plans

835. Which of the following are qualified retirement plans under IRS rules?

    I.   ESOPs

    II. 401(k)

    III. traditional IRA

    IV. SEP IRA

    (A)   II only

    (B)   II and IV

    (C)   I and III

    (D)   I, II, III, and IV

836. All of the following are TRUE about SIMPLE IRAs and SEP IRAs EXCEPT

    (A)   they both allow pretax contributions from the employee and employer

    (B)   they both require immediate vesting on all contributions

    (C)   SEP IRAs allow higher annual contributions than SIMPLE IRAs

    (D)   only businesses with 100 employees or fewer are eligible for SIMPLE IRAs

837. All of the following business retirement plans are regulated by ERISA EXCEPT

    (A)   money purchase plans

    (B)   ESOPs

    (C)   payroll deduction plans

    (D)   401(k)

838. ERISA regulations cover

    (A)   private pension plans

    (B)   public pension plans

    (C)   private and public pension plans

    (D)   none of the above

839. A self-employed carpenter has earned $200,000 this year. How much tax-deductible income may he deposit into a Keogh plan this year?

    (A) $25,000

    (B) $30,000

    (C) $40,000

    (D) $52,000

840. All of the following are TRUE about 529 plans and Coverdell ESAs EXCEPT

    (A)   deposits are made from after-tax dollars

    (B)   there are maximum annual contributions

    (C)   the beneficiary of the accounts must use the funds by age 30 for the funds not to be penalized

    (D)   money can be withdrawn tax-free if used for educational purposes

841. Which of the following would LEAST likely purchase revenue bonds?

    (A)   individual investors

    (B)   banks

    (C)   retirement plans

    (D)   mutual funds

842. Regarding qualified retirement plans, which of the following is TRUE?

    (A)   Money cannot be withdrawn until age 70½.

    (B)   Distributions are taxed at 10%.

    (C)   Contributions are made with 100% pretax dollars.

    (D)   Contributions are made with 100% after-tax dollars.

843. By what age must an individual begin withdrawing money from a retirement plan?

(A) April 1 of the year after turning age 59½.

(B) April 15 of the year after turning age 59½.

(C) April 1 of the year after turning age 70½.

(D) April 15 of the year after turning age 70½.

844. An individual has earned $80,000 in self-employed income this year. How much may the individual deposit in a Keogh plan this year without taxation?

(A) $16,000

(B) $20,000

(C) $52,000

(D) $80,000

845. Mrs. Jones withdraws money from her pension plan; how long does she have to roll over money into an IRA?

(A) 20 days

(B) 30 days

(C) 60 days

(D) 1 year

846. Which of the following is TRUE of corporate defined contribution plans?

I. The annual contribution percentage varies.

II. The annual contribution percentage is fixed.

III. Retirement benefits increase the longer the employee works for the corporation.

IV. In a bad year, the corporation may discontinue employee contributions.

(A) I and III

(B) I and IV

(C) II and III

(D) II, III, and IV

847. Which of the following securities would be LEAST suitable for a pension fund to purchase?

(A) common stocks

(B) preferred stocks

(C) corporate bonds

(D) municipal bonds

848. If an investor makes an excess contribution to an IRA, he will be assesed a

(A) 6% penalty tax

(B) 10% penalty tax

(C) 15% penalty tax

(D) 50% penalty tax

849–860 Traditional and Roth IRAs

849. What is the maximum yearly contribution allowed into a Roth IRA for a 51-year-old investor who earns $85,000 per year?

(A) $5,500 pretax

(B) $5,500 after tax

(C) $6,500 pretax

(D) $6,500 after tax

850. A 55-year-old self-employed massage therapist earns $95,000 per year and has no other retirement plan except a traditional IRA. If she deposits $4,500 into her IRA, which of the following is TRUE?

(A) It is partially tax deductible.

(B) It is not tax deductible.

(C) It is fully tax deductible.

(D) Because she is self-employed, she must open a Keogh.

851. One of your 50-year-old clients does not have a job but earns all of his money from day trading. He is quite successful and consistently makes more than $150,000 per year. He would like to open an IRA. Providing his income remains consistent, how much can he contribute to an IRA?

(A) $0

(B) $5,500

(C) $6,500

(D) $30,000

852. Prior to recommending investments for an IRA to a client, you should give maximum consideration to

(A) risk

(B) the client's tax bracket

(C) the client's marital status

(D) the client's need for current income

853. Which of the following are TRUE regarding Roth IRAs?

I. Distributions are partially taxable.

II. Distributions are not taxable providing the holding period and investor's age requirement are met.

III. Contributions are made with pretax dollars.

IV. Contributions are made with after-tax dollars.

(A) I and III

(B) I and IV

(C) II and III

(D) II and IV

854. What is the required beginning date for traditional IRAs?

(A) 59½

(B) 70½

(C) April 1 of the year after the holder turns age 70½

(D) April 15 of the year after the holder turns age 70½

855. One of your clients has rolled over money from a pension fund into an IRA; how long must your client wait before executing another rollover?

(A) 30 days

(B) 60 days

(C) 90 days

(D) 1 year

856. Mrs. Jones is leaving her job and has $40,000 in her 401(k). After she withdraws the money from the 401(k), how long does she have to roll over money into an IRA?

(A) 20 days

(B) 30 days

(C) 60 days

(D) 90 days

857. What is the last day an investor can deposit money into a traditional IRA and be able to claim it as a write-off on the current year's taxes?

(A) December 31 of the current year

(B) January 31 of the following year

(C) April 1 of the following year

(D) April 15 of the following year

858. One of your clients has left his job and would like to roll over money from his 401(k) into an IRA. You should let him know that he has up to how many days to roll the money over?

(A) 30 days

(B) 60 days

(C) 90 days

(D) 180 days

859. At what age must an investor begin withdrawals from a Roth IRA?

(A) 59½

(B) 70½

(C) April 1 of the year after turning age 70½

(D) no requirement

860. One of your 55-year-old clients needs to withdraw $10,000 from her IRA. What is her tax liability if she is in the 30% tax bracket?

(A) $0

(B) $3,000

(C) $4,000

(D) $8,000

861–864 Health Savings Accounts

861. Health savings accounts are available to

(A) individuals and families with high-deductible health plans

(B) individuals covered by Medicare

(C) individuals who have an income at or below the poverty level

(D) individuals covered by Medicaid

862. Which TWO of the following is TRUE regarding Health Savings Accounts (HSAs)?

I. Contributions are made in pretax dollars.

II. Contributions are made in after-tax dollars.

III. The funds in the account grow tax-free if used to pay qualified medical expenses.

IV. The funds in the account grow tax-deferred if used to pay qualified medical expenses.

(A) I and III

(B) II and IV

(C) I and IV

(D) II and III

863. All of the following are TRUE of Health Savings Accounts EXCEPT

(A) the amount individuals or families can contribute each year is limited under IRS rules

(B) they are available only to individuals or families who have high-deductible health plans

(C) HSA funds may be invested in mutual funds

(D) any remaining funds in the account at the end of each year must be rolled over into an IRA or IRS-approved retirement account

864. Which of the following is NOT TRUE relating to Health Savings Accounts?

(A) They may not be opened by someone on Medicare.

(B) They allow pretax contributions.

(C) If withdrawals are not related to qualified medical expenses, there is a 10% tax penalty on the amount withdrawn.

(D) Withdrawals related to qualified medical expenses are tax-free.

Chapter 12

Rules and Regulations

• •

*T*he Series 7 exam is riddled with rules and regulations. And believe it or not, they're not just in this chapter. Unfortunately, this chapter, more than any other one, requires you to remember specifics. But don't fear: A lot of the rules make sense, and the correct answer usually stands out like a sore thumb.

The number of questions in this category increased greatly when the USA Patriot Act was enacted. Due to the act, each firm must have and follow customer identification programs (CIPs) and anti-money laundering rules.

The Problems You'll Work On

In this chapter, you'll work on problems that deal with rules and regulations, including

- ✔ Understanding the different self-regulatory organizations and agent registration
- ✔ Getting deep into the USA Patriot Act and anti-money laundering rules
- ✔ Opening and transferring customer accounts
- ✔ Remembering the specifics for order tickets, trade confirmations, and account statements
- ✔ Figuring out the payment and delivery dates for different trades
- ✔ Handling customer complaints and the legal remedies
- ✔ Recognizing violations
- ✔ Acknowledging the roles of the FDIC and SIPC

What to Watch Out For

The following tips can help you determine the correct answers for questions in this chapter:

- ✔ Eliminate wrong answers when the correct one doesn't "pop out" at you right away.
- ✔ Double-check that you're not confusing your rules before picking an answer.
- ✔ Focus on the last sentence of the question to help guide you to the correct answer.

865–879 SROs and Agent Registration

865. All of the following are SROs EXCEPT

(A) FINRA

(B) MSRB

(C) SEC

(D) NYSE

866. FINRA and the NYSE have the authority to do which of the following?

I. incarcerate

II. fine

III. expel

IV. censure

(A) II and III

(B) II, III, and IV

(C) I and II

(D) I and IV

867. One of your customers has moved from New York to Alabama to avoid high property taxes. Unfortunately, you are not currently registered in Alabama. You would like to continue to do business with your customer. What do you need to do?

I. Get registered in Alabama.

II. Notify FINRA of your customer's new address.

III. Make sure your firm is registered in Alabama.

IV. Take no action until you receive written proof of your customer's new address.

(A) I only

(B) I and III

(C) II and IV

(D) I, II, III, and IV

868. While building his book, a newly registered representative would like to work weekends as a bartender for a local restaurant to earn a little extra income. He would be required to tell his

(A) broker-dealer

(B) broker-dealer and FINRA

(C) broker-dealer and the NYSE

(D) broker-dealer and the Fed

869. Mike Goldbar was a Series 7 registered representative for most of his working life. Mike had to leave the business for a while due to a family issue. Mike would be required to take his exams all over again if he has been unaffiliated with a broker/dealer for more than

(A) nine months

(B) one year

(C) two years

(D) it depends on Mike's length of employment prior to leaving the business

870. Which of the following will prohibit an individual from becoming an employee or officer of a brokerage firm?

I. The individual has been convicted of a felony within the last ten years.

II. The individual has been charged with a misdemeanor marijuana violation within the last ten years.

III. The individual has been charged with a DUI within the last ten years.

IV. The individual has been convicted of securities-related fraud within the last ten years.

(A) I, II, and III

(B) II, III, and IV

(C) I and IV

(D) I, II, III, and IV

871. Registered reps must complete the regulatory element of continuing education within _____ days of their registration anniversary date.

(A) 30

(B) 60

(C) 120

(D) 270

872. A licensed registered representative has left the securities industry to pursue his life-long ambition to become a mixed martial artist. If he decides he made a mistake and wants to return to the securities industry, he will have to retake his securities exams if he has been unaffiliated with his broker-dealer for more than

(A) one year

(B) two years

(C) three years

(D) five years

873. Joe Silber failed the Series 7 exam three consecutive times. How long must Joe wait before making a fourth attempt?

(A) 30 days

(B) 45 days

(C) 90 days

(D) 6 months

874. If a registered rep leaves a brokerage firm to join the military and serves in the military for two years or more, how much time after leaving the military does the person have to find a brokerage firm to work for and avoid the period of inactivity from starting again?

(A) 30 days

(B) 60 days

(C) 90 days

(D) 120 days

875. A registered representative has had several slow months and must file for bankruptcy. Who would the registered representative need to notify?

(A) the Fed

(B) his employing firm

(C) the FINRA

(D) the SEC

876. As of November 7, 2011, individuals who pass the Series 7 exam are limited municipal representatives. Which of the following licenses must an agent obtain to become a full municipal securities representative?

(A) Series 52

(B) Series 55

(C) Series 65

(D) Series 86/87

877. The General Securities Principal Exam is the

(A) Series 4

(B) Series 9/10

(C) Series 24

(D) Series 31

878. Agents who charge a fee for giving investment advice must pass which of the following exams?

(A) the Series 65 or Series 66

(B) the Series 65 or Series 62

(C) the Series 62 or Series 24

(D) the Series 24 or Series 10

879. An agent may be suspended from membership of the FINRA under all of the following circumstances EXCEPT

(A) the agent attempted to defraud a client

(B) the agent failed to disclose a conflict of interest regarding a transaction

(C) the agent failed to satisfy his firm's in-house requirements of sales production

(D) the agent committed a felony

880–890 The USA Patriot Act and Anti-Money Laundering Rules

880. An investor making several large cash deposits into her brokerage account may indicate that she is engaged in

(A) money laundering

(B) insider trading

(C) front-running

(D) a takeover

881. All of the following are stages of money laundering EXCEPT

(A) placement

(B) intermediation

(C) layering

(D) integration

882. You are in the process of opening a new account. Which of the following indications of money laundering should you be concerned with?

I. irrational transactions that are inconsistent with the potential client's investment objectives

II. a reluctance to provide information about business activities

III. the potential customer's concern about U.S. government reporting requirements

IV. take no action until you receive written proof of your customer's new address

(A) I only

(B) I and III

(C) II and IV

(D) I, II, III, and IV

883. One of your customers has made three cash deposits into his account over the last few weeks of $9,900 each. This is called

(A) structuring

(B) layering

(C) integration

(D) placement

884. Which of the following transactions require the filing of Form 112 with FinCEN?

(A) a check deposit of $35,000

(B) a credit card transaction of $20,000

(C) a cash deposit of $15,000

(D) all of the above

885. Suspicious activity of _____ or more must be reported to FinCEN through the filing of a SAR.

(A) $1,000

(B) $5,000

(C) $10,000

(D) $25,000

886. A customer is about to open a new account. Which of the following indicates that your new customer may be interested in laundering money?

(A) a concern with U.S. government reporting requirements

(B) a reluctance to inform you of his business activity

(C) a first trade that is inconsistent with his investment objectives

(D) all of the above

887. Which of the following customer information is NOT necessary to be verified to meet CIP standards?

(A) address

(B) Social Security number

(C) telephone number

(D) date of birth

888. As part of the USA Patriot Act of 2001, all financial institutions must maintain

(A) customer identification programs

(B) a fidelity bond

(C) SIPC coverage

(D) all of the above

889. You have a new customer whose name appears on the Specially Designated Nationals list. Your brokerage firm notifies the Office of Foreign Assets Control (OFAC). What is the likely outcome?

(A) Your customer's assets will be frozen, and your firm will be instructed to stop doing business with the customer.

(B) Your firm will be directed to let the customer know that he is on the list, and he will be asked to contact the Office of Foreign Assets Control to clear up the problem.

(C) You will be instructed to continue doing business with the customer, but each transaction must be approved by a principal and reported to the Office of Foreign Assets Control.

(D) The Office of Foreign Assets Control will immediately contract the FBI and have your customer arrested.

890. Under the USA Patriot Act, all banks and brokerage firms must maintain _____ to help prevent money laundering and the financing of terrorist operations.

(A) CIPs

(B) SDNs

(C) OFACs

(D) FinCEN

891–912 Opening Customer Accounts

891. An agent of a FINRA firm wants to open a new account at another brokerage firm. Which of the following are TRUE?

    I.   The employing firm must be notified about the opening of the account.

    II. The employing firm must receive duplicate trade confirmations if requested.

    III. The employing firm must grant written permission to the agent to open the account.

    IV. The employing firm must grant permission to execute trades in the account.

    (A) I only

    (B) I and II

    (C) I, II, and III

    (D) I, II, III, and IV

892. What type of joint account is typically set up for unrelated individuals where the estate is the beneficiary?

    (A) joint tenants with rights of survivorship

    (B) tenancy in common

    (C) discretionary account

    (D) custodial account

893. Which of the following needs permission to open a margin account at another brokerage firm?

    I.   a bank teller

    II. an insurance company clerk

    III. a credit union president

    IV. a principal of another NYSE broker-dealer

    (A) I only

    (B) II and III

    (C) I, II, and IV

    (D) I, II, III, and IV

894. Which of the following people CANNOT open a joint account?

    (A) a parent and a minor daughter

    (B) two close friends

    (C) a husband and wife

    (D) three business partners

895. All brokerage firms are required to have customer identification programs and to check the names of any new customers against

    (A) the SDN list maintained by OFAC

    (B) the SDN list maintained by the Department of Treasury

    (C) the SDN list maintained by the Secret Service

    (D) the SDN list maintained by FINRA

896. Which of the following must be verified when opening an account for a new client?

   I. citizenship

   II. whether his name appears on the SDN list

   III. whether he works at another broker-dealer

   IV. whether he has any accounts at another broker-dealer

   (A) I and IV

   (B) II and III

   (C) I, II, and III

   (D) I, II, III, and IV

897. Chael Weidman wants to open an account at MMA Broker-Dealer. Chael does not want his name to appear on the account. How would MMA Broker-Dealer handle his request?

   (A) MMA would open a numbered account for Chael.

   (B) MMA would set up a street-named account for Frederick if he is an accredited investor.

   (C) MMA would refuse to open the account until Chael agrees to have the account in his name.

   (D) MMA would provide a fictitious name for Chael from its book of approved names.

898. A registered representative may open which of the following accounts?

   I. a minor's account by a custodian

   II. a corporate account by a designated officer

   III. a partnership account by a designated partner

   IV. an account in the name of Mr. Rice for Mrs. Rice

   (A) I and IV

   (B) II and III

   (C) I, II, and III

   (D) I, II, III, and IV

899. All of the following information must be obtained from a new individual customer EXCEPT

   (A) the individual's Social Security number

   (B) the individual's date of birth

   (C) the individual's educational background

   (D) the individual's residential address

900. As a registered representative, you need to keep track of each client's investment objectives. Which of the following changes may affect a client's investment objectives?

   I. aging

   II. getting divorced

   III. having a child

   IV. winning $5 million in the lottery

   (A) I and III

   (B) II and III

   (C) I, III, and IV

   (D) I, II, III, and IV

901. Pam Platinum would like to open an UGMA account for her 10-year-old daughter. Pam is also interested in being the custodian for the account. Which of the following governs investments purchased for UGMA accounts?

   I.   the legal list

   II.   the FINRA list of approved invest-ments for minors' accounts

   III.   the prudent man rule

  (A)   I and II

  (B)   I and III

  (C)   II and III

  (D)   I, II, and III

902. You are in the process of opening a new customer account. Which of the following information do you need?

   I.   the customer's Social Security number or tax ID

   II.   the customer's investment experience

   III.   the customer's occupation and employer

   IV.   the customer's legal name and address

  (A)   I and IV

  (B)   I, II and IV

  (C)   I, III, and IV

  (D)   I, II, III, and IV

903. Which of the following needs to be filled out on a new account form?

   I.   the customer's name and address

   II.   the customer's date of birth

   III.   the type of account

   IV.   the customer's investment objectives

  (A)   I and II

  (B)   I, II and III

  (C)   I, II, and IV

  (D)   I, II, III and IV

904. Whose signature is required on a new account form?

   I.   the customer's

   II.   the registered rep's

   III.   a principal's

  (A)   I and II

  (B)   I and III

  (C)   II and III

  (D)   I, II, and III

905. You may open up a joint account for each of the following couples EXCEPT

  (A)   a parent and a minor daughter

  (B)   three unrelated individuals

  (C)   a husband and wife

  (D)   an individual and his 71-year-old mother

906. A corporate customer would like to open a cash account for his company. To open the account, you would need a copy of the

  (A)   Corporate Charter

  (B)   Corporate Resolution

  (C)   Corporate Charter and Corporate Resolution

  (D)   none of the above

907. When may a registered representative open a joint account with a client?

   I.   under no circumstances

   II.   if obtaining approval from a principal

   III.   if obtaining a signed proportionate sharing agreement from the client

  (A)   I only

  (B)   II only

  (C)   III only

  (D)   II and III

908. You have a new client who would like to open a numbered account. To open that account, what must occur?

(A) The client must sign a written statement attesting to ownership of the account.

(B) The client would need to receive permission from FINRA.

(C) The client would need to receive permission from the SEC.

(D) Choices (B) and (C)

909. Which of the following accounts may a client open up without a written power of attorney?

(A) an account for his spouse

(B) an account for his minor daughter

(C) an account for his business partner

(D) none of the above

910. If a customer wants to open a new account but refuses to provide some of the financial information requested, which of the following is TRUE?

(A) You may not open the account until the customer provides complete financial information.

(B) You may open the account and take unsolicited trades only.

(C) You may open the account if you can determine from other sources that the customer has the financial means to handle the account.

(D) You may open the account but refuse to do any trades until the customer provides complete financial information.

911. What is the minimum amount of assets your client must have to establish a prime brokerage account?

(A) $100,000

(B) $500,000

(C) $1,000,000

(D) $5,000,000

912. Principals with which of the following licenses can approve the opening of municipal fund securities accounts?

I. Series 4

II. Series 24

III. Series 51

IV. Series 53

(A) I only

(B) I and II

(C) III and IV

(D) II, III, and IV

913–929 Order Tickets, Trade Confirmations, and Account Statements

913. Diamond Broker-Dealer sent a client a confirmation of his latest trade of Mineshaft Corp. common stock. Which of the following items should be on the confirmation?

I. the trade date and the settlement date

II. whether Diamond Broker-Dealer acted as an agent or principal

III. the name of the security and how many shares were traded

IV. the amount of commission paid if Diamond Broker-Dealer acted as an agent

(A) I and III

(B) I, II, and III

(C) I, III, and IV

(D) I, II, III, and IV

914. All order tickets must be signed by

(A) a principal

(B) the customer

(C) the state administrator

(D) a compliance officer

915. Gina wants to buy 1,000 shares of Biff Spanky Corporation at $1.20 per share. As Gina's agent, you inform Gina that the investment doesn't fit into her investment profile and is probably too risky for her. If Gina still insists on buying Biff Spanky Corporation, you should

(A) refuse the order

(B) refuse the order unless Gina changes her investment profile

(C) take the order but mark it as "unsolicited"

(D) hand the phone to your principal to see if he can talk some sense into Gina

916. FINRA and SEC rules require that customer account statements be sent out at least

(A) monthly

(B) quarterly

(C) semiannually

(D) annually

917. Principals must approve trades made by registered representatives

(A) at or prior to execution

(B) at or prior to completion of the transaction

(C) the same day as execution of the order

(D) none of the above

918. Which of the following information is required on an order ticket?

  I. the registered rep' s identification number

 II. a description of the securities

III. the time of the order

IV. whether the order was solicited or unsolicited

(A) I and II

(B) I, II, and III

(C) I, II and IV

(D) I, II, III, and IV

919. One of your clients is nearing retirement age, and his main investment objective is risk aversion. However, your client is dead set on purchasing a low-priced stock that you deem too risky considering his age and investment objectives. You should

(A) refuse the order

(B) take the order and mark it as "unsolicited"

(C) not take the order until the new account form is adjusted

(D) not take the order without a principal's approval

920. How many times a year must a customer of a brokerage firm receive an account statement?

(A) 1

(B) 2

(C) 4

(D) 12

921. All of the following information would be found on an order ticket EXCEPT

(A) the name of the brokerage firm

(B) the customer's name

(C) the quantity of securities

(D) the investor's occupation

922. According to SEC Rule 10b-10, confirmations of trades executed between firms must be sent no later than

(A) the trade date

(B) one business day following the trade date

(C) the completion of the transaction

(D) three business days following the trade date

923. Your brokerage firm reports to your client that he purchased XYZ common stock at $15.80. However, the actual confirmation shows that the trade was executed at $16.00. What must your client do?

(A) Pay $15.80.

(B) Pay $15.90.

(C) Pay $16.00.

(D) Cancel the trade.

924. For member-to-customer transactions, the member firm must send a trade confirmation

(A) at or prior to the completion of the transaction

(B) no later than one business day after the trade date

(C) no later than two business days after the trade date

(D) no later than three business days after the trade date

925. According to FINRA and SEC rules, account statements must be sent to clients

I. monthly for active accounts

II. quarterly for active accounts

III. monthly for inactive accounts

IV. quarterly for inactive accounts

(A) I and III

(B) I and IV

(C) II and III

(D) II and IV

926. A client's confirmation must include

I. the markup or markdown for a principal transaction

II. the commission for an agency transaction

III. a description of the security

IV. the registered representative's identification number

(A) I and III

(B) I, II, and III

(C) II, III, and IV

(D) I, II, III, and IV

927. The certificate sent out to customers at the completion of the trade, which supplies all the details of the trade, is called a(n)

(A) proxy

(B) order ticket

(C) confirmation

(D) account statement

928. Under MSRB rules, a client's confirmation must include

(A) the markup or markdown

(B) the location of the bond resolution

(C) the settlement date

(D) whether the trade was executed on a dealer or agency basis

929. Which of the following would NOT be included on a trade confirmation?

(A) whether the trade was solicited or unsolicited

(B) the amount of commission charged on a broker transaction

(C) the trade date

(D) the address of the brokerage firm delivering the confirmation

930–946 Payment and Delivery

930. Which of the following may NOT be a factor used in determining the markup charged to customers?

(A) the market price of the security sold

(B) the price the dealer paid to purchase the security

(C) the size of the trade

(D) expenses of executing the trade

931. The return of securities previously accepted is called

(A) reclamation

(B) buy-in

(C) sell-out

(D) rejection

932. All of the following are good delivery for a trade of 670 shares EXCEPT

(A) 4 certificates for 150 shares each and 14 certificates for 5 shares each

(B) 1 certificate for 600 shares each and 7 certificates for 10 shares each

(C) 335 certificates for 2 shares each

(D) 2 certificates for 300 shares each and 70 certificates for 1 share each

933. Armbar Corporation announces a dividend with record date Thursday, October 18. When is the last day your client can buy the stock the "regular way" and receive the dividend?

(A) Monday, October 15

(B) Tuesday, October 16

(C) Wednesday, October 17

(D) Monday, October 22

934. One of your clients places an order to purchase 100 shares of LMN at $35 per share, and the trade is executed. Prior to paying for the trade, your client sees that LMN has dropped in price significantly. Your client informs you that he no longer wants the shares and is not going to pay for them. You should inform him that

(A) you will cancel the order

(B) he already purchased the shares, and he must submit the payment

(C) you will immediately sell the stock in the market and cover the loss

(D) your firm will purchase the securities for its own inventory

935. Mary Smith had her account frozen because she failed to pay for a trade. In order for Mary to purchase additional securities for her account, what must happen?

(A) She must deposit the full purchase price of the securities before the purchase order may be executed.

(B) She must get approval from a principal.

(C) She must wait until her account is no longer frozen.

(D) She must deposit the full purchase price of the securities before the settlement date.

936. When is the ex-dividend date if a corporation announces a dividend payable to shareholders of record Thursday, September 17?

(A) Monday, September 14

(B) Tuesday, September 15

(C) Wednesday, September 16

(D) Monday, September 21

937. Corporate bonds settle in

(A) one business day, and payment is due in three business days

(B) three business days, and payment is due in three business days

(C) three business days, and payment is due in five business days

(D) five business days, and payment is due in seven business days

938. The 5% markup policy applies to which of the following?

(A) IPOs

(B) the sale of mutual fund shares

(C) Regulation D offerings

(D) the over-the-counter sale of outstanding non-exempt securities

939. A client with a cash account buys stock. Five business days later, the client calls and informs you that he cannot pay for the stock. What steps would the broker-dealer follow?

(A) Send an application to the FINRA to get an extension.

(B) Give the client a two-day extension.

(C) Sell out the stock and freeze the account for 90 days.

(D) Sell out the stock and if there are no losses, there is no penalty.

940. A corporation announces a dividend with record date Thursday, August 15. If an investor wants to sell the stock and receive the dividend, when should the investor sell the stock?

I. Monday, August 12

II. Tuesday, August 13

III. Thursday, August 15 on a cash basis

IV. Friday, August 16 on a cash basis

(A) I and III

(B) I and IV

(C) II and III

(D) II and IV

941. Which of the following regulatory organizations has the authority to grant an extension for the payment of a trade?

(A) the New York Stock Exchange

(B) the Pacific Stock Exchange

(C) FINRA

(D) all of the above

942. All of the following may be reasons to reject a delivery of municipal bond certificates EXCEPT

(A) the indenture is illegible

(B) a change in the market price

(C) a missing legal opinion

(D) a misspelling of the investor's name

943. The 5% markup policy applies to which of the following types of secondary market transactions?

(A) riskless or simultaneous transactions

(B) common stock sold from a dealer's inventory

(C) proceeds transactions on non-exempt securities

(D) all of the above

944. If a client sells securities he has in his possession and fails to deliver them, what is the buy-in date?

(A) one business day after the trade date

(B) three business days after the trade date

(C) five business days after the trade date

(D) ten business days after the settlement date

945. A customer purchases 1,000 shares of XYZ common stock on Friday, October 3. What is the payment date?

(A) Monday, October 6

(B) Tuesday, October 7

(C) Wednesday, October 8

(D) Friday, October 10

946. All of the following are good delivery for a trade of 640 shares EXCEPT

(A) 1 certificate for 600 shares and 20 certificates for 2 shares each

(B) 2 certificates for 300 shares each and 1 certificate for 40 shares

(C) 2 certificates for 200 shares each and 3 certificates for 80 shares each

(D) 3 certificates for 200 shares each and 4 certificates for 10 shares each

947–952 Complaints and Legal Remedies

947. How long does a member have to respond to an arbitration complaint?

(A) 15 days

(B) 30 days

(C) 45 days

(D) 60 days

948. Miesha Silva has written a letter of complaint regarding her recent purchase of blue chip stocks to his broker-dealer. Upon receipt of the complaint, the broker-dealer must

(A) return the commission charged

(B) accept the complaint and write down any action taken

(C) guarantee to make Miesha whole

(D) repurchase the stocks at a price that is at or slightly above Miesha's purchase price

949. Simplified arbitration is used for member to non-member disputes not over

(A) $10,000

(B) $25,000

(C) $50,000

(D) $100,000

950. All of the following is TRUE about arbitration EXCEPT

(A) members may take non-members to arbitration

(B) non-members may take members to arbitration

(C) members may take other members to arbitration

(D) decisions are binding and non-appealable

951. According to FINRA rules, customer complaints must be kept on file by the brokerage firm for at least

(A) one year

(B) two years

(C) three years

(D) four years

952. Who makes the first decision regarding disputes submitted through Code of Procedure (COP) by FINRA?

(A)   FINRA Board of Governors

(B)   a panel chosen by FINRA

(C)   the NAC

(D)   the SEC

953–958 Transferring Accounts

953. MSRB rules regarding account transfers state that

I.   account transfers must be validated by the delivering firm within one business day after receiving an ACAT form

II.   account transfers must be validated by the delivering firm within three business days after receiving an ACAT form

III.   securities must be delivered within three business days after verification

IV.   securities must be delivered within four business days after verification

(A)   I and III

(B)   I and IV

(C)   II and III

(D)   II and IV

954. Your clients, a husband and wife, open a joint account as tenants in common. If one spouse dies, what must be done with the account?

(A)   The entire account is transferred to the survivor.

(B)   The deceased party's portion of the account is transferred to his or her estate.

(C)   The account is divided up on percentage invested.

(D)   None of the above.

955. Which of the following occurs under the Uniform Gifts to Minors Act when a minor reaches the age of majority?

(A)   The account must be changed to an UTMA account.

(B)   The account is transferred to the donor.

(C)   The account is closed, and the former minor receives a check from the broker-dealer equal to the market value of the securities in the account.

(D)   The account is transferred to the former minor.

956. Uniform Practice Code rules regarding account transfers state that

I.   account transfers must be validated by the delivering firm within one business day after receiving an ACAT form

II.   account transfers must be validated by the delivering firm within three business days after receiving an ACAT form

III.   securities must be delivered within three business days after verification

IV.   securities must be delivered within four business days after verification

(A)   I and III

(B)   I and IV

(C)   II and III

(D)   II and IV

957. Mr. and Mrs. Faber opened a joint account several years ago as a JTWROS. Mr. Faber was involved in a sky-diving accident and didn't survive. Upon receiving confirmation of Mr. Faber's passing, what must be done with the account?

(A)   The entire account would be transferred to Mrs. Faber.

(B)   Mr. Faber's portion of the account would be transferred to his estate.

(C)   The account is divided up depending on percentage invested.

(D)   Any one of the above is acceptable.

958. To process an ACAT, a brokerage firm must be a member of the

(A) FINRA

(B) NSCC

(C) SIPC

(D) DRS

959–982 Other Important Rules

959. Anderson Tate is a registered representative who works for KO Securities. Anderson has just learned of the death of one of his clients. Which of the following actions should Anderson take regarding his deceased client's account?

(A) Mark his client's account as deceased.

(B) Cancel all open orders.

(C) Wait for the proper legal papers.

(D) All of the above.

960. According to MSRB Rule G-39, which of the following is TRUE of cold-calling?

(A) Calls must be made after 8:00 a.m. and before 9:00 p.m. local time of the customer.

(B) Calls must be made after 9:00 a.m. and before 8:00 p.m. local time of the customer.

(C) Calls must be made after 8:00 a.m. and before 9:00 p.m. local time of the caller.

(D) Calls must be made after 9:00 a.m. and before 8:00 p.m. local time of the caller.

961. An insider of ABCD Corporation buys stock of her company on March 10 of the current year. If the insider sells the stock for a $5,000 profit on May 25 of the current year, which of the following is TRUE?

(A) The investor retains the profit.

(B) The profit is forfeited to the IRS.

(C) The profit is forfeited to the issuer.

(D) None of the above.

962. A broker-dealer must keep corporate or partnership documents for

(A) two years

(B) three years

(C) six years

(D) a lifetime

963. Mr. Silva has asked to be placed on your firm's do not call list. How long must anyone at your firm wait before contacting Mr. Silva again?

(A) one year

(B) two years

(C) five years

(D) life

964. If a client is traveling overseas, the broker-dealer may hold her mail for

(A) one month

(B) two months

(C) three months

(D) six months

965. In the event of business disruption due to a natural disaster or an act of terrorism, all brokerage firms must have a

(A) safe room

(B) business continuity and disaster recovery plan

(C) getaway vehicle

(D) duplicate records of all customers' transactions kept at a principal's home

966. All brokerage firms are required to have safeguards in place to protect customers' non-public information. The SEC regulation that outlines brokerage firm requirements to safeguard customers' information is

(A) Regulation T

(B) Regulation G

(C) Regulation S-P

(D) Regulation A

967. If an employee of a NYSE brokerage firm wants to open an account at a different brokerage firm, all of the following are TRUE EXCEPT

(A) the employee must obtain written permission from the employer to open the account

(B) the employee must obtain written approval before each trade is executed in the account

(C) the employee must make sure that the employer receives duplicate copies of all confirmations

(D) the employer must be notified about the opening of the account

968. If one of your clients dies, your brokerage firm should do all of the following EXCEPT

(A) cancel all open orders

(B) freeze the account

(C) transfer the money in the account to the executor of the estate

(D) cancel any written power of attorney

969. Regarding UGMA accounts, which TWO of the following are TRUE?

I. The minor is responsible for taxes.

II. The custodian is responsible for taxes.

III. There may be more than one custodian per UGMA account.

IV. There may be only one custodian per UGMA account.

(A) I and III

(B) I and IV

(C) II and III

(D) II and IV

970. A client of ABC Broker-Dealer owns 1,000 shares of DEF Corporation, which are held in street name. What procedure will ABC Broker-Dealer take in regard to a proxy sent from DEF Corporation?

(A) ABC Broker-Dealer must forward the proxy to the client.

(B) ABC Broker-Dealer will vote the proxy.

(C) They must inform DEF Corporation to send the proxy directly to your client.

(D) None of the above.

971. Which of the following records must be maintained by brokerage firms for six years?

I. ledgers

II. closed accounts

III. U-4 forms of terminated employees

IV. blotters

(A) I and III

(B) II, III, and IV

(C) I, II, and III

(D) I, II, and IV

972. Which of the following customers are exempt from receiving a risk disclosure document relating to penny stocks?

(A) established customers

(B) accredited investors

(C) customers who enter unsolicited orders to buy penny stocks

(D) customers of firms that generate no more than 5 percent of total commissions and markups from penny stocks

973. Which TWO of the following are TRUE?

I. The Rules of Fair Practice regulate trades between members.

II. The Rules of Fair Practice regulate trades between members and non-members.

III. The Uniform Practice Code regulates trades between members.

IV. The Uniform Practice Code regulates trades between members and non-members.

(A) I and III

(B) I and IV

(C) II and III

(D) II and IV

974. Which TWO of the following are TRUE regarding power of attorney?

I. Durable power of attorney cancels upon mental incompetence or death of an investor.

II. Durable power of attorney cancels only upon death of an investor.

III. Regular power of attorney cancels upon mental incompetence or death of an investor.

IV. Regular power of attorney cancels only upon death of an investor.

(A) I and III

(B) I and IV

(C) II and III

(D) II and IV

975. Arrange the following in the order of repayment in the event of corporate bankruptcy:

I. preferred stockholders

II. debenture holders

III. unpaid workers

IV. mortgage bondholders

(A) I, II, III, IV

(B) IV, II, III, I

(C) IV, II, I, III

(D) III, IV, II, I

976. Which of the following is NOT TRUE about UGMA accounts?

(A) Taxes are the responsibility of the minor.

(B) Certificates are endorsed by the minor.

(C) The custodian cannot give anyone else power of attorney over the account.

(D) The custodian cannot be compensated for services.

977. If your client, Sara Silver, requests a statement of a brokerage firm's financial condition, what document(s) must the brokerage firm send to her immediately?

(A) the most recent income statement

(B) the most recent balance sheet

(C) both Choices (A) and (B)

(D) neither Choice (A) nor (B)

978. Power of attorney is required for

I. discretionary accounts

II. custodial accounts

III. joint accounts

IV. fiduciary accounts

(A) I only

(B) I and II

(C) I, II, and IV

(D) I, II, III, and IV

979. An UGMA account is a(n)

(A) joint account

(B) individual account

(C) custodial account

(D) trust account

980. Which of the following statements could legally appear in advertisements or sales literature?

(A) "Our dedicated sales team is the best in the industry."

(B) "Our investment recommendations consistently outperform the market and will continue to do so."

(C) "We guarantee that we will earn each customer at least 7% on their investment each year."

(D) "Our dedicated sales team will work with you to help meet your investment goals."

981. Advertising pertaining to preferred stock recommendations must include

(A) all preferred stock positions held by your firm

(B) all securities recommendations made by your firm in the last year

(C) all preferred stock recommendations made by your firm in the last year

(D) a statement that your firm acted as a selling group member for the issuer within the last five years

982. Under FINRA Rule 2210, which of the following are considered advertising?

I. television promotions

II. billboards

III. market letters

IV. websites

(A) I only

(B) I, III, and IV

(C) I, II, and IV

(D) II, III, and IV

983–993 Violations

983. The maximum penalty for an individual convicted of insider trading is

(A) $5 million and/or 10 years in prison per violation

(B) $5 million and/or 20 years in prison per violation

(C) $2.5 million and/or 20 years in prison per violation

(D) 3 times the gain or loss avoided

984. When FINRA is considering the possibility that a brokerage account is being churned, all of the following are considered EXCEPT

(A) the profit or loss

(B) the amount of trades

(C) the client's investment objectives

(D) the amount of money in the client's account

985. All of the following are violations EXCEPT

(A) interpositioning

(B) freeriding

(C) hypothecation

(D) painting the tape

986. Two dealers are trading securities back and forth without any essential change in ownership. The dealers are engaged in a violation known as

(A) matching orders

(B) freeriding

(C) commingling

(D) interpositioning

987. A registered representative is at a fundraiser talking to an officer of ABC Corporation. The officer mentions to the registered representative that ABC plans a takeover of CBA Corporation within the next two weeks. What should the registered representative do in regard to this information?

(A) Make a recommendation to his clients that they purchase shares of ABC.

(B) Make a recommendation to his clients that they purchase shares of CBA.

(C) Purchase shares of CBA for his own account.

(D) Make no recommendations or purchases.

988. Which of the following BEST describes selling dividends?

(A) Encouraging clients to withdraw dividends from mutual funds and invest them into other securities so that you as a registered representative will receive additional commission

(B) Encouraging clients to sell equity securities right before dividends are paid so that they will be easier to sell

(C) Encouraging clients to purchase equity securities just prior to the ex-dividend date so that they will receive a dividend

(D) Encouraging a client to automatically reinvest mutual fund dividends into buying more shares of the fund

989. A client purchases a security and sells it shortly after without ever making a payment. This is a violation called

(A) matching orders

(B) freeriding

(C) commingling

(D) interpositioning

990. Judging by a client's trading pattern, you have a very strong suspicion that he is trading on inside information. You should

(A) contact a principal immediately

(B) contact the SEC and send it supporting documentation

(C) contact FINRA and send it supporting documentation

(D) all of the above

991. The CEO of OEC Corporation tells his life-long friend that OEC will be announcing an acquisition of COE, Inc., the following week. The friend acts on this knowledge and purchases shares of COE and shorts OEC. Who violated insider trading rules?

(A) the CEO

(B) the lifelong friend

(C) both the CEO and the lifelong friend

(D) neither the CEO nor the lifelong friend

992. All of the following are violations EXCEPT

(A) matching orders

(B) freeriding

(C) commingling

(D) hypothecating

993. Which of the following regulatory organizations has the authority to punish registered representatives for rule violations?

  I. SEC

  II. FINRA

  III. NYSE

  IV. MSRB

(A) I only

(B) I and II

(C) I, II, and III

(D) I, II, III, and IV

994–1001 FDIC and SIPC

994. Which of the following is TRUE about SIPC?

(A) It is an agency of the U.S. government.

(B) Investment advisers are required to be members of SIPC.

(C) Banks selling municipal securities must be SIPC members.

(D) SIPC funding is made by member assessments.

995. Mike Nugent and his wife, Mary, have individual accounts with ABCDE broker-dealer. Along with their individual accounts, they also have a joint account with rights of survivorship. Mike's individual account has $200,000 of stock, $50,000 of bonds, and $200,000 of cash. Mary's individual account has $100,000 of stock and $400,000 of cash. In the joint account, Mike and Mary have $100,000 of stock, $350,000 of bonds, and $200,000 of cash. If ABCDE declares bankruptcy, what would be the maximum SIPC coverage for all the accounts?

(A) $950,000

(B) $1,300,000

(C) $1,350,000

(D) $1,850,000

996. SIPC protects each separate customer up to

(A) $500,000 in cash and securities with no more than $250,000 cash

(B) $500,000 in cash and securities with no more than $100,000 cash

(C) $400,000 in securities and $100,000 cash

(D) $500,000 in securities and an additional $250,000 cash

997. SIPC provides coverage for which of the following securities held in a customer's account?

(A) common stock

(B) municipal bonds

(C) REITs

(D) all of the above

998. You have a new client who is going to open an individual cash account and an individual margin account in his name. At the same time, he also wants to open a joint account with his wife, a joint account with his son, and a corporate account. How many separate accounts is the investor covered for under SIPC?

(A) one

(B) two

(C) four

(D) five

999. If an investor is not fully covered under SIPC, she becomes a(n) _____ of the bankrupt broker-dealer.

(A) secured creditor

(B) general creditor

(C) owner

(D) stockholder

1000. FDIC protects each bank account up to

(A) $100,000

(B) $250,000

(C) $500,000

(D) $1,000,000

1001. Which of the following protects a broker-dealer against fraud or embezzlement by employees?

(A) SIPC

(B) fidelity bond

(C) FDIC

(D) power of substitution

Part II
The Answers

In this part . . .

You've tackled the questions; now you can check your answers. In this part, you find the correct answer and an explanation for every question listed in the first part of this book. If after reviewing your answers you decide you want more practice before taking the Series 7 exam, check out *Series 7 Exam For Dummies,* written by yours truly (and published by Wiley).

If you need help with specific business topics, check out these titles, all published by Wiley:

- ✔ *Bond Investing For Dummies,* by Russell Wild
- ✔ *Commodities For Dummies,* by Amine Bouchentouf
- ✔ *Investing For Dummies,* by Eric Tyson
- ✔ *Trading For Dummies,* by Michael Griffis and Lita Epstein

Visit www.dummies.com for more information.

Chapter 13

Answers

. . . .

1. **B. firm commitment**

A *firm commitment underwriting* is one in which any unsold securities are retained by the underwriters. *All-or-none (AON)* and *mini-max* are types of best efforts underwritings in which a certain amount of securities must be sold or the offering is canceled.

2. **D. 90 days**

Initial public offerings (IPOs) that aren't sold on an exchange have a 90-day prospectus requirement. All other new offerings have a 40-day prospectus requirement.

3. **A. 20**

The cooling-off period is when the Securities and Exchange Commission (SEC) is reviewing a company's registration statement before bringing new issues to market. The cooling-off period typically lasts about 20 days.

4. **D. None of the above.**

Although *none of the above* is rarely the correct answer, in this case, it is. You should remember that until a company files a registration statement for a new issue with the Securities and Exchange Commission (SEC), you can't do anything. You can't accept money, accept indications of interest, or send a red herring (preliminary prospectus).

5. **C. standby**

In this case, you're looking for the false answer. *All-or-none (AON), best efforts,* and *mini-max* are all types of bond underwritings. However, a *standby underwriting* is only for common stockholders. A standby underwriter purchases shares that aren't purchased by existing shareholders during a rights offering.

6. **A. selling group members**

A tombstone ad is print notice typically placed in newspapers or magazines. Companies use tombstone ads to make an announcement of a new issue of securities. Believe it or not, it got the name *tombstone ad* because the shape of the ad is typically in the shape of a headstone. The ad displays the names of the issuer, syndicate manager, and syndicate members but not selling group members.

7.

C. obtain indications of interest from investors

The correct answer is Choice (C). However, look closely at Choice (B). The Securities and Exchange Commission (SEC) (or any self-regulatory organization [SRO] for that matter) never approves or guarantees an issue of securities; the SEC just clears the issue for investment. The preliminary prospectus is released when the issue is in registration during the 20-day cooling-off period. The preliminary prospectus has no price and no effective date and may be used only to obtain indications of interest from investors.

8.

D. I and III

Remember, you're looking for the exception in this question. The preliminary prospectus (red herring) would include such items as the financial history of the company (including financial statements) and what the company is going to do with the funds being raised. However, the preliminary prospectus doesn't include the effective (release) date or the public offering price. The effective date and the public offering price would be included in the final prospectus.

9.

A. shelf registration

A *shelf registration* allows the issuer to sell securities registered with the Securities and Exchange Commission (SEC) for up to three years from the effective (release) date. A shelf registration allows an issuer to time the sale of its securities with market conditions.

10.

D. I and III

A *primary offering* is the offering of new securities from the issuer. Primary offerings raise money for the issuer and would increase the number of shares outstanding. *Treasury stock* is stock that was outstanding and was repurchased by the issuer. Because treasury stock was previously issued, it's not new stock coming to the market and wouldn't be part of a primary offering.

11.

A. I, III, and IV

Issuers can register securities on the state level by filing (notification), through coordination, or through qualification. The Series 63 and Series 66 exams explore this topic in much more detail. Communication was just thrown in there as a bogus answer choice because it looks something like the other words.

12.

A. the Securities Act of 1933

The Securities Act of 1933 covers the sale of new issues (primary market). The Securities Act of 1933 was designed to provide more transparency in financial statements and to curb fraudulent activities of issuers. The Securities Act of 1933 also goes by a myriad of other names, such as the Paper Act, New Issues Act, Full Disclosure Act, and Truth in Securities Act.

13. **B. I and IV**

Under the Securities Act of 1933, securities have to be an investment for profit and an investment risk. *Variable annuities* and *oil and gas limited partnerships* have those two elements, but *fixed annuities* and *FDIC insured negotiable CDs* don't. Fixed annuities provide guaranteed income, and FDIC insured CDs don't have the element of risk.

14. **B. the names of the selling groups**

Tombstone ads are written advertisements placed in newspapers and financial magazines informing potential investors of the offering of a security. It's called a tombstone ad because the shape of the ad resembles the shape of a grave headstone. Tombstone ads provide limited information about the issue, including the name of the issuer, the name(s) of the syndicate manager(s), the names of the syndicate members, and where investors can get a prospectus. However, a tombstone ad doesn't disclose the names of the selling group members.

15. **B. II and III**

Be careful, any time you see something about the Securities and Exchange Commission (SEC), or any self-regulatory organization for that matter, approving or guaranteeing an issue, it's a false answer. The SEC just clears the issue. During the cooling-off period, the SEC reviews registration statements and may issue stop orders.

16. **A. a price at or below the public offering price**

Stabilizing bids must be entered at or slightly below the public offering price. Stabilizing bids can't be placed above the public offering price because they can't be used to help raise the market price of an issue.

17. **C. the effective date**

The managing underwriter (syndicate manager) may determine the public offering price for a new security, the takedown (profit made by syndicate members), and the allocation of orders (the way orders are filled). However, the effective date (the first day the securities can begin trading) is determined by the Securities and Exchange Commission (SEC).

18. **D. Nothing.**

Until a corporation has filed a registration statement with the Securities and Exchange Commission (SEC) for a new issue, an account executive can't do anything. After the registration statement has been filed, account executives can start obtaining indications of interest.

19. **D. 90 days after the effective date**

If an initial public offering (IPO) will be traded initially on the Over-the-Counter Bulletin Board (OTCBB) or OTC Pink Market, brokerage firms that execute orders for customers to buy the stock must send a copy of the final prospectus with the confirmation (receipt of trade) within the first *90 days after the effective date.* For any other unlisted offering, the prospectus needs to be available for 40 days. For an IPO trading immediately on the NASDAQ or exchange, the final prospectus is necessary for the first 25 days of trading. The final prospectus includes items such as the Securities and Exchange Commission's (SEC) "we don't guarantee or approve" disclaimer, the offering price, use of proceeds, description of the underwriting, stabilization bid procedure, business history, investor risk, information about the management, financial information about the issuer, and so on.

20. **B. III and IV**

Indications of interest for a new offering aren't binding on the customer or on the broker-dealer. For example, a customer may tell you that he wants to buy 10,000 shares of Zamzow when it's available and then change his mind later. By the same token, the broker-dealer isn't obligated to have 10,000 shares available to sell to the customer when Zamzow becomes available.

21. **A. IV, I, III, II**

The normal priority for filling orders received by a syndicate is laid out in the agreement among underwriters (syndicate agreement). Here's the typical order from first- to last-filled: presale, group net (syndicate), designated, and member.

22. **C. matching orders**

Stabilization, due diligence, and *cooling-off* period are all terms that apply to a new issue of securities. However, *matching orders* is a violation that involves the illegal manipulation of securities prices by trying to make it look like the trading volume on security has increased.

23. **D. I, III, and IV**

The Securities and Exchange Act of 1934 covers margin account rules, the issuing of proxies, short sale rules, and so on. However, trust indentures are covered under the Trust Indenture Act of 1939.

24. **D. firm commitment underwriting**

When an investment banking firm (underwriter) agrees to purchase the securities directly from the issuer, it has entered into a firm commitment underwriting. In this type of underwriting, the underwriters assume all the risk of the security being sold.

25. **B. all-or-none**

An all-or-none offering is one in which the underwriter(s) is responsible for selling all the securities, or the offering is canceled. The securities and the money are held in an escrow account until the entire offering is sold. In the event that the offering is canceled, the money is returned to the purchasers, and securities are returned to the issuer. All-or-none and mini-max are types of best efforts underwritings.

26.

C. the syndicate agreement

The syndicate agreement (agreement among underwriters or syndicate letter) must be signed by all members of the underwriting and outlines the liabilities and responsibilities of all parties involved.

27.

D. I, II, III, and IV

When a company files a registration statement with the Securities and Exchange Commission (SEC), it must include the issuer's name and description of its business, the names and addresses of all the company's control persons, what the proceeds will be used for, the company's capitalization, complete financial statements, any legal proceedings against the company, and so on.

28.

B. I and IV

The nice thing about this question is that the titles *registrar* and *transfer agent* pretty much sum up what they do. The registrar works along with the transfer agent to maintain a record of stock and bondholders and to make sure that more shares aren't outstanding than there should be. The main function of a transfer agent is to transfer things like stock certificates, bond certificates, and proxies. The transfer agent also keeps a record of stock and bondholders.

29.

D. all of the above

Even though a security is exempt from registration and prospectus requirements, such as U.S. government securities and private placements, it isn't exempt from the anti-fraud provisions in the Securities Act of 1933 or the Securities Exchange Act of 1934. Anti-fraud rules always apply — all issuers must provide accurate information to the public.

30.

B. III and IV

Rule 145 is included in the Securities Act of 1933, which is designed to protect investors in the event of a corporate takeover, merger, reclassification, acquisition, consolidation, and so on. The rule is really designed to protect investors' rights in the event of a major change in the company; stock splits and stock dividends aren't considered major changes.

31.

C. green shoe provision

A green shoe provision (over-allotment option), if written into the underwriting agreement (agreement among underwriters), allows the underwriters to sell up to 15 percent more shares than the issuer had intended to sell when the securities are under high demand.

32. **D. all of the above**

An investment banking firm is a financial institution that provides a variety of services for issuers and sometimes high-net-worth investors. As related to new issues, investment bankers advise issuers how to raise money, help the issuers comply with securities laws, and often help the issuers raise money by selling securities.

33. **A. the effective date**

The effective date (the date the registration of a securities issue becomes effective) isn't determined by the syndicate manager; it's determined by the Securities and Exchange Commission (SEC).

34. **C. syndicate agreement**

The allocation of orders establishes a priority for customer orders to be filled. The allocation of orders would be found in the syndicate agreement (agreement among underwriters). The typical priority of orders is presale, syndicate (group-net), designated, and then member orders. The allocation of orders is required to be in the syndicate agreement under Municipal Securities Rulemaking Board (MSRB) rules.

35. **A. IV, I, III, II**

Typically, the largest portion goes to the takedown, which is the syndicate's portion. Next would be the concession, followed by the reallowance, and then the manager's fee.

36. **B. the underwriting spread**

The *underwriting spread* is the difference between what the issuer receives and the public offering price. The underwriting spread is equal to the takedown plus the manager's fee.

37. **C. without a markup or commission**

When a customer purchases a security during an initial public offering (IPO), he'll pay the public offering price. Remember, there's a difference between what the issuer receives and the public offering price. Within that difference is the profit for syndicate members when selling shares to the public, so no additional markup or commission would be added.

38. **A. $0.45 per share**

The additional takedown is the profit made by syndicate members on shares sold by the selling group. The syndicate members get the takedown, and the selling group gets the concession. To determine the takedown, take the spread (the difference between the public offering price and the amount that Armbar got per share) and then subtract the manager's fee:

$15.00 − $13.50 = $1.50 spread

$1.50 spread − $0.25 manager's fee = $1.25 takedown

Syndicate members get $1.25 per share if selling the shares themselves, but if the selling group helps sell the shares, they have to subtract the commission so the syndicate members get $0.45 per share:

$1.25 takedown − $0.80 concession = $0.45 additional takedown

39.   A. I and IV

The easiest one for you to remember should be the Western (divided) account. Remember, in the *wild wild west,* each man was for himself. That should help you remember that if the syndicate was set up on a Western account basis, each member is finished after its allotment is sold. Although you really don't need to do the math on this one because the answer choices give you only one choice for an Eastern (undivided) account where there was additional shares to sell, to find the answer, you'd multiply Liddell's original percentage by the offering size. Liddell Securities originally took 12.5 percent of the offering (1 million shares divided by 8 million shares); therefore, they're responsible for 12.5 percent of the shares left unsold by other members on an Eastern account basis:

(12.5%)(800,000) = 100,000

40.   D. $275,000

The selling group receives the concession. If the selling group sells all of its 500,000 shares, the total will be $275,000 ($0.55 × 500,000 shares).

41.   C. 250,000

When a syndicate is formed on an Eastern (undivided) account basis, each syndicate member is responsible not only for his or her own allotment but also for a percentage of the shares left unsold by other syndicate members. This syndicate member was responsible for selling 2.5 million shares of a 10 million share offering, which is 25 percent. After selling its entire allotment, this firm is responsible for selling 25 percent of the 1 million shares left unsold:

(25%)(1 million shares) = 250,000 shares

42.   C. $450,000

The syndicate is responsible for paying the selling group when selling new shares. If the syndicate members sell the shares themselves, they receive $0.75 per share. However, if the selling group sells shares, they receive $0.30 per share out of the syndicate member's $0.75. Therefore, the syndicate members receive $0.45 ($0.75 − $0.30) per share on shares sold by the selling group. If the selling group sells its entire allotment, the syndicate will receive

(1 million shares)($0.45) = $450,000

The $450,000 is known as the additional takedown.

43.   D. manager's fee

The manager's fee is typically the smallest portion of an underwriting spread.

44. **B. the takedown**

The takedown is the profit made by syndicate members when selling shares of a new issue.

45. **B. 200,000**

In a Western or divided account offering, each firm in a syndicate is responsible only for its original allocation. Because the firm has sold $1.8 million of the $2 million of bonds allocated to the firm, the firm is still responsible for selling the remaining $200,000 of its allocation.

46. **D. combined**

This is a combined (split) offering. The 600,000 shares that are authorized but previously unissued shares are a primary offering, and the 400,000 shares are a large block of outstanding shares, so that's a secondary offering. When you put a primary and secondary offering together, it's called a combined offering.

47. **C. secondary**

A *secondary offering* is a large block of outstanding or previously outstanding (treasury) stock. Remember, treasury stock was stock that was outstanding (trading in the market) and then at some point repurchased by the issuer.

48. **D. initial public offering**

An *initial public offering (IPO)* is the first time a corporation sells stock to the public (becomes publicly traded). When a corporation has an IPO, it can't have another one because it can go public only once. All new stock sold after the IPO is over is part of a primary offering. IPOs are usually quite risky investments and therefore aren't suitable for all investors.

49. **B. shelf offerings**

The Securities and Exchange Commission (SEC) Rule 415 outlines the rules for shelf offerings (shelf registration). Typically, a company isn't going to sell all of its shares in one shot; it may want to wait another six months, a year, or two years before selling all of its authorized shares. Under SEC Rule 415, an issuer has up to two years to sell its registered securities without having to file a new registration statement.

50. **D. II, III, and IV**

Rule 144 pertains to secondary market transactions involving restricted or control securities (securities owned by officers, directors, owners of 10 percent or more of the issuer's voting stock and their immediate family members) and therefore doesn't pertain to initial offerings.

51.   B. I and IV

A Regulation S (Reg S) offering relates to U.S. companies offering securities outside of the United States to non-U.S. residents. The transaction is exempt, and the securities must be held for one year (12 months) before they can be resold in the United States.

52.   B. I and IV

For an investor to be considered accredited, he must have a net worth that exceeds $1 million excluding the primary residence or an annual income exceeding $200,000 ($300,000 joint) in the most recent two years with an expectation of the same level in the current year. A Regulation D private placement may have up to only 35 unaccredited investors per year and an unlimited number of accredited investors.

53.   D. commercial paper

Commercial paper is corporate debt securities that mature in 270 days or less. Debt securities with a maturity of 270 days or less are exempt from Securities and Exchange Commission (SEC) registration.

54.   A. an offering of securities to no more than 35 unaccredited investors in a 12-month period

A Regulation D (Reg D; private placement) offering is a provision in the Securities Act of 1933 that exempts offerings sold to no more than 35 unaccredited (small) investors each year. Even though Regulation D offerings are limited to the number of small investors, the amount of money they can raise isn't limited.

55.   B. a U.S. issuer issuing new securities to non-U.S. investors

A Regulation S registration exemption under the Securities Act of 1933 is given to U.S. issuers who are offering securities to non-U.S. investors.

56.   C. III and IV

Don't get confused by the terminology here. Exempt securities are exempt from the Securities and Exchange Commission (SEC) registration, but non-exempt securities must register with the SEC. Out of the choices listed, *municipal bonds* and *treasury notes* are exempt from SEC registration. However, *blue chip stocks* and *variable annuities* must register with the SEC. In the case of variable annuities, they must be registered with the SEC and state insurance commission in each state in which they're to be sold.

57.   B. They are issues without using a prospectus.

Regulation A offerings are offerings of securities valued at $5 million or less within a one-year period. Regulation A offerings are exempt from the full registration requirements of the Securities Act of 1933. Companies issuing securities through Regulation A offerings make an offering circular instead of a prospectus, which is available to all potential purchasers. An *offering circular* is somewhat of an abbreviated form of a prospectus.

58. **A. an offering of securities only within the issuer's home state**

A Rule 147 offering is an intrastate (not interstate) offering that's exempt from the Securities and Exchange Commission (SEC) registration provided the issuer conducts business only in one state and sells securities only to residents of the same state. This also includes the 80 percent rule that states that at least 80 percent of the issuer's assets are located within the state, and at least 80 percent of the offering proceeds are used within the same state.

59. **D. 42,500**

When the restricted stock is to be sold, a Form 144 must be filed with the Securities and Exchange Commission (SEC), which is good for 90 days. According to Rule 144, the most the investor can sell after holding the restricted stock for at least six months is the greater of 1 percent of the outstanding shares or the average weekly trading volume for the previous four weeks. You have to be careful to take just the previous four weeks, which in this case is the top four. Start by multiplying the 1 percent by the 4 million shares outstanding:

$$(1\%)(4 \text{ million}) = 40,000$$

Next, determine the average weekly trading volume for the previous four weeks by adding together the amount of shares sold and dividing by 4:

$$35,000 + 50,000 + 40,000 + 45,000 = 170,000$$

$$\frac{170,000}{4} = 42,500$$

This investor can sell a maximum of 42,500 shares.

60. **A. limited partnership public offerings**

This question is basically asking you which security must be registered with the Securities and Exchange Commission (SEC). Out of the choices given, the only one that isn't exempt and therefore must be registered is *limited partnership public offerings*.

61. **A. at the time of sale**

Insiders must file a Form 144 with the Securities and Exchange Commission (SEC) when ready to sell restricted or control stock. After notifying the SEC, the investor has 90 days to sell the stock registered with the SEC. The maximum amount of shares that the insider may sell in the 90-day period is 1 percent of the outstanding shares or the average weekly trading volume for the previous four weeks, whichever is greater.

62. **C. I and IV**

There is a difference between securities that are exempt because of whom the issuer is and transactions that are exempt. Exempt securities include U.S. government securities, municipal bonds, securities issued by banks, public utility stocks, securities issued by nonprofit organizations, and so on. Intrastate offerings, Regulation A offerings, Regulation D offerings (private placements), and so on are exempt transactions.

63. **B. $300,000**

Regulation D private placements allow up to only 35 unaccredited investors per year and an unlimited number of accredited investors. To be considered an accredited investor, an individual must have annual income of at least $200,000, and a couple with a joint account must have an annual income of at least $300,000.

64. **C. REITs**

Securities that are exempt from the registration requirements of the Securities Act of 1933 include U.S. government securities (Treasury bonds, Treasury bills, Treasury notes, and so on), municipal bonds, securities issued by banks, public utility stocks and bonds, and so on. However, real estate investment trusts (REITs) must register with the Securities and Exchange Commission (SEC).

65. **A. I and III**

Both preferred stockholders and common stockholders have ownership of a corporation. Bondholders are creditors, not owners.

66. **B. It is stock that was previously authorized but still unissued.**

Choices (B) and (C) oppose each other, so one of them has to be the answer to the question. Treasury stock is stock that was issued and subsequently repurchased by the company. Treasury stock has no voting rights and doesn't receive dividends.

67. **C. I and II**

Stockholders can't vote for dividends. Stock and cash dividends are declared by the board of directors.

68. **C. 3,000 votes each for three candidates**

This investor has a total of 8,000 votes (2,000 shares×4 vacancies), which can be voted any which way because it's cumulative voting. The reason that Choice (C) doesn't work is because it would require 9,000 votes (3,000 votes×3 candidates), and this investor has only 8,000.

69. **A. common stock**

Out of the choices listed, common stocks are considered the riskiest. The risk is that common stockholders are the last to be paid in the event of corporate bankruptcy. However, the trade-off is that common stockholders have the greatest potential reward because their prices can fluctuate more than any of the other investment choices listed. Remember: more risk = more reward.

70.   **C. 950,000**

Macrohard could have issued up to 2 million shares, but it issued only 1.1 million at this time. Macrohard repurchased 150,000 shares of its stock, which is called treasury stock. To determine the amount of shares outstanding, use the following formula:

$$\text{Outstanding} = \text{Issued} - \text{Treasury}$$
$$= 1{,}100{,}000 - 150{,}000$$
$$= 950{,}000$$

71.   **D. repurchased stock**

Choices (A) and (B) are wrong because stock represents ownership, and you can't own a percentage of the government. Treasury stock is stock that was outstanding in the market and subsequently repurchased by the issuer. Corporations repurchase their own stock sometimes to increase the demand for their outstanding shares or to avoid a takeover.

72.   **A. 5.0%**

To determine the current yield of a stock, you need to divide the annual dividends by the market price:

$$\text{Current yield of a stock} = \frac{\text{Annual dividends}}{\text{Market price}}$$
$$= \frac{\$2.10}{\$42.00}$$
$$= 0.05, \text{ or } 5\%$$

You don't need the earnings per share (EPS) to answer this question. On the Series 7 exam, some questions may include information that you don't need just to throw you off track. Focus on the information you need to answer the question.

73.   **B. III and IV**

Common stockholders have a residual claim to the assets of the corporation at dissolution. Common stockholders are entitled to receive a report containing audited financial statements on a yearly — *not* monthly — basis. Stockholders do get to vote for stock splits but not dividends (whether cash or stock); the board of directors decides on dividends.

74.   **D. 3 years**

Shelf registration is a Securities and Exchange Commission (SEC) provision that allows an issuer to register a new issue without having to sell all the securities at one time. Shelf registration allows the issuer to hold back securities for up to three years without having to reregister them.

75. **D. 4,000**

Cain has a total of 4,000 votes (1,000 shares×4 vacancies). Because HIT allows cumulative voting, Cain can vote the shares in any way he sees fit, even if he votes them all for one candidate. Statutory or regular voting would allow Cain to vote only up to 1,000 shares for each candidate.

76. **A. I and III**

Unlike the par value of preferred stock and debt securities, the par value doesn't really matter too much to common stockholders. The par value of common stock is generally used for bookkeeping purposes of the issuer, and common stock is even sometimes issued with no par value. In the event of a stock split, the par value would be adjusted to reflect the split. And because stock is an equity security that represents ownership of the issuing corporation, there's no maturity date as there is with debt securities.

77. **C. TUV common stock**

Common stockholders are the last to be paid in the event of corporate bankruptcy, so they're subject to the greatest risk. Common stock is a junior security. Out of the choices listed, the first to be paid would be the mortgage bondholders (secured creditors), subordinated debenture holders (unsecured creditors), preferred stockholders, and, last but not least, common stockholders.

78. **B. 2.5%**

The quarterly dividend is $0.20, which makes the annual dividend $0.80 ($0.20×4 quarters). Use the following formula to determine the current yield:

$$\text{Current yield} = \frac{\text{Annual dividends}}{\text{Market price}}$$
$$= \frac{\$0.80}{\$32}$$
$$= 0.025, \text{ or } 2.5\%$$

79. **C. a stock split**

Par value for a common stock is used for bookkeeping purposes for the issuer and isn't of much use to investors. However, when a company does split its stock (such as 2 for 1), the par value would be reduced.

80. **B. 1,250 ABC at $32**

This is an uneven split. Because of the answers given, you probably don't need to set up an equation for this one. Dana is going to have five shares for every four she had before, so you know that the amount of shares must increase, and the price must decrease because Dana's overall value of securities didn't change. If you wanted to do the math to double-check your answer, first you'd multiply the 1,000 shares by 5 and then divide it by 4:

$$\frac{(1{,}000 \text{ shares})(5)}{4} = \frac{5{,}000 \text{ shares}}{4} = 1{,}250 \text{ shares}$$

Then you multiply the price ($40) by 4 and then divide it by 5:

$$\frac{(\$40)(4)}{5} = \frac{\$160}{5} = \$32 \text{ new market price}$$

81. C. 25%

When you're trying to determine how much the price of a stock is reduced for a split, use the following formula:

$$\frac{A-B}{A}$$

A represents the first number, and *B* represents the second number, so you end up with

$$\frac{4-3}{4} = \frac{1}{4} = 0.25, \text{ or } 25\%$$

82. B. $24.65

You solve this question by simply subtracting the amount of the dividend from the previous day's closing price:

$$\$24.95 - \$0.30 = \$24.65$$

83. A. another certificate representing 200 shares of ABC

This investor owns stock that was split 3 for 1, so he now owns three shares for every one that he had before. In this case, the investor had 100 shares prior to the split, so he'll have 300 shares after the split (100×3). At this point, he has only the one certificate representing 100 shares, so ABC will send him another certificate representing the additional 200 shares.

84. B. the ex-dividend date

The *ex-dividend date* is the first day a stock trades without the dividend. The market price of the stock reduces by the amount of the dividend on the ex-dividend date. Because it takes three business days for a regular-way stock transaction to settle, the ex-dividend date is automatically two business days before the record date. Therefore, there's no reason for a corporation to announce the ex-dividend date.

85. A. I and III

The *ex-dividend date* is the first day a stock trades without a previously declared dividend. The ex-dividend date is two business days before the record date (except for mutual funds), and it's the date that the stock reduces by the amount of the dividend.

86.   **A. February 11**

Regular-way settlement for common stock is three business days. For an investor to be able to purchase a stock and receive a previously declared dividend, she has to purchase at least three business days before the record date. Because you have non-business days you have to work with (Saturday and Sunday), three business days before the record date is Wednesday, February 11.

87.   **C. II and III**

When an investor receives a stock dividend, the amount of shares the investor owns increases, and the price decreases. The only answer that works is Choice (C). Remember: When an investor receives a stock dividend or stock split, the investor's overall value of investment doesn't change. You can also figure this out mathematically by multiplying the number of shares by the market price, like so:

$$(1,000 \text{ shares})(\$24 \text{ market price}) = \$24,000$$

This investor owns $24,000 worth of DIM stock, so he'll own $24,000 worth of DIM stock after the stock dividend. Your next step would be to figure out the new number of shares owned by the investor. The investor initially owned 1,000 shares and then received a stock dividend of 200 shares (20 percent × 1,000 shares):

$$1,000 \text{ shares} + 200 \text{ shares} = 1,200 \text{ shares}$$

$$\frac{\$24,000}{1200 \text{ shares}} = \$20 \text{ market price}$$

88.   **D. to increase the demand for its stock**

The main reason a corporation splits its stock is to increase the demand. The most common unit of trading stock is 100 shares, which is called a *round lot*. If a stock is trading at a relatively low price, such as $20, most investors can afford to purchase 100 shares, and it helps keep trading active. However, say that the price of the stock increased to $100 per share; it would cost $10,000 to purchase a round lot. When this happens, trading slows down because not as many investors are able to pay that much for 100 shares. If that same corporation splits its stock 4 for 1, there'd be four times as many shares outstanding at a price of $25 per share, which most investors could afford.

89.   **B. I and III**

A reverse split increases the price of the stock and decreases the amount of shares outstanding. In this case, the stock is reverse split 1 for 4, which means that there will be only one share for every four that were outstanding before, and the market price will increase to four times the amount. Because the company made the same amount of money and fewer shares are outstanding, the earnings per share (EPS) would increase.

90. **D. 525 shares valued at $52.38 per share**

Your key here is that the overall investment value doesn't change. When investors receive a stock dividend, the number of shares has to increase, and the market price has to reduce. So out of the answer choices given, only one meets the criteria: Choice (D). First, you have to figure out the overall value of investment by multiplying the number of shares by the market price:

$$(500 \text{ shares})\,(\$55 \text{ per share}) = \$27,500$$

This investor had $27,500 worth of stock and will still have $27,500 worth of stock after the dividend. When this investor gets the 5 percent stock dividend, he'll get 5 percent more shares, which means that this investor now has 525 shares: 500 shares + 25 shares (5% stock dividend) = 525 shares. Divide the $27,500 by the new number of shares to find the new stock price.

$$\frac{\$27,500}{525 \text{ shares}} = \$52.38 \text{ per share}$$

91. **B. 200**

This question is asking you how many additional shares the investor would have after the split. Because it's a 4-for-3 split, the investor would have four shares for every three that she had before. Start by multiplying the number of shares owned by four and dividing by three:

$$\frac{(600 \text{ shares})(4)}{3} = \frac{2,400 \text{ shares}}{3} = 800 \text{ shares}$$

This investor originally had 600 shares and now has 800, so she received an additional 200 shares. You should be prepared to determine how many additional shares or the number of shares after the split because a Series 7 exam question could ask you to find either answer.

92. **B. decrease**

Preferred stocks, like bonds, are affected by interest rate changes. Rates and prices have an inverse relationship. Because interest rates have increased, straight preferred stock prices would decrease.

93. **A. Treasury bill rate**

Adjustable-rate preferred stock (ARPS) has a dividend that typically varies with the Treasury bill (T-bill) rate. It's not typically set at the exact T-bill rate but at some predetermined formula tied to the T-bill rate (that is, a set percentage of the average T-bill rate for a given period of time).

94. **C. I and III**

Straight preferred stock does receive a fixed dividend and has higher preference than common stock in the event of issuer bankruptcy. However, holders of preferred stock don't have voting rights unless they don't receive expected dividends. Also, unlike bonds, preferred stock has no maturity date.

95. A. $21.50

Assume that the par value of convertible preferred stock is $100 unless stated differently in the question. As with other convertible problems, the first thing you must do is get the amount of shares it's convertible into. You can use the following formula:

$$\text{Conversion ratio} = \frac{\text{Par}}{\text{Conversion price}}$$
$$= \frac{\$100}{\$25}$$
$$= 4 \text{ shares}$$

Next, you have to get the parity price by dividing the market price of the preferred stock by the conversion ratio:

$$\frac{\$90}{4 \text{ shares}} = \$22.50$$

DEF common stock should be trading at $22.50 to be at parity with the preferred stock. However, the question states that the common stock is trading one point ($1) below parity, so the common stock is trading at $21.50 ($22.50 – $1).

96. C. It allows the issuer to issue preferred stock with a lower fixed dividend after the call date.

First, you should have crossed off Choice (D) right away because equity securities, such as preferred stock, don't have a maturity date. Callable preferred stock is issued with a higher fixed dividend rate than non-callable because it's riskier for investors (more risk = more reward) because they may not be able to hold the stock as long as they want. Issuers will typically call their callable preferred stock and/or callable bonds when interest rates decrease. If interest rates decrease, issuers would be able to issue preferred stock with a lower fixed dividend and/or bonds with a lower coupon rate.

97. C. II and III

Unlike holders of common stock, preferred stockholders typically don't have voting rights unless not receiving expected dividends. In the event of corporate bankruptcy, preferred stockholders are senior to common stockholders and would receive liquidation assets (if any) before common stockholders.

98. C. $7

If a company issues cumulative preferred stock, it's allowed to owe investors dividend payments. However, before the company pays a dividend to common stockholders, it must first make up any delinquent and current payments to the cumulative preferred shareholders. This company should be paying the preferred shareholders $4 per year (4 percent of $100 par). In the first three years, the company should have paid out $12 in dividends ($4 × 3 years). However, the company paid only $9, so it owes $3 from the first three years ($12 – $9) and $4 for the following year for a total of $7.

99. **B. convertible**

Preferred stockholders are subject to inflation risk in the same way that most bond-holders are. *Inflation risk* is the risk that the fixed interest or dividend payments will be worth less in terms of purchasing power over time. By purchasing convertible preferred stock, investors may convert their preferred stock into common stock of the same corporation at any time. Typically, common stock has a greater chance of keeping pace with inflation, which would reduce that risk.

100. **A. I only**

Unlike common stock, which can pay dividends in the form of cash, stock, or product, preferred dividends can be paid only in the form of cash.

101. **D. the issuer can replace stock with a higher dividend with stock with a lower dividend**

Although callable preferred stock would have a higher dividend than non-callable preferred stock, it's not an advantage to issuers. However, if interest rates drop, issuers of callable preferred stock can call in their high-dividend stock and issue stock with a lower dividend and save money.

102. **A. minimum yearly dividend payment**

The stated dividend for a participating preferred stock is the minimum dividend that an investor can receive. Participating preferred stock receives its own dividend and a portion of the dividend received by the common stockholders. In this case, the minimum the investor can receive is 5 percent if no common dividend was paid. If a common dividend was paid, the investor would receive greater than 5 percent.

103. **C. callable**

This is another one of those investing situations where more risk = more reward. From an investor's standpoint, purchasing callable securities is riskier than non-callable securities because the issuer decides when the security is called. For example, the issuer may call the security after one year when you were hoping to hold it at least ten years. Because an investor is taking that additional risk, callable securities pay a higher dividend or higher interest (bonds) than non-callable.

104. **D. convertible preferred stock**

Typically, preferred stock trades somewhat close to its par value. Because it trades close to its par value, investors are subject to inflation risk. Inflation risk is the risk that the value of the security doesn't keep pace with the cost of living. Your client can minimize this risk by purchasing convertible preferred stock. Convertible preferred stock allows investors to convert their preferred stock into common stock of the same company at any time. Common stock is more likely to keep pace with inflation.

105. **A. a receipt for a foreign security trading in the U.S.**

An ADR is an American depositary receipt. ADRs are receipts for foreign securities traded in the United States. Besides the normal risks of investing in securities, holders of ADRs also face currency risk.

106. **C. it has low currency risk**

American depositary receipts (ADRs) facilitate the trading of foreign securities in U.S. markets. ADRs carry currency risk because distributions on them must be converted from foreign currency to U.S. dollars on the date of distribution. The trading price of the ADR is actually quite affected by currency fluctuation, which can devalue any dividends and/or the value of the underlying security.

107. **A. they help U.S. companies gain access to foreign dollars**

American depositary receipts (ADRs) are receipts for foreign securities trading in the United States. Therefore, they help foreign companies gain access to U.S. dollars, not the other way around. Investors don't receive the actual stock certificates; they receive a receipt representing a certain number of shares of the issuer. Investors of ADRs don't have voting rights. Dividends (if any) are paid in U.S. dollars.

108. **B. II, III, and IV**

Holders of American depositary receipts (ADRs) face foreign currency risk, market risk, and political risk. However, because ADRs are actively traded, holders don't face liquidity risk.

109. **A. I and II**

Be careful when answering questions that have words such as *except* or *not* so that you don't make a careless mistake. In this case, you're looking for the false answer(s). Warrants are sometimes issued with bond offerings in a unit to make a bond offering more attractive. Warrants give the holder the right to purchase the issuer's common stock at a fixed price. Warrants trade in the market independent of the bonds. Warrants trade at a price much lower than the company's common stock; holders have a leveraged position. This means that the true answers are Statements III and V, so the correct answers for this question are Statements I and II, or Choice (A). Holders of warrants don't receive dividends because they're not holding equity securities until the warrants are exercised.

110. **C. They have voting rights.**

Warrants give investors a long-term and sometimes perpetual right to buy stock from the issuer at a fixed price. They are marketable, meaning that they may trade separately. Because warrants aren't the underlying security until the holder actually uses the warrants to purchase stock, they don't receive dividends. The answer that is *not true* is Choice (C). Warrant holders don't have voting rights.

111.

D. $2.00

The easiest way to determine the answer to this question is to set up the following equation for cum-rights (prior to ex-rights):

$$\frac{M-S}{N+1}$$

where M is the market price ($30), S is the subscription price (discount price – $24), and N is the number of rights needed to purchase one share (2).

$$\frac{\$30-\$24}{2+1}=\frac{\$6}{3}=\$2$$

After setting up the equation and plugging in the numbers, you see that the theoretical value of a right is $2.

112.

D. II and IV

Your client receives one right for each share of common stock owned. Because your client owns 80 shares of stock, the investor will receive 80 rights. Your client will need nine rights plus $10 for each share of stock purchased in the proposal. To determine the number of shares your client will be able to purchase in the rights offering, you need to divide the 80 rights by the 9 rights needed to purchase one share:

$$\frac{80 \text{ rights}}{9 \text{ rights}}=8.3 \text{ shares}$$

However, the proposal allows fractional shares to become whole shares. Therefore, 8.3 shares changes to 9 shares. Your client is actually able to purchase 9 shares for $90 (9 × $10).

113.

B. they are non-marketable securities

Warrants *are* marketable securities, which means that they can be traded separately in the market. Warrants have longer maturities than rights because they typically have a maturity of up to ten years and sometimes longer. Rights typically have a maturity of only 30 to 45 days. When initially issued, warrants are usually combined in a unit with the issuer's bonds. The exercise price of the warrants would be at a price higher than the market price of the issuer's common stock.

114.

B. I and III

Warrants are most often issued with a corporation's other securities, such as debt securities, to make an offering more attractive. Because of this, warrants are often called "sweeteners" because they're sweetening the deal. Statement II uses the word *perpetual,* which means never ending. Warrants typically provide a long-term and sometimes perpetual interest in the issuer's common stock. Holders of warrants have no voting rights until exercising their right to buy the common stock.

115.

C. $2.00

Each current shareholder receives one right for each share of common stock owned. To determine the value of a right (ex-rights), use the following equation.

$$\frac{M-S}{N}$$

where M is the market price ($45), S is the subscription price (discount price – $35), and N is the number of rights needed to purchase one share (5).

$$\frac{\$45-\$35}{5}=\frac{\$10}{5}=\$2$$

After setting up the equation and plugging in the numbers, you see that the theoretical value of a right is $2.00.

---

116. **D. rights are automatically received by preferred stockholders**

Rights are automatically received by common stockholders, not preferred stockholders. Each share of outstanding common stock receives one right. Rights are short-term (usually 30 to 45 days), and rights offerings typically have a standby underwriter to purchase the shares not purchased by stockholders.

---

117. **C. rights agent**

This is one of those examples of good answer versus better answer. If *rights agent* wasn't one of your choices, *transfer agent* would have been a good answer. However, *rights agent* is the best answer.

---

118. **B. a rights distribution to existing shareholders**

Remember, the corporation is trying to raise money. Choices (A) and (C) would cost the corporation money, and Choice (D) would be a wash. However, having a rights distribution allows existing shareholders to purchase new stock at a discount and, thus, brings more money into the corporation.

---

119. **B. I and II**

Corporations may issue unsecured bonds, such as debentures, subordinated debentures, and income bonds, or secured bonds, such as mortgage bonds, equipment trust bonds, income bonds, and guaranteed bonds. However, *double-barreled bonds* and *revenue bonds* are types of bonds issued by municipalities.

---

120. **A. a percentage of dollar price**

Term bonds are also called *dollar bonds* because they're quoted according to a percentage of dollar price. For example, a term bond that's trading for $990 would be quoted as 99 (99 percent of $1,000 par).

---

121. **B. one that is backed by the assets of another company**

A *guaranteed bond* is one that's backed by the assets of another company (typically a parent company).

122. **B. the amount an issuer must pay above par value when calling its bonds early**

A call premium is the amount over par value paid by an issuer if calling its bonds in the early years.

123. **C. an equipment trust bond**

Equipment trust bonds (or equipment trust certificates, ETCs) are typically issued by transportation companies, such as trucking companies, airlines, and railroads. These secured bonds are backed by rolling stock (assets on wheels). In the event of default, the rolling assets backing the bonds would be sold to pay off bondholders.

124. **D. a lien on property owned by HIJ Corp.**

This is one of those questions that takes you on a ride full of superfluous information you don't need. All you need to know is what the bonds are secured by. In this case, you're dealing with mortgage bonds, which are secured by a lien on property owned by HIJ. In the event that HIJ failed to pay principal and/or interest to its bondholders, property owned by HIJ would be sold to generate the money to make the payments.

125. **A. II, III, and IV**

Eurodollar bonds are denominated in U.S. dollars and issued by non-American companies outside of the United States and the issuer's home country. Because they're issued outside the United States by non-U.S. companies, they don't have to be registered with the Securities and Exchange Commission (SEC). All securities issued outside the United States are subject to currency risk.

126. **D. book entry**

Although book entry has been the most common form of delivery for U.S. government securities for some time, it's now the most common form of delivery for corporate bonds also. With a book-entry security, the investor doesn't actually receive the certificate but receives a receipt of the transaction, and the information is stored electronically.

127. **B. backed by stocks and bonds owned by the issuer**

Collateral trust bonds are typically issued by holding companies that hold securities of other companies. In the event of default, the debt holders receive the securities held in trust. A trustee hired by the issuer is responsible for the safeguarding of the securities and transferring the assets in the event of default.

128. **C. mortgage bonds**

First, eliminate the answer choices that won't work. *High-yield bonds* are also called "junk" bonds because of their high credit risk, and this investor is looking for only a moderate amount of risk, so that's not the best recommendation. *Convertible bonds* have a lower amount of income than comparable non-convertible bonds because of the conversion feature, so that won't work, either. *Mortgage bonds* may work because they provide income once every six months in the form of interest payments, and they're relatively safe because they're secured by property owned by the issuer. *Income (adjustment) bonds* are definitely out because they're issued by corporations in bankruptcy (reorganization) and are extremely risky. Therefore, out of the choices listed, *mortgage bonds* is the best recommendation.

129. C. III, II, I

Mortgage bonds are secured corporate bonds that use property owned by the issuer as collateral. The safest is the *prior lien bonds,* although they're rarely issued. Prior lien bonds allow the issuer to sell new mortgage bonds with a higher standing than the existing mortgage bonds. In the event of default, prior lien bondholders are first in line. Next safest is the *closed-end mortgage bonds*. With closed-end mortgage bonds, the trust indenture doesn't allow the issuer to issue any new mortgage bonds of the same class. The riskiest option is the *open-end mortgage bonds,* which allow the issuer to issue new bonds by using the same property as collateral, and all open-end bondholders have equal standing in the event of bankruptcy.

130. A. 4.19%

The coupon rate represents the annual rate of interest. In this case, the coupon rate is 4.25 percent, which means that the investor will receive $42.50 (4.25 percent of $1,000 par) per year broken down into two semiannual payments.

U.S. government bonds, such as Treasury bonds (T-bonds), are quoted in 32nds, not decimals, so pay close attention to the security in the question.

The market price of the bond is

$$101.16 = 101\frac{16}{32} = 101.50\% \text{ of } \$1{,}000 \text{ par} = \$1{,}015.00$$

Finally, to determine the current yield, use the following formula:

$$\text{Current yield on a bond} = \frac{\text{Annual interest}}{\text{Market price}}$$
$$= \frac{\$42.50}{\$1{,}015.00}$$
$$= 0.0419, \text{ or } 4.19\%$$

131. B. a premium

The easiest way for you to deal with questions like this is to set up a seesaw, like the following. The yields on the seesaw are always going to be in the same position. You just have to remember that higher numbers are raised up higher on the seesaw.

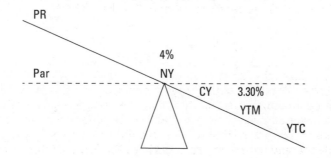

Note: PR = price of the bond, NY = nominal yield (coupon rate), CY = current yield, YTM = yield to maturity (basis), and YTC = yield to call.

The dashed line represents a bond trading at par value (normally $1,000). The NY is 4 percent, and the YTM is 3.30 percent. Because 3.30 percent is lower than 4 percent, you have to lower the right side of the seesaw. After you do this, the left side raises, and you can see that the bond would be trading at a premium to par value.

132. **A. 4.76%**

To find the yield, use this formula:

$$\frac{\text{Annual interest} + \text{Annual accretion or} - \text{Annual amortization}}{(\text{Purchase price} + \text{par})/2}$$

The annual interest is $60 because it has a 6 percent coupon rate, and par value is $1,000 (6 percent of $1,000 = $60). Because this bond was purchased at a premium, you have to determine the annual amortization by taking the difference between the purchase price and par value and dividing it by the ten years until maturity.

$$\frac{\$100}{10 \text{ years until maturity}} = \$10 \text{ per year amortization}$$

Now plug in the numbers to calculate the yield:

$$\frac{\$60 - \$10}{(\$1,100 + \$1,000)/2} = \frac{\$50}{\$1,050} = 0.0476, \text{ or } 4.76\%$$

133. **C. 4.35%**

To determine the current yield of a bond, you have to divide the annual interest by the market price. The annual interest is $40 (4 percent × $1,000 par), and the market price is $920 (92 percent × $1,000 par):

$$\text{Current yield} = \frac{\text{Annual interest}}{\text{Market price}}$$
$$= \frac{\$40}{\$920}$$
$$= 0.0435, \text{ or } 4.35\%$$

134. **D. I, II, and IV**

The best way to visualize a bond selling at a discount and how it affects the yields is by setting up a seesaw, like the following. Because the bond is selling at a discount, the price is below par value, so the left side of the seesaw has to be lowered.

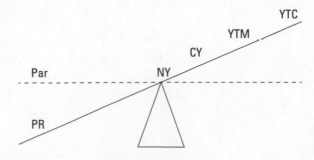

With the left side lowered, you can see that the market price (PR) is below par value, the current yield (CY) is greater than the coupon rate (NY = nominal yield), and the yield to maturity (YTM) is greater than the current yield. However, because rates and prices have an inverse relationship, if interest rates declined, outstanding bond prices would rise above par, not below par.

135. **C. $10,137.50**

The first thing you have to do is convert the fraction to a decimal. So a bond trading at 101⅜ would convert to a bond trading at 101.375 (3/8 = 0.375). Next, you have to remember that these $1,000 par value bonds aren't actually trading at 101.375. The 101.375 is a percentage of par, so the bonds are actually trading at (101.375%)($1,000 par) = $1,013.75.

Next, because the investor is purchasing ten of these bonds, you have to multiply your answer by 10: ($1,013.75)(10 bonds) = $10,137.50.

136. **A. I and III**

One point on a bond equals 1 percent ($10 on a $1,000 par bond). A basis point is 1/100 of a point, or 10 cents. In this case, because the bond increased by 50 basis points (1/2 a point), it increased by 0.50 percent or $5.

137. **B. $1,020**

This question has a lot of information that you don't need to come up with an answer. All you need to know is that you're working with a 4 percent bond and that your client held it until maturity. The fact that it was yielding 5 percent and that it's a convertible bond aren't relevant to the question. When investors hold a bond until maturity, they receive par value (usually $1,000). However, if the bond is paying interest, holders also receive their last coupon payment at maturity. It's a 4 percent bond, so investors will receive $40 per year interest ($4 percent of $1,000 par) broken down into two $20 semiannual payments. But you need to know what your client will receive, so you add the par value to the interest: $1,000 par value + $20 interest = $1,020.

138. **A. The yield to maturity is higher than the yield to call.**

This investor purchased the bond at a premium, for a price of $1,020 (102 percent of $1,000 par). The best way for you to visualize a bond selling at a premium and how it affects the yields is to set up a seesaw, like the following. Because the bond is selling at a premium, the price is above par value, so the left side of the seesaw has to be raised.

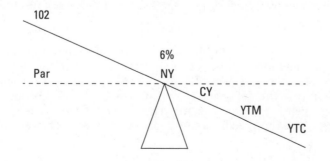

With a bond trading at a premium, the nominal yield (NY, or coupon rate) is the highest yield, the next highest is the current yield (CY), followed by the yield to maturity (YTM; basis), and the lowest is the yield to call (YTC). So the only answer choice that's true is Choice (A), which says that the yield to maturity is higher than the yield to call.

139. **D. 7.0%**

Determining the yield to call is somewhat similar to determining the yield to maturity. However, you need to use the call price rather than the maturity price. Use this formula to find the yield to call (YTC):

$$\frac{\text{Annual interest} + \text{Annual accretion to the call date}}{(\text{Purchase price} + \text{Call price})/2}$$

The annual interest is $50 because it has a 5 percent coupon rate, and par value is $1,000 (5 percent of $1,000 = $50). This bond was purchased at $950 (95 percent of $1,000 par) and was called at $1,050 in five years for a total accretion to the call date of $100. The bond price will increase from $950 to $1,050 in five years.

Take the $100 difference ($1,050 − $950) and divide it by five years to determine the yearly accretion:

$$\frac{\$100}{5\text{ years}} = \$20 \text{ per year accretion until the call date}$$

Finally, add the $50 annual interest plus the $20 per year accretion and divide it by the average price to get the yield to call: $\frac{\$50 + \$20}{(\$950 + \$1,050)/2} = \frac{\$70}{\$1,000} = 0.07$, or 7.0%.

140. **B. $20.00**

To determine the annual interest, you have to multiply the coupon rate (4 percent) by par value ($1,000): $(4\%)(\$1,000) = \$40$ annual interest.

Because bonds pay interest semiannually (twice a year), the investor will get paid $20 ($40/2) every six months.

141. **D. I, II, III, and IV**

The liquidity (marketability) of a bond depends on many factors, including the rating (the higher, the more liquid), the coupon rate (the higher, the more liquid), the maturity (the shorter, the higher the liquidity), call features (non-callable bonds are more liquid), the current market value (the lower, the more liquid), and the issuer (the more well known, the more liquid).

142. **B. I and III**

The indenture of a bond is a legal contract between the issuer and the bondholder. The indenture includes items such as the nominal yield (coupon rate), the maturity date, collateral backing the bond (if any), coupon payment dates, and callable and convertible features. The rating and the yield to maturity can't be included in the indenture because neither of them is static. The rating changes if the issuer's financial condition changes, and the yield to maturity changes when the market value changes.

143. **D. the amount that the issuer must pay to investors for calling its bonds early**

A call premium is the amount that the issuer must pay to investors for calling its bonds early. When a corporation issues callable bonds, it typically has to pay a call premium (an amount over par value) as a disincentive for calling its bonds early. The issuer, not the investor, is the one that decides when the bonds are called.

144. **C. long coupon**

You can assume that bonds pay interest semiannually (once every six months) unless it's a zero-coupon bond. In this case, the first coupon date is 6½ months from the dated date, so the first payment is a long coupon. So investors would receive a little more than their regular six-month coupon payment.

145. **D. nominal yield**

The only yield that could be included on the indenture of a corporate bond is the nominal yield (coupon rate). None of the other choices could be placed on the indenture of a corporate bond because they don't remain fixed. The yield to maturity, yield to call, and current yield change over time and when the market price changes.

146. **B. I and IV**

Liquidity relates to how tradable a security is. Securities with low liquidity are hard to trade and, therefore, aren't desirable for most investors. This question asks for bonds with the least liquidity risk, so the correct answers are *bonds with a high credit rating* and *bonds with a short-term maturity*.

147. **A. IV, III, II, I**

The top four S&P (Standard & Poor's) investment ratings — AAA, AA, A, and BBB — are considered investment grade and have a relatively high degree of safety. Each rating can be broken down even further by adding plusses and minuses. For example, in the AA rating, you'd have from highest to lowest: AA+, AA, AA–. So the first thing you need to look at is the letter rating and then whether it has any plusses or minuses. Out of the choices listed, AAA is the highest, AA is the next highest, AA– is the one after that, and A+ is the lowest. You can assume for test purposes that the lower the rating, the higher the yield (more risk = more reward).

148. **D. little call protection**

This is one of those questions where you have to look at things from a corporation's point of view rather than an investor's point of view. From a corporation's point of view, having to pay a high coupon rate, having a put feature, or having to pay a high call premium aren't desirable. However, having little call protection on callable bonds that it issued would be the best. Call protection has to do with the number of years an issuer has to wait before calling its bonds.

149. **D. IV only**

Looking at it from the issuer's point of view, the issuer will most likely refund the issue that will cost it the most money over the life of the issue. When selecting the correct answer, the first thing that an issuer would look at is the coupon rate (highest coupon first), next would be the call premium (lowest call premium first), after that, the call date (earliest call date first), and last, the maturity (longest maturity first). Out of the choices given, the one that the issuer would refund first would be Statement IV.

150. **A. default risk**

Moody's, Standard & Poor's, and Fitch rate the likelihood of default of bond issuers. The likelihood of default relates to the chances that investors won't receive their expected interest payments or par value at maturity.

151. **C. I, II, and IV**

The Trust Indenture Act of 1939 regulates all corporate bond issues exceeding $5 million. The only corporate bonds listed are equipment trust bonds. U.S. government T-bonds, municipal general obligation (GO) bonds, and municipal revenue bonds are exempt from the Trust Indenture Act of 1939.

152. **A. zero-coupon bonds**

Out of the choices listed, the best answer is *zero-coupon bonds*. Mrs. Jones is planning for a future event (her child's college tuition). Zero-coupon bonds are purchased at a deep discount from par (for example, $600 per bond), and the bonds mature at $1,000 par and don't pay interest along the way. This type of bond allows investors to invest a smaller amount of money now in return for a larger amount of money at maturity.

153. **C. I, II, and III**

The top four Moody's ratings — Aaa, Aa, A, Baa — are considered investment grade, and everything Ba and below are considered speculative or "junk" bonds. Remember, S&P, Moody's, and Fitch rate the creditworthiness of debt securities.

154. **B. income bonds**

The one you need to stay away from is income (adjustment) bonds. Income bonds are typically issued by failing businesses (bankruptcy or reorganization). As such, the bondholders receive only the interest and principal if the issuer has enough money to pay it. Income bonds are extremely risky but if the company turns around, the reward can be high. Income bonds are typically issued at a deep discount. All of the other answer choices would be proper recommendations for an investor who is risk-averse.

155. **C. serial**

Term bonds are all issued at one time and all mature at one time, so they typically have a sinking fund available to pay off the debt. Serial bonds have one issue date, but an equal amount of bonds mature each year sometime in the future (such as 20 percent on year 26, 20 percent on year 27, 20 percent on year 28, 20 percent on year 29, and 20 percent on year 30). Balloon issues are issued at the same time and mature in subsequent years like serial bonds but have a balloon payment at the end (such as 10 percent on year 26, 10 percent on year 27, 10 percent on year 28, 10 percent on year 29, and 60 percent on year 30). Series bonds are kind of the opposite of serial bonds because they're issued on different dates but all mature on the same date.

156. **D. $1,120**

The first step you have to take with convertible bond questions is to get the shares. To determine how many shares the bond is convertible into, use the following formula:

$$\text{Conversion ratio} = \frac{\text{Par}}{\text{Conversion price}}$$
$$= \frac{\$1,000}{\$25}$$
$$= 40 \text{ shares}$$

To determine the parity price of the stock, multiply the number of shares by the market price of the stock: (40 shares)($28) = $1,120.

157. **A. I and III**

First, get the shares that the bond is convertible into, using the following formula:

$$\text{Conversion ratio} = \frac{\text{Par}}{\text{Conversion price}}$$
$$= \frac{\$1,000}{\$40}$$
$$= 25 \text{ shares}$$

To determine the parity price of the stock, multiply the number of shares by the market price of the stock: (20 shares)($42) = $840.

The bond is trading for $830 (83 percent of $1,000 par), and it's convertible into $840 worth of stock. This means that the bonds are trading below parity, and converting the bonds would be profitable.

158. **B. $1,000**

When holding a bond until maturity, an investor will receive par value. Assume par value is $1,000 unless stated differently in the question.

159. **A. a forced conversion**

In this situation, you have to determine which would be most profitable for your client. The bond is being called at $1,040 (104 percent of $1,000 par) or is convertible into common stock valuing $1,140 ($28.50 × 40 shares). In this case, it'd make much more sense for investors to convert because they'd be losing $100 ($1,140 − $1,040) by accepting the call and not converting. Situations like this are called *forced conversions*. Corporations may also issue reverse convertible bonds that gives them the opportunity to convert the bonds at a predetermined date.

160.   A. Allow the bond to be called.

The best way to determine what's best for the investor is to determine the amount of money he'll receive for the call, for selling the bond in the market, and for converting the bond. Whichever is highest is the best for the investor.

> Allowing the bond to be called: $1,020 (102 percent of $1,000 par)
>
> Selling the bond in the market: $980 (98 percent of $1,000 par)
>
> Converting the bond and selling the stock: $1,000 (25 shares × $40)

For an investor holding the convertible bond, the best alternative is to allow the bond to be called because the investor will receive $1,020, which is higher than the other two alternatives.

161.   D. 25

As with some of the questions you'll see on the real Series 7 exam, this question includes information that isn't necessary to answer the question. Don't let the test writers take you on a ride that you don't need to be on. Just focus on the information you need to answer the question.

The conversion ratio is the amount of shares a convertible bond (or stock) is convertible into. You can use the following formula:

$$\text{Conversion ratio} = \frac{\text{Par}}{\text{Conversion price}}$$
$$= \frac{\$1,000}{\$40}$$
$$= 25 \text{ shares}$$

In this case, assuming that the par value for the bonds is $1,000, an investor would receive 25 shares of TUV's common stock if converting one of his bonds.

162.   C. $17.64

When dealing with convertible bond questions, you need to determine the amount of shares the bond is convertible into. In this case, the bond is convertible at $20, which gives you the following equation:

$$\text{Conversion ratio} = \frac{\text{Par}}{\text{Conversion price}}$$
$$= \frac{\$1,000}{\$20}$$
$$= 50 \text{ shares}$$

Next, to determine parity price, you have to divide the market price (98 percent of $1,000 par, or $980) of the bond by the conversion ratio:

$$\frac{\$980}{50 \text{ shares}} = \$19.60$$

So if parity price of the stock is $19.60, the stock has to be at $17.64 ($19.60 − $1.96) to be at 10 percent below parity.

163. **B. convertible bonds**

It's important for holders of convertible securities to have an anti-dilution clause (anti-dilutive covenant) to protect the conversion rights. For example, say that you have a bond that's convertible into 20 shares of common stock. If the issuer splits its stock 2 for 1, you wouldn't be happy having your bond convertible into 20 shares of stock worth half as much. So with an anti-dilution clause, in this case, if the issuer splits its stock 2 for 1, you'd receive 40 shares of stock (2 for 1).

164. **C. II and III**

When a corporation declares a stock dividend, investors receive more shares at a lower market price.

When the corporation lowers the market price due to the stock dividend, it also lowers the conversion price. If the conversion price decreases, the conversion ratio (the amount of shares the bond is convertible into) increases.

165. **A. II, III, and IV**

The keyword to this question is *farm*. The Federal Farm Credit System is comprised of the Federal Intermediate Credit Banks (FICB), Bank for Cooperatives (COOPs), and Federal Land Banks (FLBs). These institutions give loans to farmers, not to homeowners, as in Statement I.

166. **B. I, II, and III**

This is an *except* question, so you're looking for the false answer. Treasury bills (T-bills)) are short-term U.S. government debt securities. T-bills have initial maturities of one month, three months, six months, and one year and are sold in increments of $100. T-bills are sold at a discount and don't make semiannual interest payments. Because T-bills are short term, they're not callable. The one true statement is that they're traded on a discount yield basis because they're quoted in yields, not prices.

167. **D. $10,037.50**

Government notes and bonds are quoted in 32nds. Therefore, a quote of 100-12 means $100\frac{12}{32}$, which translates to 100.375 (12/32 = 0.375). Next, you have to move the decimal point over one position to the right because bonds are quoted as a percentage of $1,000 par. So the price of each bond is $1,003.75, and because the investor purchased ten, the overall cost is ($1003.75)(10 bonds) = $10,037.50.

168. **B. Treasury bill**

Typically, when you're looking at the bid and ask prices, the number on the left is smaller than the number on the right. However, in this case, the number on the left is larger. That means that this has to be the quote for a Treasury bill (T-bill). T-bills are quoted on a discount yield basis where the bid is higher than the ask. If the yields were converted to prices, you'd see that the number on the left would be lower than the one on the right, just like other securities.

169. **C. between 10 and 30 years**

Treasury bonds (T-bonds) have the longest maturity and have an initial maturity of anywhere between 10 and 30 years.

170. **A. I and II**

Ginnie Maes (GNMAs) are mortgage-backed securities issued by the U.S. government and are considered safer investments than Freddie Macs (FHLMCs). GNMAs pay interest monthly, and the interest is taxed on all levels (federal, state, and local). The minimum investment for GNMAs is $25,000.

171. **D. ten years**

Treasury securities have the following maximum maturities:

T-bills: 1 year

T-notes: 10 years

T-bonds: 30 years

T-STRIPS: 30 years

172. **C. investment grade bonds**

Out of the choices listed, the safest investment is *investment grade bonds*. For the most part, people who hold investment grade bonds receive par value at maturity, no matter whether the market is up or down. *Blue chip stocks* are stocks of well-established companies, but the stock is still subject to market fluctuation. *Warrants* and *call options* are the riskiest of the choices because investors have a higher likelihood of losing all money invested.

173. **D. $1,027.50**

Remember, you always buy at the ask (offer) price and sell at the bid price. The ask price in this case is $102.24. Because this is a Treasury bond (T-bond), it's quoted in 32nds. Therefore, 102.24 is actually $102\frac{24}{32}$. To get this into a decimal, divide the fraction 24 by 32:

$$102\frac{24}{32} = 102.75$$

This means that the bonds are selling for 102.75, or 102.75 percent of $1,000, which gives you a purchase price of (102.75%)($1,000 par) = $1,027.50.

174. **B. I, II, and IV**

This question is a little tricky. The keyword to this question is *earn*. Although holders of Treasury bills and Treasury STRIPS don't receive interest payments, they do receive interest. Treasury bills and Treasury STRIPS are issued at a discount and mature at par value, and that difference is considered interest. Treasury bondholders receive interest payments once every six months. However, Treasury stock is stock that was issued and subsequently repurchased by issuing corporation. Stockholders never receive interest but sometimes receive dividends.

175. **C. III, I, II**

Treasury bills are issued with maturities of one month, three months, six months, and one year. Treasury notes are issued with maturities of more than one year to ten years. Treasury bonds are issued with maturities of 10 years to 30 years.

176. **C. They are sold at face value.**

Series EE savings bonds are the type of bonds that many grandparents used to give to their grandchildren as a Christmas or birthday present. EE bonds have a minimum face value of $25 and earn a fixed rate of interest. Currently, people can't buy paper versions of EE bonds, and they're no longer issued at a discount. Because they're issued by the U.S. government, default risk is virtually nonexistent. The interest received from these bonds is subject to federal tax but exempt from state and local tax.

177. **A. book entry**

The U.S. government has issued securities in book-entry form since the mid-1980s. Book-entry securities are sold without delivering a certificate. A central agency keeps the ownership records, and investors receive a receipt representing the securities owned.

178. **C. II and III**

Treasury STRIPS (T-STRIPS) are purchased at a discount and mature at par value. As such, the principal and interest aren't received until maturity. However, holders must pay taxes on the accretion (the difference between the previous year's cost basis and current year's cost basis) every year.

179. **A. a guaranteed profit**

Treasury inflation-protected securities (TIPS) are marketable U.S. government securities with 5-, 10-, and 30-year maturities. TIPs pay interest semiannually at a fixed rate tied to the principal. Because the principal of the bond is tied to the Consumer Price Index (CPI), the interest payments may rise or fall depending on whether the economy is in a period of inflation or deflation. At maturity, holders receive the greater of the original face value or the adjusted principal. Even though these are low-risk securities, investors aren't guaranteed a profit because they may end up being sold at a lower price than the investor's cost basis.

180. **D. I, II, III, and IV**

All of the choices listed are U.S. government securities. U.S. government securities include Treasury bills (T-bills), Treasury notes (T-notes), Treasury bonds (T-bonds), Treasury STRIPS (T-STRIPS), Treasury inflation-protected securities (TIPS), floating rate notes (FRNs), EE/E savings bonds, HH/H savings bonds (no longer available), and I savings bonds.

181. **C. I bonds**

Series EE bonds, Series HH bonds, and Series I bonds are non-marketable, but only Series I bonds have an adjustable interest rate, which is made up of a fixed interest rate plus an inflation rate that's tied to the Consumer Price Index (CPI). The interest is accrued over the life of the bond and is paid when the bond is redeemed. Therefore, *I bonds* is the best recommendation for your client.

182. **B. bankers' acceptance**

Bankers' acceptances (BAs) are money market instruments used to provide short-term financing for importers and exporters. BAs trade at a discount and mature at face value.

183. **C. $100,000**

Negotiable certificates of deposit (CDs) aren't appropriate investments for smaller investors. The minimum denomination is $100,000, and they're often traded in blocks of $1 million. Because of the high minimum denomination, negotiable CDs are typically purchased and traded only by institutional investors.

184. **A. short-term debt**

Money market instruments are short-term debt securities that typically have maturities of one year or less.

185. **B. Your broker-dealer sold securities to the customer with an agreement to buy them back at a predetermined date.**

Repurchase agreements (repos) are money market instruments that involve using U.S. government securities as collateral. In this case, the broker-dealer sold the U.S. government securities to the large institutional investor with an agreement to buy them back at a higher price at a later date (often the following day). These are securitized loans using the U.S. government securities as collateral. The difference between the initial selling price and the repurchase price represents interest paid. Choice (A) is called a reverse repurchase agreement (reverse repo).

186. **B. The interest rate is determined from the discount rate set by the FRB.**

Eurodollar deposits are dollar-denominated deposits held in banks outside of the United States; thus, the risk and interest paid is higher, but the rate has nothing to do with the Federal Reserve Board (FRB). Investors making Eurodollar deposits are attempting to take advantage of the higher interest rates.

187. **D. 270 days**

Corporate commercial paper is a money market instrument. To be exempt from the Securities and Exchange Commission (SEC) registration, commercial paper has a maximum expiration of 270 days.

188. **C. jumbo CDs**

The only money market instrument (short-term debt security) that trades with accrued interest is certificates of deposit (CDs). All the other money market instruments are issued at a discount and mature at par value. Holders of CDs receive interest payments; therefore, investors purchasing CDs are required to pay the seller any accrued interest due.

189. **A. I, III, and IV**

Corporate commercial paper matures in 270 days or less and is exempt from the Securities and Exchange Commission (SEC) registration. It's issued at a discount and matures at par value and, therefore, trades without accrued interest. Unlike some other corporate debt securities, commercial paper isn't backed by the issuer's assets.

190. **D. 50 days**

Because the question refers to a new municipal bond, no previous coupon date exists, so you need to use the dated date. The dated date is the first day a bond starts accruing interest. Municipal bonds settle in three business days. As such, this transaction settled on February 21 (2/21). So subtract the previous dated date of January 1 (1/1) from that:

$$
\begin{array}{ccc}
2 & / & 21 \\
-\ 1 & / & 1 \\
\hline
\end{array}
$$
1 month and 20 days

Corporate and municipal bonds assume 30-day months so you end up with $30 + 20 = 50$ days.

191. **D. 88 days**

Accrued interest is owed when a bond is purchased in between coupon dates. Corporate bonds settle in three business days so the settlement date is Thursday, May 13 (5/13). From that, you need to subtract the previous coupon date of February 15 (2/15):

$$
\begin{array}{ccc}
5 & / & 13 \\
-\ 2 & / & 15 \\
\hline
\end{array}
$$
3 months and −2 days

Corporate and municipal bonds assume 30-day months, so you end up with 90 days (3 months × 30 days) less 2 days for a total of 88 days.

192. **A. from the previous coupon date up to but not including the settlement date**

When purchasing a bond in between coupon dates, the purchaser owes the seller accrued interest. Typically, the question will ask you to determine the amount of days of accrued interest as you see in some of the other questions. However, if you're asked a question similar to this one, the standard answer is *Accrued interest is calculated from the previous coupon date up to but not including the settlement date.*

193. **C. the date on which a bond begins accruing interest**

The dated date is the date on which bonds start accruing interest. When determining the amount of days of accrued interest for new bonds, you start counting from the dated date because there's no previous coupon date.

194. **B. I and IV**

Corporate and municipal securities calculate accrued interest assuming 30-day months and a 360-day year. However, U.S. government securities calculate accrued interest using actual days per month and actual days per year (normally 365).

195. **D. $11.85**

This is definitely a difficult question. Corporate and municipal bonds calculate accrued interest using 30-day months and 360-day years. The first thing you must determine is the settlement date. Corporate and municipal bonds settle in three business days from the trade date, so the settlement date is Friday, March 20 (3/20). Next, you have to subtract the previous coupon date of January 1 (1/1).

$$\begin{array}{ccc} 3 & / & 20 \\ -\ 1 & / & 1 \\ \hline \end{array}$$
2 months and 19 days

Then, multiply the 2 months by 30 days to get a total of 60 days. Add the 19 days, and you have a total of 60 + 19 = 79 days.

Now you have to figure out the dollar amount. This bond has a 5 percent coupon rate, so it pays $54 per year in interest (5.4 percent of $1,000 par). Because corporate bonds use a 360-day year, you have to divide $54 by 360 days to determine the amount of accrued interest per day:

$$\frac{\$54}{360 \text{ days}} = \$0.15 \text{ per day accrued interest}$$

The last step is to multiply the $0.15 per day accrued interest by the 79 days of accrued interest owed: ($0.15)(79 days) = $11.85.

You're more likely to get questions asking you to determine the amount of days of accrued interest, but you do stand a chance of getting one of these monsters.

196. **C. 97 days**

This question is a little more difficult because you're calculating the days of accrued interest for a U.S. government bond and not a municipal or corporate bond. U.S. government bonds settle in one business day rather than three and calculate accrued interest, using actual days per month instead of 30-day months. So the first thing you need to do is get the settlement date of Friday, October 20 (10/20), and subtract the previous coupon date of July 15 (7/15).

$$\begin{array}{ccc} 10 & / & 20 \\ -\ 7 & / & 15 \\ \hline \end{array}$$
3 months and 5 days

The best way to start is by assuming 30-day months and then adding additional days where needed. So you have 90 days (3 months × 30 days) plus 5 days for a total of 95 days. Next, because you're going through the end of July, August, and September, you have to add extra days for the months that have more than 30 days. In this case, July and August have 31 days, so you need to add 2 extra days:

$$90 \text{ days} + 5 \text{ days} + 2 \text{ extra days (July and August)} = 97 \text{ days}$$

197. D. income bonds

Income (adjustment) bonds are issued by corporations in bankruptcy (reorganization). These bonds are typically sold at a deep discount, and holders won't receive interest unless the issuing corporation becomes popular. Therefore, income bonds typically trade flat (without accrued interest).

198. A. certificates of deposit

Because collateralized mortgage obligations (CMOs) are such unique investments, they may be compared only to other CMOs.

199. B. they are always backed by mortgages

Collateralized debt obligations (CDOs) are asset-backed securities secured by loans, such as credit cards, auto loans, and rarely mortgages. The assets backing the CDOs aren't very liquid on their own, so they have been pooled together and repackaged to make them available to investors. As with CMOs, CDOs are broken down into tranches with varying degrees of risk and varying maturities.

200. A. I and II

Because collateralized mortgage obligations (CMOs) are backed by U.S. government and U.S. government agency mortgages, they typically have a Standard & Poor's (S&P) rating of AAA or AA.

201. D. PAC

The planned amortization class (PAC) tranche is considered the safest because a large portion of the prepayment risk and extension risk associated with collateralized mortgage obligations (CMOs) is absorbed by a companion tranche. The targeted amortization class (TAC) tranche isn't quite as safe as the PAC tranche because it's more subject to prepayment and extension risk. A companion tranche absorbs the prepayment and extension risk associated with PAC and TAC tranches and is risky because the average life varies greatly with interest rate changes. A Z-tranche is the most volatile of the CMO tranches because investors receive no payments until all the CMO tranches are retired.

202. D. II, III, and IV

Collateralized debt obligations (CDOs) are asset-backed securities similar to collateralized mortgage obligations (CMOs). However, the main difference is that CMOs are backed by mortgages, and CDOs are backed by other debt, such as credit cards and auto loans. CDOs add liquidity to the loan market. However, the individual loans aren't liquid because they include loans of small amounts. Therefore, CDOs are more liquid than the individual loans on their own.

203. **C. SLMA**

Collateralized mortgage obligations (CMOs) diversify their investments in mortgages issued by Ginnie Mae (GNMA), Fannie Mae (FNMA), and Freddie Mac (FNMA). Sallie Mae (SLMA) is an agency that issues bonds to fund student loans and can't be part of a CMO.

204. **B. $1,000**

Collateralized mortgage obligations (CMOs) have a minimum denomination of $1,000.

205. **C. II and III**

The average maturity on collateralized mortgage obligations (CMOs) depends highly on mortgage interest rates. If interest rates fall, more homeowners will refinance to take advantage of the lower rates, and the amount of prepayments will increase. If interest rates rise, homeowners won't refinance, and the amount of prepayments will decrease.

206. **D. they are subject to prepayment and extension risk**

Collateralized mortgage obligations (CMOs) are subject to prepayment and extension risk depending on the amount of people refinancing or moving. Prepayment risk and extension risk are highly tied to prevailing mortgage interest rates. CMOs aren't guaranteed by the U.S. government, they carry varying amounts of risk, and they're taxable on all levels.

207. **C. They pay interest semiannually.**

Unlike a majority of other debt securities, interest on Ginnie Maes (GNMAs) is paid monthly just like people pay their mortgages. Interest is not paid semiannually.

208. **A. PAC**

Planned amortization class (PAC) and targeted amortization class (TAC) tranches are supported by companion tranches. Companion tranches absorb the prepayment risk associated with collateralized mortgage obligations (CMOs).

209. **B. II, III, and IV**

General obligation (GO) bonds are issued to fund non-revenue-producing facilities and are backed by the taxing power of the municipality. Because the people living in the municipality will be paying additional taxes to back the bonds, they do need voter approval. Also, GO bonds are subject to a debt ceiling, which is the maximum amount of money that a municipality may borrow to meet its needs.

210. **A. because they are usually thin issues**

Remember, when investors sell a security short, they're borrowing securities for immediate sale in the market. Short sellers must cover their short positions by purchasing the securities in the market so that they can be returned to the lender. The problem with selling any municipal securities short is that typically they're thin issues and don't have national interest. As such, there are no good securities to sell short because it would likely be difficult for investors to cover their short positions.

211. **C. state governments**

States don't collect property taxes. Local governments, such as school districts, counties, and towns, collect property taxes.

212. **C. long-term**

Because Uriah believes that interest rates are going to drop over the next 20 to 30 years, he should lock in at a high interest rate right now. Buying long-term bonds makes sense for Uriah because he believes that the rates are high right now, and if interest rates drop like he expects them to, he'd be locking in a high rate for a long period of time. Additionally, if interest rates drop, the price of his bonds will increase, because interest rates and outstanding bond prices have an inverse relationship.

213. **D. refunding**

Refunding is when an issuer issues new bonds and uses the proceeds to call outstanding bonds. *Pre-refunding* or *advance refunding* is when an issuer issues new bonds a long time prior to the call date of existing bonds to take advantage of low interest rates. The money received is held in an escrow account and invested in U.S. government securities until the existing bonds can be called. Because the money is there to pay off the bondholders, pre-refunded bonds are typically rated AAA.

214. **C. the call feature makes the bonds more marketable**

Looking at Choices (A) and (C), you'll notice that they directly oppose each other, so the chances are extremely high that one of those is the correct answer. You're looking for the answer that's the exception in this case, so it has to be Choice (C). The call feature of a bond doesn't make the bond more marketable; it makes it less marketable, therefore, the issuers would have to pay higher coupon rates to attract investors.

215. **A. property tax**

The largest backing for municipal general obligation (GO) bonds is property taxes. The credit rating of GO bonds is highly dependent on the municipality's tax collection record, the number of people living in the municipality, property values, whether it's a limited tax GO bond or unlimited tax GO bond, and so on. Unlike revenue bonds, GO bonds typically require voter approval prior to being issued.

216.   **B. I and II**

General obligation (GO) bonds require voter approval prior to being issued because they're mostly backed by taxes on people living in the municipality. GO bonds are issued to fund non-revenue-producing facilities, such as schools and jails. A municipality would issue revenue bonds to fund revenue-producing projects, such as toll roads and airports. Revenue bonds are backed by users, not taxes.

217.   **C. $3,290**

Ad valorem (property) taxes are the largest source of backing for general obligation (GO) bonds. They're based on the assessed property value, not the market value. These taxes are based on mills (0.001). To determine the ad valorem tax, multiply the assessed property value by 0.001 and then multiply by the tax rate in mills (14):

$$(\$235,000)(0.001)(14) = \$3,290$$

218.   **B. I and III**

Municipal general obligation (GO) bonds and double-barreled bonds are backed by the full faith and credit and taxing power of the municipal issuer. Double-barreled bonds are backed by a revenue-producing facility, and, if the revenues are insufficient to be able to pay the principal and interest on the bonds, they're backed by the municipality.

219.   **C. property taxes**

Property taxes (ad valorem taxes) are the largest source of funding for municipal general obligation (GO) bonds, not revenue bonds.

220.   **D. I, II, and IV**

Revenue bonds are backed by the revenue-producing facility and are supposed to be self-sustaining. Raising money by issuing revenue bonds to build toll roads, airports, and sports stadiums all make sense because the revenues from these projects would be used to pay off bondholders. However, if a municipality wanted to build a new library, it would issue GO bonds because libraries don't make enough money to be self-sustaining.

221.   **D. double-barreled bonds**

Double-barreled bonds are kind of a combination of revenue and general obligation bonds. Revenue bonds are typically 100 percent supported by revenues generated by the revenue-producing facility. If it's a double-barreled bond and if the revenues aren't high enough to pay interest and/or principal on the bonds, the revenues are supplemented with municipal taxes.

222.   **B. I, III, and IV**

The indenture of a revenue bond would include items such as the maturity date, interest payment dates, the coupon rate, the legal opinion, covenants, the flow of funds, and so on. However, anything that's subject to change, such as the rating, wouldn't be placed on the indenture of a bond.

223. **A. the maturity date of the issue will typically exceed the useful life of the facility backing the bonds**

In this case, you need to find the exception. The maturity of revenue bonds may be 25 to 30 years, but the facility being built by the income received from the revenue bond issue is usually expected to last a long time, if not a lifetime. Revenue bonds may be issued by interstate authorities, such as tolls, and the interest and principal on the bonds is paid from revenue received from the facility backing the bonds. In addition, revenue bonds aren't subject to a debt ceiling (maximum tax that can be imposed on people living in the municipality); general obligation bonds are.

224. **A. property taxes**

Property taxes are the largest source of backing for general obligation (GO) bonds, not revenue bonds. Revenue bonds are self-supporting and backed by user fees of the revenue-producing project or facility.

225. **B. backed by excise taxes**

Special tax bonds are a type of municipal bond that's funded (backed) by taxes on certain items (excise taxes). Excise taxes are taxes on nonessential goods, such as gasoline, alcohol, and tobacco.

226. **C. They are backed by a corporation.**

An industrial development revenue (IDR) bond is a municipal bond that's backed by a private company. The municipality uses the lease payments that the private company makes to pay principal and interest on the bonds. Therefore, IDRs are the riskiest municipal bonds.

227. **A. They are backed by charges on the benefitted property.**

Special assessment bonds are types of municipal bonds that are backed by taxes on the properties that benefit. For example, say that people who live a few blocks from you got all new streetlights and sidewalks. Why should you pay additional taxes to pay for their streetlights and sidewalks? The answer is, you shouldn't, and that's where special assessment bonds come into play. In this case, just the properties that benefit will be taxed at a higher level, while yours stays the same.

228. **B. direct payment BABs**

Direct payment BABs (build America bonds) are bonds issued to fund infrastructure projects, such as bridges, roads, and tunnels, where municipalities receive tax credits from the U.S. government of 35 percent of interest paid to investors. Because municipality is receiving a tax credit, it can issue the bonds with higher coupon rates than comparable bonds.

229. **D. I and IV**

A double-barreled bond is a combination of revenue and general obligation (GO) bonds. If the revenues from the revenue-producing facility fall short, the bonds will be backed by the full faith and credit (taxing power) of the municipality.

230. **A. BABs**

BABs (build America bonds) are taxable municipal bonds issued to raise money for infrastructure projects, such as bridges, tunnels, and roads. There are two types of BABs: *tax credit BABs,* where holders receive tax credits from the U.S. Treasury equal to 35 percent of the coupon rate, and *direct payment BABs,* where the issuer receives tax credits from the U.S. Treasury equal to 35 percent of the coupon rate. Direct payment BABs are more commonly issued than tax credit BABs. Therefore, investors would likely receive a higher coupon rate than tax credit BABs.

231. **B. the type of tax that can be used to back the bond issue**

A limited tax general obligation bond (LTGO) is typically backed by a specific tax. As an example, an LTGO may be backed by revenue only from sales taxes and not necessarily property taxes. Therefore, LTGOs are riskier investments and would likely have a higher coupon rate than a regular GO bond.

232. **B. public housing authority bonds**

Public housing authority (PHA) bonds are municipal bonds issued to finance the repair or construction of low-income housing. These bonds are extra safe because even though they're technically municipal bonds, they're guaranteed by the federal government. As with most other municipal bonds, their interest is exempt from federal taxation.

233. **A. they are backed by U.S. government subsidies**

New housing authority (NHA) bonds are also known as public housing authority (PHA) bonds or simply housing authority bonds. NHA bonds are issued to build or repair low-income housing. Besides the rental income, these bonds are considered quite safe because they're backed by a subsidy from the U.S. government and are typically rated AAA.

234. **A. provide short-term financing**

Municipalities issue short-term notes, such as RANs (revenue anticipation notes), BANs (bond anticipation notes), TANs (tax anticipation notes), and CLNs (construction loan notes), to provide interim financing until a permanent long-term bond issue is floated, until tax receipts increase, or until revenue flows in.

235. **B. AONs**

Municipal notes are short-term debt securities issued by municipalities to provide interim financing while waiting for other revenues to come in. Municipal notes include TANs, RANs, TRANs, BANs, CLNs, PNs, and GANs. AON (all-or-none) is an order qualifier, not a type of municipal note.

236. **C. MIG1**

A bond anticipation note (BAN) issued by municipalities is backed by bonds that will be issued. Municipal notes are short term and are rated by Moody's, using the Moody's investment grade (MIG) scale. MIG1 is the best rating available for a municipal note.

237. **D. GOs**

Moody's investment grade (MIG) determines the creditworthiness of municipal notes (short-term municipal bonds). PNs (project notes), TRANs (tax and revenue anticipation notes), and CLNs (construction loan notes) are all types of municipal notes. However, GOs are general obligation bonds issued to provide long-term financing for a municipality and can't have an MIG rating.

238. **B. tax anticipation notes**

The key phrase in this question is *temporary cash flow shortage,* which tells you that the municipality needs to issue short-term debt securities. So you can cross off Choices (C) and (D) because revenue bonds and general obligation (GO) bonds are long term. That leaves you with the *construction loan notes* or *tax anticipation notes.* Because construction wasn't mentioned anywhere in the question, the best answer is *tax anticipation notes* because a municipality is always collecting taxes.

239. **B. municipal notes**

Moody's investment grade (MIG) ratings are applied to municipal notes, such as BANs, RANs, TANs, CLNs, and so on.

240. **D. I, II, III, and IV**

All of the choices listed are municipal notes. Municipal notes are issued to provide short-term financing. The maturity of municipal notes is one year or less.

241. **C. II and III**

Certificates of participation (COPs) are revenue bonds. As such, COPs don't require voter approval to be issued. The holders of COPs receive interest backed by lease or loan payments received from land or facilities owned by the municipality. In the event of issuer default, COP holders could actually foreclose on the asset associated with the bond certificate.

242. **A. reset bonds**

Reset bonds are also known as variable rate demand obligations (VRDOs). These bonds have relatively stable prices because the coupon (interest) rate varies based on other specified interest rates as stated in the indenture. Outstanding bonds with fixed coupon rates see their prices drop when interest rates increase and prices increase when interest rates drop.

243. **A. a moral obligation bond**

A moral obligation bond is a revenue bond in which the state legislature has the authority, but no legal obligation, to provide financial backing for the issuer in the event of default.

244. **B. They have stable prices and a variable coupon rate.**

Auction rate securities (ARS) are long-term variable rate bonds that have stable prices because coupon rates are variable. The coupon rates are reset based on future Dutch auctions of the same issuer that are successful with enough bidding institutions. In theory, the coupon rate of an ARS should move in the same direction as interest rates overall. However, the reset of the coupon rate won't occur if the auction is unsuccessful.

245. **A. The discount is accreted annually and not taxed on the federal level.**

The interest received from municipal bonds is federally tax-free. When investors purchase municipal bonds that were issued at a discount, the difference between the purchase price and par value is also treated as part of the tax-free income. The discount would be accreted over the 30 years until maturity and wouldn't be taxed on the federal level. An investor of these bonds wouldn't be subject to a capital gain or loss unless the bond(s) is sold.

246. **A. I only**

Interest on municipal bonds is federally tax-free, but capital gains on all securities are fully taxed. Interest on U.S. government bonds is state tax-free but is taxed at the federal level. Cash dividends on stock are always taxable.

247. **D. It is exempt from federal, state, and local taxes.**

When purchasing a municipal bond issued within your home state, the interest received is triple tax-free and is exempt from federal, state, and local taxes. Additionally, if you purchase a bond issued by a U.S. territory (such as Puerto Rico, U.S. Virgin Islands, Guam, Samoa, and Washington, D.C.), the interest is also triple tax-free. If you purchase a bond issued by another state, the interest is exempt from federal taxes only.

248. **B. GO bonds**

For Series 7 purposes, you can assume that municipal bonds have the lowest yields of all bonds. You may have chosen T-bonds (Treasury bonds) because they would be the safest, but then you didn't take into consideration the tax advantage of investing in municipal bonds. Municipal GO (general obligation) and municipal revenue bonds have lower yields because the interest investors receive is federally tax-free. Therefore, municipalities are able to offer lower pre-tax yields to investors than with other debt security investments.

249. **B. Tito's tax bracket**

To determine the best investment for Tito, you must do a taxable equivalent yield (TEY) calculation. To accomplish this, you need to know Tito's tax bracket. Remember, the interest received from municipal bond investments is federally tax-free, and investors in higher tax brackets will save more money by investing in municipal bonds when compared to other debt securities. The formula for TEY is as follows:

$$TEY = \frac{\text{Municipal yield}}{100\% - \text{Investor's tax bracket}}$$

250. **A. \$0**

Municipal OID (original issue discount) bonds must be accreted; the discount is treated as part of the client's tax-free interest. Because these municipal discount bonds must be accreted, the cost basis will be equal to the par value and, as a tax consequence, your client will have no losses or gains if the bond is held until maturity.

251. **C. 4% GO bond**

To determine the best after-tax investment for an individual investor, look for municipal bonds. A general obligation (GO) bond is a municipal bond in which the interest received is exempt from federal taxation. To compare all the listed bonds equally, you need to determine the GO bond's taxable equivalent yield (TEY), using this formula:

$$TEY = \frac{\text{Municipal yield}}{100\% - \text{Investor's tax bracket}}$$
$$= \frac{4\%}{100\% - 28\%}$$
$$= \frac{4\%}{72\%}$$
$$= 5.56\%$$

For this investor, the taxable equivalent yield is 5.56 percent, which is higher than all the other bonds listed. The 5.56 percent represents the coupon rate needed on a taxable bond to be equal to the 4 percent that he'd be receiving on the federally tax-free bond.

252. **D. IDRs**

IDRs (industrial development revenue bonds; also IDBs or IRBs) are municipal bonds backed by a corporate lessee. Because they may be non-public purpose bonds, the interest received from these bonds may be subject to alternative minimum tax (AMT).

253. **A. The general obligation bond has a higher after-tax yield.**

Because the interest on municipal general obligation bonds is federally tax-free, you have to work out the taxable equivalent yield (TEY) by using the following formula:

$$TEY = \frac{\text{Municipal yield}}{100\% - \text{Investor's tax bracket}}$$

$$= \frac{5\%}{100\% - 28\%}$$

$$= \frac{5\%}{72\%}$$

$$= 6.94\%$$

For this investor in the 28 percent tax bracket, purchasing a 5 percent municipal bond is equivalent to purchasing a 6.94 percent corporate bond. This means that the 5 percent municipal bond has a higher after-tax yield than the 6 percent corporate bond.

254.

B. 4.14%

As compared to starting with a municipal yield and trying to find the taxable equivalent yield (TEY), in this case, you're starting with a corporate bond and trying to find the municipal equivalent yield (MEY). You can use the following formula to determine the MEY:

$$MEY = (\text{Taxable bond yield})(100\% - \text{Investor's tax bracket})$$

$$= (6\%)(100\% - 31\%)$$

$$= (6\%)(69\%)$$

$$= 4.14\%$$

The MEY is 4.14 percent, which means that for an investor in the 31 percent tax bracket, purchasing a 4.14 percent municipal bond is equivalent to purchasing a 6 percent taxable bond.

255.

A. the interest charges on the debit balance are not tax-deductible

Typically, when an investor purchases securities on margin, the interest charges on the debit balance (DR) are deductible. However, when buying tax-free municipal bonds on margin, the interest charges on the debit balance aren't deductible. Because the interest on these bonds is exempt from federal tax, the IRS won't allow investors to take a deduction when they're receiving no money.

256.

D. industrial development revenue bonds

Industrial development revenue bonds (IDRs, IRBs, or IDBs) are typically issued to fund buildings or acquire factories for private sector companies. As such, the interest income from the IDRs is subject to alternative minimum tax (AMT) calculation.

257.

C. $40 federally tax-free interest and $5 taxable accretion

Because this bond was purchased at a discount in the secondary market (outstanding) instead of as an original issue discount (OID), the bond must be accreted, and the annual accretion is taxable. Forty dollars (4 percent of $1,000 par) would be federally non-taxable interest, and the $5 per year annual accretion ($50 discount divided by 10 years) is taxable.

258.

B. $900 return of capital and $500 federally tax-free interest over the life of the bond

Because this municipal bond is an original issue discount (OID), the annual accretion is treated as part of the investor's federally tax-free income. This investor originally purchased the bond for $900 (90 percent of $1,000 par), so when he receives $1,000 at maturity, $900 of that is a return of capital. The other $100 had to be accreted over the life of the bond, which added an extra $10 ($100/10 years) of federally tax-free interest each year.

259.

C. I, II, and III

Interest received from municipal bonds issued by the U.S. territories Guam, Puerto Rico, and U.S. Virgin Islands is triple tax-free (exempt from federal, state, and local taxes). You'd probably also want to let your client know that purchasing municipal bonds issued by his/her own state would also be triple tax-free.

260.

C. the proposal with the lowest interest cost

When a municipality, such as Suffolk County, New York, is issuing bonds through a competitive offering, it means that it's allowing syndicates to bid on the issue. Suffolk County will accept the bid with the lowest interest cost to the taxpayer. For example, if Syndicate A said that it could sell the bonds with a 5 percent coupon and Syndicate B said that it could sell the bonds with a 4.75 percent coupon, Syndicate B would be the winner.

261.

A. the bond rating

The official notice of sale is an official invitation from a municipality, asking for broker-dealers to bid on a new issue of municipal bonds. The official notice of sale includes the date, time and place of sale, the bond maturity date, interest payment dates, any call provisions, the amount of good faith deposit, a description of the issue, and so on. The rating of the bond issue comes from ratings companies, such as Moody's and Standard & Poor's, and isn't determined until the bond is issued.

262.

A. short-term bonds

If the municipality had the choice of issuing bonds now or later, it would obviously wait until later because with lower interest rates it could issue bonds with a lower coupon rate and save money. However, if it needs money now and interest rates are expected to drop, it would issue short-term bonds. By issuing short-term bonds, it would have to pay the higher coupon rate only for a short period of time. When the interest rates drop, it can issue long-term bonds with a lower coupon rate.

263.

C. I, II, and III

If you take a quick glance at the answers choices, you'll notice that they all include Statements II and III, which means that you don't have to look closely at those answers. So you have a choice of Statement I or IV being correct. When determining the marketability of municipal bonds, the maturity is important because bonds with short-term maturities are more marketable. The dated date (the first day that bonds start accruing interest) doesn't affect a bond's marketability.

Part II: The Answers

264. **C. notice of sale**

When a municipality wants to inform potential underwriters that it's taking bids for a new issue, it would post an official notice of sale in *The Bond Buyer*.

265. **D. covenants**

Covenants are promises stated on the indenture and are important for investors of revenue bonds, not general obligation bonds. An example is an insurance covenant where the issuer promises to adequately insure the income-producing facility backing the bonds.

266. **D. I, II, III, and IV**

The official notice of sale is published in *The Bond Buyer* and is designed to solicit bids from underwriters for a new issue of municipal bonds. Included in the official notice of sale is all the information needed by underwriters to come up with a bid for the new issue, such as the name of the issuer, a description of the issuer, type of bond (GO, revenue, double-barreled), any bidding restrictions, required interest payment dates, the dated date, any call provisions, maturity structure (long term, short term), denomination of certificates, the name of the bond counsel, the name of the trustee, and so on.

267. **C. a syndicate that could sell the issue with the lowest cost to the municipality**

The issuer will determine the winning bid on the lowest cost. The issuer will take into consideration the coupon rate (the lower, the better) and the selling price (the higher, the better).

268. **A. 0%**

If the syndicate was set up on a divided (Western) account basis, after a syndicate member is done selling his allotment, he's done. However, if done on an Eastern (undivided) account basis, a syndicate member is responsible for selling a percentage of the issue left unsold. In this case, it would be 10 percent because the member was originally responsible for 10 percent ($2 million/$20 million) of the issue.

269. **C. reoffering yields**

The reoffering yield (reoffering scale) is the yield to maturity (YTM) that investors receive when purchasing bonds from the underwriter(s). Because it doesn't affect the issuer directly, reoffering yields aren't required as part of the bid.

270. **B. true interest cost**

The two methods of interest evaluation are true interest cost (TIC) and net interest cost (NIC). In this case, the issuer is taking into consideration the timing of interest payments or the time value of money. That means that the issuer is determining the bids based on the true interest cost because it's discounting future interest payments to arrive at a present value.

271. **B.** *The Bond Buyer*

The Bond Buyer provides the best source of information about municipal bonds in the primary market. *The Bond Buyer* includes the 40-Bond Index, 20-Bond index, 11-Bond Index, Revenue Bond Index (RevDex), the visible supply, and the placement ratio.

272. **A. to get assistance from another brokerage firm in selling unsold securities**

A firm quote with a recall option is used to give another brokerage firm a chance to sell securities that a dealer has difficulty selling. One firm gives another firm the opportunity to try and sell securities for a limited time. If the other firm is successful, the two firms in the agreement split the commissions or markups from the transaction.

273. **C. insurance covenants**

You're looking for the exception in this question. Covenants are promises placed on the indenture of revenue bonds, not general obligation bonds. However, general obligation (GO) bonds are subject to a debt ceiling and are backed by items such as property taxes and traffic fines.

274. **A. I and II**

When analyzing municipal general obligation (GO) bonds, investors should be concerned with the tax base, efficiency of the government, existing debt, debt per capita, and so on. If investing in municipal revenue bonds, an investor should be concerned about covenants and flow of funds.

275. **D. the official statement**

The official statement is similar to a prospectus but for a municipality, not a corporation. In the official statement, investors would be able to find out what the bond funds will be used for, the tax base, tax collection history, interest payment dates, the maturity date, insurance backing the bonds, and so on.

276. **B. I and II**

The Bond Buyer's 11-Bond Index is made up of a select group of municipal general obligation (GO) bonds found in the 20-Bond Index. The 11 bonds have an average Standard & Poor's rating of AA+ and are made up of bonds rated AAA and AA.

277. **A. the placement ratio**

The Bond Buyer's placement ratio indicates the demand for new issues by disclosing the number of new municipal issues that have sold within the last week as compared to the amount available. You can set this up mathematically as

$$\text{Placement ratio} = \frac{\text{New issue municipal bonds sold during the week}}{\text{New issue municipal bonds available during the week}}$$

278. **D. a state**

Overlapping (coterminous) debt is important to not only taxpayers but also purchasers of municipal general obligation (GO) bonds. Overlapping debt has to do with debt being shared by more than one municipality. An example would be a town that's responsible for a portion of the county's debt. People who live in a county are also responsible for a portion of the state's debt. However, states can't be overlapped because one state isn't responsible for a portion of another state's debt.

279. **B. 3 to 1**

Because these bonds were issued under a net revenue pledge (which almost all are), bondholders are paid from net revenues after operation and maintenance are paid. To calculate this question, remember that net revenue equals gross revenue minus operating and maintenance expenses. Here, net revenue is $76 million – $40 million = $36 million. You also need to calculate debt service, which is the combination of interest and principal repayment. Here, debt service is $10 million + $2 million = $12 million. Finally, to compute the debt service ratio, you divide the net revenue by the debt service:

$$\text{Debt service coverage ratio} = \frac{\text{Net revenues}}{\text{Debt service}}$$
$$= \frac{\$36,000,000}{\$12,000,000}$$
$$= 3$$

This means that the debt service coverage ratio is 3 to 1 (3:1).

280. **D. revenue bonds**

The flow of funds is used for municipal revenue bonds. The indenture specifies whether the municipal bond principal and interest is paid using net or gross revenues.

281. **A. $357.14**

The direct debt per capita is the amount of debt that Phoenix residents owe directly. Although the residents of Phoenix are responsible for a percentage of Arizona's debt, that doesn't come into play unless the question asks you for overall debt per person or overlapping debt per person. All you need to do for this question is divide the $500 million debt by the 1.4 million residents to get an answer of $357.14.

282. **B. III and IV**

What's nice about this question is that if you know you can eliminate Statement I, you can quickly come up with the correct answer of Choice (B). *Direct debt per capita* and *net debt per assessed valuation* are important to purchasers of general obligation bonds, not revenue bonds. Items that are important to purchasers of revenue bonds include the *debt service coverage ratio* (how much money is netted as compared to how much is owed in principal and interest) and *flow of funds* (whether bondholders are paid first or operating and maintenance is paid first).

283. **D. guaranteeing timely payment of interest**

A municipal bond counsel prepares the legal opinion for new municipal bonds. The main function of a municipal bond counsel is to make sure that it's valid and binding on the issuer and meets the laws that will make it federally tax-free. However, municipal bond counsels don't guarantee timely payment of principal and interest.

284. **C. liquidity**

The problem with most municipal bonds is that they're thin issues and don't have a national interest. White's Rating Service looks at municipal bonds and determines how marketable or liquid they are. This would be important to investors buying municipal bonds, because they'd want to make sure they'd have no problem selling them if needed.

285. **C. II, III, and IV**

The coupon on a variable rate municipal bond is adjusted periodically to keep pace with the current interest rates. Because the coupon rate keeps pace with interest rates, the bond price stays relatively stable. Therefore, variable rate municipal bonds aren't subject to interest rate risk (the risk that a securities value will decline due to rising interest rates). However, variable rate municipal bonds are still subject to market risk, default risk, and liquidity risk.

286. **A. official statement**

Municipal bonds don't have a prospectus, but they do have an official statement. The official statement gives investors the most information about the issuer and the bond issue.

287. **B. property taxes**

Property taxes are the largest source of backing for general obligation (GO) bonds, not revenue bonds. What's important to revenue bond investors is the *feasibility study* (how much sense the income producing project makes), *the flow of funds* (priority of payments from revenues), and *rate covenants* (a promise to adequately charge users of the facility).

288. **C. default risk**

Municipal bond insurance is a credit enhancer that insures municipal bonds against default risk. Default risk is the risk that interest and principal payments won't be received. In the event that the issuer fails to make expected payments, the insurance company will make them. Insured municipal bonds are typically rated AAA.

289. **B. Treasury bonds**

Because the largest source of backing for general obligation bonds is taxing power, they're usually ranked only second as far as their credit rating to Treasury bonds issued by the U.S. government.

290. **A. rate covenants**

A rate covenant would be on the indenture of a revenue bond, not a general obligation (GO) bond. However, per capita debt (debt per person), assessed property values, and the tax collection history of the municipality would all certainly affect the credit rating of a GO bond.

291. **B. it increases the credit rating and marketability of the bonds**

Municipal bond insurance is called a *credit enhancer* because it increases the credit rating of the bonds. Insured municipal bonds typically have a Standard & Poor's credit rating of AAA. The higher the credit rating, the more marketable the bonds.

292. **B. I and II**

The Bond Buyer's 11-Bond Index uses a select group of general obligation bonds taken from the 20-Bond Index rated AAA or AA. The average rating is AA+ (Standard & Poor's) or Aa1 (Moody's).

293. **D. MSRB RTRS**

The Real-Time Reporting System (MSRB RTRS) gets information from services that execute municipal trades to the public within 15 minutes of execution. The MSRB RTRS is open from 7:30 a.m. to 6:00 p.m. every business day.

294. **C. II and IV**

Geographical diversification is purchasing municipal bonds from different areas of the country. Geographical diversification would protect investors against economic and business risks that may affect only certain areas or regions of the country. Geographical diversification wouldn't protect against purchasing power risk because municipal bonds have long-term maturities. In addition, diversification can't eliminate interest risk because if interest rates increase, outstanding bond prices fall.

295. **D. I, II, and III**

Actually, all of the choices listed are important. The *state of residence* is important because if a client purchases a municipal bond issued by his own state, he'll receive triple tax-free interest. *The tax bracket* is important because the interest on municipal bonds is federally tax-free, so they're more advantageous to investors in higher tax brackets. And, finally, if municipal bonds don't fit into a client's *investment objectives,* they shouldn't be recommended.

296. **B. *The Bond Buyer***

The Bond Buyer (www.bondbuyer.com) provides the best information on new municipal bonds (primary market). *The Bond Buyer* has an online subscription service that provides up-to-date information.

297. **A.** *The Bond Buyer*

The 30-day visible supply is published in the Friday edition of *The Bond Buyer*. The visible supply is the dollar volume of municipal bonds expected to reach the market within the next 30 days.

298. **C. the RevDex**

Credit ratings from ratings agencies, such as Moody's and Standard & Poor's, the placement ratio, and the visible supply, are all important in helping determine the marketability of municipal general obligation (GO) bonds. However, the RevDex (Revenue Bond Index) discloses the average yield of 25 revenue bonds with 30-year maturities and has nothing to do with GO bonds.

299. **B. the dated date**

The dated date is the first day that a bond starts accruing interest and isn't a factor in the marketability of a bond. However, the credit rating, the maturity date, and the issuer's name are all important and would affect the marketability of a bond.

300. **A. bond principal and interest**

Under a gross revenue pledge, the issuer will pay principal and interest (debt service) prior to any other expenses. Most municipalities issue revenue bonds under a net revenue pledge in which the net revenues (after operation and maintenance are paid) are used to cover the debt service.

301. **D. the issuer meets all conditions without restrictions**

As funny as it sounds, an unqualified legal opinion as related to municipal bonds is actually a good thing. It's not saying that the bond counsel is unqualified but that the bond counsel found no problems with issue. Remember, the bond counsel (attorney) has to examine the issue and make sure that the issue is legally binding on the issuer and that it meets the tax laws to provide federally tax-free income. By contrast, a qualified legal opinion may mean that the issuer may not have clear title to a property, the issuer may have liens or judgments against property he owns, and so on.

302. **D. I, II, III, and IV**

All of the choices listed are important. General obligation (GO) bonds are backed by the full faith, credit, and taxing power of the municipality. Although the largest backing for GO bonds is property (ad valorem) taxes, they're also backed by items such as license fee and fines. The issuer's home state is important because if purchasing a tax-free municipal bond within your own home state, the interest will be triple tax-free. You'd also want to see a growing population trend because that means that more people will be backing the bonds. Obviously, bonds being backed by a wealthy community are better than ones backed by a poor community. You'd also want to see a diversity of industry within the tax base because that would help a community grow.

303. C. I, II, and IV

Typically, insured municipal bonds have an S&P credit rating of AAA or a Moody's rating of Aaa because of the insurance guaranty. As such, insurance is known as a credit enhancement. In the event of issuer default, the insurance company is obligated to pay off the bondholders. The companies that insure municipal bonds include the National Public Finance Guarantee Corp., FGIC (Financial Guaranty Insurance Company), AGC (Assured Guaranty Corporation), and AMBAC (American Municipal Bond Assurance Corporation). SIPC (Securities Investor Protection Corporation) insures investors due to broker-dealer bankruptcy and doesn't insure municipal bonds.

304. B. operation and maintenance

You'll find that most revenue bonds and industrial development revenue bonds have a net revenue pledge. This means that the first priority of revenue goes to pay operation and maintenance on the facility, which makes sense. If they don't keep the facility running, they'll never be able to pay off bondholders. Next is the debt service (principal and interest on bonds), followed by a debt service reserve fund, a reserve maintenance fund, a renewal and replacement fund, and, finally, a surplus fund.

305. A. EMMA

EMMA (electronic municipal market access) is a centralized online site that provides information about municipal securities to retail, non-professional investors. The site gives access to official statements for most new municipal bond offerings and provides real-time access to prices.

306. C. amount

When looking at a client's portfolio of securities, you should make sure that they're diversified. A client shouldn't have too many of his eggs in one basket, so to say. Relating to municipal bonds, diversification could be buying bonds of different types (revenue, GO, notes), buying bonds with different credit ratings (AAA, A, BBB), buying bonds from different geographical locations (New York, California, Guam), buying bonds with different maturities (short term, intermediate term, long term), and so on. However, buying a different amount of one security doesn't figure into the diversified portfolio mix.

307. B. EMMA

EMMA (electronic municipal market access) provides information about municipal securities for retail, non-professional investors. The official statements for most new municipal bond offerings are available on EMMA. In addition, EMMA provides access to prices and rates regarding auction-rate securities.

308. A. pre-refunded municipal GO

Even if the word *pre-refunded* wasn't in front of the municipal GO (general obligation) bond, it still would have been the best answer. Remember: GO bonds are backed by the full faith, credit, and taxing power of the municipal issuer. The fact that it's pre-refunded makes it even safer. Pre-refunding involves an issuer issuing new bonds and putting the money it receives in an account and using the interest money received to pay off existing bondholders. Issuers do this to take advantage of low interest rates. Their intention is to use the money to call the existing higher coupon rate bonds at some time in the future. This allows the issuer to extend the debt until a later date while saving interest money. The money received from pre-refunding is typically invested in U.S. government securities such as T-bills.

309. **D. bond anticipation notes**

Market risk is the risk that the price of a security will decline due to negative market conditions. Because bond anticipation notes (BANs) are short term, they're not in the market as long and, therefore, are less subject to market risk.

310. **B. the bond price should remain stable**

Variable rate bonds have no fixed coupon rate. The rate on these bonds is tied to a particular market rate, such as the yield to T-bonds, and is subject to regular change. Because the coupon rate varies, the bond price remains close to its par value.

311. **C. bond indenture**

The flow of funds is the way that a municipality distributes income generated from a revenue-producing facility backing revenue bonds. The flow of funds would be found in the bond indenture (bond contract).

312. **A. trustee acting for the bondholders**

The bond resolution (indenture) outlines the characteristics of the offering (interest payment dates, coupon rate, maturity date, and so on) and the obligations that the issuer has to holders of the issue. In the event of issuer default, the trustee will act to protect the bondholders.

313. **B. The facility backing the bond has been condemned due to a hurricane.**

A catastrophe call (calamity call) is just what it sounds like. It means that something catastrophic has happened to the revenue-producing facility backing the bonds. In this event, the outstanding bonds would be called, and investors would be paid par value and any accrued interest (typically by an insurance company).

314. **D. I, II, III, and IV**

Actually, all of the choices given are important. The higher your client's tax bracket, the bigger the advantage for buying municipal bonds. If a client purchases municipal bonds issued from within his home state, he'll have the advantage of them being triple tax-free. The bond's rating and maturity are important depending on the risk tolerance of your client.

315.   A. 4 to 1

The question didn't state whether it was a net revenue pledge or gross revenue pledge, so you can assume net. To get the net revenues, subtract the operating and maintenance expenses from the gross revenues.

$$\text{Net revenues} = \$30,000,000 - \$12,000,000 = \$18,000,000$$

Next, to determine the debt service coverage ratio, divide the net revenues by the combined principal and interest ($1,500,000 interest + $3,0000,000 principal = $4,500,000):

$$\text{Debt service coverage ratio} = \frac{\text{Net revenues}}{\text{Principal and interest}}$$

$$= \frac{\$18,000,000}{\$4,500,000}$$

$$= 4$$

That means that the debt service coverage ratio is 4 to 1 (4:1).

316.   C. $360 million

Net overall debt is debt that Richmond owes directly plus any overlapping debt. Richmond is directly responsible for $200 million in debt and responsible for $160 million (20 percent of $800 million) of Virginia's debt. Add those together to get Richmond's overall debt:

$$\$200 \text{ million} + \$160 \text{ million} = \$360 \text{ million}$$

317.   A. I and III

With revenue bonds, a feasibility report (engineering report) is required to estimate the costs and revenues of the facility paying off the debt. In addition, the flow of funds must be included on the indenture of the revenue bonds to indicate how the money raised from the facility is spent by the municipality. Debt limitation and debt per capita are related to general obligation bonds rather than revenue bonds.

318.   A. $769.23

Direct debt is the debt owed by a municipality that doesn't include overlapping debt. The question states that Fort Myers has $50 million in debt. To calculate debt per capita, divide the debt by the population:

$$\frac{\$50,000,000}{65,000} = \$769.23$$

319.   B. municipal GO bonds

Because your client is in a high income tax bracket, municipal bonds are ideal. Remember, the higher the customer's tax bracket, the better benefit they get out of buying municipal bonds. Therefore, you can cross off Choices (C) and (D). Because your client is looking for income, you wouldn't recommend a zero-coupon bond because your client wouldn't receive any income until maturity. The best answer is *municipal GO bonds*.

320. **D. geographical**

Mr. Mullahy has purchased bonds from municipal bonds from different geographical locations. Other types of municipal diversification include buying bonds with different ratings, different maturities, different types (such as revenue, GO, IDRs), and so on. All investors should have a diversified portfolio.

321. **A. 25 various revenue bonds with 30-year maturities**

The Bond Buyer's Revenue Bond Index (RevDex) is the average yield of 25 revenue bonds with 30-year maturities rated A+ or better.

322. **B. 20 years**

The Bond Buyer's Municipal Bond Index (40-Bond Index) provides the average dollar price of 40 highly traded revenue and general obligation (GO) bonds with an average maturity of 20 years and a rating of A or better.

323. **D. the interdealer market**

Trades between dealers take place in the interdealer market.

324. **D. the total dollar amount of municipal bonds expected to reach the market in the next 30 days**

The visible supply is published in the Friday edition of *The Bond Buyer* and is the total dollar amount of municipal bonds expected to reach the market in the next 30 days. If the visible supply is much larger than normal, interest rates are likely to rise to entice investors to buy.

325. **B. $250 per election**

According to MSRB Rule G-37, the maximum contribution allowed for a municipal finance professional (MFP) to a candidate running for a local government office is $250 per election. If a particular candidate is running in a primary and a general election, the MFP may contribute a total of $500 ($250 for the primary election and $250 for the general election).

326. **A. I and IV**

A municipal dealer must notify the employing firm in writing before opening an account for an employee of another firm. In addition to notifying the employing firm, the municipal dealer must also send duplicate confirmations of each trade to the firm.

327. **C. An employee of a broker-dealer holds a position of authority over the municipal issuer.**

According to MSRB rules, a control relationship exists when a firm or employee of a firm has a position of authority over the issuer of the securities being recommended (such as an employee of a firm is on the school board in the municipality of the municipal securities being recommended).

All control relationships must be disclosed prior to the execution of the trade verbally or in writing. If the first disclosure is verbal, written disclosure is required no later than the completion of the transaction. The same rule applies if the brokerage firm is a syndicate member or investment adviser of the issuer.

328. **C. II and III**

Registered reps are subject to a 90-day apprenticeship period. During this time, registered reps may not transact business with public customers or be compensated for municipal securities transactions. In addition, the rep may earn a salary but not a commission. Exams to become reps must be passed within 180 days of the beginning of the apprenticeship period.

329. **D. three business days of receipt of an ACAT form, and transfers must be completed within four business days of validation**

What makes this question especially difficult is that the MSRB, FINRA, and the CBOE all have different rules. However, under MSRB rules, account transfers must be validated within three business days of receipt of an account transfer (ACAT) form, and the transfers must be completed within four business days of validation.

330. **C. 5% bond trading at 4.5% basis maturing in 2025**

Municipal bond confirmations must disclose the yield to maturity (YTM, or basis) or yield to call (YTC), whichever is lower. The best way to visualize the bond price and yields is to set up a seesaw. Remember, the higher the number, the higher it goes on the seesaw. Choices (A) and (B) would make a seesaw that has the left side down and right side up, so those would have to be quoted yield to maturity. Choice (D) would be flat, so it would trade on its coupon rate. However, by plugging in the numbers from Choice (C), you get the following situation:

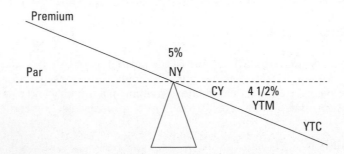

In this case, the NY (coupon rate) is 5 percent, and the YTM (basis) is 4.5%, so the right side has to be lowered. Therefore, this bond would have to be quoted YTC because it's lower than the YTM. Also, as you can see from the seesaw, municipal bonds trading at a premium and callable at par must show YTC on the confirmation, which means that municipal bond trading at a discount and callable at par must show YTM on the confirmation.

Note: Zero-coupon bonds (bonds making no interest payments), variable rate bonds, and bonds in default would trade on the bond price.

331. **C. buying a client season passes to the Yankees**

According to MSRB rules, no municipal securities brokers or dealers shall give (directly or indirectly) a gift in excess of $100 per year to any person other than a partner or employee of the dealer. However, normal business expenses, such as business meals, airline tickets, and hotel expenses, are exempt. So sending a client a picture of yourself in an $80 frame may be inappropriate (or not), but it's not a violation. However, buying season tickets for the Yankees would go way and beyond the $100 limit and wouldn't be deemed a business expense.

332. **D. a municipal securities principal**

All advertisements relating to municipal securities must be approved by a municipal securities principal (manager) or general securities principal prior to being sent to customers or potential customers. All advertising sent out by a firm (municipal or otherwise) must be approved by a principal.

333. **C. II and III**

Remember, a broker, as compared to a dealer, acts as a middleman in between trades and doesn't deal from his own inventory. So that makes Statement III correct. Also, as the name suggests, broker's brokers are brokers for brokers, so they don't deal with public customers. That means that Choice (C) is correct.

334. **D. bond counsel**

The legal opinion is a statement by a bond counsel (attorney) affirming that the interest received from a bond issue meets the requirements to be exempt from federal taxation. All municipal bonds must be accompanied by a legal opinion unless the issue is marked as ex-legal (a municipal bond that trades without a legal opinion).

335. **A. arbitration**

According to MSRB rules, disputes must be settled through arbitration.

336. **A. issuers**

The Municipal Securities Rulemaking Board (MSRB) establishes rules that broker-dealers, bank-dealers, and municipal advisors must follow when engaging in transactions of municipal securities. Issuers aren't subject to MSRB rules.

337. **A. I and III**

A municipal finance professional (MFP) is a person associated with a broker-dealer who is primarily engaged in municipal securities other than retail sales to customers or is engaged in the solicitation of municipal securities business for the broker-dealer.

338. **D. the preliminary official statement**

Because a municipal issuer prepares the preliminary and official statements, they don't need to be approved by a municipal securities principal. However, most of the things that happen within your firm, such as opening accounts, transactions in accounts, and advertisements sent out by your firm, do need to be approved by a principal (manager) of the firm.

339. **D. I, II, and III**

A control relationship exists when a municipal securities broker-dealer controls, is controlled by, or is under a common control of a municipal securities issuer. In other words, investors have the right to know that you or your firm are recommending a municipal securities that the firm has ties to. Control relationships must always be disclosed. A verbal disclosure at the time of the trade is acceptable as long as the customer receives a written disclosure before the completion of the transaction.

340. **D. the MSRB**

Believe it or not, the Municipal Securities Rulemaking Board (MSRB) doesn't enforce MSRB rules; they just make them. FINRA and the SEC enforce MSRB rules for broker-dealers, and the FDIC, the Fed, and Comptroller of Currency enforce MSRB rules for bank-dealers.

341. **D. Tuesday, October 8**

The regular-way settlement for municipal bonds is three business days after the trade date. Business days are Monday through Friday. Because you have a weekend in the way, the settlement date is Tuesday, October 8. If this had been a cash trade, the settlement date would have been the same as the trade date (Thursday, October 4).

342. **D. I, II, III, and IV**

Under MSRB Rule G-15, the confirmation (receipt of trade) must include the customer's name, the capacity of the broker-dealer (agency or principal trade), the par value of the securities, trade date, execution price, whether it was a purchase or sale, the settlement date, yield or dollar price, CUSIP number (if there is one), and so on.

343. **B. Accept the complaint and record any action taken.**

Upon receipt of any complaint from the customer, a municipal securities dealer must accept the complaint and record any action taken. All actions and responses become part of the complaint file.

344. **C. six years**

According to MSRB rules, complaints regarding the trading of municipal securities must be kept on file with the broker-dealer for at least six years.

345. **B. I, II, and IV**

Broker's brokers execute trades of municipal bonds for broker-dealers and bank-dealers for a fee. When the trades are executed, the broker's brokers keep the identities of the firms involved in the transaction anonymous. They don't rate the credit of bonds — that's done by credit rating agencies, such as Moody's and Standard & Poor's. By definition, brokers don't carry any inventory or underwrite new issues.

346. **B. the delivery of a mutilated bond ertificate**

Out of the choices listed, the only one that would be considered a fail to deliver (bad delivery) is *the delivery of a mutilated bond certificate.* If a bond has a legal opinion, it should be attached to the bond; if it's marked *ex-legal,* it'd be delivered without a legal opinion.

347. **C. a bona fide quote**

You should have been able to cross out Choices (A) and (D) right away because nominal and subject quotes mean the same thing. When a municipal dealer gives or publishes a quote for a municipal security, it must be a bona fide (firm) quote. Because it's a bona fide quote, the dealer must be prepared to trade the security at that price.

348. **C. yield to call**

Because it's a pre-refunded (advance-refunded) municipal bond that's going to be called in two years, the yield shown must be yield to call. For municipal bonds that aren't pre-refunded, the confirmation must show yield to maturity or yield to call, whichever is lower.

349. **C. III and IV**

Municipal bonds used to be available in bearer, registered as to principal only, fully registered, and book-entry form. However, at the present time, new issues of municipal bonds can only be fully registered or book entry. Book entry is now becoming the most common form of delivery.

350. **A. Friday, October 4**

Any trade for cash settles on the same day as the trade date. Regular-way settlement is three business days after the trade date.

351. **D. II and IV**

Like corporate bonds, the accrued interest on municipal bonds is calculated by using 30-day months and a 360-day year.

352. **A. before 8:00 a.m. or after 9:00 p.m. local time of the person being called**

Prospecting calls may not be made before 8:00 a.m. or after 9:00 p.m. local time of the person being called. The caller must disclose his name, the name of his firm, the firm's phone number, the firm's address, plus the fact that he's calling to solicit the purchase of municipal securities. The 8:00 a.m. to 9:00 p.m. rule doesn't apply to established customers.

353. **C. I, III, and IV**

Because of the additional risk taken in margin accounts, customers must sign a margin agreement before executing any trades. The margin agreement is broken down into the credit agreement, a hypothecation agreement, and a loan consent form. A risk disclosure document needs to be sent out prior to opening an options account.

354. **A. the credit agreement**

The credit agreement discloses the terms for borrowing, which includes the interest rate to be charged on the debit balance, the broker-dealer's method of computation, and how and when the interest rate may change. There's no such thing as a *margin interest rate form,* so Choice (D) is obviously wrong.

355. **B. allows the broker-dealer to loan a customer's margined securities to other investors**

A loan consent form is required only for margin accounts, not cash accounts. Although technically it isn't required, almost all firms require that customers sign it prior to opening a margin account. The loan consent form allows the broker-dealer to loan a margin customer's securities to other investors or broker-dealers, typically for the short sale of securities.

356. **D. risk disclosure document**

Because of the additional risk involved when purchasing securities on margin, all margin customers must receive a risk disclosure document prior to opening the account. The risk disclosure document covers some of the broker-dealer's rules and outlines the risks like "investors may lose more money than initially deposited." Because of the additional risk involved, not all investors are good candidates for margin accounts. As far as the other answers go, the credit agreement, the hypothecation agreement, and the loan consent form are all part of the margin agreement.

357. **C. $2,000**

You have to pay particular attention to whether it's an initial transaction because different rules apply. Because this customer is opening the margin account, it's an initial transaction. This customer is selling short as an initial transaction, so he must deposit a minimum of $2,000. If the customer had an existing margin account, he'd have had to deposit 50 percent (Regulation T) of the $1,500 short sale, or $750.

358.

B. $1,800

Because this is the initial transaction in a margin account, different rules apply. After the margin account is open, the customer would just have to deposit Regulation T (Reg T; 50 percent) of the purchase. However, in an opening transaction for a long margin account, the investor must pay in full, deposit $2,000, or pay the Reg T amount. If the customer is purchasing less than $2,000 worth of securities, he'd have to pay in full. If the amount of securities purchased is greater than $2,000 but Reg T is less than $2,000, the customer would have to deposit $2,000. If the amount of securities being purchased is greater than $2,000 and Reg T is greater than $2,000, the customer would pay the Reg T amount.

The best way to deal with this situation is to take the three numbers — the value of the securities, Reg T, and $2,000 — and then choose the number in the middle. This will always work for an initial transaction in a margin account. For this question, you have $1,800 in securities, $900 Reg T amount, and $2,000. The middle number is $1,800, so that's the answer.

359.

C. $2,500

In an initial transaction for a short margin account, the investor has to deposit Regulation T (Reg T; 50 percent) of the amount of securities shorted, or $2,000, whichever is more. Because this investor is shorting $5,000 worth of securities, he has to deposit ($5,000)(50%) = $2,500.

360.

D. all of the above

U.S. government bonds (T-bills, T-notes, T-bonds, and so on), U.S. government agency securities, and municipal securities can be purchased on margin but are exempt from the Regulation T (50 percent) margin requirement. The margin requirement for these securities is much lower than for other securities.

361.

A. I and II

Securities that are marginable include stock and bonds listed on an exchange, NASDAQ stocks, non-NASDAQ stocks approved by the Fed, and warrants. However, mutual funds and IPOs (initial public offerings) can't be purchased on margin because they're new issues. New issues can't be purchased on margin for at least 30 days. However, after you've held mutual fund shares for more than 30 days, they can be transferred to a margin account.

362.

D. five business days after the trade date

The deadline for customers meeting margin calls is five business days after the trade date. The customer must deposit 50 percent of the purchase (or short) amount or deposit fully paid securities worth twice the amount of the margin call. If needed, the broker-dealer may request an extension from a designated examining authority. In the event that the customer is less than $1,000 short, the broker-dealer isn't required to take action.

363. C. $25,000

A day trader is an individual who purchases and sells the same security within the same day in an attempt to take advantage of price fluctuations. Pattern day traders are individuals who execute four or five more day trades within five business days. The minimum equity for a pattern day trader is $25,000.

364. C. $3,800

Normally, the customer would just have to deposit either $1,900 if it was an existing margin account or $2,000 for a new margin account. However, because the customer is shorting a low priced security, different rules come into play. They are as follows:

Price per share	Margin and maintenance requirement
$0 - $2.50	$2.50 per share
$2.50 - $5.00	100% of SMV
$5.00 - $10.00	$5.00 per share

Because this investor is selling short stock at $3.80 per share, he's in that $2.50 to $5.00 range and must deposit 100 percent of the SMV (short market value) for a total of ($3.80)(1,000 shares) = $3,800.

365. C. $13,500

This investor is opening a combined (long and short) margin account. The best way to deal with this is to treat each transaction separately. The investor is purchasing ($15)(1,000 shares) = $15,000 worth of ABC and shorting ($12)(1,000 shares) = $12,000. Assuming Regulation T at 50 percent, this investor would have to come up with 50 percent of each transaction.

($15,000)(50%) = $7,500

($12,000)(50%) = $6,000

$7,500 + $6,000 = $13,500

This investor would have to deposit $13,500 as a result of the two transactions.

366. D. $3,000

Even though Regulation T may be set at 50 percent and minimum maintenance at 25 percent for long accounts, the broker-dealer (house) can increase those percentages if he chooses not to take as much risk. Because the house margin requirement is 60 percent, the investor must come up with 60 percent of the $5,000 purchase: (60%)($5,000) = $3,000.

367. B. $6,700

The brokerage firm is allowed to rehypothecate (use as collateral) 140 percent of the debit balance. Check out the following formula:

$$LMV - DR = EQ, \text{Regulation } T = 60\%$$
$$\$12,00 - \$4,800 = \$7,2000$$

Here, LMV is the long market value of the stock (500 shares × \$24 = \$12,000), DR is the debit balance (the amount borrowed from the broker-dealer), and EQ is the equity (the investors portion of the account: (12,000 LMV × 60% Regulation T = \$7,200)

The brokerage firm may rehypothecate 140 percent of the debit balance, so it can rehypothecate (140%)(\$4,800) = \$6,720.

368.   C. \$8,000

You can tell that this is a long margin account because it has a debit balance (DR), not a credit balance (CR). In this particular equation, you have to ignore the SMA (special memorandum account) because it doesn't help you get the answer you need. Use the following equation to help you get your answer:

$$LMV - DR = EQ$$
$$\$30,000 - \$22,000 = \$8,000$$

Here, LMV is the long market value of the securities, DR is the debit balance (the amount owed to the broker-dealer), and EQ is the equity (the owner's portion of the account).

369.   B. \$5,000

Minimum maintenance is the minimum percentage an investor must have in equity in a margin account. You have to start by adding the market value of all the investments together. This investor has \$1,500 (100 × \$15) of TUV, \$6,000 (200 × \$30) of XYZ, and \$12,500 (500 × \$25) of LMN, so you get \$1,500 + \$6,000 + \$12,500 = \$20,000.

The minimum maintenance for a long margin account is 25 percent of the long market value (LMV): (25%)(\$20,000) = \$5,000.

370.   A. \$5,400

You have to start by getting the long market value (LMV) of all the securities held in the account. Mr. Flanagan has \$6,000 of CSA (100 × \$60 per share), \$4,800 of TUV (200 × \$24 per share), and \$1,800 of LMN (100 × \$18 per share) for a total of \$12,600. Next, pop it into the equation to see where he stands:

$$LMV - DR = EQ$$
$$\$12,600 - \$7,200 = \$5,400$$

Mr. Flanagan has \$5,400 in equity (EQ) with the long market value (LMV) at \$12,600 and the debit balance (DR) at \$7,200.

371.   C. stock dividends

Choices (A), (B), and (D) bring money into the margin account and thus would help pay down the debit balance (DR; the amount owed to the broker-dealer). However, receiving a stock dividend doesn't affect the overall value of investment and doesn't bring money into the account to help pay down the debit balance.

372. **A. I and II**

The debit balance is the amount of money borrowed from the broker-dealer in long margin accounts. A change in the market value of the securities doesn't change the amount borrowed, so Statements III and IV are out. That leaves you with Choice (A). Broker-dealers charge interest on the money borrowed, so when that interest is charged, it's added to the debit balance. In addition, if an investor withdraws his SMA, he's borrowing more money from the account, and the debit balance would increase.

373. **C. $40,000**

When shorting securities, investors lose money when the price of the security increases. To determine how high the short market value of the securities can increase before the investor receives a maintenance call, use the following formula:

$$\frac{CR}{1.3} = \frac{\$52,000}{1.3} = \$40,000$$

You may also see this equation as CR/130% and (10×CR)/13. Feel free to use whichever one you're more comfortable with.

374. **C. $45,000**

The short selling of securities must always be executed in a margin account. Set up the equation as follows, where SMV is the short market value, EQ is the equity, and CR is the credit balance:

$$SMV + EQ = CR$$
$$\$30,000 + \$15,000 = \$45,000$$

The investor sold short 1,000 shares of LMN at $30, so you have to place $30,000 (1,000×$30) under the SMV. You can assume that Regulation T is 50 percent, so the investor had to come up with $15,000 (50 percent of $30,000). Place the $15,000 under the EQ (the investor's portion of the account), and you can see that the credit balance (CR) has to be $45,000 ($30,000+$15,000).

375. **B. $7,500**

Minimum maintenance on short accounts is 30 percent of the short market value. So simply multiply $25,000 by 30 percent:

$$(\$25,000)(30\%) = \$7,500$$

376. **B. $27,000**

Your client has a combined long and short margin account. You can either take each equation for each account and plug the numbers in separately to determine the equity or use the following formula:

$$\text{Combined equity} = LMV + CR - DR - SMV$$
$$= \$30,000 + \$40,000 - \$18,000 - \$25,000$$
$$= \$27,000$$

Note that the SMA (special memorandum account) has no effect on the combined equity.

377. **C. $5,000 increase in equity**

When you purchase securities, you want the price to increase, and when you short securities, you want the price to decrease. In this case, both things happened, which is great for this investor. A direct correlation exists between the market value of the stock and the equity (1 to 1). Therefore, because the long account went up by $3,000 ($35,000 to $38,000) and the short account went down by $2,000 ($28,000 to $26,000), the combined equity increased by $3,000 + $2,000 = $5,000.

378. **D. $30,000**

The first thing that you have to do is set up the short margin account equation. The short market value (SMV) is $80,000 (1,000 × $80), and the investor had to deposit 50 percent (Reg T) of that amount, which gives her an equity (EQ) of $40,000. Plugging these values into the equation, you can see that her credit balance (CR) is $120,000.

$$SMV + EQ = CR$$
$$\$80,000 + \$40,000 = \$120,000$$

Next, the market value drops to $70,000 (1,000 × $70), and the credit balance (CR) stays the same, so that means that the EQ had to increase to $50,000. At this point, you can cross off the top set of numbers because you don't need them anymore.

$$SMV + EQ = CR$$
$$\cancel{\$80,000 + \$40,000 = \$120,000}$$
$$\$70,000 + \$50,000 = \$120,000$$

Next, multiply Reg T (50 percent) by the new short market value of $70,000 to get $35,000. Compare the $35,000 needed to be at 50 percent with the $50,000 in equity, and you see that this investor has $50,000 − $35,000 = $15,000 more than needed in equity. With Regulation T being set at 50 percent, Mrs. Diamond can purchase (or short) $30,000 worth of securities with having excess equity of $15,000.

379. **A. $5,500**

Normally, an investor purchasing $25,000 worth of stock on margin would have to deposit $12,500 to meet the margin call (you can assume Regulation T is 50 percent of the purchase). First, you have to find out whether this investor has any excess equity in his margin account to help offset the $12,500 payment by using the following equation:

$$LMV - DR = EQ$$

Here, you use the market value of the securities for the long market value (LMV) and the $18,000 debit balance for the debit record (DR).

$$LMV - DR = EQ$$
$$\$50,0000 - \$18,000 = \$32,000$$

You come up with an equity (EQ) of $32,000. Now, multiply Regulation T (50 percent) by the LMV to get the amount of equity the customer should have in the account to be at 50 percent: (50%)($50,000)=$25,000. This investor needs only $25,000 in equity to reach 50 percent, and this investor has $32,000, which is $32,000 – $25,000 = $7,000 more than necessary.

The $7,000 is excess equity (also known as special memorandum account, SMA), which he can use to help offset the margin call for the $25,000 worth of stock he wants to buy. To determine how much the investor needs to deposit, use the following formula:

$12,500 margin call – $7,000 excess equity = $5,500 to deposit

380.   B. $7,000

Buying power is the amount of additional securities that you can purchase on margin with the SMA (excess equity) in the account. You must first set up the equation so you can determine the SMA.

There is a debit balance (DR); therefore, you know that it has to be a long margin account. The long market value minus the debit balance (the amount borrowed from the broker-dealer) equals the equity (the investor's portion of the account).

$$LMV - DR = EQ$$
$$\$46,000 - \$19,500 = \$26,500$$
$$Reg\ Tx\quad LMV\quad -\$23,000$$
$$\$3,500$$

Next, you have to multiply the LMV by the Regulation T margin requirement (50 percent) to determine the amount of equity the investor should have in the account to be at 50 percent margin: (50%)($46,000)=$23,000. Because the investor has $26,500 in equity, the investor has an excess equity (SMA) of $26,500 – $23,000 = $3,500. This $3,500 is additional money that the investor can use (if he chooses to) to purchase additional securities. Assuming Regulation T is at 50 percent, the investor can purchase $7,000 worth of securities on margin with $3,500 SMA.

381.   B. $7,000

Normally, an investor purchasing $30,000 worth of stock on margin would have to deposit $15,000 to meet the margin call (you can assume Regulation T is 50 percent of the purchase). First, you have to find out whether Mr. Jones has any excess equity in his margin account to help offset the $15,000 payment. Use the following equation:

$$LMV - DR = EQ$$

After setting up the equation, enter the $60,000 market value of the securities under the long market value (LMV). Next, enter the $22,000 under the debit record (DR), also known as the debit balance.

$$LMV - DR = EQ$$
$$\$60,000 - \$22,000 = \$38,000$$

Multiply Regulation T (50 percent) by the LMV to get the amount of equity the customer should have in the account to be at 50 percent: (50%)($60,000) = $30,000. This investor needs only $30,000 in equity to reach 50 percent, and this investor has $38,000, which is $8,000 more than necessary.

The $8,000 is excess equity (SMA; special memorandum account), which he can use to help offset the margin call for the $30,000 worth of stock he wants to buy:

$15,000 margin call − $8,000 excess equity = $7,000 to deposit

382. A. increase

The excess equity (SMA) in a margin account is built in to the equity. If your client removes equity from a margin account, he's borrowing more money from the account, and the debit balance (the amount owed to the broker-dealer) will increase.

383. D. $3,750

Whenever an investor sells securities short, the sale has to be executed in a margin account. Short sellers are bearish and want the price of their securities to decrease. Mr. Steyne will end up with a restricted account because the value of his securities increased. To determine how much the account is restricted, use the following equation:

$$SMV + EQ = CR$$

Here, SMV (short market value) = $42,000, EQ (equity) = $21,000 (the Regulation T amount, or 50 percent of the SMV, because that's how much the investor has to deposit into the account).

$$\$42,000 + \$21,000 = \$63,000$$

Now, change the SMV to $44,500 to adjust for the change in the market price and then calculate the new equity. Bring the CR down because that number doesn't change as the SMV goes up or down. Now that the SMV is $44,500 and the CR is $63,000, the EQ has to be $18,500 ($63,000 − $44,500). You can draw a line through the top numbers because you don't need them from this point on.

SMV + EQ = CR
$42,000 + $21,000 = $63,000
$44,500 + $18,500 = $63,000

Multiply Regulation T (you can assume 50 percent) by the new SMV to find the amount of equity (EQ) the investor should have to be at 50 percent: (50%)($44,500) = $22,250.

This investor needs $22,500 to be at 50 percent of the SMV. He has only $18,500; therefore, the account is restricted by $22,250 − $18,500 = $3,750.

384. C. $7,000

The standard equation for long margin accounts is

$$LMV - DR = EQ$$

Here, LMV is the long market value of the securities, DR is the debit balance (the amount owed to the broker-dealer), and EQ is the equity (the owner's portion of the account). In this case, the long market value is $50,000 ($3,000 + $2,000 = $5,000). Then, you find the EQ by multiplying the LMV by 50 percent (Reg T requirement), which equals $25,000. So the DR also must be $25,000.

$$LMV - DR = EQ$$
$$\$50,000 - \$25,000 = \$25,000$$

Now, change the long market value to $40,000 ($40 × 1,000 shares). The DR remains the same because the customer didn't borrow any additonal money from the broker-dealer. This means that the EQ reduces to $15,000. Place all of those numbers in the equation and cross off the initial numbers because you don't need them anymore.

$$LMV - DR = EQ$$
$$\cancel{\$50,000} \quad \cancel{\$25,000} = \cancel{\$25,000}$$
$$\$40,000 - \$25,000 = \$15,000$$

Next, you have to multiply Reg T (50 percent) by the new LMV ($40,000) to determine how much the investor should have in EQ to be at 50 percent: (50%)($40,000) = $20,000. This investor should have at least $20,000 in equity in order not to have a restricted account. He has only $15,000 in equity, so the account is restricted by $5,000.

385. C. $48,000

Minimum maintenance on a long account is 25 percent of the long market value (LMV) unless increased through in-house rules. To determine how low the account can drop before the investor receives a maintenance call, divide the debit balance (DR) by 0.75.

$$\frac{DR}{0.75} = \frac{\$36,000}{0.75} = \$48,000$$

For this investor, if the long market value drops to $48,000, he is at the lowest it can go before receiving a maintenance call.

386. A. I only

If a customer's margin account is restricted, the equity (EQ) has fallen below the 50 percent Regulation T requirement, so Statement I is true. Therefore, you know that Statement II is false. She may borrow additional money by depositing Regulation T (50 percent) of any new purchases. She doesn't have to take the account out of restricted status, and the only time she has to deposit money immediately is if the account falls below minimum maintenance (25 percent of the LMV).

387. C. Regulation U

The Federal Reserve regulation that covers bank loans made to customers for the purpose of buying securities is Regulation U. Regulation T covers broker-dealer loans to customers.

388. **A. 50% initial and 25% maintenance**

Under Regulation T, the initial margin requirement for long accounts is 50 percent of the market value, and minimum maintenance is 25 percent. For short accounts, the initial margin requirement is 50 percent of the market value, and minimum maintenance is 30 percent. However, broker-dealers may increase the initial margin requirement and minimum maintenance through house rules.

389. **A. on demand**

If a margin account falls below minimum maintenance (25 percent for a long account and 30 percent for a short account), payment must be made right away. If the payment isn't made, the broker-dealer has the right to sell securities in the account to bring it out of restricted status. The customer can deposit fully paid marginable securities or cash to meet the maintenance call.

390. **B. twice the margin call**

When an account is restricted, the equity in the account is below the Regulation T (50 percent) margin requirement. Investors can still purchase securities on margin when the account is restricted, but they must come up with 50 percent of the new purchase. If the investor fails to pay for the purchase, the broker-dealer will sell stock out of the account worth two times the margin call.

391. **C. commingling**

Mixing a customer's securities with that of the broker-dealer is a violation called commingling.

392. **D. I, II, and IV**

Margin accounts are always held in street name (in the name of the broker-dealer for the benefit of the customer). Because the customer borrowed money from the broker-dealer to purchase the securities, the customer would be required to pay interest on the money borrowed (the debit balance; DR). In addition, a portion of the securities (140 percent of the DR) may be pledged as collateral for a bank loan by way of rehypothecation. However, a decrease or increase in the market value of the securities doesn't affect the debit balance.

393. **C. They charge commissions to customers who purchase shares.**

Open-end investment companies (mutual funds) don't charge a commission; they charge a sales charge added to the NAV.

394. **D. II, III, and IV**

Closed-end investment companies make a one-time offering of new shares and then trade in the market like other equity securities. Also, closed-end investment companies may issue preferred stock and bonds in addition to common stock.

395. **A. UIT**

UITs (unit investment trusts) invest in a fixed portfolio of securities. Because the trust is a fixed portfolio, the trust wouldn't need a manager to supervise the money invested. Therefore, UITs don't charge a management fee.

396. **B. closed-end**

In both open- and closed-end funds, the NAV indicates the performance of the fund's portfolio. If the NAV (net asset value) and POP (public offering price) move in opposite directions, the fund must be a closed-end fund. The price of a closed-end fund depends not only on the performance of the securities held but also on supply and demand. In an open-end fund, the NAV and POP must move in the same direction because the price depends solely on the performance of the securities held by the fund.

397. **C. $27.52 plus a commission**

Closed-end funds charge a commission added to the POP (public offering price). Open-end funds charge a sales charge, which is built into the POP, except for no-load funds, which don't charge a sales charge.

398. **A. II and III**

Closed-end funds are typically listed on an exchange and have a fixed number of shares outstanding. Closed-end funds must be sold to another investor and aren't redeemable. In addition, closed-end funds may issue common stock, preferred stock, and bonds.

399. **D. investment objectives**

Although all of the choices listed are important, investors should start at a fund's investment objectives. For example, is the customer looking for growth, income, growth and income, a tax-advantaged investment (municipal bond fund), and so on? After the client determines the type of fund, she can then start comparing the performance and expenses of those types of funds from several issuers prior to making a decision.

400. **B. Investors are prohibited from redeeming the money market fund for a year.**

Money market funds are types of mutual funds that hold short-term debt securities. The NAV of the fund is set at $1. They do offer a check-writing feature, they're no-load (no sales charge), and they compute dividends daily and credit them monthly. However, investors aren't prohibited from redeeming their funds for a year; they can redeem at any time.

401. **C. II and III**

The interest on municipal bonds is federally tax-free. When purchasing a municipal bond fund, the tax-free interest is passed through to investors by way of a dividend. However, capital gains, even on municipal bonds, are always taxable.

402.   **B. life-cycle fund**

Life-cycle funds are pretty interesting and would meet this client's needs perfectly. As investors grow older, they typically don't have the ability to assume as much risk as younger investors. In most cases, investors adjust their portfolio every so often to move a larger percentage into fixed-income securities as they get older to minimize risk. Life-cycle (target-date) funds adjust the portfolio of securities held on their own. The investment adviser for the fund will rebalance the securities held by the fund every so often by selling off equity securities held by the fund and purchasing more fixed-income securities. Clients interested in investing in life-cycle funds should choose one with a target retirement date in line with their own needs.

403.   **A. specialized**

If an investor is looking for capital appreciation, you should recommend some type of stock fund. Out of the choices listed, a specialized (sector) fund would be the best fit for this customer. Specialized funds invest in stocks of a particular industry or region with a main objective of capital appreciation.

404.   **D. income fund**

Although hedge funds, growth funds, and aggressive growth funds have capital appreciation potential, they don't provide current income. Income funds invest in stocks paying dividends and bonds paying interest. Therefore, the best choice for this investor would be an income fund or some sort of bond fund.

405.   **C. growth funds**

In this case, you aren't told what the couple's investment objectives are. However, because they've already invested the maximum for the year into their IRAs and are young, growth funds would be ideal. Younger investors can afford to take more risk than older investors. Growth funds invest in a diversified portfolio of stocks that have capital appreciation potential.

406.   **B. a municipal bond fund**

The interest received on municipal bonds is federally tax-free. Therefore, they're of a bigger advantage to investors in higher income tax brackets. When purchasing municipal bond funds, the dividends received by investors that represent the flow-through of interest received from the municipal bonds held by the fund aren't taxable.

407.   **A. HOLDRs**

HOLDRs (holding company depositary receipts) are products issued by brokerage firms and are somewhat similar to exchange-traded funds (ETFs). One of the differences is that HOLDRs pass through voting rights of the stocks purchased to investors. Another difference is that investors can choose to own a group of stocks that are traded together or can unbundle the stocks owned by the HOLDR and trade the stocks as separate investments.

408. **D. a structured fund**

Structured funds specify the percentage of assets allocated toward stocks and the percentage toward bonds. The asset allocation remains constant for the entire life of the fund. For example, if the asset allocation is 50-50 and the stocks have been outper-forming the bonds, the investment adviser would sell off some stocks and buy more bonds to remain at 50-50.

409. **B. a sector fund investing in high-tech stocks**

Investors interested in current income would purchase some sort of bond or income fund. They wouldn't purchase a fund that invests in high-tech stocks because they're growth companies. Growth companies usually don't pay dividends but invest their earnings back into the company to expand or purchase new equipment.

410. **A. mutual funds can't be purchased on margin**

New securities can't be purchased on margin for at least 30 days. Because mutual funds are new securities, they're not marginable. However, investors who have held onto mutual fund shares for more than 31 days can place them in margin accounts and borrow money against them.

411. **B. an inverse exchange-traded fund**

Exchange-traded funds (ETFs) are funds that track a basket of securities or an index, such as the S&P 500, NASDAQ 100, Russell 2000, or even specific sectors. Inverse ETFs (short funds) are constructed to take advantage of a declining market. Inverse ETFs are often purchased by investors to hedge their portfolios against falling prices. Choices (A) and (D) are out because mutual funds can't be sold short.

412. **C. special situation fund**

Funds that hold stocks of corporations that are releasing new products, have new man-agement, have patents pending, and so forth are called *special situation funds*.

413. **C. hedge funds**

ETFs (exchange-traded funds) and inverse ETFs are easily tradable, and money market funds are easily redeemable, so they all have a high degree of liquidity. Hedge funds are the least liquid because they're unregulated and require a minimum holding period (lock-up provision) before investors can make withdrawals. Hedge funds are speculative and employ strategies unavailable to regulated investment companies. Hedge funds may purchase securities on margin, sell securities short, purchase or sell options, and so on.

414. **A. an insured municipal bond fund**

Out of the choices listed, the only fund that provides tax-free interest is a municipal bond fund. The interest received on the municipal bonds held by the fund is passed through to investors by way of federally tax-free dividends. The fact that the municipal bonds held by the fund are insured adds another level of safety.

415. **D. I, II, and IV**

In this question, you're looking for the differences between exchange-traded funds (ETFs) and mutual funds. Unlike mutual funds, ETFs can be sold short, they can be purchased on margin, and provide real-time pricing, not forward pricing like mutual funds. What is similar is that both ETFs and mutual funds represent a basket or portfolio of securities.

416. **A. $32.26**

This question isn't quite as easy as it looks. Most people take the numbers, add them together, and then divide by 5. Unfortunately, that may give you the average price per share but not average cost per share. What your client has set up here is dollar cost averaging. Dollar cost averaging is depositing the same amount periodically into the same security. By sticking with this plan, it allows investors to purchase more when the price is low and less when the price is high. The benefit of dollar cost averaging can be demonstrated by seeing what happens with this client by looking at how many shares he was able to purchase each month.

Month 1: 50 shares ($1,000/$20)

Month 2: 40 shares ($1,000/$25)

Month 3: 25 shares ($1,000/$40)

Month 4: 20 shares ($1,000/$50)

Month 5: 20 shares ($1,000/$50)

So this investor deposited a total of $5,000 over the past five months and was able to purchase 155 shares (50 + 40 + 25 + 20 + 20). To determine the average cost per share, just divide $5,000 by 155 shares:

$$\frac{\$5,000}{155 \text{ shares}} = \$32.26 \text{ per share}$$

417. **B. fixed share averaging**

Fixed share averaging is buying the same amount of shares periodically. Dollar cost averaging is buying the same dollar amount of securities periodically. A constant dollar plan is keeping the same amount of money invested in a security at all times. Market timing has to do with switching between different types of funds to take advantage of bullish or bearish markets.

418. **C. 90 days**

By signing a letter of intent, an investor is able to take advantage of a breakpoint (reduced sales charge) right away, even though not purchasing enough to receive a breakpoint. A letter of intent allows an investor up to 13 months to purchase enough to receive the breakpoint. Letters of intent can be backdated for up to 90 days (3 months) so they can apply to previous purchases.

419.

C. You should remind your client that he has another month to invest an additional $5,000 into ABC.

Your client signed a letter of intent (LOI) to receive a breakpoint (a discounted sales charge for large dollar purchases). A letter of intent is good for 13 months, which means that your client has 13 months to purchase $20,000 worth of ABC. The fact that ABC has appreciated to more than $20,000 doesn't come into play. This means that your client has one more month to deposit the additional $5,000, or ABC will sell shares held in escrow to make up for the money it lost in sales charges by providing the discount.

420.

B. 5.7%

To determine the sales charge percent, use the following formula:

$$\text{Sales charge }\% = \frac{\text{POP} - \text{NAV}}{\text{POP}}$$

where POP is the public offering price, and NAV is the net asset value per share. In this case, the POP is $14.00, and the NAV is $13.20, so you get

$$\text{Sales charge }\% = \frac{\$14.00 - \$13.20}{\$14.00}$$
$$= \frac{\$0.80}{\$14.00}$$
$$= 5.7\%$$

421.

B. 1,298.701 shares

Notice that the answer choices include a decimal point because mutual funds can sell fractions of shares. This investor is going to receive a breakpoint for purchasing more than $20,000 worth of the fund, so he won't be paying the public offering price (POP) of $31.40 per share. To determine how much he'll be paying per share, use the following formula:

$$\text{POP} = \frac{\text{NAV}}{100\% - \text{Sales charge }\%}$$

POP equals the Public Offering Price and NAV equals the Net Asset Value. In this case, the NAV is $29.26. To whittle down to this investor's public offering price, plug in the numbers:

$$\text{POP} = \frac{\$29.26}{100\% - 5\%}$$
$$= \frac{\$29.26}{95\%}$$
$$= \$30.80$$

So this investor will be paying $30.80 per share instead of $31.40. Now, you need to determine how many shares he can purchase when depositing $40,000 and paying $30.80 per share. You can figure that out by simply dividing the deposit amount by the price per share, like so:

$$\frac{\$40,000 \text{ invested}}{\$30.80 \text{ per share}} = 1,298.701 \text{ shares}$$

Because this investor received a breakpoint, he was able to purchase 1,298.701 shares. Without the breakpoint, he would have been able to purchase only 1,273.885 shares.

422. D. 8.5% of the amount invested

The maximum sales charge for a mutual (open-end) fund is 8.5 percent of the amount invested.

423. A. the net asset value + the sales charge

The public offering price (POP) of a mutual fund is the net asset value (NAV) plus the sales charge, so the answer is Choice (A). If the mutual fund is no-load, the net asset value and the public offering price are the same.

424. B. I, III, and IV

Mutual fund performance statistics must show results for one, five, and ten years, or the life of the fund, whichever is less.

425. A. the custodian bank

The custodian bank is responsible for the safekeeping of securities and cash held by the mutual fund.

426. B. $100,000

A mutual fund must have at least $100,000 in private capitalization prior to making a public offering. In addition, they must have at least 100 investors and investment objectives that are clearly defined.

427. C. the next computed bid price

When investors redeem shares of a mutual fund, they're essentially selling shares back to the issuer. When investors sell, they sell at the bid price. The bid price for a mutual fund is the net asset value (NAV). Because mutual funds hold so many different securities, there's no current bid or ask price. Mutual funds use *forward pricing* so investors selling shares are selling them at the next computed bid price, which is typically at the end of the trading day.

428. D. 8.5% of the amount invested

The maximum sales charge (load) for a mutual fund is 8.5 percent of the amount invested (the public offering price). However, most mutual funds charge much less.

429. A. I and III

When an investor purchases a mutual fund that provides automatic reinvestment of dividends and capital gains, the reinvestment must be at the NAV (net asset value).

430. **D. on the date set by the board of directors**

The ex-dividend date for common and preferred stock is automatically two business days before the record date. However, mutual funds may set the ex-dividend date at any time determined by the board of directors.

431. **D. seven calendar days**

A mutual fund must redeem shares of a mutual fund within seven calendar days of the request.

432. **D. annually**

Regulated investment companies must distribute at least 90 percent of net income after expenses to investors at least once a year. Investors are taxed on the distributions received each year.

433. **C. semiannually**

Under the Investment Company Act of 1940, mutual (open-end) funds must send out account statements at least semiannually. Regarding account statements and how often they must be sent out, remember AIM:

Active accounts: monthly

Inactive accounts: quarterly

Mutual funds: semiannually

434. **B. Any gains or losses on DIMCO Aggressive Growth Fund would be recognized for tax purposes.**

Even though this investor is keeping within the same family of funds (DIMCO), he'd need to report any gains or losses on his tax form. When switching funds (even within the same family), it's treated as a sale and a purchase. In this event, the investor can't defer any of his losses or gains.

435. **C. 90%**

A REIT (real estate investment trust) must distribute at least 90 percent of its income to shareholders to avoid taxation as a corporation.

436. **A. The REIT must generate at least 75% of income from construction and mortgage loans.**

A mortgage REIT must generate at least 75 percent of gross income from construction and mortgage loans and doesn't invest in ownership of properties. An equity REIT invests in ownership of properties. A Hybrid REIT invests in a combination of loans and properties. Because a REIT must generate at least 75 percent of gross income from real estate investments, dividends, and interest, 25 percent of income may be earned from securities, such as stocks and bonds.

437.   **C. REITs**

REITs (real estate investment trusts) are actively traded in the secondary market. However, open-end funds and unit investment trusts (UITs) must be redeemed with the issuer and don't trade in the secondary market.

438.   **A. I only**

REITs (real estate investment trusts) raise money from investors to invest in real estate–related projects. At least 75 percent of the trust's gross income must be earned from real estate–related projects. They may invest a small portion of their assets in non–real estate investments, such as stocks and other securities. They do have to register with the SEC, and they don't issue redeemable securities.

439.   **C. double-barreled**

Double-barreled bonds are ones issued by municipalities and aren't types of REITs (real estate investment trusts). The three basic types of REITs are

- Equity REIT: Purchases properties
- Mortgage REIT: Invests in construction and/or mortgage loans
- Hybrid REIT: A combination of equity and mortgage REITs

440.   **B. raw land**

Equity, mortgage, and hybrid (a combination of equity and mortgage) are all types of real estate investment trusts (REITs). But *raw land* is a type of real estate limited partnership.

441.   **D. single payment deferred annuity**

This investor has a large amount of money right now, so he'll likely make a single (lump-sum) payment. Because he's only 25 years old, he'll defer payments until he retires. Single payment deferred annuity would work best for this investor. As a side note, Choice (A) is bogus because the insurance company won't pay out without an investor depositing money first.

442.   **C. I and IV**

In variable life insurance policies, the minimum death benefit is guaranteed, but the cash value isn't. Based on the performance of the securities held in the separate account, the death benefit may increase but may never decrease below the minimum. The cash value (surrender value) varies depending on the performance of the separate account and isn't guaranteed.

443.

B. $840

Because it's a non-qualified annuity, the investor was already taxed on the $38,000 invested. This means that she wasn't taxed on the $9,000 ($47,000 − $38,000 = $9,000) that the account appreciated in value. So the first money withdrawn will be the taxable part: $9,000(28%) = $2,520.

444.

B. It will be higher.

If the return in the separate account is higher than the AIR (assumed interest rate) for a particular month, the payout for the following month would be higher. Conversely, if the return is lower than the AIR, the payout would be lower than the AIR for the following month.

445.

A. life income annuity

Because the life income annuity (life annuity) payments cease at the death of the annuitant, they have the highest monthly payments. Joint and last survivor annuities have the lowest monthly payments.

446.

B. fixed annuities

The payout on a fixed annuity is guaranteed, so fixed annuities aren't regulated by the Investment Company Act of 1940. Fixed annuities are exempt from SEC registration, and the payouts are made out of the insurance company's general account, not a separate account. Because fixed annuities have a fixed payout, they're subject to purchasing power risk. You need an insurance license but not a securities license like a Series 7 to sell fixed annuities.

447.

D. the designated beneficiary

If the owner of a variable annuity dies during the accumulation (pay-in) phase, the death benefit will be paid to the designated beneficiary. The death benefit is typically the total of all investments plus any earnings. It's typically paid in a lump sum, and the beneficiary would be responsible for paying taxes on the earnings (amount received over the deceased's cost basis) at the beneficiary's tax rate.

448.

C. investors are protected against capital loss

Variable annuities have a separate account that's professionally managed and often contains mutual funds. Variable annuities are much more likely to keep pace with inflation than fixed annuities. However, variable annuity investors aren't protected against capital loss the way that holders of fixed annuities are.

449.

B. mortality guarantee

Actually, the only answer that wasn't made up was Choice (B). Holders of variable annuities receive payments for life even if they live beyond their life expectancy. The insurance company assumes the mortality guarantee.

450.   **A. II only**

Accumulation units are similar to shares of a mutual fund. A variable annuity holder purchases accumulation units during the pay-in phase. During the pay-out phase, the accumulation units are converted into annuity units. So for a variable annuity to have accumulation units, there had to be a pay-in phase. Out of the choices listed, the only one that had a pay-in phase was the *periodic payment deferred annuity.*

451.   **A. straight life annuity**

Annuities are retirement plans issued by insurance companies. Straight-life annuities are annuities with no beneficiaries and, therefore, provide the largest monthly payout. After the investor dies, the insurance company isn't required to pay a beneficiary. *Life annuity with period certain, joint and survivor annuities,* and *unit-refund annuities* have named beneficiaries to be paid if the policyholder dies early.

452.   **B. Mr. Silver, who is 56½ years old, has thousands available to invest, and has been investing the maximum into his IRA and 401(k) plan**

The best answer out of the choices listed is Choice (B) because Mr. Silver is already investing the maximum amount into his retirement plans and has additional money to invest. Mrs. Platinum would be another possibility except for her advanced age. You have to remember that variable annuities don't have a guaranteed payout. The payout on variable annuities varies depending on the performance of the securities held in the separate account.

453.   **A. the holder of the policy**

Annuities are retirement plans issued by insurance companies. The big difference with fixed and variable annuities is that in variable annuities, the investment risk is on the policyholder. In a fixed annuity, the insurance company holds the investment risk. Variable annuities are riskier but more likely to keep pace with inflation.

454.   **C. I and III**

This one is a little tricky. Most of the securities you will be dealing with only have to be registered with the SEC (Securities and Exchange Commission). However, variable annuities are a security that has to be registered with the SEC and an insurance product that must be registered with the State Insurance Commission.

455.   **D. a fixed number of annuity units based on the value of his accumulation units**

When a variable annuity is annuitized during the payout phase, investors receive a fixed number of annuity units based on the value of the accumulation units. The part that's variable with a variable annuity is that the payouts vary based on the value of the securities held.

456. **A. $4,100**

Investors that withdraw money from most retirement plans are assessed a 10 percent penalty for withdrawals before the age of 59½ except in cases of death, disability, and in some cases first-time homebuyers. Variable annuities are non-qualified retirement plans where contributions are made from after-tax dollars. Upon withdrawal, the investor is taxed only on the income earned by the investments in the separate account. Of the $20,000 withdrawn, $10,000 is taxable from the money earned on the investments held in the separate account. Therefore, because this investor was charged an extra 10 percent added to his tax bracket, he'll have to pay taxes at 41 percent:

$$\$10,000 \times 41\% = \$4,100$$

457. **B. voting on which partnership assets should be liquidated to pay creditors**

Limited partners have voting rights in a limited partnership. Partners can't vote on which assets should be liquidated to pay creditors because that's a decision the general partner makes.

458. **B. general partners assume the most risk**

The risk assumed by a limited partner is limited to the amount invested plus any additional loans. However, because general partners can be sued as a result of the partnership, they assume unlimited risk.

459. **A. an active role and unlimited liability**

A general partner has an active role in managing the partnership and has unlimited liability. A limited partner has an inactive role and limited liability.

460. **B. It could jeopardize the status of the limited partner.**

The role of a limited partner is supposed to be limited. If a limited partner gets involved in business activity that is supposed to be handled by a general partner, he could lose his limited liability status.

461. **C. providing a bulk of the capital for the partnership**

The general partner is responsible for running and making decisions for the partnership. However, the limited partners provide the bulk of the capital.

462. **A. I, II, and III**

Limited partners can't make management decisions for the partnership; that is the job of the general partner(s). However, limited partners may inspect the books, compete with the partnership (invest in another competing partnership), and vote to terminate the partnership.

463. **C. I, II, and IV**

Limited partnerships require a subscription agreement to accept new limited partners, a certificate of limited partnership to be filed with the Securities and Exchange Commission (SEC) and states, and a partnership agreement (agreement of limited partnership) that outlines the rights and responsibilities of the general and limited partners.

464. **D. I, II, and III**

The certificate of limited partnership must be filed with the Securities and Exchange Commission (SEC) and states. Included would be things such as the partnership's name, type of business, amount of time the partnership expects to be in business, the amount of contribution made by the limited and general partners, and so on.

465. **D. an oil and gas limited partnership**

Limited partnerships require written proof of the customer's financial background. Both the broker-dealer and the general partners must verify that the customer has a high enough net worth, enough money to invest now, and more money to invest in the future if necessary.

466. **D. a subscription agreement**

A general partner would sign a subscription agreement to accept a new limited partner.

467. **A. certificate of limited partnership**

A limited partnership (DPP) must file a certificate of limited partnership with the SEC (Securities and Exchange Commission) prior to a public offering. The subscription agreement is the paperwork a general partner must sign prior to accepting a new limited partner. The agreement of limited partnership states the rights and responsibilities of the limited and general partners.

468. **C. historic rehabilitation**

The objective of a historic rehabilitation direct participation program is to develop historic sites for commercial use. Because they invest in historical sites, investors receive tax credits from the government for preserving historic structures.

469. **D. sold**

Depletion has to do with reducing the amount of a mineral resource, such as oil and gas. Depletion deductions are based on the amount of oil and gas sold, not extracted from the ground and put in storage.

470. **A. I only**

Direct participation program (DPP) losses are deemed to be passive losses under IRS rules. Passive losses can be used to offset only passive gains from another direct participation program (partnership).

471. **D. real estate**

Non-recourse debt is available to limited partners in real estate direct participation programs (DPPs) only. Non-recourse debt involves pledging partnerships assets as collateral for a loan, and the limited partners aren't held personally responsible.

472. **C. The partnership is fully taxed by the IRS.**

Remember, you're looking for a false answer for this question. If you look at Choices (C) and (D), you can see that they're opposing answers, so it has to be one of them. One of the advantages of being a partner in a limited partnership is that all gains, losses, expenses, and income flows through to the limited and general partners. Remember that partnership passive gains and passive income can be written off only against passive losses.

473. **C. $60,000**

The cost basis is the maximum loss for the limited partner. In this case, Matt had deposited a total of $190,000.

$150,000 initial investment + $40,000 recourse debt = $190,000

However, Matt had $20,000 in cash distribution, $60,000 in depreciation deductions, and $50,000 in depletion deductions.

$190,000 − $20,000 − $60,000 − $50,000 = $60,000

474. **B. depreciation recapture**

Depreciation is reducing the value of a fixed asset as it gets older or becomes more obsolete. Recapture happens when depreciation deductions have been taken that exceed the value of the asset.

475. **D. $60,000**

This investor can lose the $25,000 initially deposited and is personally responsible for the recourse note he signed for $35,000, so his initial cost basis is $60,000.

476. **B. cash distributions**

When a limited partner receives a cash distribution, it reduces the cost basis because the limited partner is receiving some money back. The cost basis is derived from cash contributions, recourse and non-recourse debt of the partnership, and any property contributed to the partnership.

477. **A. the crossover point**

Typically, it takes partnerships a while to generate a positive cash flow. The point when partnership income exceeds deductions is called the crossover point.

478. **A. exploratory**

IDCs are intangible drilling costs and are associated only with oil and gas partnerships. IDCs are highest in the first year of operation; therefore, exploratory (wildcatting) is the best answer. IDCs are usually completely deductible in the first year, and they include expenses, such as fuel costs, insurance, wages, and supplies.

479. **B. II only**

Out of the choices given, the only partnership that could claim depletion deductions is oil and gas. Depletion deductions can be claimed only on a natural resource that has been used up (depleted). However, all three of the types of partnerships listed can claim depreciation deductions.

480. **C. the sales proceeds and the adjusted cost basis**

To determine the gain or loss, you have to compare the sales proceeds with the adjusted cost basis. The adjusted cost basis includes the amount invested plus any recourse loans minus any distributions taken.

481. **B. $870,000**

To determine the cash flow, use the following formula:

Cash flow = net income + depreciation + depletion

To determine the net income, take the revenues and subtract all of the expenses:

Net income = $2,000,000 − $800,000 − $150,000 − $1,200,000 − $180,000 = −$330,000

In this case, the net income was –$330,000. To determine the cash flow, you have to add the depreciation back in:

Cash flow = −$330,000 + $1,200,000 = $870,000

Notice that even though the net income is negative, the partnership still had a positive cash flow because depreciation is a write-off and not an out-of-pocket expense.

482. **C. appreciation**

The main concern of investors of undeveloped (raw) land limited partnerships is appreciation potential. Their hope is that land purchased by the partnership can be purchased cheaply and sold sometime in the future at a much higher price.

483. **D. It is one in which 25 percent or more of its sites have not been identified at the time of the offering.**

Blind pool can relate to oil and gas or real estate direct participation programs (DPPs). Typically, a large oil and gas DPP is offered in the form of a blind pool. In this case, investors aren't sure of all the properties that the partnership is investing in because they aren't all identified at the time of the offering. Investors of blind-pool offerings are relying on the general partner to choose sites that will become profitable.

484. **C. depletion deductions**

Depletion deductions can be claimed only on natural resources that can be used up. Because real estate can't be used up, real estate partnerships can't claim depletion deductions.

485. **B. oil well drill heads**

Equipment leasing partnerships generate revenue by leasing out equipment purchased by the partnership. Oil well drill heads are used by oil and gas drilling programs and aren't leased out by equipment leasing programs.

486. **A. I, II, III**

Income programs have the least risk because they purchase income-producing wells and sell what comes out of the ground. And exploratory (wildcatting) programs are the riskiest because they purchase land in unproven areas, hoping they find oil.

487. **A. oil and gas exploratory program**

You should direct John to invest in a partnership that produces immediate write-off to offset the gains from the real estate DPP. Oil and gas exploratory (wildcatting) programs have immediate write-offs as they're searching and/or drilling for oil. Oil and gas exploratory programs drill in unproven areas. Write-offs include things such as payroll, equipment, fuel, and leasing or purchasing land. Exploratory programs are the riskiest oil and gas DPPs but have the highest return if oil or gas is reached.

488. **C. Section 8**

Although your client may be limiting his upside potential, investing in a partnership specializing in Section 8 housing would provide stability of income. Section 8 housing is backed by U.S. government subsidies and is therefore considered quite safe.

489. **C. capital appreciation potential**

You're looking for the false answer in this question. Equipment leasing limited partnerships make money by leasing out equipment. The equipment leased out gets worn out or outdated, so capital appreciation potential makes no sense. However, a steady stream of income, depreciation deductions, and operating expenses to offset revenues are all advantages of investing in an equipment leasing program.

490. **B. an oil and gas limited partnership**

If Marge is looking to add some liquidity (ease of trading) to her portfolio, an oil and gas limited partnership wouldn't make sense. Limited partnerships (direct participation programs, DPPs) are some of the most difficult investments to get in and out of. Limited partnerships require approval not only of the registered rep but also of the general partner of the limited partnership. Limited partnership investors need a certain minimum deposit and need to have liquidity in other investments in case the limited partnership needs additional funds to meet its goal.

491. **B. developmental program**

Oil and gas exploratory programs drill in unproven areas. Oil and gas developmental programs drill in proven areas. Oil and gas income programs take over existing, productive areas. Oil and gas combination programs are a combination of all three.

492. **C. an income program**

Because your client is set on investing in an oil and gas program and is risk-averse, you should put him in the safest program, which is an income program. Income programs invest in already producing wells, so the risk is minimal as compared to the other programs. However, the potential reward isn't going to be as high as the other programs.

493. **D. You should not recommend a limited partnership.**

The key to this question is that Mary has all of the rest of her money tied up in non-liquid investments. Partnerships require not only an initial investment but also the limited partners to come up with additional funds if needed. It's your job as a registered rep to pre-screen investors prior to having an investor submit a subscription agreement to a general partner. Part of that pre-screening process is to make sure that a potential limited partner has liquidity in other investments. In this case, Mary isn't a good fit for a limited partnership. However, you may want to recommend that she invest in real estate investment trusts.

494. **A. III, IV, I, II**

In the event of a bankruptcy, the secured creditors would be paid before the unsecured creditors. After that, any assets remaining would be paid to the limited partners and finally to the general partner(s).

495. **D. real estate investment trusts**

You'll notice that all the partnerships require proof of the investor's financial status. The reason is because investors are not only responsible for an initial investment but may also be required to invest more money if needed. Such is not the case for real estate investment trusts (REITs).

496. **C. a combination program**

Oil and gas combination programs offer diversification between exploratory, developmental, and income producing areas.

Answers
401–500

497. **B. I and II**

The purchase of call options and the sale of covered call options may be executed in cash accounts. Because of the additional risk, short sales, the sale of naked options, and spreads must be executed in margin accounts.

498. **A. strike price minus the premium**

When writing (selling) a naked (uncovered) call option, the maximum loss is unlimited. However, when writing a naked put option, the maximum loss is the strike (exercise) price minus the premium. Put options go in the money when the price of the stock drops below the strike price. This means that a put option can go only so far in the money because the price of the underlying stock can drop only to zero. Therefore, the maximum loss per share is the strike price less whatever Mr. Drudge received per share when he sold the option.

499. **B. I and IV**

Buying calls is a bullish strategy because the investor wants the price of the underlying security to increase. For example, if an investor purchased an ABC 30 call option, the investor would want the price of the stock to go above 30. If the price of ABC increases above 30, the investor could exercise the option to buy the stock at 30 and sell it in the market for a higher price. In addition, selling in-the-money put options is also a bullish strategy because the seller wants the price of the underlying security to increase. When selling a naked option, the most an investor can hope to make is the premium received. Therefore, the seller wouldn't want the put option to go into the money more; he'd want the underlying stock to increase in value.

500. **C. ABC May 50 call**

The phrase *call up and put down* will help you remember that call options go in the money when the price of the stock goes above the strike price, and put options go in the money when the price of the stock goes below the strike price. Choice (A) is in the money because the price of the stock is below the put price of 45. Choice (B) is in the money because the price of the stock is above the 35 call strike price. Choice (D) is in the money because the price of the stock is below the 55 put strike price. However, Choice (C) is out of the money because the price of the stock is below the 50 call strike price.

501. **B. 4**

To determine the time value of an option, you can use the following equation:

$$P = I + T$$

where P is the premium of the option, I is the intrinsic value of the option (how much it's in the money), and T is the time value of the option. In this case, you're looking for the time value, so plug in the numbers for the premium and intrinsic value and then solve for time. The premium is 9, and the intrinsic value is 5 because call options go in the money when the stock price goes above the strike price. To determine the intrinsic value, just subtract the 50 strike price from the market price of $55, which equals 5.

$$9 = 5 + T$$
$$T = 9 - 5$$
$$T = 4$$

502.   **C. II and III**

You have to remember that sellers (writers or shorters) of options always face more risk than the buyers. The buyers' risk is limited to the amount they invest. However, sellers of put options don't face a maximum loss potential that's unlimited because put options go in the money when the price of the stock drops below the strike price, and it can go down only to 0.

Sellers of uncovered calls face an unlimited maximum loss potential because call options go in the money when the price of the stock increases above the strike price, and the seller would have to purchase the stock at a price that could keep going higher. Additionally, investors who short stock (Statement II) face an unlimited maximum loss potential because they're bearish and lose money when the price of the security increases, and nothing stops the price from increasing. Investors who have sold covered calls don't face an unlimited maximum loss potential because they already have the stock to deliver if exercised.

503.   **A. above the exercise price plus the premium paid**

In order for an investor to profit from a long call position, he'd have to exercise the option when the market price is above the exercise (strike) price plus the premium paid.

504.   **D. The option is exercised when the price of the underlying stock is below the strike price minus the premium.**

When selling an uncovered put option, an investor takes a bullish position. The maximum potential gain is the premium received. In other words, the investor doesn't want the option to be exercised because he'll start losing money and possibly even end up taking a loss. Therefore, Choice (D) is the correct answer.

505.   **A. I, III, and IV**

Call options go in the money when the market price is greater than the strike (exercise) price. Put options go in the money whenever the market price is lower than the strike price. Therefore, the only option that isn't in the money when UPP is trading at 43.50 is short a 40 put.

506. **C. long a put or short a call**

Investors who are long a put or short a call deliver a stock when the option is exercised. Here's the breakdown:

- *Long a call* is the right to buy the stock.
- *Long a put* is the right to sell the stock.
- *Short a call* is the obligation to sell the stock.
- *Short a put* is the obligation to buy the stock.

507. **B. buying a DWN put option**

You should have knocked out Choice (A) right away because buying a call option is a bullish strategy used when you believe the price of the security is going to increase. Choices (C) and (D) would work, but they aren't the cheapest options. Buying a straddle is ideal when you aren't sure which direction the stock is going because you're buying a put and buying a call. When shorting a stock, an investor has to come up with 50 percent of the market value. *Buying a put* is the best answer because it's a bearish strategy, and investors can have an interest in a large amount of securities for a small outlay of money.

508. **B. The premium decreases the cost basis.**

Selling covered calls reduces the cost basis. The best way to see this is to use sample numbers. Say that an investor purchased stock for $50 per share and then sold a covered call for $3. He originally spent $50 per share and then got $3 back, so his cost basis was reduced from $50 to $47 ($50 – $3).

509. **D. I, II, III, and IV**

Options of the same series have the same stock, expiration month, strike price, and type (calls or puts).

510. **C. the strike price minus the premium**

The best way to determine a break-even point for an investor who has only an option position is to remember *call up* and *put down*. Because this is a put option, you need to put down by subtracting the premium from the strike price. This answer would apply whether the investor was long the put or short the put.

511. **A. a capital gain**

All option transactions will result in a capital gain, a capital loss, or a break-even position.

512. **C. 100 shares of the underlying security**

Most option contracts represent 100 shares of the underlying security.

513. **B. one business day prior to expiration**

Unlike American-style options, which can be exercised at any time, European-style options can be exercised only one business day prior to expiration. Almost all options are American-style but world-currency options may be either American-style or European-style.

514. **D. I, II, and III**

All of the choices listed are important factors in an option's premium. If the underlying security is subject to wide price swings, the option has more of a chance of going in the money, and sellers would expect a higher premium for taking more risk. Also, when comparing two options with everything equal except the expiration month, the one with the longer time until maturity would have a higher price because it has more of a chance of going in the money. *Remember:* An option's premium is made up of intrinsic value (how much the option is in the money) and time value. If the intrinsic value goes up, the premium goes up.

515. **C. selling uncovered calls**

When purchasing an option, the most you can lose is the premium. Therefore, option sellers always face more risk than option buyers. When selling uncovered call options, the maximum loss potential is unlimited because call options go in the money when the price goes above the strike price. In theory, the price of the stock can keep going up. Put options go in the money when the price of the stock goes below the strike price. Because the price can go only to zero, the maximum loss potential when selling an uncovered put isn't unlimited.

516. **C. obligation to buy stock at a fixed price if exercised**

The purchasers of options always have the right, and the writers (sellers) have the obligation to live up to the terms of the contract if exercised. Here it is in a nutshell:

- *Buy a call* is the right to buy stock.
- *Buy a put* is the right to sell stock.
- *Sell a call* is the obligation to sell stock.
- *Sell a put* is the obligation to buy stock.

517. **D. 3.5**

The premium of an option is made of intrinsic value (how much the option is in the money) and time value (the longer the maturity, the higher the premium). In this case, the option isn't in the money because put options go in the money when the price of the stock goes below the strike price. That means that the price of the stock would have to be below $45, which it isn't. So because there's no intrinsic value, the premium is made up entirely of time value, which is 3.5.

518. **B. 9 months**

Standard option contracts are issued with nine-month expirations. Long-term equity anticipation securities (LEAPS) have expirations of up to 39 months.

519. **C. 12.25**

An options premium (P) is made up of intrinsic value (I) and time value (T). This option has an intrinsic value (an in-the-money amount) of 12 because it's a 40 call option, and the stock is at 52. Call options go in the money when the price of the stock goes above the strike price. So the premium has to be at least 12. Because the option is only two days away from expiration, the time value has to be really small. The only answer that works is Choice (C).

520. **A. 34**

The easiest way to determine the break-even point for an individual option is to remember *call up* and *put down:*

- Call up: Add the premium to the call strike price.
- Put down: Subtract the premium to the put strike price.

In this case, you must *put down:* $40 - 6 = 34$.

521. **A. $700**

This question is relatively easy. You can use an options chart, but it's probably not really necessary. The question doesn't mention anything about this investor having any other stock or option positions, so you're just dealing with the individual option. Because this investor sold the option, the most she can hope to make is the premium received. The premium received is $700 (7 premium × 100 shares per option).

522. **B. $75 gain**

The easiest way for you to see what's going on is to set up an options chart. This investor wrote (sold) the RST put for a premium of 3.25, so you have to put $325 ($3.25 × 100 shares per option) in the *Money In* side of the chart because the investor received the money for selling the option. Next, the option was exercised, so you have to put $4,000 (the $40 strike price × 100 shares per option) in the *Money Out* side of the chart because "puts switch," meaning that the exercised option has to go on the opposite side of the chart from the premium. After that, the investor sold the 100 shares of stock in the market for $37.50 per share for a total of $3,750, which goes in the *Money In* side of the chart because the investor received money for selling the stock. Total up the two sides, and you'll see that the investor had received $4,075 and spent $4,000 for a miniscule profit of $75.

Money Out	Money In
$4000	$325
	$3750
$4000	$4075

523. **C. (strike price – the premium) × 100 shares × 10 options**

When selling an uncovered (naked) put option, the most the seller could lose is the strike price minus the premium multiplied by 100 shares and then by 10 options. Put options go in the money when the price of the stock goes down below the strike (exercise) price. Because the stock can go down only to zero, the seller can lose money from the strike price down to zero less the premium received. However, because options are for 100 shares, you have to multiply that answer by 100 shares and then by the 10 options the customer sold.

524. **A. 31.5**

Put options go in the money when the price of the stock goes below the strike price. Therefore, this stock has to go 3.5 points below the strike price of 35 for this investor to break even.

$$35 - 3.5 = 31.5 \text{ break-even point}$$

525. **D. $41.75**

When you're determining the break-even point for an individual option, the current market value doesn't fit into the equation. You just have to look at what the investor paid for the option and the strike price. Call options go in the money when the price of the stock goes above the strike price. In this case, Mr. Couture paid 1.75 for the option, so the break-even point would be $40 + 1.75 = \$41.75$.

526. **C. $65.00**

This is a fairly easy question if you remember that options are for 100 shares, unless otherwise stated in the question. It's as simple as taking the premium increase and multiplying it by 100:

$$0.65 \times 100 = \$65.00$$

527. **B. $415**

When selling an individual option, the maximum potential gain is the premium. When looking at the exhibit, the first column is the market price of RST, the second column is the strike prices, and everything to the right of that column is the premiums. To find the premium for a Dec 50 put, find where the *Dec* column (the last one) and the *50p* row (the bottom one) intersect. In this case, it's 4.15, which represents a price of $415 because options are for 100 shares.

528. **C. 68.38**

This question includes a lot of information that isn't needed to get the answer. Put options go in the money when the price of the stock goes below the strike (exercise) price. To get the answer, all you need to do is "put down" (subtract the premium from the strike price). In this case, you need to subtract 6.62 from 75.

$$75 - 6.62 = 68.38$$

529. **B. long combination**

Because the investor purchased both options, it has to be long because *long* means to buy. Therefore, you can knock out Choices (C) and (D) right away. Next, you have to determine whether it's a combination or a straddle. To be a straddle, the call and put purchased would have to have the same stock, same expiration month, and same strike price. Because the strike prices are different, it's a combination.

530. **B. Write a DUD straddle.**

To generate income, your client has to sell something. The only answer choice that has your client selling something is Choice (B). Writing (selling) a straddle would allow your client to generate income on a stock that's remaining stable because he'd receive the premiums for selling the straddle. Your client would be able to profit if neither the call option nor put option that are part of the straddle go too much in the money.

531. **A. $200 gain**

You can best work out this question in an options chart. Look at the following setup:

Money Out	Money In
$400	$3500
$700	
$2200	
$3300	$3500

This investor bought the CDE Nov 35 call for 4, so you enter $400 (4 × 100 shares per option) on the *Money Out* side of the options chart. The investor also bought the CDE Nov 35 put for 7, so enter $700 (7 × 100 shares per option), again on the *Money Out* side.

Next, the investor bought the stock in the market at the market price of $22 per share for a total of $2,200 ($22 per share × 100 shares) to cover the put option. The investor spent $2,200 for the stock; therefore, that amount also goes on the *Money Out* side of the options chart. After that, you exercise the put. You have to exercise the put at its strike price of 35. Calculating 35 × 100 shares per option gives you a price of $3,500, which you enter on the *Money In* side of the chart because "puts switch" (go on the opposite side of the options chart from its premium). Add up each side, and you see that this investor had a gain of $200 ($3,500 in and $3,300 out).

532. **C. 25 and 50**

This investor sold the two options for a combined premium of $10 per share (7 + 3). Therefore, this investor would break even when either the call option goes 10 in the money or the put goes 10 in the money. Call options go in the money when the price of the stock goes above the strike price, and put options go in the money when the price of the stock goes below the strike price.

$$40 \text{ call} + 10 = 50$$
$$35 \text{ put} - 10 = 25$$

533. **D. unlimited**

This question is a lot easier than the answer choices suggest. When purchasing a straddle, you're buying a call and buying a put. The maximum potential gain is unlimited on the call side. Purchasing a put along with a call doesn't change that fact.

534. **D. short one TUV Sep 40 put**

First, to create a *short* anything, you can't have a *long* in it. Therefore, you can eliminate Choices (A) and (B) right away. A short combination is selling (shorting) a call and selling a put on the same stock, with the same strike price, and the same expiration month. The only answer choice that fits that description is Choice (D).

535. **C. remain stable**

Selling a straddle is selling a call and selling a put on the same stock, same strike price, and same expiration month. When selling a straddle, the most you can hope to make is the premiums that you received. In this case, the investor would hope that the stock price of XYZ stays right at the strike price of 35 so that neither option will be exercised. If that happens, he gets to keep the premiums he received for selling the options. Remember, the buyer and the seller want opposite things to happen — the seller wants stability, and the buyer wants volatility.

536. **C. neutral on DEF**

When an investor sells an at-the-money straddle, the investor has already maximized his profit. If the price of the underlying stock moves in either direction, one of the options will go in the money, and the seller will start losing money. Therefore, this investor wants the stock to stay at the same price and is neutral on DEF.

537. **D. II and IV**

Sellers of straddles and combinations maximize their profits when the underlying security doesn't go in the money. They make their profit on the premium received and start to lose it if the underlying security goes in the money.

538. **B. short combination**

Sellers always face more risk than buyers. When shorting (selling) a combination, a straddle, or uncovered call option, the seller faces an unlimited maximum loss potential. There's no unlimited maximum gain or loss potential, whether long or short a spread.

539. **A. $400 gain**

Start by setting up an options chart. Look at the following setup:

Money Out	Money In
$900	$5,800
$500	
$4,000	
$5,400	$5,800

This investor bought the ABC May 40 call for 9, so you enter $900 (9 × 100 shares per option) on the *Money Out* side of the options chart. The investor also bought the ABC May 40 for 5, so enter $500 (5 × 100 shares per option), again on the *Money Out* side. Next, the investor exercised the call, so you have to put $4,000 (40 strike price × 100 shares per option) on the same side as its premium because "calls same" (the exercised option goes on the same side of the options chart as its premium). Next, the investor received $5,800 ($58 × 100 shares) for selling the stock in the market, so you have to put $5,800 on the *Money In* side of the chart. Total up, and you see that the investor had a $400 gain ($5,800 – $5,400).

540. **C. I and III**

When you're holding a straddle, you're holding a call and holding a put on the same security. This means that you're neither bullish nor bearish, but you want the underlying security to move enough in either direction for you to make a profit. Therefore, you're looking for volatility.

541. **A. $44.70**

This investor has established a long straddle. The investor purchased the call for 6.5 and the put for 3.2 for a combined premium per share of 9.7 (6.5 + 3.2). To find the points where the investor breaks even, you have to add the 9.7 to the call strike price and subtract the 9.7 from the put strike price:

$$55 + 9.7 = 64.7$$
$$55 - 9.7 = 45.3$$

The break-even points for this investor are 64.7 and 45.3. For this investor to see a profit, the stock would have to be trading below 45.3 or above 64.7. The only answer that works is $44.70.

542. **A. I or II**

With straddles, you must add the premiums and use "call up" (add the combined premiums to the strike price) and "put down" (subtract the combined premiums from the strike price) to figure out the break-even points. An investor who is long a straddle has a loss, unless the price of the underlying security goes below the put break-even point or above the call break-even point.

543. **C. long straddle**

Beta tells you how volatile a stock is in relation to the market. A stock with a high beta is a volatile stock. Holders of long straddles and long combinations are looking for volatility of the underlying security.

544. **D. $300 loss**

Start by setting up an options chart. In the *Money Out* side, place the $600 (6 × 100 shares per option) and the $200 (2 × 100 shares per option) that the customer paid to purchase the two options. To *close* means to do the opposite. Because the customer originally purchased the two options, to close, he has to sell the two options. Place the closing transactions in the *Money In* side of the chart. He sold the call for $100 and the put for $400.

Money Out	Money In
$600	$100
$200	$400
$800	$500

The customer has $300 more out than in, so that is his loss.

545. **D. long one HIJ Dec 80 call/short one HIJ Nov 70 call**

To create a spread, you need to buy a call and sell a call or buy a put and sell a put with the same stock. To create a bearish spread, you have to buy the option with the higher strike price and sell the option with the lower strike price.

Remember: Buy low, sell high is bullish, and buy high, sell low is bearish.

You may have inadvertently picked Choice (C), but if you look closely, you'll notice that you're dealing with two different stocks, so it's not a spread.

546. **B. $900**

Using an options chart to answer the question, you first need to put the premiums in the chart. Mr. Levin wrote (sold) the 60 put for 6, so you need to put $600 (6 premium × 100 shares per option) on the *Money In* side of the chart. Next, he bought the 75 put for 12, so you have to place $1,200 ($12 premium × 100 shares per option) in the *Money Out* side of the chart. Stop and take a look at the chart to see whether you have more money in than out. At this point, you see that you have $600 more out than in, so that is Mr. Levin's maximum potential loss.

To get the maximum potential gain, you need to exercise both options. First, exercise the 60 put option and place the $6,000 (60 strike price × 100 shares per option) on the opposite side of its premium because "puts switch" (the exercised option goes on the opposite side of the chart from its premium). Then, place the $7,500 (75 strike price × 100 shares per option) in the chart across from its premium for the same reason.

Answers
501–600

Money Out	Money In
$1,200	$600
$6,000	$7,500
$7,200	$8,100

Total up the two sides, and you see that you have $900 more money in than money out, so that is Mr. Levin's maximum potential gain.

---

547. **C. diagonal spread**

To create a spread, an investor has to buy a call and sell a call or buy a put and sell a put on the same security. In this case, Mrs. Jones has indeed created a spread. To determine whether it's a vertical, horizontal, or diagonal spread, you need to look at the strike prices and expiration months. If just the strike prices are different, it's a vertical spread. If just the expiration months are different, it's a horizontal spread. If both the strike prices and the expiration months are different, as in this case, it's a diagonal spread.

---

548. **D. buying a put at a low strike price and selling a put at a high strike price**

To create a spread, you're buying an option and selling an option on the same security. To create a short (credit) spread, you have to have received more money for the option sold than the money you paid for the option purchased. This question is particularly tough because you weren't given the premiums. However, using a little bit of logic, you can get the answer. When comparing two options where everything is the same except the strike (exercise) price, the one that's in the money first will have a higher premium. So Choice (D) is correct. Put options go in the money when the price of the stock goes down. Therefore, the one with the higher strike price will be in the money first and therefore have a higher premium. Because you're buying the one with the lower premium and selling the one with the higher premium, you have created a credit spread.

---

549. **A. I or III**

To answer this question, you need to determine whether you're dealing with a credit or debit spread. Start out by placing the premiums in an options chart, like the following:

Money Out	Money In
$200	$700

This investor bought the STU Sep 30 put for a premium of $200 (2 × 100 shares per option). Because the investor bought for $200, place this amount in the *Money Out* portion of the options chart. Next, the investor sold the STU Sep 40 put for a premium of $700 (7 × 100 shares per option). Put that premium in the *Money In* portion of the options chart, because the investor received money for selling that option. This investor has a credit spread, because he has more money in than money out. When an investor has a credit spread, he wants the premium difference to narrow (premiums narrow as the options get closer to expiration or move further away from being in the money), and he wants the options to expire so he can keep the profit.

550.

D. $425

You can cross out the ZAM Dec 45 put and the ZAM Dec 50 put right away because you can't create a call spread with puts. To create a debit call spread, the investor has to pay more for the option purchased than he receives for the one he sold. Investors always buy at the offer (ask) price and sell at the bid price. Having this knowledge, the only thing that makes sense is the investor's buying the ZAM Dec 45 call for 5.25 and selling the ZAM Dec 50 call for 1. Place these values in the options chart to get your answer:

Money Out	Money In
$525	$100

Because the investor purchased the Dec 45 call for 5.25, place $525 (5.25 × 100 shares per option) in the *Money Out* side of the chart. Then the investor sold the Dec 50 call for 1, so you need to place $100 (1 × 100 shares per option) in the *Money In* side of the chart. Total up, and you see that the investor had an out-of-pocket expense of $425 ($525 – $100).

551.

A. the difference between the exercised strike prices minus the difference between the premiums

The easiest way to see this is to set up an options chart, using made-up numbers. To create a debit call spread, you have to purchase a call option with a higher premium and sell an option with a lower premium. Call options go in the money when the price of the stock goes above the strike price, so to create a debit spread, you have to purchase the one with the lower strike price because it will be in the money first. Here's an example:

Buy 1 ABC Oct 40 call for 8

Sell 1 ABC Oct 50 call for 2

Now set up an options chart.

Money Out	Money In
$800	$200

The option was purchased for $800 (8 premium × 100 shares per option), so you have to place $800 in the *Money Out* side of the chart. Next, the 50 call option was sold for $200 (2 premium × 100 shares per option), so you have to place $200 in the *Money Out* side of the chart. At this point, you have established a maximum loss of $600 ($800 – $200). So to get the maximum potential gain, you have to exercise both options.

Money Out	Money In
$800	$200
$4000	$5000
$4800	$5200

Exercise the 40 call option by placing $4,000 (40 strike price × 100 shares per option) under its premium because "calls same" (the exercised strike price goes on the same side of the chart as its premium). Then, put $5,000 under its premium of $200 for the same reason. Total up, and you come up with a maximum potential gain of $400 ($5,200 − $4,800).

The only answer choice that works is Choice (A). Here's the proof: The difference between the exercised strike prices is $1,000 ($5,000 − $4,000). The difference between the premiums is $600 ($800 − $200). And $1,000 − $600 = $400.

552.

C. II and III

If an investor creates a spread, it means that he's long a call and short a call or long a put and short a put. When creating a debit spread, when just looking at the premiums, the investor already has a loss. So he'd want the options to be exercised. Also, if the premium difference widens, he could sell himself out of the position for more money than he paid for creating the debit spread to begin with.

553.

C. $46

To determine the break-even point for spreads, you have to subtract the premiums and then call up (add the adjusted premium to the lower call price) or put down (subtract the adjusted premium from the higher strike price). Your client purchased the one option at 8 ($800) and sold the other one at 2 ($200) for a net cost of $6 per share (8 − 2). That means that the option that your client owns has to go in the money by $6 for her to break even. The one she purchased was the $40 call, so you just need to call up from the $40 strike price by adding $6 to it: $40 + $6 = $46.

554.

B. $62

To determine the break-even point for spreads, you have to subtract the premiums and then call up (add the adjusted premium to the lower call price) or put down (subtract the adjusted premium from the higher strike price). Stan sold the one option at 5 ($500) and purchased the other one at 2 ($200) for a net profit of $3 per share (5 − 2). To determine the break-even point, you need to subtract the $3 from the higher strike price of $65: $65 − $3 = $62.

555.

C. $1,300

Using an options chart to answer the question, you first need to put the premiums in the chart. The investor bought the 40 call for 9, so you need to put $900 (9 premium × 100 shares per option) on the *Money Out* side of the chart. Next, he wrote (sold) the 60 call for 2, so you have to place $200 ($2 premium × 100 shares per option) in the *Money In* side of the chart. Stop and take a look at the chart to see whether you have more money in than out. At this point, you have $700 more out than in, so that is the investor's maximum potential loss.

To get the maximum potential gain, you need to exercise both options. First, exercise the 40 put option and place the $4,000 (40 strike price × 100 shares per option) on the same side as its premium because "calls same" (the exercised option goes on the same side of the chart from its premium). Then, place the $6,000 (60 strike price × 100 shares per option) in the chart on the same side as its premium for the same reason.

Money Out	Money In
$900	$200
$4000	$6000
$4900	$6200

Total up the two sides, and you see that you have $1,300 more money in than money out, so that is the investor's maximum potential gain.

556. **A. vertical spread**

Because Mrs. Smith has spent more money for the option she purchased than she received for the option sold, she has a long (debit) spread. To tell whether it's vertical, horizontal, or diagonal, you have to look at the strike prices and expiration months of the options. If just the strike prices are different, it's a vertical (price) spread. If just the expiration months are different, it's a horizontal (calendar) spread. If both are different, it's a diagonal spread. In this case, just the strike prices are different, so it's a vertical spread.

557. **C. bullish/neutral on LMN**

Your client received more money for the option sold than he paid for the one purchased, so he has a short (credit) spread. At this point, neither option is in the money, and he has the maximum profit that he can make. If the options start going in the money, he'll start losing money, which wouldn't be good. Because put options go in the money when the price of the stock goes down, he's okay with the stock sitting at the price it is now (neutral position) and with the stock price going up (bullish).

558. **B. $100 loss**

Start by setting up an options chart. This investor purchased the 70 put for 4, so you need to put $400 (4 × 100 shares per option) in the *Money Out* side of the chart. Next, the investor wrote (sold) the 90 put for 12, so you need to put $1,200 (12 × 100 shares per option) in the *Money In* side of the chart. This investor closed the 70 put by selling it at 6, so you need to put $600 in the *Money In* side of the chart. Finally, he closed the 90 put by purchasing it for 15, so you need to put $1,500 in the *Money Out* side of the chart. Total up the two sides, and you see that this investor had a $100 loss.

Money Out	Money In
$400	$1200
$1500	$600
$1900	$1800

Remember, for an investor to close himself out of a position, he has to do the opposite of what he did initially. If he originally bought an option, to close, he'd have to sell the option. If he originally sold the option, to close, he'd have to buy the option.

559. **D. II and IV**

This question is a bit more difficult because you aren't given the premiums. However, because the options are on the same stock and have the same expiration month, the one that goes in the money first would have to have a higher premium. Call options go in the money when the price of the underlying stock goes up, so the 50 call has to have a higher premium than the 60 call. That means that it has to be a credit spread because the investor received more money for the option sold than he paid for the option purchased. The easiest way to tell whether it's a bullish position or a bearish position is to look at the strike prices. If the investor is buying the low one and selling the higher one (like he did in this case), he is bullish. If he's buying the higher one and selling the lower one, he is bearish. Whether you're dealing with a put spread or call spread doesn't make a difference here.

560. **D. $325**

You can cross out the GHI Sep 40 put and the GHI Sep 50 put right away because you can't create a call spread with puts. To create a debit call spread, the investor has to pay more for the option purchased than he receives for the one he sold. Investors always buy at the offer (ask) price and sell at the bid price. Having this knowledge, the only thing that makes sense is the investor's buying the GHI Sep 40 call for 5.25 and selling the GHI Sep 50 call for 2. Place these values in the options chart to get your answer:

Money Out	Money In
$525	$200

The investor bought the GHI Sep 40 call for $525 (5.25 premium × 100 shares per option), so that goes on the *Money Out* side of the options chart. Next, enter the $200 (2 premium × 100 shares per option) on the *Money In* side of the options chart, because the investor received $200 for selling that option. The investor paid $325 more for the option purchased than he received for the option sold.

561. **B. I and IV**

A vertical spread means that the strike prices of the two options used to create the spread are different. When creating a long (debit) call spread, an investor is buying the call option that's going to be in the money first and selling the one that's going to be in the money second. Therefore, creating a vertical long call spread is bullish. When shorting a put spread, the investor is selling the option that's going to be in the money first if the price of the stock goes down and buying the one that's going to be in the money second. This means that the investor already has a profit and doesn't want the price of the stock to go down. Investors of vertical short put spreads are bullish or neutral.

562. **C. long 1 JKL Sep 40 call/short 1 JKL Sep 30 call**

To create a credit spread, you have to sell the option that has the higher premium and purchase the option with the lower premium. Choice (C) is a credit spread because you're short the 30 call and long the 40 call. Call options go in the money when the price of the stock increases and it has to hit 30 before 40. This means that the 30 call option sold has to have a higher premium.

563. **B. bearish call spread**

This customer bought one option and sold the other on the same stock, so it's a spread position. Because the customer bought the option with the higher strike price and sold the one with the lower strike price, he created a bearish spread.

564. **C. 56**

When determining the break-even point for spreads, you have to start by subtracting the premiums. In this case, he shorted (sold) the one option for 6 and longed (purchased) the other one for 2 for a net gain of 4 (6 − 2). Next, because it's a put spread, you have to subtract that 4 from the higher strike price (60) to get the break-even point: $60 - 4 = 56$.

565. **A. different expiration months**

A horizontal spread is also known as a calendar spread because the two options that make up the spread have different expiration months.

566. **D. II and IV**

Because both the expiration months and the strike prices are different, it's a diagonal spread. This investor paid more for the option purchased (13) than he received for the option sold (9), so it's also a debit spread.

567. **C. ratio spread**

Ratio spreads are when a customer writes more contracts than he purchased. This exposes the customer to a maximum potential loss that's unlimited because three call options were sold that are uncovered (naked).

568. **B. bearish**

A debit put spread is purchasing a put with a higher strike price and selling a put with a lower strike price. Debit means that the investor paid more for the option purchased than he received for the option sold. The investor would need his put option to go in the money to have any chance of making money. Because put options go in the money when the market price of the security goes down, holders of debit put spreads are bearish.

569. **A. I and III**

To create a spread, you have to have one long and one short option. Therefore, you can eliminate Statement II, which leaves you with Choice (A). Statement IV is also out because you need either two calls or two puts.

570. **B. $4,425**

The first thing you should do is put the stock and the option in an options chart. Because Mr. Goldshack purchased the stock for $4,750 ($47.50 × 100 shares), you need to put that in the *Money Out* side of the chart. And he sold the option for $325 ($3.25 × 100 shares per option), so you need to put that in the *Money In* side of the chart.

Money Out	Money In
$4750	$325

At this point, you stop to take a look to see whether you have your answer. Because the question is asking for the maximum potential loss, you don't need to go any further because you already have more money out than in. Subtract the two numbers to get the answer: $4,750 − $325 = $4,425.

571. **D. $47.50**

When shorting a stock, an investor makes money when the price of that stock decreases and loses money when the price increases. In this case, the investor received $44.50 per share for shorting the stock and another $3 per share for selling the covered put. That means that the investor's break-even point is $44.50 + $3 = $47.50.

572. **B. fall sharply**

Buying a protective put on a stock owned protects the investor if the market falls quickly. Even though the investor will be losing money on the stock owned, the put will be gaining in value to offset some of the loss.

573. **B. $495**

The easiest way for you to see what's going on is to set up an options chart. Your customer purchased 100 shares of DEFG at 45.10, so you have to put $4,510 (45.10 × 100 shares) in the *Money Out* side of the chart. Next, your customer purchased an OEX put for 4.50, so you have to put $450 (4.50 × 100 shares per option) in the *Money Out* side of the chart. If your customer closes the stock position (to close means do the opposite — so if he originally bought, to close, he has to sell) for 43.55, you have to put $4,355 (43.55 stock price × 100 shares) in the *Money In* side of the chart. Then, because you're dealing with an option that settles in cash instead of delivery of the underlying security, you need to put the profit of $1,100 in the *Money In* side of the chart. To get to the

$1,100, you have to remember that put options go in the money when the price of the stock goes below the strike price, which it is by 11 (790 – 779), and options are for 100 shares. Total up the two sides, and you see that your customer had a profit of $5,455 – $4,960 = $495.

Money Out	Money In
$4510	$4355
$450	$1100
$4960	$5455

---

574.   **A. buy an LMN call option**

To *hedge* means to protect. If Mr. Gold wants to hedge his position, he should buy a call on LMN above the market price. Remember that Mr. Gold is short the stock and must buy LMN back at some point to close his short position. Buying an LMN call gives him the right to buy back LMN at a fixed price, which would allow him to protect the position and not face an unlimited maximum loss potential.

---

575.   **B. $1,600**

To make this question easier, use an options chart. Because the investor purchased 100 shares of TUV at $40, you need to put $4,000 on the *Money Out* side of the chart because that's how much the investor spent. Next, the investor wrote (sold) a 50 call for $600 (6 premium × 100 shares per option), so you need to put that in the *Money In* side of the chart because the investor received $600 for selling the option. Before going any further, stop to see if that answered your question. At this point, you have $3,400 more money out than in so that is the maximum potential loss, not maximum potential gain. This tells you that you need to exercise the option to get the answer you need. Take $5,000 (50 strike price × 100 shares per option) and put it in the *Money In* side of the options chart because calls same, meaning that the exercised strike price goes on the same side of the chart as its premium. Total up the sides to get your answer.

Money Out	Money In
$4000	$600
	$5000
$4000	$5600

After totaling the two sides, you see that you have $1,600 more money in than money out, so that is the investor's maximum potential gain.

---

576.   **D. $825 gain**

The easiest way for you to see what's going on is to set up an options chart. Todd purchased 100 shares of HLP at 25, so you have to put $2,500 (25 × 100 shares) in the *Money Out* side of the chart. Next, Todd wrote (sold) an HLP call for 3.25, so you have to put $325 (3.25 × 100 shares per option) in the *Money In* side of the chart. After the stock increased, the call was exercised, so you have to put the exercised strike price of

$3,000 (30 strike price × 100 shares per option) under its premium of $325 because "calls same," meaning that for call options, the premium and the exercised strike price go on the same side of the chart. Total up the two sides, and you see that Todd had a gain of $825 ($3,325 in − $2,500 out).

Money Out	Money In
$2500	$325
	$3000
$2500	$3325

577. A. write a TUF call

The key to this question is that Mr. Hendricks is trying to generate some additional income. This means that he has to sell something because buying something costs him money. Because Mr. Hendricks has the stock to deliver if the option is exercised, his best option is to write a covered call on TUF.

578. A. $44.25

This investor sold short DWN at $47.50 per share. When an investor sells short, he stands to make a profit when the security decreases in price. Because this investor purchased the protective call for 3.25, the stock that he shorted would have to decrease by that amount for him to break even: $47.50 − $3.25 = $44.25.

579. A. $25 gain

The easiest way for you to see what's going on in this question is to set up an options chart. Zeb bought the put for $275 (2.75 × 100 shares per option) and the stock for $5,100 (51 × 100 shares), so you need to put $275 and $5,100 in the *Money Out* side of the chart. Next, Zeb sold the stock for $5,350 (53.50 × 100 shares) and closed the option — that is, he sold (remember to close, you have to do the opposite) — for $50 (0.50 × 100 shares per option), so you put $5,350 and $50 in the *Money In* side of the chart. Total up the two sides, and you see that he had a $25 gain.

Money Out	Money In
$275	$50
$5100	$5350
$5375	$5400

580. B. $1,100

When you get a question like this, look for the action words, such as *buys, purchases, writes, exercises,* and *sells.* Every time you see an action word, you need to enter something into the options chart. Your client *purchased* 100 shares of DEF at 54, so you have to put $5,400 into the chart on the *Money Out* side. Next, your client *wrote* a call for 5, so you have to place the $500 (5 × 100 shares per option) on the *Money In* side of the chart. After that, the call was *exercised,* so you have to put $6,000 (the call strike price) below its premium because "calls same," meaning the exercised call has to go on the same side as its premium. Total up the two sides, and you see that your client had a gain of $1,100 ($6,500 in – $5,400 out).

Money Out	Money In
$5400	$500
	$6000
$5400	$6500

A mistake people often make in questions like this is that they want to put the stock price (73 in this case) in the chart. You have to remember that by your client selling the call at a 60 strike price, he sold the right to someone else to purchase the stock at 60. The stock price could have gone to $150 per share, and it wouldn't have changed the outcome of this equation.

581. **A. $2,925**

To determine your client's maximum potential loss, set up the equation in an options chart, like the following:

Money Out	Money In
$3250	$325

Your client purchased 100 shares for $32.50 per share, totaling $3,250. Because he paid $3,250, enter $3,250 in the *Money Out* portion of the options chart. Next, enter the $325 ($3.25 premium × 100 shares per option) that your client received for selling the WIZ Jun 35 call in the *Money In* side of the options chart. Stop at this point to see whether the chart lets you answer the question. Because you're looking for the maximum potential loss and you have more money out than money in, you have your answer. The totals are on opposite sides of the chart, so subtract the two numbers to get the maximum potential loss: $3,250 – $325 = $2,925.

582. **B. the stock price minus the premium**

For this question, use some logic. A *covered call* means that the investor has the stock to deliver if exercised. Say that the investor purchased the stock at $50 per share and then sold the call for $4 per share. Now, the investor's cost basis or break-even point is $46 ($50 – $4). In essence, the price of the stock could go down to $46 per share before the investor starts losing money. You get that answer by taking the stock price minus the premium.

583. **D. 72**

Although you could set up an options chart to answer this question, you probably don't need to. The easiest way is to break it down to a "per share" price. Mrs. Gold paid $65 per share to purchase the stock and then paid $7 per share to purchase the option. This means that she spent $72 ($65 + $7) per share, which is how high the stock must go for her to break even.

584. **D. 100 shares of DLQ stock**

When looking at whether an investor is covered or uncovered (naked), you're looking to see whether the investor has the security to deliver if exercised. An investor who sells a DEF call option would be considered covered if the investor owns 100 shares DEF stock or owns anything convertible into 100 shares of DEF stock. An escrow receipt for DEF stock is proof of ownership. An investor may also sell a covered call option if owning a call option with the same strike price or lower on the same stock with the same expiration or later because the investor may buy the stock at the same price or less for just as long as the other investor. Obviously, owning the stock of another company, such as DLQ, wouldn't cover the seller of a DEF call option.

585. **B. buy an ABC put option**

This investor should buy a protective put option on ABC. His main concern is losing money in the event that ABC decreases in value. By purchasing an ABC put option, the option would go in the money if the price decreases and would offset some of the loss from the stock decreasing in price.

586. **D. long 1 XYZ Aug 70 put**

To be covered for the sale of an XYZ Aug 60 put, the investor would either have to be short 100 shares of XYZ stock or own an XYZ put with the same or longer expiration and the same or higher strike price. In this case, Choice (D) works because put options go in the money when the price of the stock goes down, and a 70 put would go in the money before a 60 put.

587. **C. 55**

Mr. Steele purchased the stock for $60 per share and then received $5 per share for selling the option, so his break-even point is $55 ($60 – $5). Mr. Steele is bullish on the stock because he owns it, and he sold the covered call against it to generate additional income.

588. **B. owning stock with a cost basis of 51**

Because the investor purchased the stock and bought the protective put on the same day, it's a *married put*. As a result of the two transactions being married together, the investor won't experience a capital loss by the option expiring worthless. However, his cost basis was adjusted for purchasing the put. He spent $48 per share for the stock and $3 per share for the put for a cost basis of $51.

589. **D. unlimited**

This investor has an unlimited maximum potential gain on the stock he owns. The fact that the investor purchased puts to protect herself in the event that the stock drops in value doesn't affect the maximum gain potential.

590. **D. 40**

When determining the break-even point, it doesn't matter that the client purchased more than one option and more than 100 shares. The client purchased the ABC stock for $36 per share and purchased the options for $4 per share. This means that the client has $40 ($36 + $4) out of his pocket, so the stock would have to go to $40 for him to break even.

591. **A. $6,000**

The original purchase of the three HIJ Sep 40 calls for 3 had to be paid for in full. When the investor exercises the calls, the stock is purchased at the strike price of $40. The investor is purchasing 300 shares (3 options at 100 shares each) for a total of $12,000 (300 × $40). Assuming that the Regulation T margin requirement is 50 percent, the investor would have to deposit $6,000 ($12,000 × 50%).

592. **D. No deposit is required.**

Your client owns the calls that he's exercising. Your client is exercising at a profit of $10 per share (less the premium) and is selling the stock immediately, so no deposit is required. It wouldn't make much sense to have your client pay $30 per share when exercising the options and then have your firm send him a check for $40 per share. The key here is that your client exercised the option and sold the stock on the same day.

593. **D. II and IV**

Because this is a long debit spread (more money out than in from the premiums), the investor would profit if the premium difference widens and the options are exercised. This investor already has a loss, so he needs the options he owns to go in the money to be able to make money. If that happens, the premium difference will widen, and he can either exercise or close his positions and be able to make a profit. Therefore, the investor would lose money if the premiums narrow or the options expire unexercised.

594. **D. 37**

Melissa purchased 300 shares of stock and 3 options representing 300 shares (100 shares per option). Because Melissa purchased the same amount of both the stock and options representing the same amount of shares, you can ignore the multiple when determining the break-even point. Breaking it down to a per-share basis, Melissa purchased the stock at $35 per share and then purchased the options at $2 per share for a break-even point of $37.

595. **C. $1,050 loss**

The easiest way for you to see what's going on in this question is to set up an options chart. Sandy purchased two calls and two puts, so the first thing that you should do is put the multiplier of × 2 on the outside of the chart, as if you're dealing with single options. Because Sandy bought the calls for 450 each (4.5 × 100 shares per option) and the puts for 200 each (2 × 100 shares per option), you need to put 450 and 200 in the

Money Out side of the chart. Next, Sandy closed her options for their intrinsic value (the in-the-money amount). Because call options go in the money when the price of the stock goes above the strike price, only the call option is in the money, not the put option. With the stock price at $36.25 and the strike price at 35, the call is 1.25 in the money ($36.25 – $35.00), so you need to put $125 (1.25 × 100 shares per option) in the *Money In* side of the chart because Sandy is closing the option (to *close* means to do the opposite — so if you originally bought, to close, you have to sell). Total up the two sides, and you see that Sandy had a loss of $525 per option. Because Sandy bought two options, she had a total loss of $1,050.

(x2) Money Out	Money In
$450	$125
$200	
$650	$125

596. **D. $120 gain**

Set up an options chart so you're less likely to make a mistake. First, because Mike shorted (sold) and subsequently closed three options, move the multiplier × 3 to the side of the chart, as if you're dealing with one option. Mike sold the options, so you have to put $300 in the *Money In* side of the chart. Next, he closed (in this case, purchased) the options for $260 per option, so you have to place that number in the *Money Out* side of the chart. At this point, you see that Mike had a $40 gain ($300 – $260).

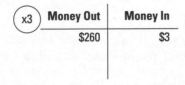

(x3) Money Out	Money In
$260	$3

Now, you can go back to the multiplier to figure out the final answer. Because Mike sold three options, you have to multiply the $40 gain by 3: $40 × 3 = $120.

597. **C. $800**

Set up an options chart to get this answer quickly. Because the investor purchased two options and shorted (sold) two options, move the multiplier (× 2) to the outside of the chart, as if it's one option on each side. The investor purchased the 40 call for 6, so put $600 (6 × 100 shares per option) in the *Money Out* side of the chart. He sold the 50 call at 2 so put $200 (2 × 100 shares per option) in the *Money In* side of the chart.

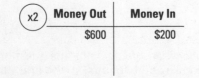

(x2) Money Out	Money In
$600	$200

At this point, you can see that the investor has a maximum loss of $400 ($600 – $200) per option. Now you have to multiply that by 2 to get the answer: $400 × 2 = $800.

598. **D. $37.00**

The easiest way to calculate the break-even point for stock/option problems is to take a look at what's happening. This investor purchased the stock for $32.50 per share and then purchased the options for $4.50 per share. This investor paid $37 ($32.50 + $4.50) per share out of pocket and would need the stock to be at $37 per share to break even.

599. **C. $2,400**

Start by setting up an options chart. The investor purchased four puts and sold (wrote) four puts, so the first thing that you should do is put the multiplier of × 4 on the outside of the chart, as if you're dealing with single options. Because the investor bought the puts for $600 each (6 × 100 shares per option), you need to put $600 in the *Money Out* side of the chart. Next, the investor sold the 50 put options for $200 each (2 × 100 shares per option), so you have to place $200 in the *Money In* side of the chart.

Stop at this point to see if that's answered the question. Because more money is out than in at this point, you need to exercise the options to get the maximum gain. Place the $6,000 (60 premium × 100 shares per option) in the *Money In* side of the chart because it goes opposite its premium (that is, *puts switch* — the exercised option goes opposite its premium). Then, place $5,000 (50 premium × 100 shares per option) in the *Money Out* side of the chart opposite its premium. Total up the two sides, and you see that there's a gain of $600 ($6,200 – $5,600).

x4	Money Out	Money In
	$600	$200
	$5000	$6000
	$5600	$6200

At this point, you have to go back to the multiplier of 4 to get the maximum gain: 4 × $600 = $2,400.

600. **B. The number of shares per contract will increase, and the stock price will decrease.**

As with stock splits, when a company provides a stock dividend, option contracts are adjusted. Stock dividends are treated like uneven splits; the number of shares per contract is increased, and the strike price is decreased.

601. **B. one HIJ contract for 120 shares with a strike price of 25**

An option contract doesn't change for cash dividends, but it does change for stock dividends. Because options are normally for 100 shares, it would have to be increased for a stock dividend. In this case, there'd be 120 shares after the dividend (20 percent more shares). If the amount of shares per option contract is increased, the strike price would have to be reduced to make up for it. The only answer that works is Choice (B).

602. **A. The number of contracts will increase, and the strike price will decrease.**

When a corporation splits its stock evenly (2 for 1, 3 for 1, 4 for 1, and so on), the number of contacts will increase, and the strike price will decrease.

603. **C. four HIJ Oct 16 calls, 250 shares each**

This one is a little bit tougher than a regular something-for-1 split. This is an uneven split, so the rules are a little different. First, show what the options looked like prior to the split:

four HIJ Oct 40 calls (100 shares per option)

Because this is an uneven split, you change the number of shares per option instead of the amount of options. So because it's a 5-for-2 split, you have 5 shares for every 2 you had before.

$$\frac{5 \times 100 \text{ shares}}{2} = 250 \text{ shares}$$

Next, you have to take the strike price of 40 and multiply it by 2/5 (the reciprocal of 5/2).

$$\frac{40 \text{ call} \times 2}{5} = 16 \text{ new strike price}$$

Now, the option will read as follows:

four HIJ Oct 16 calls (250 shares per option)

604. **C. 12 LMN Oct 20 calls, 100 shares each**

First, list the options prior to the split:

four LMN Oct 60 calls (100 shares per option)

Because this is an even split, you change only the number of options and the strike price. You don't need to change the amount of shares per option. And because it's a 3-for-1 split, you have 3 options for every 1 you had before, which means that the investor is now going to have 12 options (3 × 4). Next, because you multiplied the amount of options by 3, you have to divide the strike price by 3.

$$\frac{60}{3} = 20 \text{ strike price}$$

After the 3-for-1 split, the investor will have

12 LMN Oct 20 calls (100 shares per options)

605. **B. I and IV**

SPX options are based on the S&P 500, and VIX options are based on the S&P 500 volatility index. Because your client is bullish on the market, he'd buy SPX calls. However, the VIX is the fear index and usually moves the opposite way of the S&P 500. When investors are bullish on the market, they're more confident, and market volatility is reduced. Therefore, because the VIX would probably decrease, the client would buy VIX puts.

606. A. $300

Prices of Japanese yen options are quoted in units of 0.0001 and have a contract size of 1,000,000 yen. Because 1,000,000 × 0.0001 = $100, the premium and strike price may be multiplied by 100 to calculate the full cost of the strike price or premium. The cost of the option is the premium, so 3 × 100 = $300.

607. C. U.S. dollar

There are no options on the U.S. dollar available in U.S. markets. However, all of the other choices are traded in the United States.

608. B. $3,000

Most options can't be purchased on margin. However, LEAPS (Long-Term Equity Anticipation Securities), which have more than nine months until maturity, can be purchased on margin by coming up with 75 percent of the premium. The premium for each option is $400 (4 × 100 shares per option), and this investor purchased 10 of them for $4,000, so the margin call is 75% × $4,000 = $3,000.

609. D. long-term capital loss

Options are always taxed as capital gains or capital losses. This investor purchased an option that expired worthless, and therefore he lost money. The investor held the LEAPS for over one year, so he would be taxed as a long-term capital loss.

610. C. II and III

The thing that makes this question a little difficult is that you have to remember that interest rates and prices have an inverse relationship. An investor who believes that interest rates are going to increase believes that outstanding bond prices are going to decrease. As such, the proper investments would be buying T-bond puts and writing (selling) T-bond calls because both are bearish strategies.

611. B. They are available only on index options.

LEAPS (Long-Term Equity Anticipation Securities) are long-term options. They may be exercised at any time, they have a longer life than other options, and they have higher premiums because holders have a longer time to use the options. However, LEAPS are available on both individual stocks and indexes.

612. B. cash equal to the intrinsic value of the option times 100 shares at the end of the exercise day

OEX is an index option on the S&P 100. The rule for index options is that exercises are settled in cash instead of delivering, in this case, 1 share of each of the securities that are part of the index. The holder of the index option being exercised is expected to deliver cash equal to the intrinsic value (the in-the-money amount) of the option multiplied by 100 shares per option based on the closing price of the index at the end of the exercise day.

613. **A. bearish on the market**

SPX options are options on the S&P 500 index rather than an individual security. Index options are always settled in cash. As with other securities, an investor who buys a put option is bearish. In this case, the investor is bearish on the market.

614. **C. Buy Canadian dollar calls.**

You can cross off Choices (A) and (B) because there are no options on U.S. dollars. And because U.S. currency and foreign currency have an inverse relationship, your investor should buy Canadian dollar calls because she believes that the Canadian dollar will increase in value over the U.S. dollar.

615. **B. Treasury securities**

Yield-based options are based on the yields of U.S. Treasury securities, such as T-bonds, T-notes, and T-bills. An investor who purchases a yield-based call is expecting yields to increase. As with index options, yield-based options are also settled in cash.

616. **B. I and IV**

The easiest way to think about this is that good news is bullish and bad news is bearish. And when bullish, you buy calls and sell puts; when bearish, you buy puts and sell calls.

Because England had good news, an investor would buy calls or sell puts on the British pound. Japan had bad news, so an investor would buy puts or sell calls on the Japanese yen.

617. **C. II and III**

If your client believes that interest rates are going to increase, he's bullish on yields (rates), so he'd buy yield calls. Now, you have to remember that yields and outstanding bond prices have an inverse relationship. If an investor is bullish on yields, he's bearish on outstanding bond prices. Therefore, this investor may also be interested in purchasing T-bond puts.

618. **A. Buy interest rate calls.**

Preferred stock is similar to debt securities in that they're both subject to price decreases if interest rates rise. Preferred stock typically pays a fixed dividend, and if interest rates increase, the preferred stock will decrease in value. A customer can protect himself by buying interest rate (yield) calls. If interest yields increase, the value of the preferred stock decreases, but the value of the calls increases to help offset the loss.

619. **B. I and IV**

Investors who are bullish on a security should buy calls or sell puts. Investors who are bullish on the market should buy index calls or sell index puts. Remember, index options are always settled in cash.

620.

C. II, III, and IV

There are no options available for the U.S. dollar on U.S. exchanges. However, U.S. investors can buy currency options on the euro, Japanese yen, Canadian dollar, New Zealand dollar, Australian dollar, British pound, and Swiss franc.

621.

A. NASDAQ OMX PHLX

The NASDAQ OMX PHLX (Philadelphia Exchange) is the exchange where world currency (foreign currency) options trade. The NASDAQ OMX PHLX offers options settled in U.S. dollars on the euro, Canadian dollar, Australian dollar, British pound, Mexican peso, New Zealand dollar, Norwegian krone, South African rand, Swedish krona, Japanese yen, and the Swiss franc.

622.

A. the premium paid

Whenever an investor purchases an individual option, the maximum potential loss is the premium paid.

623.

C. cash equal to the intrinsic value of the option at the end of the day of exercise

OEX index options are based on the movement of the S&P 100 index. Index options may be exercised only in cash. The money received by the owner must be equal to the intrinsic value of the option at the end of the day of exercise.

624.

C. call options

Options aren't marginable except for LEAPS, which have more than nine months until maturity. LEAPS can be purchased on margin by coming up with 75 percent of the premium. All other options must be paid for in full.

625.

D. 4:30 p.m. CST on the third Friday of the expiration month

Stock options expire on the Saturday following the third Friday of the expiration month. The last time a customer can exercise an option is 4:30 p.m. CST (5:30 p.m. EST) on the business day prior to expiration.

626.

C. within 15 days after approval of the account

Investors must receive an options risk disclosure document (ODD) at or prior to the approval of the account. However, investors must sign and return an options account agreement within 15 days after approval of the account.

627.

B. No, because it is impossible to profit from these option positions.

These trades aren't suitable for any investor because it's impossible for the investor to make a profit. You can see this by setting up an options chart. First, put the premiums for the options in the chart. Because the investor bought the Oct 35 call option at 7, you have to put $700 (7 premium × 100 shares per option) in the *Money Out* side of the chart. Next, put $200 (2 premium × 100 shares per option) in the *Money In* side of the chart because the investor sold that option. Because the investor has $700 out and $200 in, it tells you that the investor's maximum loss potential is $500 ($700 – $200). To get the maximum gain, you have to exercise both options. Because "calls same," you have to put the exercised strike prices below their respective premiums in the chart. Place $3,500 (35 strike price × 100 shares per option) under its premium of $700, and place $4,000 (40 strike price × 100 shares per option) under its premium of $200. After that, you have to total the sides to see that because the *Money In* side and the *Money Out* side of the chart each equal $4,200, the investor can't make a profit.

Money Out	Money In
$700	$200
$3500	$4000
$4200	$4200

---

628. **D. closing sale**

Break this question down into two parts. First, look at whether it's an initial purchase or sale or whether the customer is getting rid of an option position. In this case, the customer is getting rid of (closing) an option position. Next, is the customer buying (purchasing) or selling himself out of the position? This customer owns the option, so he has to sell himself out of the position. This means that you'd mark the option order ticket as a *closing sale*.

---

629. **C. short 8,000 GHI calls**

Options have certain position limits, meaning there can't be more than a certain number of options on the same security on the same side of the market (bullish or bearish). In this case, the investor can't have more than 10,500 bullish option positions or 10,500 bearish option positions.

Remember: *Bullish* means buying calls and selling puts, and *bearish* means selling calls and buying puts.

This investor is already long 5,000 GHI calls, so she can't purchase more than 5,500 more calls on GHI or sell more than 5,500 puts on GHI without violating position limits. Therefore, the only answer choice that works is Choice (C) because shorting calls is bearish.

---

630. **A. III, I, IV, II**

Prior to opening an options account for a client, the client must first receive an options risk disclosure document (ODD), which outlines the risks of investing in options. Next, the registered options principal (ROP) would have to approve the account. After that, you can finally execute the trade for the client. The last thing that has to happen is that the client must send in a signed options account agreement (OAA) within 15 days after approval of the account.

631. **A. in one business day**

Listed option transactions settle in one business day after the trade date.

632. **A. 0.01 in the money**

If an investor doesn't exercise his option and it's at least 0.01 in the money at expiration, it will automatically be exercised by the Options Clearing Corporation (OCC).

633. **B. random selection**

The OCC (Options Clearing Corporation) chooses which firm to receive the exercise notice randomly only. When the firm receives the exercise notice, it chooses which customer's options to exercise randomly, first-in, first-out, or any other method fair and reasonable.

634. **C. 3:00 p.m. CST on the business day prior to expiration**

The last time an investor can trade an option is 3:00 p.m. CST (4:00 p.m. EST) on the business day prior to expiration of the option.

635. **D. I, II, III, and IV**

All option confirmations must include the option type, the underlying security, the strike price, the number of contracts, the premium, and commission.

636. **A. a registered options principal**

A registered options principal (ROP) is responsible for approving all options accounts. In addition, he must approve all options transactions and approve all options advertising. To become a ROP, you must pass a Series 4 exam.

637. **A. It is halted.**

A stock option's value is derived from the value of the underlying stock, so if the stock stops trading, so do the options. When the stock starts trading again, the options will start trading again.

638. **C. OBO**

Options market makers on the CBOE (Chicago Board Options Exchange), Pacific Exchange, and the Philadelphia Exchange are called order book officials (OBOs).

639. **B. II, I, IV, III**

When a customer is interested in purchasing or selling options, you must first send them an ODD (options risk disclosure document). The ODD isn't an advertisement but lets the customer know the risks of investing in options. Next, a ROP (registered options principal) must approve the account. Then, the trade can be executed. Finally, within 15 days of the approval of the account, the customer must sign and return the OAA (options account agreement). The OAA basically states that the customer understands the risks and rules regarding option transactions.

640. **B. II and III**

Options advertisements don't require an options risk disclosure document (ODD) because advertisements are untargeted promotions. However, options sales literature must be accompanied or preceded by an ODD because sales literature is targeted. Because the CROP (compliance registered options principal) is responsible for approving promotions to the public. The senior ROP is responsible for supervising the reps and the accounts of the firm.

641. **D. the client's investment objectives**

The most important consideration is the client's investment objectives. You'd hope that the client's age, marital status, and financial needs should help your client determine his or her investment objectives. Investment objectives include current income, capital growth, tax-advantaged investments, preservation of capital, diversification, liquidity, and speculation.

642. **A. Treasury bills**

Although your client has a main investment objective of aggressive growth, she may have to put that on hold for a short while because she's purchasing a home. Actually, Choices (B), (C), and (D) are ideal for an aggressive growth strategy; they're too risky for someone purchasing a home in the near term. In this case, you should let your client know that purchasing Treasury bills is a safe investment, which ensures that she has the funds available when needed to purchase the new home.

643. **B. I, III, and IV**

If one of your customers has a primary investment objective of *preservation of capital,* you wouldn't recommend speculative investments, such as an exploratory direct participation program. However, AAA-rated corporate bonds, blue chip stocks (such as IBM, Ford, and GE), and U.S. government bonds are all proper recommendations.

644. **C. the stock of new corporations**

Investors looking for capital growth are more speculative investors. These investors are looking to invest money now, hoping that the investment will grow at a rapid rate. To meet that objective, the investor should invest in stock of new corporations.

645. **A. I and II**

Liquidity has to do with ease of trading. The more liquid a security is, the easier it is to trade. To get the answer for this question, you have to find the two answers that aren't liquid. Municipal bonds usually aren't very liquid because they're usually thinly traded. Direct participation programs are some of the most difficult investments to get in and out of, so they're not liquid.

646. **D. I, II, III, and IV**

All of the choices listed would likely change the investor's investment objectives. Typically, as investors grow older, they want to take less risk. By the same token, investing for one person or two people, as in someone getting married or divorced, would change the investment objectives. Also, as people gain investment experience, they're likely open to more speculative investments. And you can assume that as investors acquire more family responsibilities, they'll want to take less risk.

647. **B. I and III**

Clients' investment decisions should be based on their own risk tolerance and investment needs. However, registered representatives should take a client's needs and risk tolerance into consideration before making a recommendation.

648. **D. all of the above**

When opening an account for a client, you should help determine the risk tolerance and investment goals. Part of that includes looking at the client's financial and nonfinancial considerations. Some of the nonfinancial considerations are the customer's age, marital status, number of dependents, employment status, and employment of other family members.

649. **A. 40% in stocks and 60% in bonds and cash equivalents**

This question gives you very limited information. Knowing how much risk this investor would like to (or should) take would certainly be helpful. However, as a baseline, you can use the equation 100 – the investor's age = % invested in stocks, and you put what's left in bonds and cash equivalents, such as money market funds. Using this equation helps limit risk as investors get older. Out of the answer choices given, Choice (A) is the best choice for this investor. If an investor is risk-averse or willing to take more risk, you can adjust those percentages.

650. **A. Treasury bills**

Reinvestment risk is the additional investment risk taken with interest or dividends received. Treasury notes, revenue bonds, and GO (general obligation) bonds all have reinvestment risk because they pay interest. However, Treasury bills (T-bills) don't have reinvestment risk because they're issued at a discount and mature at par value. Therefore, there are no interest payments made along the way to reinvest.

651.

D. corporate bonds

Your client is looking for total return, which is growth and income. At the current time, 100 percent of his portfolio is invested in stocks, which provide only growth potential. He also needs to invest in fixed-income securities, like corporate bonds, which provide income to meet his investment objective.

652.

C. I and IV

An investor who has an investment objective of speculation (aggressive growth) would purchase securities that have a potential for growth, such as sector funds or technology stocks. The risk of investing in sector funds and technology stocks is high, but if the investments become profitable, the reward can be quite high. Speculative investors are looking to purchase securities at a low price and sell them at a much higher price.

653.

B. sell some of his stocks and purchase more bonds

As investors age, they should start shifting more of their investments from stocks into bonds and cash equivalents, such as money market instruments. The thought is that older investors can't afford to take as much risk. The standard asset allocation model suggests that you subtract the person's age from 100 to determine the percentage that he should invest in stocks. In this case, the investor is 60, so he should have 40% (100 − 60) invested in stocks and the balance in bonds and cash equivalents.

654.

A. The registered representative must determine the client's suitability.

The registered representative should get the customer's investment objectives and suitability prior to making a recommendation. A principal's approval isn't required for a registered representative to make an investment recommendation to a client.

655.

B. municipal bonds

Because your client is in the highest tax bracket, he should have some tax-advantaged investments, like municipal bonds or municipal bond funds, in his portfolio. Because the interest received from municipal bonds is federally tax-free, high income tax bracket investors save more tax money by investing in them.

656.

D. Take the order and mark the order ticket as "unsolicited."

You don't have to refuse the order unless the order is to purchase a direct participation program. In this case, you just have to mark the order ticket as "unsolicited" and take the trade.

657.

C. DPPs

DPPs (direct participation programs; limited partnerships) wouldn't be a proper recommendation because of the difficulty of buying and selling them. Not only do you have to prequalify a DPP investor, but also the investor has to be accepted by a general partner. All of the other choices would be considered quite liquid and would meet Mr. Steele's needs.

658. **D. I, II, III, and IV**

You'd do well to advise all your clients to have a well-diversified portfolio. Smaller investors can build a well-diversified portfolio by purchasing mutual funds. Diversification happens in many ways, such as buying different types of securities, buying securities from different industries, buying debt securities with different maturity dates, buying securities with different ratings, and buying securities from different areas of the country or world. Most investors diversify in several ways to limit their risk.

659. **A. purchasing several different mutual funds**

Because this investor has no other investments and has only $10,000 to invest, it's impossible to build a diversified portfolio without mutual funds. Mutual funds are designed for investors who don't have enough money and/or expertise to build a diversified portfolio. Each mutual fund in itself is diversified because the fund invests in several different securities.

660. **A. I and III**

If the Fed (or Federal Reserve Board, FRB) is trying to tighten the money supply, it could increase the reserve requirements (the percentage of deposits banks must keep on hand), or it could raise the discount rate (the rate that the FRB charges member banks for loans).

661. **C. II and III**

A tight money (inverted) yield curve is opposite of what you'd expect. Normally short-term bonds have lower yields than long-term bonds. A tight money yield curve indicates that interest rates have recently increased, and short-term bonds are yielding more than long-term bonds. The following figure can help you visualize an inverted yield curve.

———— Tight money (inverted) yield curve

- - - - - - Normal (easy-money) yield curve

662.

B. the interest rate that the Fed charges banks for loans

The *discount rate* is the rate that the Fed charges banks for loans. The discount rate is the lowest of all rates. The *prime rate* is the rate that banks charge their best customers for loans. The *federal funds rate* is the rate that banks charge each other for overnight loans. The *broker loan (call loan) rate* is the rate that customers are charged on the debit balance in their margin accounts.

663.

D. inflation increases

If the Fed increases the discount rate, you can assume that all rates will increase across the board. Therefore, bond yields and the federal funds rate would increase. When the discount rate is increased, it also tends to hurt the market and lower stock prices. Typically, one of the reasons the Fed increases the discount rate is to help curb inflation. This means that if the Fed increases the discount rate, the inflation rate would decrease; not increase.

664.

C. supply-side theory

The supply-side theory is also known as Reaganomics. Supply-side economics lowers taxes and allows people to keep and spend more of their own money. The money spent by individuals helps stimulate the economy and create more jobs. When more people are working, tax revenues actually increase.

665.

B. U.S. imports of foreign goods increase

The best way to deal with competitive problems is to substitute the word *cheap* for *competitive*. Something that's *more competitive* is *more cheap* or cheaper. In this case, you're looking for the false answer. If the value of the U.S. dollar declines in relationship to foreign currencies, you can't buy as much of their goods and vice versa. Therefore, Choice (B) is the false one because it says that the United States would buy more foreign goods with a weaker dollar.

666.

C. T-bonds

T-bonds (Treasury bonds) have the longest-term maturity, so they'd decrease the most in price. Remember, when the discount rate (the rate the Fed charges banks for loans) changes, all rates across the board change, including yields on bonds. Bond prices and yields have an inverse relationship, so if yields increase, outstanding bond prices fall.

667.

B. I and IV

If the U.S. dollar is falling against the euro, it shows a weakening in U.S. currency. When the U.S. dollar is weak, it costs more to purchase foreign goods, and it costs foreign companies less to buy U.S. goods. Therefore, U.S. imports would likely decrease, and U.S. exports would likely increase. The weakening of the U.S. dollar typically happens during easy-money periods.

668. **C. money available for bank loans**

An increase in the money available for bank loans would show an easing of the money supply, not a tightening.

669. **A. open market operations**

Although the Fed does control the discount rate and reserve requirements, the tool most commonly used by the Fed to control the money supply is open market operations. Open market operations is when the Fed buys and sells U.S. government securities, which happens on a continuous basis.

670. **B. setting the federal funds rate**

The Federal Reserve Board (FRB) is responsible for open market operations (buying and selling U.S. government securities), setting the discount rate (the rate the Fed charges banks for loans), and setting the minimum margin requirements. However, the federal funds rate is the rate that banks charge each other for loans and is determined by the banks, not the FRB.

671. **B. I and IV**

What you have to do with questions like this is look at which way the money is flowing. The question indicates a trade deficit, meaning that more money is going to foreign countries than what's coming in from foreign countries. If that deficit is increasing even more, you have to look at which choices send more money out of the country. If the U.S. is buying more foreign goods, it has to pay for them, so that increases the deficit. Also, if U.S. investors are purchasing ADRs (American depositary receipts), they're buying interest in foreign countries and increasing the deficit more.

672. **A. CPI**

The CPI (Consumer Price Index) is the best measure of inflation or deflation. The CPI measures price changes in consumer goods and services. The GDP (gross domestic product) is the sum of all goods and services produced by a country in one year, and it measures how much the economy is growing. M1 is a measure of the money supply that includes currency in circulation, checking accounts, and NOW accounts (interest-bearing checking accounts). M3 is a measure of the money supply that includes everything in M1 plus savings accounts and CDs.

673. **A. recession**

A recession is defined as a six-month (two consecutive quarters) or more decline in business activity and stock prices. A depression is an 18-month (six consecutive quarters) or more economic decline.

674.   **D. real GDP**

The real GDP (gross domestic product) is the sum of all goods and services produced by a country in a one-year period. It's measured in constant dollars, meaning that it takes inflation into consideration to determine how a country is doing from year to year.

675.   **C. 5% bond with a 15-year maturity**

Long-term bonds have more volatility and duration than short-term bonds because investors have to wait a longer time to receive par value at maturity. If two bonds have the same or similar maturity date, the bond with the lowest coupon rate has the highest volatility or duration because investors receive less interest annually to reinvest.

676.   **B. Long-term interest rates are less volatile than short-term interest rates.**

Whether during a time of an easy-money (normal) yield curve or a tight-money yield curve, short-term interest rates are always more volatile than long-term interest rates. What this means is that when interest rates change, short-term interest rates adjust faster than long-term interest rates.

677.   **C. building permits**

Leading economic indicators are statistics that indicate how the economy is going to do. Leading indicators include the money supply, stock prices, the discount rate, the federal funds rate, reserve requirements, orders for durable goods, and so on. Industrial production and GDP (gross domestic product) are coincidental indicators, and the unemployment rate is a lagging indicator.

678.   **D. trend lines**

Fundamental analysts decide what to buy, and technical analysts decide when to buy. A fundamental analyst compares the earnings per share (EPS) of different companies as well as balance sheets and income statements. However, trend lines are something that a technical analyst examines.

679.   **B. 5**

The *P* in PE ratio stands for market price, the *E* stands for earnings per share, and the word *ratio* lets you know that you need to divide. So set up the equation like so:

$$\text{PE Ratio} = \frac{\text{Market Price}}{\text{EPS}}$$

The market price is $40, and the earnings per share is $8, so that means that the PE ratio is 5

$$\text{PE Ratio} = \frac{\$40}{\$8}$$
$$= 5$$

680. **A. earnings trends**

Fundamental analysts compare companies to help determine what to buy. Technical analysts examine the market to try to determine when to buy. Knowing that, fundamental analysts are definitely interested in earnings trends. Technical analysts are interested in such things as support and resistance and the breadth of the market.

681. **A. inventory**

Current assets (assets convertible into cash within a one-year period) include inventory, marketable securities held by the corporation, cash, and so on. However, when dealing with quick assets, you have to take inventory out of the equation. Quick assets are convertible into cash within a three- to five-month period. In most cases, inventory takes longer to sell than three to five months.

682. **C. net income + depreciation + depletion**

Cash flow helps measure the financial health of a company. Cash flow is determined by taking the net income (after-tax income) and adding back in the depreciation and depletion deductions (if any). You need to add depreciation and depletion back in because they're write-offs for a company but aren't out-of-pocket expenses. So the equation looks like this:

$$\text{Cash flow} = \text{net income} + \text{depreciation} + \text{depletion}$$

683. **A. the market price divided by the earnings per share**

The PE ratio is a tool that technical analysts use to help determine whether a stock is overpriced or underpriced. Typically, they'll compare the PE ratios of several different companies within the same industry to see whether there's a good investment opportunity. Actually, the lower the PE ratio, the better. A company with a low PE ratio means that the earnings per share (EPS) are high compared to its price. The equation for PE ratio is

$$\text{PE ratio} = \frac{\text{Market price}}{\text{EPS}}$$

684. **C. 50%**

To determine the dividend payout ratio (DPR), use the following formula and then just plug in the numbers from the question:

$$\text{DPR} = \frac{\text{Annual dividends per common share}}{\text{Earnings per share (EPS)}}$$
$$= \frac{\$0.30}{\$0.60}$$
$$= 50\%$$

685.

B. EPS

When determining the EPS (earnings per share) of a company, a fundamental analyst looks at the income statement, not the balance sheet.

686.

D. II and IV

Intangible assets are listed on a corporation's balance sheet and don't have any physical properties, such as trademarks, patents, formulas, and goodwill (based on the reputation of the corporation). Inventory is part of a corporation's current assets, and equipment is part of a corporation's fixed assets.

687.

C. current assets – current liabilities

You can calculate working capital by working with the numbers on a corporation's balance sheet. Working capital is the amount of money that a corporation has to work with, and the basic formula is

$$\text{Working capital} = \text{current assets} - \text{current liabilites}$$

Current assets are items convertible into cash in a one-year period (such as cash, securities owned, and accounts receivable). Current liabilities are expenses due in a one-year period (such as accounts payable, debt securities due to mature, cash dividends, and taxes).

688.

C. 3:1

To determine the current ratio, you have to divide the current assets (all assets convertible into cash within a one-year period) by the current liabilities (everything that must be paid within a one-year period). When looking at the exhibit, the current assets are cash, securities, accounts receivable, and inventory. Machinery and land are fixed assets. The current liabilities are accounts payable and bonds due this year. Bonds due in ten years are a long-term liability. The equation sets up like this:

$$\text{Current ratio} = \frac{\text{Current assets}}{\text{Current liabilities}}$$
$$= \frac{\$60,000,000}{\$20,000,000}$$
$$= 3:1$$

689.

C. $7.33

To determine a stock's earnings per share (EPS), you can divide the stock's price by the PE (price earnings) ratio.

$$\text{EPS} = \frac{\text{Stock price}}{\text{PE ratio}}$$
$$= \frac{\$44}{\$6}$$
$$= \$7.33$$

690. **A. book value per share**

To determine the book value per share, you need to use numbers from a balance sheet, not an income statement. Book value per share is based on the net worth of the company. The book value per share formula is

$$\text{Book value per share} = \frac{\text{Net worth} - \text{intangible assets} - \text{par value of preferred stock}}{\text{Number of common shares outstanding}}$$

691. **B. Liabilities increase.**

When a corporation declares a cash dividend, its liabilities increase. Liabilities are something that is owed. When a corporation declares a dividend, it must pay it. The assets will remain the same until it pays the dividend, and then the assets will decrease. The working capital and stockholder's equity decrease when a corporation declares a cash dividend.

692. **D. earned surplus**

Earned surplus (retained earnings) is the amount of money a corporation has left after paying all expenses, interest, taxes, and dividends. Paid-in capital (capital surplus, paid-in surplus) is the amount of money a company receives above par value for issuing stock. You determine net worth by subtracting a corporation's liabilities from its assets:

$$\text{Net worth} = \text{Assets} - \text{Liabilities}$$

693. **C. net worth**

When a company issues bonds, net worth doesn't change. The assets and the liabilities increase by the same amount when a company borrows money. Therefore, the net worth would have to remain the same.

Because the bonds are a long-term liability, the working capital (the amount of money the corporation has to work with) increases.

694. **B. I and II**

Investment grade bonds and AAA-rated industrial development bonds are both considered safe investments. However, income bonds are issued by corporations in bankruptcy, and high-yield bonds are also known as junk bonds. This investor should definitely stay away from purchasing income bonds and high-yield bonds.

695. **B. inflationary risk**

All long-term bonds have inflationary (purchasing power) risk. Inflationary risk is the risk that the return on the investment doesn't keep pace with inflation. To limit inflationary risk, investors should purchase stocks. Over the long haul, stocks have more than kept pace with inflation.

696. **D. regulatory risk**

Regulatory risk is the risk that the price of a security declines due to new regulations placed on specific corporations.

697. **A. countercyclical**

Precious metal stocks, such as gold stocks, are countercyclical and tend to move in the opposite direction of the economy. Cyclical stocks move in the same direction as the economy.

698. **C. I, II, and III**

Your client would face political risk, market risk, and currency risk but not interest rate risk because he isn't buying fixed income securities. *Political (legislative) risk* is the risk that laws may change that may adversely affect the securities purchased. *Market risk* is the risk that the securities might decline due to negative market conditions. *Currency risk* is the risk that the security declines in value due to an unfavorable exchange rate between the U.S. dollar and foreign currencies.

699. **D. countercyclical stock**

Cyclical stock moves in the same direction as the economy. So countercyclical stock moves in the opposite direction of the economy. Investors buy countercyclical stocks to balance out their portfolios and to protect themselves in the event of economic decline. Precious metals stocks, such as gold, tend to be countercyclical because they usually do well when the market is doing poorly and vice versa. Defensive stocks tend to do well no matter what. Some examples of defensive stocks are food companies, alcohol, tobacco, pharmaceuticals, and so on. Blue chip stocks are from well-established companies (such as IBM, Ford, and Microsoft) with a history of good earnings.

700. **B. III and IV**

Defensive stocks are ones that perform consistently no matter how the economy's doing. Companies that sell goods such as alcohol, food, tobacco, and pharmaceutical supplies, issue defensive stocks. Automotive and appliance company stocks aren't defensive because when the economy is doing poorly, investors wait a little longer to purchase these items.

701. **C. utilities**

Utilities are highly leveraged companies because they issue a lot of bonds (debt securities). If interest rates increase, they'll have to issue bonds with higher coupon rates, which affects their bottom line more than other companies that aren't as highly leveraged.

702.   **C. II and III**

Portfolio diversification doesn't reduce systematic (market) risk because a bearish market can affect all securities. However, portfolio diversification does reduce non-systematic (business) risk because some companies may perform better than expected, even though others may not be performing as well.

703.   **A. II, III, and IV**

Defensive industries are ones that perform well no matter how the economy is doing. Utilities, food, clothing, alcohol, tobacco, cosmetics, healthcare, and pharmaceutical are examples of defensive industries. Household appliances are cyclical, and their performance depends on the economy.

704.   **D. Treasury STRIPS**

Reinvestment risk is the additional risk taken with interest and dividends received each year. All securities making interest or dividend payments have reinvestment risk. Treasury STRIPS have no reinvestment risk because they're issued at a discount and mature at par value without making interest payments along the way.

705.   **C. an increase in the DJIA and the DJTA**

According to the Dow theory, trends must be confirmed by the DJIA (Dow Jones Industrial Average) and the DJTA (Dow Jones Transportation Average). For it to be a real trend, both need to be going the same direction. This makes sense because it isn't enough that industries are selling and producing goods unless they're also being shipped.

706.   **A. reversal of a bullish trend**

A head and shoulders top formation pattern indicates that the stock has possibly hit a high and is reversing. A head and shoulders top formation pattern is a bearish sign because it's the reversal of a bullish trend. Check out the following figure to see what a head and shoulders top formation looks like.

Head and shoulders top formation

The highest peak is the head, and the two shorter peaks are the shoulders.

707. **A. bullish indicator**

Short sellers are bearish, meaning that they want the price of a security to decrease. However, looking at it from a technical analyst's point of view, if short interest increases, it's a bullish sign. Remember, short sellers must eventually cover their short positions by buying stock. When the market starts to increase, short sellers will be buying stock at a rapid rate, thus accelerating a bullish market.

708. **A. support**

The lower portion of a securities trading range is called the support. The upper portion of a securities trading range is called the resistance. A breakout occurs when a security breaks out of its normal trading range.

709. **C. the stock is more volatile than the market**

Beta is a measure of how volatile a stock is compared to the market. A stock with a beta of 1 is equally volatile to the market, meaning that if the market increased 5 percent over a given period of time, you'd expect the price of your stock to increase 5 percent. If the market declines by 5 percent, you'd expect the price of your stock to decline by 5 percent. If you're purchasing a stock with a beta greater than 1, it's more volatile than the market. In this case, you're dealing with a stock with a beta of 1.6, meaning that if the market increased or decreased by 10 percent over a given period of time, you'd expect the price of your stock to increase 16 percent or decrease 16 percent. A stock with a beta less than 1 is less volatile than the market.

710. **D. reversing from a bearish trend**

A saucer formation is similar to an inverted head and shoulders pattern in that it's a reversal of a bearish trend. However, a saucer formation is a more gradual change in direction. A saucer formation is a bullish sign, and an inverted saucer formation is a bearish sign.

711. **C. the trading volume on the NASDAQ OMX PHLX**

Technical analysts follow the market to determine when to buy or sell securities. One of the things that they look at is trading volumes.

712. **B. odd-lot theory**

Smaller investors are more likely to engage in odd-lot trading (trading for less than 100 shares). Investors who subscribe to the odd-lot theory believe that by the time smaller investors get their information and execute trades, it's too late. Therefore, believers in the odd-lot theory buy when smaller investors are selling and sell when smaller investors are buying.

713.   **D. trend lines**

Technical analysts look at the market and decide when to buy. Technical analysts look at things like trend lines, trading volume, and short interest. Fundamental analysts look at things like the price earnings ratio, income statements, and balance sheets.

714.   **C. the earnings**

Technical analysts look at the market and price movements. Corporate earnings is something that a fundamental analyst would examine.

715.   **A. consolidating**

When a stock stays within a narrow trading range (trading channel), it's consolidating. A breakout occurs when a stock breaks out of its normal trading range.

716.   **D. I, II, III, and IV**

All of the choices listed are broad-based indexes. Broad-based indexes reflect the movement of the entire market as compared to narrow-based indexes, which focus on a certain sector or a few sectors.

717.   **D. Lipper**

Lipper indexes allow investors to compare mutual fund investments against active indexes based on sectors, industries, countries, market capitalization, and so on.

718.   **C. Transportation**

The Dow Jones 65 Composite is broken down into the Dow Jones Industrial Average (DJIA), which is made up of 30 listed industrial stocks, the Dow Jones Transportation Average (DJTA), which is made up of 20 listed transportation stocks, and the Dow Jones Utility Average (DJUA), which is made up of 15 listed utility stocks.

719.   **B. the S&P 500 declining by 20% in a day**

If the S&P 500 declines by 20 percent (Level III market decline) in a day compared to the previous day's close between 9:30 a.m. and 4:00 p.m. EST, the NASDAQ OMX PHLX and NYSE Euronext would halt for the remainder of the trading day.

720.   **A. DJIA**

The DJIA (Dow Jones Industrial Average) is made up of 30 broad-based listed common stocks and is the most widely used to indicate the performance of the market. The DJIA is part of the Dow Jones Composite, which is made up of the industrial stocks, transportation stocks, and utility stocks.

721. **B. I, II, and III**

NASDAQ OMX PHLX, ECN (electronic communications network), and NYSE Euronext are all exchange markets. However, the OTCBB (over-the-counter bulletin board) is an over-the-counter negotiated market.

722. **D. I, II, and III**

Options orders can be executed on the CBOE (Chicago Board Options Exchange), the NYSE, and the NASDAQ OMX PHLX.

723. **A. Level I**

As a registered rep, you likely have a computer with Level I access on your desk. NASDAQ Level I includes the inside market (highest bid and lowest ask) prices. These are subject quotes because they're subject to change. Levels I and II include all firm quotes. Level II displays all market maker quotes, while Level III is where market makers enter their firm quotes. The NASDAQ market doesn't include Level IV.

724. **B. a negotiated market**

The over-the-counter (OTC) market is a negotiated market where buyers and sellers negotiate the trading price of a security. Exchanges are considered auction markets where prices and trading volumes are shouted out on the exchange floor.

725. **B. II, III, and IV**

The OTCBB (Over-the-Counter Bulletin Board) is a negotiated market where buyers and sellers negotiate on price. Unlisted securities typically trade on the OTCBB or the OTC Pink Market. NYSE Euronext, NASDAQ OMX PHLX, and NYSE Arca are all examples of auction markets, where buyers and sellers bid or offer securities. Auction markets have a centralized trading floor, and all trades are executed at the same location.

726. **D. a minimum dividend payout**

To be listed on an exchange such as the NYSE Euronext, a corporation must have a minimum number of publicly held shares, a minimum number of round lot (100 shares) shareholders, national interest, a minimum trading price, a minimum total market value of the outstanding shares, and so on. However, to be listed, a stock doesn't have to be paying a dividend. You won't be tested on the actual numbers.

727. **D. 3**

OTC (Over-the-Counter) Bulletin Board and Pink Market securities are non-NASDAQ securities and are subject to the three-quote rule. If at least two market makers aren't displaying firm quotes, it's up to the broker-dealer to contact at least three dealers to get the best price for the customer.

728. **C. listed securities trading OTC**

A third market trade is listed securities trading OTC (over-the-counter).

729. **A. combined offering**

The first time a company ever offers securities is an IPO (initial public offering). A primary offering is new shares coming to the market from a company that has already gone public. A secondary offering is a large block of securities sold by existing shareholders. In this case, it's a combined offering because the 1 million shares are new, and the 800,000 shares are being sold by existing shareholders.

730. **C. I, II, and III**

The secondary market is the trading of outstanding securities whether OTC (over-the-counter) or securities listed on an exchange. The underwriting of new issues is executed in the primary market.

731. **D. fourth market trade**

A trade between institutions without using the services of a broker-dealer is considered a fourth market trade. Fourth market trades usually take place using ECNs (electronic communications networks).

732. **A. a syndicate selling new issues of municipal GO bonds to the public**

Remember, new issues are always sold in the primary market regardless of whether they're municipal GO bonds or any other security. By contrast, sales of outstanding securities or previously outstanding securities (treasury stock) always take place in the secondary market. The secondary market is broken down into the following:

- **First market:** Listed securities trading on an exchange
- **Second market:** Unlisted securities trading over-the-counter
- **Third market:** Listed securities trading over-the-counter
- **Fourth market:** Institutional trading without using the services of a broker-dealer

733. **C. I, II, and III**

If dark pools of liquidity execute trades, the trades are reported as over-the-counter (OTC) transactions, not exchange transactions. Dark pools of liquidity represent pools of institutions, large retail clients, and firms trading for their own inventory. Because the clients and sizes of accounts remain anonymous, dark pools reduce transparency of the markets.

734. **D. unlisted securities trading OTC**

The second market, not to be confused with the secondary market, is unlisted securities trading OTC (over-the-counter). The secondary market is broken down into the first market, the second market, the third market, and the fourth market. The first market is listed securities trading on an exchange, the third market is listed securities trading OTC, and the fourth market is institutional trading without using the services of a broker-dealer.

735. **B. $17.00**

The dealer has to sell at the current offering (ask) price, which is $17.00. The fact that the dealer paid more than that to purchase the stock for his own inventory doesn't come into play. Remember, dealers are speculating that the price of a security that they have in inventory will appreciate, just like investors hope that the prices of securities that they have in their portfolios will appreciate. Because the price decreased, the dealer lost money.

736. **C. principal**

When broker-dealers make a market in a particular security, they're acting as a principal or market maker. This means that they're willing to buy securities for their own inventory or sell securities from their own inventory. Broker-dealers not acting from their own account are acting as a broker or agent.

737. **D. II and IV**

When a securities firm buys securities for or sells securities from its own inventory, it's acting as a dealer (principal or market maker). When a dealer sells securities from his own inventory, he charges a price that includes a markup.

738. **A. 100**

All firm quotes entered by market makers are an obligation to buy or sell 100 shares unless otherwise stated.

739. **B. position trading**

When dealers buy securities for their own inventory, they're taking a position in that security. In this case, they're expecting the price of outstanding bonds to increase because interest rates and bond prices have an inverse relationship.

740. **A. includes a markup**

Dealers (principals) sell securities out of their own inventory and buy securities for their own inventory. Dealers charge a markup when selling securities from their own inventory and a markdown when purchasing securities for their own inventory. Brokers act as middlemen and charge a commission.

741. **D. I, II, and III**

All the choices listed are discretionary orders and require a written power of attorney signed by the customer in order to be accepted. To not need a power of attorney, the customer must provide or agree to the number of shares (or bonds), whether to buy or sell, and the specific security. Discretionary orders don't require a customer's verbal approval to be executed.

742. **A. buy stop order on FFF**

Remember that stop orders are used for protection, so you can cross off Choices (B) and (D) right away. Because your client has a short position on FFF, he'd have to buy himself out of the short position. Therefore, the answer is Choice (A), *buy stop order on FFF.* Your client would enter a buy stop order above the current market price.

743. **B. buy limits and sell limits**

By placing a limit order, an investor guarantees that the order will be executed at a specific price or better if it ever hits that price. Stop orders are triggered when hitting the stop order price or better but may be executed at a price at, above, or below the stop price.

744. **D. triggered at $24.88, executed at $25.25**

BLiSS (buy limit, sell stop) orders are triggered at or below the market price. The order is triggered (elected) at or below $25.00 ($24.88) and is executed at the next price ($25.25).

745. **C. II and III**

An immediate-or-cancel (IOC) order must be attempted to be filled immediately by the firm handling the order but may be filled partially. It's a one-time order and doesn't allow the order to be executed in several attempts.

746. **D. all of the above**

Stop orders are used to help protect investors from losing too much money when holding either long or short positions. For argument's sake, say that you purchased stock for $30 per share, so you could enter a sell stop order at $28. If the market price touched or passed through the $28 per share, your stock would be sold at the next price. By the same token, if you purchased the stock at $30 per share and the stock subsequently rose to $37 per share, you could enter a sell stop order below that price to protect your profit. Buy stop orders are used to limit the loss on a short position or protect the profit on a short position. Unlike sell stop orders, which are entered below the market price, buy stop orders are entered above the market price. Investors who sell securities short lose money when the price of security increases.

747. **C. sell stop at $46**

Stop orders (not limit orders) are used for protection. Therefore, none of the answer choices that include the word *limit* would fit. A sell stop order would be entered below the market price of the security, so the correct answer is Choice (C).

748. **C. triggered at $20.50, executed at $20.40**

This client has entered a sell stop limit order. You must first take care of the sell stop portion of the order. Sell stop orders are BLiSS (buy limit, sell stop) orders that are triggered at or below the order price. Follow the ticker from left to right and look for the first transaction at or below $20.50. The first transaction at or below $20.50 is $20.50, so that's where the order is triggered. From that point forward, you need to take care of the sell limit portion. Sell limit orders are SLoBS (sell limit, buy stop) orders that are executed at or above the order price. From where the order was triggered, the first transaction that was at or above $20.40 was $20.40.

749. **B. must be executed in their entirety or the order is canceled**

Unlike fill-or-kill (FOK) orders and immediate-or-cancel (IOC) orders, all-or-none (AON) orders don't have to be executed immediately. However, like FOK orders, they must be filled entirely or the order is canceled. AON orders remain active until they're executed or canceled.

750. **D. stop**

Stop (stop loss) orders become market orders for immediate execution as soon as the underlying security passes the stop price. Stop orders are used for protection.

751. **A. below the current market price**

Investors who own a security use sell stop orders for protection. Because these investors are concerned about the price dropping, they enter sell stop orders below the current market price of the security. If the market price of the security hits or passes the sell stop order price, the sell stop order becomes a market order for immediate execution.

752. **A. I and III**

Fill-or-kill (FOK) orders must be executed immediately in their entirety, or the order must be canceled.

753. **B. buy 600 shares at 25 stop**

When you're talking about cash dividends, only BLiSS (buy limit, sell stop) orders are reduced. However, when you're talking about stock dividends, all orders in the book are adjusted. In this case, there's a 20 percent stock dividend, so you have to add 20 percent more shares:

$$500 \text{ shares} \times 20\% = 100 \text{ additional shares}$$

$$500 \text{ shares} + 100 \text{ additional shares} = 600 \text{ shares}$$

Because the amount of shares increased, the price of the stock has to decrease. The order was initially for $15,000 (500 shares × $30), so you have to divide the $15,000 by 600 shares to get the stop price.

$$\frac{\$15,000}{600 \text{ shares}} = \$25$$

754. **C. The order should be sent to the floor broker immediately.**

This is an *at-the-close order* (or market on close, MOC, order). The registered rep should take the order and mark the order ticket at close. The firm will then transfer the order to its floor broker who will make sure that the order is executed properly.

755. **A. I and III**

The customer specified a price, so it's a limit order. In this case, it would be a limit order to buy 100 shares at a price of 50 or lower. Market orders aren't price specific; they're used to buy or sell at the best price available. All stop and limit orders are good for the day unless the customer specifies that he wants the order in place for a longer time. If the day order isn't executed that day, the order is canceled.

756. **B. bearish**

Short sellers borrow securities for immediate sale in the market. Their hope is that the price of the security drops, and they can repurchase it in the market at a lower price and return it to the lender. Therefore, short sellers are definitely bearish because they want the price of the security to decrease. If they were neutral, they would want the price of the security to stay the same. If this were the case, they wouldn't make money, and they'd still have to pay a commission, which is a losing proposition.

757. **C. II, III, and IV**

Although short sales against the box used to be used as a tax deferral, IRS rules have changed, and investors would be responsible for any capital gains due on the long position at the time they go short against the box. All of the other answer choices are true.

758. **B. the short sale of securities**

Regulation SHO covers the rules for short sales. Under SHO rules, all order tickets must be marked as short sale as compared to long sale, which is when an investor is selling securities that are owned. In addition, all brokerage firms must establish rules to locate, borrow, and deliver securities that are to be sold short. All brokerage firms must make sure that the security can be located and delivered by the delivery date prior to executing a short sale.

759. **A. I, III, and IV**

Short sellers face unlimited risk, the trades must be executed in margin accounts, and listed securities may be sold short. However, because OTCBB (Over-the-Counter Bulletin Board) stocks aren't marginable, they can't be sold short.

760. **D. municipal bonds**

Although municipal bonds may be sold short, they typically aren't. The reason is that the security must be borrowed and later found to cover the short position. Because municipal bonds are usually thin issues, they're not very liquid and therefore not good candidates for selling short.

761. **A. $5,000 short-term gain**

When you're looking at whether something is long term or short term, you have to look at the holding period. When selling securities held for more than one year (at least a year and a day) the gain or loss is long term. When selling securities held for one year or less, the gain or loss is short term. However, relating to this question, the investor had a short position and never held the stock. When buying back securities to cover a short sale, the gain or loss is always short term. Because the investor sold the stock initially for $35,000 ($35 × 1,000 shares) and then purchased it for $30,000 ($30 × 1,000 shares), the investor had a $5,000 short-term gain.

762. **D. OTCBB stocks may be sold short**

All short sales must be executed in margin accounts. Therefore, because OTCBB (Over-the-Counter Bulletin Board) stocks aren't marginable, they can't be sold short.

763. **B. The DMM needs permission from an exchange official.**

When a DMM (designated market maker specialist) stops stock, he's guaranteeing a trading price to a floor broker for a public order while the floor broker attempts to get a better price. DMMs have the ability to trade out of their own accounts, so they don't need permission to stop stock.

764. **C. I, III, and IV**

A designated market maker (DMM) uses priority, parity, and precedence to determine which orders get executed first.

- **Priority:** Orders at the best price will be executed first.

- **Parity:** If more than one order comes in at the best price, the one that came in first will be executed first.

- **Precedence:** If more than one order came in at the best price and at the same time, the largest order will be executed first.

765. **B. 46.02 to 46.06**

When you're looking at an exhibit such as this, you must ignore the stop orders. Then find the highest bid, which is 46.02, and the lowest offer (ask), which is 46.06, to get the inside market.

766. **A. NH**

A designated market maker can't hold NH (not held) orders. NH orders are ones in which your client gives you (the registered rep) authority over the price and time that the order is placed. These are used in the case where you believe that you can get a client a better price later in the day. NH orders aren't discretionary orders and don't require a written power of attorney.

767. **C. II and III**

On the ex-dividend date (ex-date), buy limit and sell stop orders are reduced to reflect the cash dividend unless marked DNR (do not reduce). Sell limit and buy stop orders remain the same.

768. **D. market orders**

A display book keeps track of stop orders, limit orders, and GTC orders but not market orders. Remember, market orders aren't price specific but are for immediate execution at the best price available. Therefore, they wouldn't need to be kept in a book for later execution.

769. **B. designated market makers**

Designated market makers (DMMs) are responsible for maintaining a fair and orderly market on the NYSE floor and helping to keep trading as active as possible.

770. **C. any order can be entered regardless of the amount of shares traded**

The SDBK (Super Display Book) is a computerized routing and trading system used on the NYSE (New York Stock Exchange). The SDBK will automatically pair orders that it can, and the rest will be left for the DMM (designated market maker) to keep in the display book for later execution. The SDBK is used only for orders of 6.5 million shares or less.

771. **D. The order would be canceled.**

Unlike forward splits, reverse splits cancel all stop and limit orders on the ex-split date. *Open order* is just another way of saying good-till-canceled (GTC).

772. **C. as a good-till-canceled (GTC) order**

Orders placed in market makers' order books are stop and limit orders, which are good for the day or good-till-canceled (GTC). In this case, the order would be entered into the market maker's book as a GTC order, and it would be up to the brokerage firm to cancel it at the end of the week if not executed. All GTC orders that haven't been executed or removed from the market maker's book by the last trading day in April or the last trading day in October are automatically canceled.

773. B. 22 × 13

When you're looking at the NYSE Display Book, the first thing you have to do is ignore the stop orders. Then, you need to look for the highest bid price and the lowest ask (offer) price. The highest bid price is 30.02, and the lowest ask price is 30.05. That's the inside market. Next, add up the numbers at each price to get 22 (8 Southwest B/D + 18 Southeast B/D) × 13 (4 Atlantic Sec. + 9 Gulf B/D). This is the amount of round lots (100 shares); therefore, another acceptable answer would be 2,200 × 1,300.

774. D. It has not been executed.

This is a buy stop limit order. The first thing you must do is handle the buy stop portion. Buy stop orders are SLoBS (sell limit, buy stop) orders that are triggered or executed at or above the order price. In this case, the order would be triggered (activated) at or above 40.25. The first trade at or above 40.25 is 40.25. Next, you have to take care of the buy limit portion. Buy limit orders are BLiSS (buy limit, sell stop) orders, which are triggered or executed at or below the order price. So starting from the 40.25 trigger price, you're looking for a trade at or below 40.25. None exist, so this order was triggered but has not yet been executed.

775. C. bonds

The consolidated tape doesn't show bonds, new issues, options, or odd-lot trades (trades smaller than 100 shares).

776. B. do not include markups or commissions

Trade reports on the consolidated tape don't include markups, markdowns, or commissions.

777. A. 26.80

Although they don't have to be, in this case, the stop and limit prices are the same. You have to separate the sell stop and the sell limit portions. First, you have a sell stop order at 27, which is a BLiSS (buy limit, sell stop) order. BLiSS orders are triggered (elected) or executed at or below the order price. The first trade at or below the order price is 26.80, so that is the answer. To take it to the next step, which is the price at which the trade takes place, you have to do the sell limit portion. Sell limit orders are SLoBS (sell limit, buy stop) orders that are triggered or executed at or above the order price. After being triggered, the first trade at or above the order price is 27.

778. C. The trade is reported out of sequence.

The symbol SLD on the tape indicates that the trade was reported out of sequence.

779. D. FINRA and the exchanges

FINRA and the exchanges are responsible for reporting the trading volume and last sale prices to the consolidated tape system.

780. **A. a delayed opening print**

If the trading of a security has been delayed and doesn't trade at the opening of the market, the first trade will be reported with an OPD next to it.

781. **C. II and III**

TRACE (Trade Reporting and Compliance Engine) reports trades of all long-term corporate bonds and U.S. government agency bonds but not convertible bonds. All trades must be reported by the buyer and seller within 15 minutes of execution. TRACE displays the trade date, time of execution, amount of the trade, price of the trade, yield of the bond, and so on. However, TRACE doesn't provide the names of the brokerage firms who executed the order.

782. **C. entire life of an order from entry to execution**

The Order Audit Trail System (OATS) is an automated computer system that tracks the life of an over-the-counter (OTC) order from entry to execution or cancellation. OATS tracks all OTC securities including OTCBB (Over-the-Counter Bulletin Board) stocks and OTC Pink Market stocks.

783. **D. RTRS**

RTRS (Real-Rime Transaction Reporting System) provides up-to-the-minute pricing information regarding municipal bond transactions. The information is made available within 15 minutes of the trade.

784. **B. TRACE**

TRACE (Trade Reporting and Compliance Engine) is the FINRA-approved trade reporting system for OTC long-term corporate bonds, CMOs, CDOs, and U.S. government agency bonds.

785. **B. It facilitates the reporting of trade data for NASDAQ-listed securities and exchange-listed securities occurring off the exchange floor.**

The Trade Reporting Facility (TRF) is an automated system that expedites the reporting of trade data for NASDAQ-listed securities and exchange-listed securities occurring off the exchange floor.

786. **D. OATS**

OATS (Order Audit Trail System) tracks the life of an order entered OTC from entry to execution or cancellation. OATS tracks orders of all listed and unlisted stocks where the order is negotiated by brokerage firms without the use of an exchange.

787. **A. within 30 seconds of the trade**

Market makers for NASDAQ securities are required to report trades within 30 seconds of the transaction.

788. **C. Regulation M**

Regulation M of the Securities Exchange Act of 1934 outlines rules to prevent market manipulation. It's broken down into Rules 101 to 105. Think *M* for *market manipulation*.

789. **A. I, III, and IV**

The Securities and Exchange Commission (SEC), which was created under the Securities and Exchange Act of 1934, regulates the trading of securities. Commodities aren't considered securities and therefore aren't regulated by the SEC. A Series 7 license doesn't allow you to trade commodities, which is something you should keep in mind when answering Series 7 questions.

790. **D. the full and fair disclosure required on new offerings**

The full and fair disclosure that's required on new offerings is covered under the Securities Act of 1933, not the Securities Exchange Act of 1934. The Securities Act of 1933 deals with the registration of new issues, and the Securities Exchange Act of 1934 deals with the trading of outstanding issues.

791. **B. the Securities and Exchange Act of 1934**

The Securities and Exchange Act of 1934 created the Securities and Exchange Commission (SEC).

792. **B. It regulates trades of securities in the primary market.**

The Securities Act of 1933 regulates trading of securities in the primary (new issue) market. The Securities Exchange Act of 1934 regulates trades of outstanding securities in the secondary market.

793. **C. II, III, and IV**

Regressive taxes are ones in which all individuals are taxed at the same rate regardless of income level. Regressive taxes include sales, gas, and alcohol. Progressive taxes, where individuals with higher income pay a higher rate, include income, gift, and estate taxes.

794. **C. appreciation**

At this point, the investor just has appreciation of securities. You don't know whether the investor is going to have a profit or loss until the securities are sold. Capital gains or losses take place when a security is sold, and ordinary income would be from interest or dividends received.

795.   **B. II, III, and IV**

Portfolio income includes net capital gains from the sale of securities (including municipal bonds), dividends, and interest. Income, gains, and losses from a DPP (direct participation program) are passive.

796.   **D. sales**

Progressive taxes are taxes that increase depending on an individual's tax bracket. Progressive taxes affect individuals with high incomes more than individuals with low incomes. Personal income, gift, and estate taxes are progressive taxes. Sales tax and excise taxes (gas, alcohol, tobacco, and so on) are regressive taxes because everyone is taxed at the same rate.

797.   **A. capital gains**

Earned (active) income includes salaries, bonuses, and any income received from active participation in a business. Capital gains are considered portfolio income.

798.   **A. I and III**

Property tax is a flat or regressive tax in which taxes are levied equally regardless of the individual's income level. Flat taxes include sales, gasoline, excise, payroll, and property tax.

799.   **D. 28%**

When dealing with bond interest, the holding period doesn't come into play. Unlike qualified dividends and long-term capital gains, corporate bond interest is taxed at the investor's tax bracket.

800.   **B. I and IV**

Municipal bond interest is exempt from federal tax. However, unless purchasing a municipal bond within your home state or from a U.S. protectorate (such as Guam, U.S. Virgin Islands, or Puerto Rico), the interest is subject to state tax.

801.   **A. I and III**

Dividends received from stock and interest received from bonds are always taxed as ordinary income. Passive income is income that an investor receives from limited partnerships only. Long-term capital gains are for securities held for longer than one year. Because this investor held the stock for exactly one year, it's taxed as a short-term capital gain.

802.   **D. $4,500**

Cash dividends are always fully taxable for the year in which they were received.

803.

B. III and IV

Stock dividends and stock splits aren't taxable events. However, cash dividends and interest payments on corporate bonds are taxable.

804.

A. It will be treated as a tax credit on your client's U.S. tax return.

Your client would receive a tax credit on his U.S. tax return. This tax credit would reduce your client's U.S. tax liability.

805.

C. 20%

Unless qualified, dividends are taxed at the holder's tax bracket. Qualified dividends are ones on stock that has been held for more than 60 days during the 121-day period, which begins 60 days prior to the ex-dividend date. The tax rate on qualified dividends is as follows:

- Zero percent for investors who are in the 10 or 15 percent tax bracket

- Fifteen percent for investors who are taxed at a rate higher than 15 percent but below 39.6 percent

- Twenty percent for investors who are taxed at 39.6 percent

806.

B. federal tax but not state tax

Interest on U.S. government T-bonds (treasury bonds) is subject to federal tax but not state tax.

807.

C. He has a $3,000 loss for the current year and $3,500 carried over to the following year.

Capital losses can be used to offset capital gains. In this case, your client had losses exceeding his gains by $6,500 ($21,000 losses – $14,500 gains). Out of the $6,500, the client can write a total of $3,000 against his ordinary income each year. This means that your client would be carrying a $3,500 loss ($6,500 – $3,000) into the following year.

808.

B. $600 capital gain

When an investor buys and sells the same security several times, gains and losses are figured out by FIFO (first in, first out) unless specified otherwise by the investor. Therefore, the first stock purchased is the first stock sold, and the stock sold in February is the stock purchased in January.

809.

C. long-term capital gain or long-term capital loss

Short-term gains or losses are ones that take place in one year or less. The fact that Dirk purchased a call option on the same security doesn't affect his holding period on the stock that he purchased. Because Dirk has held the stock for one year and eight months (6 months + 9 months + 5 months = 20 months), the sale of the stock would be treated as a long-term capital gain or long-term capital loss.

810. **A. appreciation**

In this case, the shares just appreciated in value. The investor wouldn't have a capital gain or loss unless selling the securities at a price other than his cost basis. Passive income is income received from limited partnerships, and ordinary income is interest received from bonds or dividends received from stock.

811. **C. all gains or losses are considered short term**

Short selling is selling a borrowed security. Investors are hoping that the price of the security drops so that they can purchase the securities in that market at a lower price and return the securities to the lender. Short selling is a bearish strategy because investors want the price of the security to decrease. Because the investor isn't actually holding the securities, all gains and losses from selling short are considered short term, and the investor is taxed at his tax bracket.

812. **C. October 1 of the following year**

This is somewhat of a trick question. Securities become long term after holding them for more than a year. In this case, you may think that September 31 would be the answer. However, September has only 30 days, so there's no September 31; the correct answer is October 1 of the following year.

813. **D. I, II, III, and IV**

All cash dividends are subject to federal taxation. Interest on T-notes is state tax-free but not federally tax-free. In addition, investors must pay taxes on accretion unless purchasing a municipal bond in the primary market at a discount. All capital gains are subject to state and federal taxation.

814. **B. I, II, and III**

Short-term capital gains are taxed at the investor's tax bracket. Long-term capital gains are ones realized after holding a security for more than a year. Long-term capital gains are taxed at the same rate as qualified dividends:

- Zero percent for investors who are in the 10 or 15 percent tax bracket

- Fifteen percent for investors who are taxed at a rate higher than 15 percent but below 39.6 percent

- Twenty percent for investors who are taxed at 39.6 percent

815. **D. identified shares**

Because the price has been fluctuating, this investor would be best to identify which shares are to be sold. To minimize the tax burden, he'd choose to sell the shares with the highest purchase price. Unless specified, it's assumed that the first shares purchased are the ones that are going to be sold (FIFO — first in, first out).

816. **C. $500**

Amortization reduces the cost basis of bonds purchased at a premium (over $1,000 par) over several years.

Your client purchased the bonds for a price of $11,000 (110 percent of $1,000 par × 10 bonds), and they mature in eight years at $10,000.

Divide the $1,000 difference ($11,000 purchase price – $10,000) by eight years until maturity.

$$\frac{\$1,000}{8 \text{ years}} = \$125 \text{ per year amortization}$$

Your client is losing $125 per year on the value of his bonds (at least as far as the IRS is concerned) — he'll lose $500 ($125 × 4 years) over the course of four years.

817. **B. I and IV**

All new municipal bonds purchased at a discount must be accreted. The accretion would be part of Sally's tax-free interest. If she holds the bond until maturity, the difference won't be taxed as a capital gain or loss. To have a capital gain or loss, Sally would have had to sell the security at a price that differs from her cost basis.

818. **D. no gain or loss**

You use amortization for premium bonds (bonds purchased at a price greater than $1,000 par) to reduce the cost basis over several years. This investor purchased the bond for a price of $1,060 (106 percent of $1,000 par), and it matures in 12 years at $1,000 par.

Take the $60 difference ($1,060 purchase price – $1,000 par) and divide it by the 12 years until maturity.

$$\frac{\$60}{12 \text{ years}} = \$5 \text{ per year amortization}$$

If this investor is losing $5 per year on the value of his bond (at least as far as the IRS is concerned), he'll lose $20 ($5 × 4 years) over the course of four years. Next, subtract the $20 from the purchase price of the bond to determine the investor's cost basis after six years: $1,060 – $20 = $1,040. This investor's cost basis is $1,040, and he sold the bond at $1,040 (104 percent of $1,000 par); therefore, he saw no gain or loss.

819. **A. $28 loss**

Because Mrs. Jones purchased the bond at a discount, you're going to accrete the bond. Accretion is the act of adjusting the cost basis of the bond and bringing it closer to par over the number of years until maturity. Accretion is taxable yearly in addition to whatever interest Mrs. Jones receives. The first thing you must do is take the purchase price of $920 (92 percent of $1,000 par) and adjust it toward par over the ten years until maturity.

$$\frac{\$80}{10 \text{ years}} = \$8 \text{ per year accretion}$$

After doing the math, you see that there's an $8 per year accretion. Take that $8 and multiply it by the number of years Mrs. Jones held the bond before selling it: $8 × 6 years = $48.

Next, you must get the new cost basis by adding the $48 to Mrs. Jones' purchase price of $920.

$920 + $48 = $968 new cost basis

As the final step, you have to compare the new cost basis to the selling price to determine the amount of gain or loss.

$968 cost basis − $940 selling price = $28 loss

---

820.   **D. $55**

You should be able to eliminate Choices (A) and (B) right away. Because it's a 5 percent bond purchased at a discount, this investor has to claim at least $50 (5 percent × $1,000 par). The next thing you have to do is accrete the bond by spreading the discount over the number of years until maturity. The bond was purchased at $950 (95 percent of $1,000 par) and matures at $1,000 in ten years.

Take the $50 discount ($1,000 − $950) and divide it by the number of years until maturity.

$$\frac{\$50}{10\ years} = \$5\ per\ year\ accretion$$

Accretion is a taxable event, so you need to add the $5 accretion to the $50 interest to see how much this client will have to claim each year:

$50 + $5 = $55

---

821.   **D. II and IV**

Under IRS rules, all municipal bonds purchased at a premium must be amortized. Amortization of a bond decreases its cost basis and decreases the reported bond interest income.

---

822.   **B. I and IV**

All corporate bonds purchased at a discount, either in the secondary market or as an OID (original issue discount), *must* be accreted. However, if a corporate bond is purchased at a premium as a new issue or in the secondary market, it doesn't have to be amortized. In this case, the investor *may* amortize or elect to take a capital loss at maturity.

---

823.   **D. unlimited**

There is no gift tax between spouses, so the tax deduction limit is unlimited.

824. **D. $1,750**

Michelle received a gift of securities that has increased in value since purchase, so she'd assume the original purchase price of the securities. Because the securities were purchased at $4,250 ($42.50 × 100 shares) and sold at $6,000 ($60 × 100 shares), she'd have a capital gain of $1,750 ($6,000 – $4,250).

825. **B. The $6.50 loss per share deduction is disallowed.**

According to the wash sale rule, if an investor sells a security at a loss, the investor can't buy or sell the same security or anything convertible into the same security for 30 days (prior and after) and be able to claim the loss. Because Uriah sold GNP Corporation stock at a loss, he can't buy GNP call options within 30 days because GNP call options give him the right to buy GNP stock. In this case, the loss would be disallowed, and the cost basis of GNP stock would be adjusted for the $6.50 per share loss.

826. **D. DEF preferred stock**

The IRS wash sale rule states that investors can't sell a security at a loss and buy back the same security or anything convertible into the same security for 30 days (before or after). If an investor violates the wash sale rule, he wouldn't be able to claim the loss on his or her taxes (it would increase the cost basis of the securities repurchased). In this case, DEF convertible bonds are convertible into DEF common stock, DEF call options give the holder the right to buy DEF common stock, and DEF warrants give the holder the right to purchase DEF common stock at a fixed price. DEF preferred stock is allowable because it's a different security and isn't convertible into DEF common stock.

827. **A. I and III**

Each person may give an individual a gift of up to $14,000 per year that's exempt from gift tax. This gift is for $52,000 worth of securities; therefore, Gary (the donor) is subject to paying a gift tax. When receiving a gift of securities, the recipient assumes the donor's original cost basis (in this case, $42).

828. **B. $10**

Because the securities are inherited, the cost basis to the beneficiary (Clay) is the closing price on the day of his grandfather's death. Therefore, the cost of the stock is $52, and the stock is sold at $62. Clay realizes a $10 capital gain per share.

829. **A. I and II**

An IRS unified tax credit is one that's allowed for every man, woman, and child in America. This credit allows each person to gift a certain amount of his or her assets to other parties without having to pay gift or estate taxes.

830. **C. 401(k) plan**

Deferred compensation plans, payroll deduction plans, and 457 plans are all non-qualified retirement plans. 401(k)s are qualified salary reduction plans that allow investors to deposit pretax money.

831. **B. 100% taxable at the investor's tax bracket**

403(b) plans are also known as tax-sheltered annuities (TSAs). TSAs are available to school employees, tax-exempt organizations, and religious organizations. These are salary reduction plans in which the contributions are made on a pretax basis. Because the investor didn't pay any taxes on the contributions, the distributions are 100 percent taxable at the investor's tax bracket.

832. **A. a corporate executive who receives $10,000 in stock options from his employer each year**

Only individuals with self-employed income may participate in Keogh plans. As you can see, Choices (B) and (D) include the term *self-employed* right in the answer. However, if you read Choice (C) carefully, you see that although this person has a job working for someone else, she also has a side business giving lectures and makes some self-employed income. Stock options, or for that matter, capital gains, dividends, and/or interest aren't considered self-employed income and therefore don't allow the investor to contribute into a Keogh plan.

833. **A. I and III**

Contributions to IRS qualified retirement plans are made with pretax dollars, and the distributions are 100 percent taxed at the holder's tax bracket.

834. **C. Keogh plans**

401(k)s, SIMPLEs, and profit sharing plans are all types of corporate defined contribution plans. Defined contribution plans have the contribution amount specified in the plan, and it's typically a percentage of the employee's income. However, the amount received at retirement varies. Keogh (HR-10) plans are for self-employed income and aren't corporate retirement plans.

835. **D. I, II, III, and IV**

All of the choices listed meet the IRS requirements to be considered qualified retirement plans. Qualified plans allow investors to contribute pretax money and the retirement account to grow on a tax-deferred basis.

836. **A. they both allow pretax contributions from the employee and employer**

SEP IRAs allow contributions from the employer only, and SIMPLE IRAs allow contributions from both the employer and employee. Both plans allow for qualified pretax contribution, and all contributions are fully vested immediately. SIMPLE IRAs are allowed only for businesses with 100 employees or fewer who earn at least $5,000 in salary. SEP IRAs don't require a minimum number of employees.

837. **C. payroll deduction plans**

Payroll deduction plans are non-qualified plans that aren't required to include all full-time employees. ERISA (Employee Retirement Income Security Act) regulates only qualified plans that are available to all full-time employees of a company.

838. **A. private pension plans**

ERISA (Employee Retirement Income Security Act) regulations cover private pension plans only.

839. **C. $40,000**

The maximum amount of self-employed income that can be contributed into a Keogh plan each year is 100 percent of self-employed income or $52,000, whichever is less. The maximum amount of self-employed income that investors may write off is 20 percent of gross income or $52,000, whichever is less. This investor may write off 20 percent of his gross income, which is $40,000 (20 percent of $200,000).

840. **C. the beneficiary of the accounts must use the funds by age 30 for the funds not to be penalized**

Coverdell ESAs (educational savings accounts) and 529 plans (qualified tuition plans) are non-qualified plans designed to provide money for higher education. All of the answer choices given are true except for Choice (C). In a Coverdell ESA, the funds must be used by age 30 or transferred to another candidate. In a 529 plan, there are no age requirements.

841. **C. retirement plans**

Revenue bonds are types of municipal bonds. Revenue bonds have a federal tax advantage because the interest received is federally tax-free. Therefore, because retirement plans already have a nice tax advantage (money isn't taxed until it's withdrawn), it wouldn't make much sense to purchase low-yielding municipal bonds.

842. **C. Contributions are made with 100% pretax dollars.**

Under IRS laws, qualified retirement plans allow investors to invest money for retirement with pretax dollars. This means that investors can write it off. In addition, earnings accumulate on a tax-deferred basis (the investor isn't taxed until withdrawal). However, distributions (tax-deferred earnings and contributions) for which the participant received a tax deduction are 100% taxable at the investor's tax bracket.

843. **C. April 1 of the year after turning age 70½.**

Individuals may begin withdrawing money without penalty at age 59½ but must begin withdrawing no later than April 1 of the year after turning 70½. You may have accidentally jumped at April 15, but that's the day that your tax return is due.

844.   A. $16,000

Keogh plans are retirement plans designed for individuals with self-employed income. The maximum that may be contributed to a Keogh plan without taxation is 20 percent of gross self-employed income (25 percent net) or $52,000 per year, whichever is less. So in this case, the individual can deposit $80,000 × 20% = $16,000 into his Keogh plan.

845.   C. 60 days

After withdrawing money from a pension plan, individuals have 60 days to roll over the money into an IRA in order not to be taxed as if taking a withdrawal.

846.   C. II and III

In a defined contribution plan, the annual contribution percentage remains fixed. Certainly, the longer the employee stays with the corporation, the more money is contributed into the retirement plan and the more money the employee will receive at retirement. Contributions will continue even in bad years.

847.   D. municipal bonds

Because pension funds and other retirement plans are tax-deferred, it wouldn't make much sense to purchase municipal bonds because of their low yield. Remember, because the interest in municipal bonds is federally tax-free, they typically have the lowest yields of all bonds.

848.   A. 6% penalty tax

If an investor makes an excess contribution to an IRA, the excess contribution is subject to a 6 percent penalty tax.

849.   D. $6,500 after tax

Normally, the maximum contribution to a Roth IRA per year is $5,500. However, because this investor is over 50 years old, there's $1,000 additional catch-up contribution allowed. Unlike traditional IRAs, all contributions are after tax, but all withdrawals after age 59½ and holding the account for at least five years are tax-free.

850.   C. It is fully tax deductible.

Because the therapist has no other retirement plan, the IRA contributions are fully tax deductible. She may deposit up to $5,500 per year and be able to write it off on her taxes. If she had another retirement plan, she could still contribute to the IRA, but the contribution may or may not be tax deductible depending on the amount of earned income.

851. **A. $0**

For an investor to open an IRA, he must have earned income. In this case, the investor is making income only from trading and doesn't have a job. Therefore, he can't contribute money into an IRA.

852. **A. risk**

When recommending securities for a retirement plan, the maximum consideration should be given to risk. Investments within retirement plans shouldn't have a high degree of risk. The idea is preservation of capital and a steady rate of return.

853. **D. II and IV**

Unlike traditional IRAs, contributions made to Roth IRAs are made with after-tax dollars. Providing the investor has held the Roth IRA for at least five years and is at least 59½ years old, distributions are 100 percent tax-free.

854. **C. April 1 of the year after the holder turns age 70½**

Payouts for traditional IRAs must begin no later than April 1 of the year after the holder turns age 70½ (required beginning date, RBD). In the event that the holder doesn't withdraw the required minimum distribution (RMD) by April 1 of the year after turning age 70½, he or she will be hit with a 50 percent tax penalty on the amount that should have been withdrawn.

855. **D. 1 year**

Your client would have to wait at least one more year before executing another rollover.

856. **C. 60 days**

After withdrawing money from a pension plan, individuals have 60 days to roll over the money into an IRA without being taxed as a withdrawal.

857. **D. April 15 of the following year.**

Investors can deposit money into a traditional IRA up to April 15 (tax day) of the following year and claim it as a write-off on the previous year's taxes.

858. **B. 60 days**

After withdrawing money from his IRA, he has up to 60 days to roll it over into another eligible retirement plan without being taxed as a withdrawal.

859. **D. no requirement**

A Roth IRA is different than a traditional IRA because the money deposited into a Roth IRA is not tax deductible. However, all of the money withdrawn from a Roth IRA after age 59½ is tax-free, including the gains in the account. Therefore, because the IRS won't be taxing the money withdrawn, there's no requirement as to when the money has to be withdrawn.

860. **C. $4,000**

When withdrawing money from a retirement plan prior to age 59½, there's a 10 percent tax penalty under IRS Rule 72(t) (except in cases of death, disability, and in some cases first-time home buyers) added to the investor's tax bracket. Because your client withdrew $10,000 prior to age 59½, she'd be taxed at 40 percent (30 percent tax bracket + 10 percent penalty) and have a tax liability of $4,000.

861. **A. individuals and families with high-deductible health plans**

Health savings accounts (HSAs) are tax-exempt trust or custodial accounts set up with a qualified trustee. The trustee for a health savings account can be a bank, insurance company, or anyone approved by the IRS. HSAs may be set up only for individuals or families who have high-deductible health plans (HDHP). Any individual covered by Medicare isn't eligible to have an HSA.

862. **A. I and III**

Contributions to HSAs are made in pretax dollars, which are limited under IRS rules. The money in the HSA grows on a tax-free basis, and withdrawals are tax-free when used for qualified medical expenses.

863. **D. any remaining funds in the account at the end of the year must be rolled over into an IRA or IRS-approved retirement account**

Health Savings Account (HSA) funds may be invested in certain mutual funds, the amount that each family or individual can contribute each year is limited, and they're available only to individuals or families who have high-deductible health plans (HDHPs). Funds left over in the account at the end of each year can be left in the account and don't need to be rolled over into a retirement plan.

864. **C. If withdrawals are not related to qualified medical expenses, there is a 10% tax penalty on the amount withdrawn.**

Health Savings Accounts (HSAs) are available for individuals with high-deductible health plans (HDHPs) to save money for medical expenses that insurance doesn't cover. Money may be contributed on a qualified (pretax) basis. Money may be withdrawn tax-free if withdrawn for qualified medical procedures that insurance doesn't cover fully. If money is withdrawn for any other reason, there will be a 20 percent tax penalty assessed.

865. **C. SEC**

SROs are self-regulatory organizations that are unaffiliated with the federal government. The SEC (Securities and Exchange Commission) is a government agency.

866. **B. II, III, and IV**

As self-regulatory organizations (SROs), FINRA and the NYSE can fine, expel, and/or censure members. However, because FINRA and the NYSE aren't affiliated with the government, they can't imprison members.

867. **B. I and III**

To sell a security in a state, you, your firm, and the security must be registered in the state. You don't have to notify FINRA of the customer's new address, and you don't need to receive written proof of the customer's new address.

868. **A. broker-dealer**

When a registered representative takes a job outside of his firm, he is moonlighting. Moonlighting rules for registered representatives require the individual to disclose this information to his employing broker-dealer only.

869. **C. two years**

If a registered rep leaves the brokerage industry for more than two years, he would be required to take his exams all over again.

870. **C. I and IV**

An individual who has been *convicted* (not charged) within the past ten years of any felony is prohibited from working in the securities industry. In addition, an individual who has been convicted of any securities- or money-related misdemeanors can't work in the securities industry. Just because an individual is charged doesn't mean that he'll be convicted.

871. **C. 120**

Under Financial Industry Regulatory Authority (FINRA) rules, all registered reps must complete their computer-based regulatory element of their continuing education within 120 days of their second anniversary of becoming a registered rep and every third anniversary after.

872. **B. two years**

After an individual has been unaffiliated with a broker-dealer for more than two years, his licenses are no longer valid, and he'd have to take the licensing exams again.

873. **D. 6 months**

The rules for taking FINRA exams are as follows:

- If you fail an exam once, you have to wait 30 days before another attempt.
- If you fail the exam twice, you have to wait 30 days before another attempt.
- If you fail the third time, you have to wait six months before another attempt.

So make sure you're ready to pass the first time so you don't have to worry about those rules.

874. **C. 90 days**

After leaving the military, a person who was previously a licensed registered representative and has served in the military for two years or more must find a brokerage firm to work for within 90 days of leaving the military to prevent the period of inactivity from being counted.

875. **B. his employing firm**

If a registered representative has to file for bankruptcy, he's responsible for notifying only his firm.

876. **A. Series 52**

An agent must pass a Series 52 exam to become a full municipal securities representative. The Series 55 is a license to become an equity trader for a brokerage firm. A Series 65 or 66 is required to become an investment adviser. The Series 86/87 are exams individuals need to take to become research analysts of a brokerage firm.

877. **C. Series 24**

Most principals (managers) of a firm are Series 24 licensed. This license allows them to supervise trades of most securities.

878. **A. the Series 65 or Series 66**

Under the Investment Advisers Act of 1940, if you're charging a fee for giving investment advice, you must register as an investment adviser. If your sole business is charging for giving investment advice, you can take the Series 65. However, if you plan on passing the Series 7 so that you can execute trades for customers and charge a commission, you can take the Series 66. The Series 66 exam is an investment adviser exam but is good only in combination with the Series 7.

879. **C. the agent failed to satisfy his firm's in-house requirements of sales production**

An agent (registered rep) can't be suspended by FINRA just because he failed to meet his employer's sales quota.

880. **A. money laundering**

Although the depositing of large amounts of cash in itself isn't illegal, it may be a sign of the possibility of money laundering.

881. **B. intermediation**

The three stages of money laundering are placement, layering, and integration.

- *Placement* is when illegally obtained money is placed into a financial institution.
- *Layering* is an activity intended to disguise an illegal activity.
- *Integration* is when illegal money is mixed with legal money.

882. **D. I, II, III, and IV**

All of the answer choices listed are potential indications of money laundering.

883. **A. structuring**

Structuring is an indication of money laundering. Structuring occurs when an investor makes deposits just under $10,000, which don't need to be reported to the U.S. government.

884. **C. a cash deposit of $15,000**

A Form 112 is used to report cash transactions or money order transactions of $10,000 or more. Cash deposits over $10,000 in one day may be an indication of money laundering and must be reported to FinCEN (U.S. Treasury Financial Crimes Network) by filling out a currency transaction report (CTR).

885. **B. $5,000**

Suspicious activity of $5,000 or more must be reported to FinCEN (U.S. Treasury Financial Crimes Network) through a SAR (suspicious activity report). Suspicious activity includes financial transactions that are illogical and serve no apparent purpose.

886. **D. all of the above**

All of the choices listed may be signs that your customer is planning on laundering money.

887. **C. telephone number**

Brokerage firms must verify the customer's name, address, date of birth, and Social Security number through a valid government issued photo ID. However, a customer's telephone number isn't required to be confirmed to determine customer identity.

888. **A. customer identification programs**

Under the USA Patriot Act, all financial institutions must maintain customer identification programs (CIPs). It's up to the financial institution to verify the identity of any new customers, maintain records of how they verified the identity, and determine whether the new customer appears on any suspected terrorist list or terrorist organization. As part of the identification program, they must obtain the customer's name, date of birth, address (no P.O. boxes), and Social Security number.

889. **A. Your customer's assets will be frozen, and your firm will be instructed to stop doing business with the customer.**

If a new customer's name appears on the Specially Designated Nationals (SDN) list, it indicates that your customer is being watched or may have been involved in terrorism, trafficking in narcotics, and so on. In this case, the customer's assets will be frozen, and your firm will be instructed to cease doing business with the customer.

890. **A. CIPs**

The USA Patriot Act requires financial institutions, such as broker-dealers and banks, to maintain CIPs (customer identification programs) to help prevent money laundering and the financing of terrorist organizations. Financial institutions are required to look at the Specially Designated Nationals (SDNs) list published by the Office of Foreign Asset Control (OFAC) to see whether any of their new customers are on the list. If a new customer is on the list, his assets will be frozen, and your firm must cease doing business with him.

891. **B. I and II**

Because the agent works for a FINRA firm, the agent needs to notify his firm about the opening of the account. The agent doesn't need permission to open or trade the account. However, if the agent worked for an NYSE firm, he'd need permission from his firm to open the account. The FINRA or NYSE firm always must receive a duplicate confirmation of all trades executed in the other account. The agent never needs permission to execute trades in the other account.

892. **B. tenancy in common**

In a joint tenancy in common (TIC) account, if one investor dies, that investor's portion of the account is transferred into the investor's estate while the remainder of the assets are transferred to the survivors. Persons may or may not have equal ownership of the account. The account may be divided based on percentage of money contributed.

893. **C. I, II, and IV**

Employees of financial institutions need permission to open margin accounts at brokerage firms but not cash accounts. Officers of financial institutions don't need any permission to open brokerage accounts. All employees of NYSE brokerage firms need permission to open any type of account at another brokerage firm.

894. **A. a parent and a minor daughter**

A joint account is one in the name of more than one adult. An account for an adult and a minor would be an UGMA (Uniform Gifts to Minors Act) or UTMA (Uniform Transfer to Minors Act) account. Both UGMA and UTMA accounts are custodial accounts in the name of the adult for the benefit of the minor.

895. **A. the SDN list maintained by OFAC**

All financial institutions, such as banks and broker-dealers, must have customer identification programs (CIPs) in place. As part of that program, the names of all new customers must be checked against the SDN (Specially Designated Nationals) list maintained by OFAC (Office of Foreign Assets Control).

896. **C. I, II, and III**

Although it may be helpful, you're not required to know whether a new customer has an account at another brokerage firm. However, you do need to know the customer's citizenship, whether his name appears on the SDN (Specially Designated Nationals) list, and whether he works for another broker-dealer.

897. **A. MMA would open a numbered account for Chael.**

Numbered (street-named) accounts are very common at broker-dealers. If Chael wants to remain anonymous, he can have the broker-dealer set up his account as a numbered account. All order tickets would contain a number or code; however, the broker-dealer must have a signed document on file by Chael, stating that he is the owner of the account.

898. **C. I, II, and III**

A registered rep may open a minor's account by a custodian (UGMA account), a corporate account by a designated officer, and a partnership account by a designated officer. However, registered reps aren't permitted to open an individual account in the name of a third person.

899. **C. the individual's educational background**

The individual's Social Security number, date of birth, and residential address are all required from a customer when opening an account. Although the individual's educational background would be helpful to have, it's not required.

900. **D. I, II, III, and IV**

Logically, all of the choices listed would change an investor's investment objectives. Certainly, aging and having a child would most likely mean that an investor wouldn't take as much risk. Depending on the terms of a divorce, an investor may want to invest in something that would provide regular income. However, winning a lot of money in a lottery would most likely mean that an investor would be able to take additional risk.

901.

B. I and III

Fiduciary accounts, such as UGMA and UTMA accounts, are required to follow the prudent man rule or legal list of the state in which the account is set up. The prudent man rule or legal list establishes a guideline of appropriate investments for fiduciary accounts. There isn't a FINRA list of approved investments for minors' accounts.

902.

C. I, III, and IV

Statements I and IV were probably a given. But you also need the type of account that the customer is opening (cash, margin, corporate, and so on), the customer's age and marital status, and the customer's occupation and employer. You don't need the customer's educational background.

903.

D. I, II, III, and IV

All of the information listed needs to be on the new account form. In addition, you also need the Social Security number (or tax ID if a business), the occupation and type of business, bank references, net worth, annual income, if the customer is an insider of a company, and the signature of the registered rep and a principal.

904.

C. II and III

Yes, believe it or not, a customer's signature isn't required on a new account form. However, if you're opening a new account for a customer, you'd have to fill out and sign the new account form and have it signed by a principal (manager) of the firm.

905.

A. a parent and a minor daughter

A joint account is an account in the name of more than one adult. That means that Choice (A) doesn't work. UGMA accounts are designed for situations when you have one minor and one adult.

906.

B. Corporate Resolution

For a corporation to open a cash account, you or your firm would need to receive a copy of the Corporate Resolution. The Corporate Resolution tells you who has trading authority for the account. If the corporation was opening a margin account, you'd need a copy of the Corporate Resolution and the Corporate Charter. The Corporate Charter (by-laws) lets you know that the corporation is allowed to purchase securities on margin according to their own by-laws.

907.

D. II and III

A registered representative may open a joint account with a client if obtaining approval from a principal of the firm. In addition, the registered representative and the client must agree in writing to share gains and losses based on the percentage of money invested.

908. **A. The client must sign a written statement attesting to ownership of the account.**

Numbered accounts are also known as street-name accounts. To open an account for a client in street name, the customer must sign paperwork attesting to responsibility for the account. Because accounts of different investors can't be commingled (combined), the firm must keep this client's account segregated from other clients' accounts held in street name.

909. **B. an account for his minor daughter**

An individual may open an account and trade the account for a minor without a written power of attorney. However, if a client wants to open and trade an account for his wife or for his partner, he'd need her to sign a power of attorney, giving him the authorization to open the account and execute trades.

910. **C. You may open the account if you can determine from other sources that the customer has the financial means to handle the account.**

Unfortunately, this situation isn't unusual. When you're opening an account for a new customer, he may not feel comfortable sharing all of his financial information. However, you can still make recommendations and do trades for the customer if you can determine financial information from other sources, such as Dun & Bradstreet (D&B) cards.

For argument's sake, say that the D&B card says that your new customer is the owner of a company that made $500 million last year. In this case, you can assume that the customer has a lot of money. Recommendations made to customers should be suitable to their investment objectives and financial situation. If you can't determine the information from other sources, you can still make trades and recommendations that would be suitable for all investors, such as U.S. government securities and mutual funds.

911. **B. $500,000**

Your client must have at least $500,000 in assets available for investments to establish a prime brokerage account, although the minimum requirement is only $100,000 if the account is established through an investment adviser. Prime brokerage firms consolidate information from all brokerage accounts the client has to provide one statement for the customer.

912. **C. III and IV**

Municipal fund securities are 529 plans. To approve 529 accounts, a principal must have either a Series 51 or a 53 license. A Series 51 licensed principal may approve only municipal fund securities transactions while a Series 53 licensed principal may approve municipal fund securities transactions and municipal bond transactions.

913. **D. I, II, III, and IV**

When a client receives a confirmation (receipt of trade), the confirmation has to include the trade and settlement date, the name and type of the security, how many shares were traded, and the amount of commission if traded on an agency basis. In the event that the trade was made on a principal basis, the amount of markup doesn't need to be disclosed.

914. **A. a principal**

New account forms and order tickets must be signed by a principal (manager) of the firm. Order tickets don't have to be signed prior to placing the order for trade but must be signed by the end of the day. This means that you can do trades while your principal is out to lunch.

915. **C. take the order but mark it as "unsolicited"**

Even though the shares of Biff Spanky Corporatoin may not fit into Gina's investment objectives, you can still accept the order. However, to protect yourself, you need to mark the order ticket as "unsolicited." The only unsolicited orders that you wouldn't be able to accept are on options (unless her options account was approved) and DPPs (direct participation programs).

916. **B. quarterly**

FINRA (Financial Industry Regulatory Authority) and the SEC (Securities and Exchange Commission) require member firms to send customer account statements at least quarterly (once every three months) for inactive accounts. To help you remember how often account statements should be sent out, think "AIM": **a**ctive accounts (monthly), **i**nactive accounts (quarterly), and **m**utual funds (semiannually).

917. **C. the same day as execution of the order**

Principals (managers) must approve trades on the same day as execution but not necessarily before execution. This would allow the order to be entered as quickly as possible. Principals must approve trades as soon as possible after execution but no later than the end of the day at the latest.

918. **D. I, II, III, and IV**

When you become a registered rep, you receive your own unique identification number. This number has to be placed on any order ticket you fill out along with a description of the securities (such as ABC common stock), the time the order was placed, and whether the order was solicited or unsolicited. An unsolicited order is when a client tells you the securities she wants to purchase or sell without your input.

919. **B. take the order and mark it as "unsolicited"**

You probably want to let your client know about the risks of investing in low-priced stocks and let him know that it doesn't fit his investment objectives. However, you should definitely take the order and mark the order ticket as "unsolicited." By marking the order ticket as "unsolicited," you're putting the responsibility for the order on your client's shoulders.

920. C. 4

If a question doesn't specify whether an account is active or inactive, assume that the client is inactive and will receive quarterly statements. If a customer places any trade orders in a particular month, she must receive an account statement that month.

921. D. the investor's occupation

The investor's occupation is something that's on the new account form, not the order ticket.

922. B. one business day following the trade date

Don't spend too much, or any, time remembering the rule number because it's extremely unlikely that you'll see the rule number on the exam. However, you should know that confirmations for trades between firms must be sent no later than one business day following the trade date. Confirmations to customers must be sent at or prior to the completion of the transaction.

923. C. Pay $16.00.

If a brokerage firm accidentally reports a trade executed at a different price than shown on the actual confirmation, the client must accept the price on the actual confirmation. In this case, your client would have to pay the $16.00 per share.

924. A. at or prior to the completion of the transaction

For member-to-customer transactions, the member firm must send the trade confirmation at or prior to completion of the transaction (the settlement date). For member-to-member transactions, the firms must send each other confirmations no later than one business day after the trade date.

925. B. I and IV

If trading was done during the month, the account is active. Account statements must be sent out monthly for active accounts and quarterly for inactive accounts.

926. C. II, III, and IV

A confirmation must include the amount of commission charged for an agency transaction, a description of the security purchased or sold, the registered representative's identification number, and so on. However, the markup or markdown doesn't need to be disclosed for principal transactions.

927. C. confirmation

All member firms are required to send a trade confirmation to a customer at or prior to the completion of each transaction. The confirmation provides all the specifics of the trade, such as the trade date, whether the customer bought or sold, the amount of securities, the name of the security, the price of the security, and so on.

928. **D. whether the trade was executed on a dealer or agency basis**

MSRB (Municipal Securities Rulemaking Board) rules require that confirmations include whether a trade was executed on a principal (dealer) or agency (broker) basis. The amount of the commission on an agency trade does need to be disclosed, but the dealer's markup or markdown on a principal trade doesn't have to be disclosed. The trade date (the day the transaction was executed) would need to be disclosed but not the settlement date because that's assumed to be three business days after the trade date.

929. **A. whether the trade was solicited or unsolicited**

Whether an order is solicited or unsolicited is on an order ticket, not the confirmation. Order confirmations include items such as the customer's account number, the agent's ID number, the trade date, whether the security was bought (BOT) or sold (SLD), the number or par value of securities, the yield (if bonds), the CUSIP number (if any), the price of the security, the total amount paid, and the commission charged.

930. **B. the price the dealer paid to purchase the security**

The 5 percent markup policy (FINRA 5% policy) states that a brokerage firm may use all relevant factors of a trade to determine the markup or commission charged to a customer except dealer cost (the price that the firm paid to have the security in inventory).

931. **A. reclamation**

Reclamation is the return of securities previously accepted. Rejection is the refusal of securities at the time of delivery.

932. **A. 4 certificates for 150 shares each and 14 certificates for 5 shares each**

The number of shares on each stock certificate must be in multiples of 100 (100, 200, 300, and so on), divisors of 100 (1, 2, 4, 5, 10, 20, 25, 50), or in units that add up to 100 (70 + 30, 85 + 15, 60 + 40, and so on). Choice (A) is the exception because150 isn't a multiple or divisor of 100. In addition, the odd-lot (less than 100 shares) portion of the trade is exempt from the rule. For example, in this case, you could have three certificates for 200 shares each and one certificate for 70 shares.

933. **A. Monday, October 15**

The last day that your investor client can buy the stock the "regular way" and still receive the dividend is on the business day before the ex-dividend date. The ex-dividend date is on Tuesday, October 16, so an investor must buy the stock no later than Monday, October 15, to receive the dividend.

934. **B. he already purchased the shares, and he must submit the payment**

As soon as the purchase order is executed, your client owns the securities and must pay for them no matter what happens to the market price of the securities.

935. **A. She must deposit the full purchase price of the securities before the purchase order may be executed.**

A client's account would be frozen for 90 days if he failed to pay for securities he purchased or failed to deliver securities he sold. In this case, Mary must pay for the securities in full before any order would be entered or deliver securities before they will be sold.

936. **B. Tuesday, September 15**

The ex-dividend date (ex-date) is two business days before the record date.

937. **C. three business days, and payment is due in five business days**

Corporate bonds settle in three business days, and payment is due in five business days.

938. **D. the over-the-counter sale of outstanding non-exempt securities**

The 5 percent markup policy doesn't apply to primary (new issue) offerings, mutual funds (continuous offering of new shares), or Regulation D (exempt) offerings.

939. **C. Sell out the stock and freeze the account for 90 days.**

If a client fails to pay for the trade by the payment date, the security is sold out and the account is frozen for 90 days. To apply for an extension with the FINRA, a customer must disclose a legitimate reason for needing the extension.

940. **D. II and IV**

The record date is Thursday, August 15, so the ex-dividend date is Tuesday, August 13. If a regular-way trade is executed on the ex-dividend date, the seller of the stock receives the dividend. In a cash trade, the trade needs to be executed after the record date to receive the dividend.

941. **D. all of the above**

An extension to pay for a trade may be granted by FINRA, the Fed, or any national securities exchange. The extension generally grants customers an extra five business days to pay for the trade.

942. **B. a change in the market price**

Securities can't be rejected due to a change in market price. Securities are rejected if the transfer agent doesn't follow the good delivery rules.

943. **D. all of the above**

The 5 percent markup policy is a guideline for broker-dealers to use when executing trades of outstanding securities for public customers. For a standard-sized trade of non-exempt securities, broker-dealers typically shouldn't charge a commission, markup, or markdown that is greater than 5 percent. However, some situations may warrant a charge more than 5 percent, such as a small trade or extra work involved in executing the trade. The 5 percent policy applies to both commission charges on agency transactions and to markups and markdowns on principal transactions, including proceeds transactions, and riskless (simultaneous) transactions.

944. **D. ten business days after the settlement date**

If a client sold securities in his possession and failed to deliver them within ten business days after the settlement date, your firm must buy them from another seller. Remember, once the order ticket is executed, your client's securities were sold. If your client fails to deliver them, your firm is still responsible for getting them to the purchaser. In this case, your client's account would be frozen for 90 days, and he wouldn't be able to purchase securities without paying first and wouldn't be able to sell securities in his possession without delivering them first.

945. **D. Friday, October 10**

The stock settlement date for stock purchases is three business days, but the payment date is five business days after the trade date. Remember, Saturday and Sunday aren't business days, so the payment date would be Friday, October 10.

946. **C. 2 certificates for 200 shares each and 3 certificates for 80 shares each**

In order to be considered good delivery, the trade has to be in multiples of 100 shares (100, 200, 300, 400, and so on), divisors of 100 shares (1, 2, 4, 5, 10, 20, 25, 50, and so on), or shares that add up to 100 (20 +80, 35+65, 15+85, and so on). The odd-lot portion (the portion less than 100 shares) is exempt. The odd-lot portion in this case is 40 shares.

The answer choice that doesn't work in this question is Choice (C). The two certificates for 200 shares each is okay, but the three certificates for 80 shares isn't good because there's nothing to match up with the 80 shares to make it 100.

947. **C. 45 days**

When a member receives an arbitration complaint, the member has 45 days to respond if guilty or not.

948. **B. accept the complaint and write down any action taken**

After receiving Meisha's written complaint, the broker-dealer must accept the complaint and write down any action taken to resolve the complaint. All broker-dealers should keep a complaint file for each client and keep accurate records of any communications or actions taken regarding a complaint.

949. **C. $50,000**

Simplified arbitration is used for member to non-member disputes not over $50,000. Simplified industry arbitration is used for member to member disputes not over $50,000. Most arbitration complaints are judged by a three-person panel, but simplified arbitration is decided by one person.

950. **A. members may take non-members to arbitration**

Members can't force non-members to submit a dispute to arbitration. The non-member (customer) decides if the dispute is settled through arbitration or COP (Code of Procedure). However, many firms require customers to sign an arbitration agreement when opening an account that requires disputes to be settled through arbitration only.

951. **D. four years**

According to FINRA Rule 4513 — don't worry about remembering the rule number — complaints must be kept by the brokerage firm for at least four years (previously three years).

952. **B. a panel chosen by FINRA**

If a complaint is submitted by FINRA (Financial Industry Regulatory Authority), the first decision on a dispute that is handled through the FINRA Code of Procedure is made by a hearing panel chosen by FINRA. The decision may be appealed to the NAC (National Adjudicatory Council).

953. **D. II and IV**

According to MSRB (Municipal Securities Rulemaking Board) rules, account transfers must be validated by the delivering firm within three business days after receiving the ACAT (account transfer) form. The securities must be delivered within four business days after verification. What makes this question more difficult is that according to FINRA rules, broker-dealers have one business day to validate and three business days to transfer.

954. **B. The deceased party's portion of the account is transferred to his or her estate.**

In a joint account with tenants in common (TIC), if one investor dies, the deceased party's portion of the account is transferred to his or her estate. In a joint account with rights of survivorship, the entire account is transferred to the survivors of the account.

955. **D. The account is transferred to the former minor.**

Under the terms of the Uniform Gifts to Minors Act (UGMA), the account must be handed over to the former minor when he or she reaches the age of majority. You won't be expected to know the age of majority because it varies from state to state, but it's typically between the ages of 18 and 21.

956. **A. I and III**

Upon receiving a signed ACAT (account transfer) form, the delivering firm has one business day to validate the positions in the account. After validating the positions, the delivering firm must cancel any open orders and freeze the account. Then, the delivering firm must deliver the securities within three business days. Note that MSRB rules are different than Uniform Practice Code rules.

957. **A. The entire account would be transferred to Mrs. Faber.**

This account was set up as joint tenants with rights of survivorship (JTWROS). When an investor with a JTWROS account dies, the investor's portion of the account is transferred to the remaining survivors of the account (in this case, Mrs. Faber). Most married couples set up their joint accounts this way to avoid probate issues.

958. **B. NSCC**

To process an ACAT (Automated Customer Account Transfer), a brokerage firm must be a member of the NSCC (National Securities Clearing Corporation). When a brokerage firm is a clearing firm, the firm is assuming financial responsibility if a customer doesn't pay for a trade or doesn't deliver certificates that are sold.

959. **D. All of the above**

When learning of the death of a client, you should mark the account as deceased, freeze the account (don't do any trading), cancel all open orders (GTC), cancel all written powers of attorney, and await the proper legal papers for instructions about what to do with the account.

960. **A. Calls must be made after 8:00 a.m. and before 9:00 p.m. local time of the customer.**

According to Rule G-39, all cold calls (calls to potential customers) must be made after 8:00 a.m. and before 9:00 p.m. based on the local time of the customer.

961. **C. The profit is forfeited to the issuer.**

If an insider of a company realizes a profit within six months or less on stock of the company, it's considered a short-swing profit and must be forfeited back to the issuer. This rule was designed to curb insider trading abuses.

962. **D. a lifetime**

Documents that establish the broker-dealer as a corporation or partnership must be kept for the firm's lifetime.

963. **C. five years**

Individuals placed on a firm's do not call list can't be contacted for five years.

964. **C. three months**

A brokerage firm may hold customer mail (such as account statements and confirmations) for two months if traveling within the United States or three months if traveling outside of the United States.

965. **B. business continuity and disaster recovery plan**

In the event of a major business disruption, FINRA requires that all brokerage firms create and maintain a business continuity and disaster recovery plan. As part of the plan, all brokerage firms must have hard copy and electronic backups of all of their data, an alternate location for all of their employees, a way to communicate with regulators, an alternate means of communication between the firm and its employees, an alternate means of communication between the firm and its customers, and a way to provide fast customer access to funds and securities in case the firm is unable to stay in business.

966. **C. Regulation S-P**

All brokerage firms must have safeguards to protect customer records from unauthorized use (Gramm-Leach-Bliley Act). The safeguards must be disclosed in writing to all new customers at the time of the opening of the account and to all existing customers annually. Non-public information includes customers' Social Security number, transaction history, account balance, and so on.

967. **B. the employee must obtain written approval before each trade is executed in the account**

A NYSE registered rep needs permission from his firm of employment to open an account at another firm. Approval of each trade isn't necessary after the account is opened.

968. **C. transfer the money in the account to the executor of the estate**

If a client dies, all open orders should be canceled, the account should be frozen (no trading), and any written power of attorney needs to be canceled. No assets should be transferred until receiving instructions from the executor of the estate.

969. **B. I and IV**

UGMA (Uniform Gifts to Minors Act) accounts are custodial accounts set up with one minor and one custodian per account. Any taxes due are paid by the minor, not the custodian.

970. **A. ABC Broker-Dealer must forward the proxy to the client.**

Street-name accounts are numbered accounts held in the name of the broker-dealer for the benefit of the client. In this case, DEF Corporation would send the proxy to ABC Broker-Dealer who must in turn forward the proxy to its client.

971. **D. I, II, and IV**

U-4 forms of terminated employees must be maintained by brokerage firms for only three years. All other choices listed must be maintained by brokerage firms for a minimum of six years.

972. **A. established customers**

Established customers are exempt from penny stock signature requirements on suitability statements. However, established customers aren't exempt from the requirement of receiving the risk disclosure document. Established customers are customers of the brokerage firm for at least one year or who have purchased at least three different penny stocks on three different days through the firm. All of the other answers mentioned are exempt from risk disclosure and suitability statement requirements.

973. **C. II and III**

The Uniform Practice Code regulates trades between members. The Rules of Fair Practice or Conduct Rules regulate trades between members and non-members. The Code of Procedure is a process of handling complaints.

974. **C. II and III**

A durable power of attorney cancels only upon death of an investor. A regular power of attorney cancels upon death or mental incompetence of the investor. If the investor is declared mentally incompetent by a state court, the state court would choose a guardian to manage the investor's assets.

975. **D. III, IV, II, I**

In the event of corporate bankruptcy, the first to be paid would be unpaid workers; then the IRS; secured creditors, such as mortgage bondholders; unsecured creditors, such as debenture holders; preferred stockholders; and, lastly, common stockholders.

976. **B. Certificates are endorsed by the minor.**

UGMA (Uniform Gifts to Minors Act) accounts are custodial accounts set up with one minor and one custodian per account. The accounts are set up in the custodian's name for the benefit of the minor. Because the minor is legally too young to endorse any paperwork or certificates, the custodian endorses them.

977. **B. the most recent balance sheet**

If a client requests a copy of a broker-dealer's balance sheet, the brokerage firm must send a copy of the most recent one to the client immediately.

978. **A. I only**

A power of attorney or trading authorization is required for discretionary accounts. In this case, an individual is giving trading authorization to his registered rep or broker-dealer. All discretionary orders must be marked as such at the time they're entered for execution. These types of accounts must be monitored closely by a principal to make sure that there's no excessive trading for the purpose of generating commission (churning).

979. **C. custodial account**

UGMA (Uniform Gift to Minors Act) accounts are custodial accounts. These accounts are managed by a custodian for the benefit of the minor. The custodian has full control over the account and has the right to buy or sell securities, exercise rights or warrants, hold securities, and so on. The custodian must do what is in the best interest of the minor. Once the minor reaches the age of majority, which varies from state to state, the account is transferred to the former minor. A UGMA account can have only one custodian and one minor.

980. **D. "Our dedicated sales team will work with you to help meet your investment goals."**

Choices (B) and (C) aren't legal because they're guarantees, and a firm can't guarantee that its investment recommendations will outperform the market, even if they did for the last ten years. Also, a firm can't guarantee customers that it will earn them at least 7 percent on their investments each year. Additionally, there's no way to prove that this broker-dealer's "dedicated sales team" is the best in the industry. However, stating that its sales team will help investors meet their investment goals is fine and is what every broker-dealer should be doing.

981. **C. all preferred stock recommendations made by your firm in the last year**

The reason for this rule is that investors have the right to see all recommendations of a similar kind (in this case, common stock) for the last year. If a broker-dealer is claiming his expertise by making recommendations, investors have the right to see how successful the recommendations are. Did the broker-dealer pick right 70 percent of the time or only 30 percent of the time?

982. **C. I, II, and IV**

For you to determine whether something is advertising, you have to look at who it's directed toward. Advertisements aren't directed or targeted to specific individuals. Advertisements include TV ads, radio ads, websites, billboards, and tombstone ads. Sales literature is directed toward specific individuals. Sales literature includes market letters, form letters, abstracts of prospectuses, and research reports. A principal must approve advertising and sales literature.

983. **B. $5 million and/or 20 years in prison per violation**

If an individual is convicted of insider trading, he faces up to a $5 million dollar fine and/or 20 years in prison per violation.

984. **A. the profit or loss**

Churning is the excessive trading of a client's account for the sole purpose of generating commissions and is a violation. Yes, believe it or not, when FINRA (Financial Industry Regulatory Authority) is looking to see whether an account has been churned, the client's profit or loss doesn't come into play.

985. **C. hypothecation**

Hypothecation isn't a violation. Hypothecation takes place when a brokerage firm lends money to a customer when purchasing securities or margin.

986. **A. matching orders**

Trading securities back and forth without any essential change of ownership is a violation known as matching orders. The idea behind it is to make it look like there's a large trading volume on a particular security to help drive the price up.

987. **D. Make no recommendations or purchases.**

This registered representative has received inside information. Inside information is information that hasn't been made public through the media. The registered representative can't act on or make recommendations based on this inside information. The registered representative should bring this information to a principal.

988. **C. Encouraging clients to purchase equity securities just prior to the ex-dividend date so that they will receive a dividend**

Selling dividends is a violation in which a registered rep (agent) encourages an investor to purchase an equity security in time to receive a previously declared dividend. This is a violation because there's no advantage to purchasing a security prior to the ex-dividend date (the first day the security trades without a dividend). Remember, the price of the stock is reduced by the amount of the dividend on the ex-dividend date. As such, even though a customer might receive a $0.25 cash dividend, the price of the stock is reduced by $0.25, so there's no advantage.

989. **B. freeriding**

Clients must pay for trades even if selling the securities at a profit shortly afterward. You can imagine the problems that would occur if clients never paid for trades and just waited to see whether there was a profit. In this case, the client's account would be frozen for 90 days, and she wouldn't be able to purchase securities without paying for them first.

990. **A. contact a principal immediately**

If you suspect that one of your clients is using inside information, you must immediately inform a principal. Any further action will be decided by your firm. The Insider Trading and Securities Fraud Enforcement Act of 1988 requires all broker-dealers to have written supervisory procedures that address insider information.

991. **C. both the CEO and the lifelong friend**

Because the friend used the inside information (information not yet released to the public), both the CEO and the friend violated insider trading rules.

992. **D. hypothecating**

Hypothecating isn't a violation. Hypothecation takes place when a brokerage firm lends money to a customer to purchase securities in a margin account.

993. **C. I, II, and III**

The SEC has the authority to punish individuals inside or outside of the brokerage industry. The NYSE and FINRA may penalize an individual within the industry. However, because the MSRB doesn't enforce MSRB rules, the MSRB may not punish any individual for rules violations.

994. **D. SIPC funding is made by member assessments.**

SIPC (Securities Investor Protection Corporation) is funded by annual fees paid by brokerage firms. SIPC isn't a U.S. government agency. Banks and investment advisers aren't required to purchase SIPC insurance.

995. **B. $1,300,000**

SIPC (Securities Investor Protection Corporation) covers each separate customer account up to $500,000, of which no more than $250,000 can be cash. So in this case, Mike's account would be covered for $450,000 ($200,000 stock + $50,000 bonds + $200,000 cash), Mary's account would be covered for $350,000 ($100,000 stock + $250,000 cash), and the joint account would be covered for $500,000 ($100,000 stock + $350,000 bonds + $50,000 cash). Added together, that's $450,000 + $350,000 + $500,000 = $1,300,000.

996. **A. $500,000 in cash and securities with no more than $250,000 cash**

SIPC (Securities Investor Protection Corporation) covers investors in the event of broker-dealer bankruptcy. SIPC covers each investor up to $500,000, of which no more than $250,000 can be cash.

997. **D. all of the above**

SIPC (Securities Investor Protection Corporation) provides coverage for all types of securities held in customer accounts. SIPC provides protection for customers in the event of broker-dealer bankruptcy. SIPC coverage covers each separate account up to $500,000, of which no more than $250,000 can be cash.

998. **C. four**

The customer has a cash account and a margin account in his name, which counts as one separate customer according to SIPC. The joint account with his wife, the joint account with his son, and the corporate account are three other separate accounts.

999. **B. general creditor**

SIPC (Securities Investor Protection Corporation) protects each separate account only up to $500,000, of which no more than $250,000 can be cash. If the investor had more held in the account than would be covered by SIPC, she would become a general creditor of the firm for the remainder.

1000. **B. $250,000**

FDIC (Federal Deposit Insurance Corporation) covers each depositor up to $250,000 in the event of bank failure.

1001. **B. fidelity bond**

A fidelity bond protects a firm against fraud or embezzlement by employees of the brokerage firm. SIPC protects customers against broker-dealer bankruptcy.

Index

Notes

Notes

Notes

Notes

Notes

Notes

About the Author

After earning a high score on the Series 7 exam in the mid-1990s, **Steven M. Rice** began his career as a stockbroker for a broker dealership with offices in Nassau County, Long Island, and in New York City. In addition to his duties as a registered representative, he also gained invaluable experience about securities registration rules and regulations when he worked in the firm's compliance office. But it was only after Steve began tutoring others in the firm to help them pass the Series 7 exam that he found his true calling as an instructor. Shortly thereafter, Steve became a founding partner and educator in Empire Stockbroker Training Institute (www.empirestockbroker.com).

In addition to writing *Series 7 Exam For Dummies* and *1,001 Series 7 Exam Practice Questions For Dummies* (published by Wiley), Steve developed and designed the Empire Stockbroker Training Institute online (Series 7, Series 6, Series 63, Series 66, and more) exams. Steve has also coauthored a complete library of securities training manuals for classroom use and for home study, including the Series 4, Series 6, Series 7, Series 11, Series 24, Series 63, Series 65, and Series 66. Steve's popular and highly acclaimed classes, online courses, and training manuals have helped tens of thousands of people achieve their goals and begin their lucrative new careers in the securities industry. Steve continues to tutor students online through his two tutoring websites (www.series7tutoring.com and www.insightprofessionaltraining.com).

Dedication

I dedicate this book to my beautiful wife, Melissa. Melissa is the love of my life, my joy, my inspiration, and my best friend.

Author's Acknowledgments

There is a phenominal team at Wiley that made this book possible. I would like to start by thanking my acquisitions editor, Erin Calligan Mooney, for seeing something in me that told her that I was the right guy for the job. She is a professional through and through, and I appreciate all of her help.

A load of thanks also goes to senior project editor Tim Gallan, for his rapid-response emails, which provided guidance and helped to keep me moving in the right direction.

I would also like to thank my copy editor, Jennette ElNaggar, for making suggestions and tweaking my writing to make it more in line with *For Dummies* style. Her input ultimately made this book more fun to read for all of you.

Next, I would like to thank the entire composition team and the technical editor, Christopher Rohn. Although I didn't get a chance to communicate with any of you directly, this book wouldn't be possible without every one of you. I sincerely appreciate all of your hard work.

I would also like to thank my dad, Tom Rice, his wife, Maggie, my sisters Sharlene and Sharlet, and my son Jim for all of their love and support.

Publisher's Acknowledgments

Acquisitions Editor: Erin Calligan Mooney

Senior Project Editor: Tim Gallan

Copy Editor: Jennette ElNaggar

Technical Editor: Christopher Rohn

Art Coordinator: Alicia B. South

Project Coordinator: Emily Benford

Illustrator: Rashell Smith

Cover Image: ©iStock.com/leungchopan

pple & Mac

ad For Dummies,
th Edition
78-1-118-72306-7

hone For Dummies,
th Edition
78-1-118-69083-3

lacs All-in-One
or Dummies, 4th Edition
78-1-118-82210-4

S X Mavericks
or Dummies
78-1-118-69188-5

logging & Social Media

acebook For Dummies,
th Edition
78-1-118-63312-0

ocial Media Engagement
or Dummies
78-1-118-53019-1

/ordPress For Dummies,
th Edition
78-1-118-79161-5

usiness

ock Investing
or Dummies, 4th Edition
78-1-118-37678-2

vesting For Dummies,
th Edition
78-0-470-90545-6

Personal Finance
For Dummies, 7th Edition
978-1-118-11785-9

QuickBooks 2014
For Dummies
978-1-118-72005-9

Small Business Marketing Kit
For Dummies, 3rd Edition
978-1-118-31183-7

Careers

Job Interviews For Dummies,
4th Edition
978-1-118-11290-8

Job Searching with Social
Media For Dummies,
2nd Edition
978-1-118-67856-5

Personal Branding
For Dummies
978-1-118-11792-7

Resumes For Dummies,
6th Edition
978-0-470-87361-8

Starting an Etsy Business
For Dummies, 2nd Edition
978-1-118-59024-9

Diet & Nutrition

Belly Fat Diet For Dummies
978-1-118-34585-6

Mediterranean Diet
For Dummies
978-1-118-71525-3

Nutrition For Dummies,
5th Edition
978-0-470-93231-5

Digital Photography

Digital SLR Photography
All-in-One For Dummies,
2nd Edition
978-1-118-59082-9

Digital SLR Video &
Filmmaking For Dummies
978-1-118-36598-4

Photoshop Elements 12
For Dummies
978-1-118-72714-0

Gardening

Herb Gardening
For Dummies, 2nd Edition
978-0-470-61778-6

Gardening with Free-Range
Chickens For Dummies
978-1-118-54754-0

Health

Boosting Your Immunity
For Dummies
978-1-118-40200-9

Diabetes For Dummies,
4th Edition
978-1-118-29447-5

Living Paleo For Dummies
978-1-118-29405-5

Big Data

Big Data For Dummies
978-1-118-50422-2

Data Visualization
For Dummies
978-1-118-50289-1

Hadoop For Dummies
978-1-118-60755-8

Language & Foreign Language

500 Spanish Verbs
For Dummies
978-1-118-02382-2

English Grammar
For Dummies, 2nd Edition
978-0-470-54664-2

French All-in-One
For Dummies
978-1-118-22815-9

German Essentials
For Dummies
978-1-118-18422-6

Italian For Dummies,
2nd Edition
978-1-118-00465-4

Available in print and e-book formats.

Available wherever books are sold. **For more information or to order direct visit www.dummies.com**

Math & Science

Algebra I For Dummies,
2nd Edition
978-0-470-55964-2

Anatomy and Physiology
For Dummies, 2nd Edition
978-0-470-92326-9

Astronomy For Dummies,
3rd Edition
978-1-118-37697-3

Biology For Dummies,
2nd Edition
978-0-470-59875-7

Chemistry For Dummies,
2nd Edition
978-1-118-00730-3

1001 Algebra II Practice
Problems For Dummies
978-1-118-44662-1

Microsoft Office

Excel 2013 For Dummies
978-1-118-51012-4

Office 2013 All-in-One
For Dummies
978-1-118-51636-2

PowerPoint 2013
For Dummies
978-1-118-50253-2

Word 2013 For Dummies
978-1-118-49123-2

Music

Blues Harmonica
For Dummies
978-1-118-25269-7

Guitar For Dummies,
3rd Edition
978-1-118-11554-1

iPod & iTunes For Dummies,
10th Edition
978-1-118-50864-0

Programming

Beginning Programming
with C For Dummies
978-1-118-73763-7

Excel VBA Programming
For Dummies, 3rd Edition
978-1-118-49037-2

Java For Dummies,
6th Edition
978-1-118-40780-6

Religion & Inspiration

The Bible For Dummies
978-0-7645-5296-0

Buddhism For Dummies,
2nd Edition
978-1-118-02379-2

Catholicism For Dummies,
2nd Edition
978-1-118-07778-8

Self-Help & Relationships

Beating Sugar Addiction
For Dummies
978-1-118-54645-1

Meditation For Dummies,
3rd Edition
978-1-118-29144-3

Seniors

Laptops For Seniors
For Dummies, 3rd Edition
978-1-118-71105-7

Computers For Seniors
For Dummies, 3rd Edition
978-1-118-11553-4

iPad For Seniors
For Dummies, 6th Edition
978-1-118-72826-0

Social Security For Dummies
978-1-118-20573-0

Smartphones & Tablets

Android Phones
For Dummies, 2nd Edition
978-1-118-72030-1

Nexus Tablets For Dummies
978-1-118-77243-0

Samsung Galaxy S 4
For Dummies
978-1-118-64222-1

Samsung Galaxy Tabs
For Dummies
978-1-118-77294-2

Test Prep

ACT For Dummies,
5th Edition
978-1-118-01259-8

ASVAB For Dummies,
3rd Edition
978-0-470-63760-9

GRE For Dummies,
7th Edition
978-0-470-88921-3

Officer Candidate Tests
For Dummies
978-0-470-59876-4

Physician's Assistant Exam
For Dummies
978-1-118-11556-5

Series 7 Exam For Dummies
978-0-470-09932-2

Windows 8

Windows 8.1 All-in-One
For Dummies
978-1-118-82087-2

Windows 8.1 For Dummies
978-1-118-82121-3

Windows 8.1 For Dummies,
Book + DVD Bundle
978-1-118-82107-7

𝑒 **Available in print and e-book formats.**

Available wherever books are sold. **For more information or to order direct visit www.dummies.com**

Take Dummies with you everywhere you go!

Whether you are excited about e-books, want more from the web, must have your mobile apps, or are swept up in social media, Dummies makes everything easier.

Leverage the Power

For Dummies is the global leader in the reference category and one of the most trusted and highly regarded brands in the world. No longer just focused on books, customers now have access to the For Dummies content they need in the format they want. Let us help you develop a solution that will fit your brand and help you connect with your customers.

Advertising & Sponsorships

Connect with an engaged audience on a powerful multimedia site, and position your message alongside expert how-to content.

Targeted ads • Video • Email marketing • Microsites • Sweepstakes sponsorship

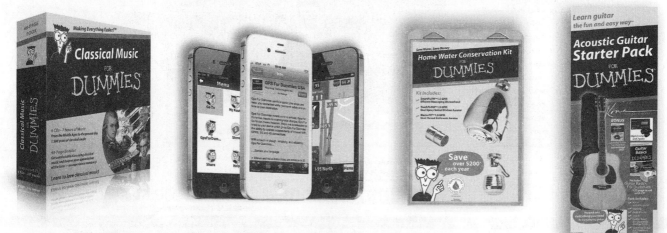

Dummies products make life easier!

- DIY
- Consumer Electronics
- Crafts

- Software
- Cookware
- Hobbies

- Videos
- Music
- Games
- and More!

For more information, go to **Dummies.com** and search the store by category.

FOR
DUMMIES

A Wiley Brand

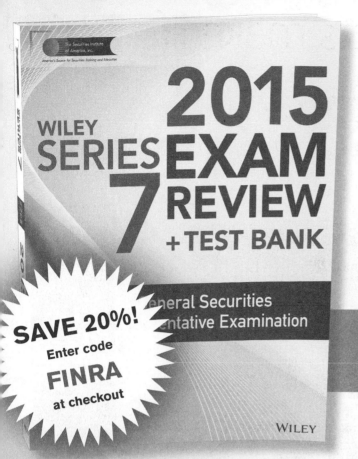
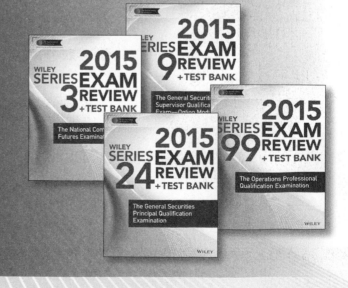